The Texas Indians

Number Ninety-five:
Centennial Series of the Association of Former Students,
Texas A&M University

The Texas
Indians

David La Vere

TEXAS A&M UNIVERSITY PRESS • College Station

The paper used in this book meets the minimum requirements
of the American National Standard for Permanence
of Paper for Printed Library Materials, z39.48–1984.
Binding materials have been chosen for durability.
⊗

Library of Congress Cataloging-in-Publication Data

La Vere, David.
The Texas Indians / David La Vere.—1st ed.
p. cm.—(Centennial series of the Association of Former
Students, Texas A&M University ; no. 95)
Includes bibliographical references and index.
ISBN 1-58544-301-8 (cloth : alk. paper)
1. Paleo-Indians—Texas. 2. Indians of North America—Texas—History.
3. Indians of North America—Texas—Government relations. 4. Indians of North
America—Texas—Social conditions. I. Title. II. Series.
E78.T4 L32 2004
976.4004'97—dc21
2003014561

For my friends,
Theda Perdue, Mike Green, and Brian Hosmer

Contents

Preface

Texas Indian history is very fertile ground. As any resident will tell you, Texas itself is a vast country, encompassing virtually the entire Southern Plains, but with a good dose of forests, prairies, deserts, mountains, canyons, rivers, and coastline. A multitude of Indian peoples made use of these environments for thousands of years. Apaches, Comanches, and Kiowas traveled the plains, Wichitas and Tonkawas on the prairies, Caddos in the East Texas forests, Atakapas and Karankawas on the Gulf Coast, Coahuiltecans in South Texas, and Jumanos and Tiguas along the Rio Grande and Pecos. Of course, these were just the major nations. There were also a multitude of much smaller, virtually autonomous bands whose members saw themselves as a single people but who have long since vanished from the land and the history books: Beitonijures, Achubales, Cujalos, Toremes, Gediondos, Siacuchas, Suajos, Isuchos, Dijus, Colabrotes, Unojitas, Juanas, Yoyehis, Humez, Bibis. And these are just a scant few of the many peoples who made Texas home at one time or another.

Sometimes it is easy for us to forget that the Indians of Texas had a history long before Spaniards ever showed up in the Western Hemisphere. And that ancient history, as well as how Indian peoples saw their world, ordered their societies, put food in their stomachs, and determined how they interacted with each other. All this is certainly meal for the historian's metate. Add the Spanish, French, English, Mexicans, Americans, and such migrant Indians as the Alabama-Coushattas, and you have a mix that has attracted historians for more than forty years and continues to do so in ever-growing numbers.

Unfortunately, the story of European and American colonists has overshadowed that of Texas Indians. Because historians rely so much on written records, which the Spanish, French, Mexicans, and Americans left in vast quantities, we often overplay the roles of the Spanish or Americans and virtually ignore that of the Indians. Too often Texas Indian history has devolved into Spanish-Indian relations or American-Indian relations. In 1961 anthropologist W. W. Newcomb, with the publication of *The Indians of Texas,* was the first to really examine the Indians themselves and their own history. Providing both a cultural and historical study of the Indian peoples of Texas, it has remained the classic history of Texas Indians. Nevertheless, Professor Newcomb would certainly agree that much new information on Texas Indians has come to light in the last forty years. However, I have tried to follow in his footsteps. This book is a history of the Texas Indians, not a history of Europeans or Americans in Texas. At every step I have tried to keep the Indians at center stage. Rather than just rudderless victims of Europeans, Indians had their own agendas and utilized strategies to realize them. This is not to say they did not suffer greatly at the hands of Europeans and Americans, only that Indian peoples were players in their own drama and tried to arrange things to their benefit. Sometimes it worked. Sometimes it did not.

As the reader begins this historical adventure, a few caveats might make the road a little easier to travel. First, historians examine change and continuity over time, and the Indians of Texas certainly experienced both. Outside pressures, fresh ideas, and new products helped change their societies. A Wichita in 1542 was certainly different from a Wichita in 1842. But Indian peoples had an ancient history during which they developed beliefs, traditions, outlooks, and approaches that provided a foundation for their societies. These often changed little, and many can still be found among Wichitas and other Indians at the turn of the twenty-first century.

Another caution is that readers should be prepared for the changeability of Indian identity. Over time and for a variety of reasons, bands and nations might break apart and their people scatter to the winds. Some might form a new band with a new name. Some might go live with other bands. Some might be absorbed by wholly different peoples. Or they might welcome outsiders into their bands. To put it in perspective, one could think of the Celts, Angles, Saxons, and Jutes, the different peoples who helped make modern Britain. What did it take to be a Saxon? How did a person know she was an Angle and not a Jute or a Celt? What became of them? And what happened after 1066 when the French settled in England? Were there "full-blooded" Jutes then? Where are they now? Similarly, one would be hard-pressed in these early years of the twenty-first century to find a Rio Grande Jumano either in or outside of Texas. Some Jumanos became Apaches; some became Mexican peasants; and others went to live with other Indians. Nevertheless, one can still find people up and down the Rio Grande who might trace their ancestry back to the Jumanos.

For many Europeans and Americans, Indians seemed to run willy-nilly around Texas with plenty of madness but little method. Over the years, many historians have viewed Indians in similar lights, often using such words as "treacherous" or "renegade" to describe them. These concepts fade when one looks closer at Indian politics and diplomacy or even admits that Indians possessed such things. Indian history becomes clearer when we view Indians as people hoping to navigate their way through an increasingly confusing world. Rival chiefs offered competing views of the direction their people should take. Indian peoples long understood the value of trade networks and worked to be a part of them or even dominate them. They also had a sense of territoriality, knowing where theirs ended and other people's began. And they were quick to prevent intruders from invading their land or having access to valuable resources, such as the Southern Plains buffalo herds. They also understood the need for economic and military allies and went out of their way to make alliances in order to solidify their own advantages or press a war against their enemies.

Indians, however, wanted not only to navigate through life but also, like most people, to maximize their economic well-being while adhering to traditional values and mores. If we can acknowledge this, then much of what Indians did in Texas makes sense even to non-Indians in the twenty-first century. Indians lived in a world that made sense to them. That a buffalo might be a buffalo or maybe a spirit come to impart knowledge would not have surprised many Indians. That a dream could tell people what to do or even change the direction of their life was accepted by virtually every Indian of Texas. Everyone knew that life needed to be kept in balance and this entailed a host of obligations ranging from where to place a tepee or house, the way to smoke a pipe, how to dispose of a baby's umbilical cord, or when to take revenge in order to restore harmony and allow the victim's spirit to pass on to the next world. Kin took care of kin, and while people were free to display individual character traits, their first duty lay not in advancing themselves but in protecting and sustaining their community. Nevertheless, sustaining one's community through bravery, generosity, and wisdom accorded status, something all men and women craved and which in turn brought political and spiritual power.

Rather than "red devils" or "noble savages," Indians had all the same virtues and vices of people the world over. And they usually wanted the same thing. Like all human beings, the Indians of Texas, deep down, wanted safety and security in this world and the next. At the most basic, Indian people wanted full bellies, peaceful sleep, good families, friendly neighbors, prosperous times, helpful gods, and an easy afterlife. Over the millennia they developed religious beliefs, political structures, social configurations, and economic strategies to achieve these goals. Consensus, community welfare, lines of kinship, obligations of reciprocity, harmony and balance, the divinity of nature all shaped the Indian worldview.

This "red road" clashed lethally with European and American concepts of individual rights, authoritarian leadership, property ownership, capitalism, and a dynamic, conversion-oriented religion. European and American men also sought status, which came through land ownership and wealth, rather than generosity. Europeans and Americans lived in a world in which white was better than red and Christianity better than anything the Indians had. They believed what they had was "civilization" and what the Indians had was "savagery." Therefore Europeans and Americans did not take Indians seriously. Certainly they took Indian threats to heart, but never the Indians themselves nor their culture. Few settlers or officials believed that Indians truly utilized the land or had legal claim to it. Nor did they believe that Indian culture possessed anything of value, that Indians suffered the same emotions that non-Indians did, or that an Indian might be one's equal before God or the law.

Over the last five hundred years, this Euroamerican way of viewing the world gradually triumphed. Helping it along were European diseases and superior technology combined with the Indians' own fluid political structure, the inability of their societies to rapidly modernize, and the Indian determination to adhere to traditional ways in the face of a changing world. Of course, history is long and continues its march. So who knows what the next five hundred years will bring to Texas and the Indians who once called it home, and indeed still do.

A word also needs to be said about some of the terminology and organization in this book. The debate goes on about what to call Indian people. Wherever possible, I have tried to call them by their national names—Comanches, Caddos, Kiowas, and such. Naturally, this may not be what they originally called themselves, but it is what they call themselves today and it is how most people know them.

When it came to grouping them together as a whole, then I have opted for "Indian" over "Native American." Most Indian people I know do not mind the term "Indian" and many prefer it over "Native American." It is also less confusing than trying to get around "Native American" and the similar "Native- born American." When referring to non-Indians, I've tried to be specific and use such national identities as Spain, France, England, Mexico, United States, and Texas. When I need to be very specific about non-Indians, sometimes I employ such terms as "Mexican," "Anglo," "African American," "Tejano," or "Texan." When being a little more general, I've used "European" for colonial peoples and "American" for those who came to Texas after the colonial period. "Euroamerican" comes in to play when I want to differentiate between "Indian" and "non-Indian" characteristics.

In organizing this book, one question I had to consider was "are those Indians who were pushed out of Texas into Oklahoma during the second half of the nineteenth century still Texas Indians?" I believe they are, and I know that many of them still consider Texas home. Just as I believe that those Indian people who migrated in to Texas became Texas Indians in their own right. Therefore, both the immigrant and emigrant Indians have their story told here. Unfortunately, Texas Indians pushed into Oklahoma do not get much press. While there are hundreds, even thousands, of works on Texas Indians prior to 1880, there are scant few once they are defeated and placed on reservations. Much historical and anthropological work needs to be done on Texas (and Oklahoma) Indians in the twentieth and twenty- first centuries. It is an open field.

Finally, in writing this book, I have learned just how much research on Texas Indians has been done in the last forty years. To be sure, a considerable number of historical and anthropological books and articles have been published and more are coming out every day. I have tried to use as many and as large a variation of published sources as time and space would allow. However, I know that I have missed some and I hope these fine historians and anthropologists will forgive me.

As always, a book such as this does not write itself. I owe much thanks and a tremendous amount of appreciation to friends and colleagues who have made this work possible. First and foremost, Sophie Williams, Madeleine Bombeld, and Mary Corchoran in the Inter-Library Loan Department at the University of North Carolina at Wilmington. They worked hard to get me the articles and books I needed. A great thank-you also goes to my "boss," Kathleen Berkeley, chair of the Department of History at UNCW. She has always been in my corner, always supported me and my penchant for researching and writing. Others at UNCW to whom I owe a nod of thanks include Andrew Clark and Renee Vincent. Both have listened to me for hours talking about Texas Indians. And both have offered constructive advice on how to approach certain subjects. Friends and colleagues around the country also helped in their own way. These include Gary Anderson at the University of Oklahoma, Brian Hosmer at the Newberry Library in Chicago, Mike Green and Theda Perdue at the University of North Carolina at Chapel Hill, Terri Baker at Northeastern State University in Tahlequah, Oklahoma, and her husband, Tom, Greg Cantrell, Donald Chipman, and F. Todd Smith at the University of North Texas, Wendy St. Jean now at Boston University, Clyde Ellis at Elon University, and the staff at Texas A&M University Press. As always, gratitude goes to my mother, Ann, my late father, Dick, and my two sisters, Tracy and Rhonda. Many friends in Wilmington and around the country also gave support in one way or another: Floyd Ebron, Jake Sulzbach, Gary Baer, Maureen Hankins, Kevin Sands, Kay Parks, Carrie Griffin, and Caryn Mills. I hope all will take pride in the part they played in making this history possible but none should shoulder any blame for errors. That is for me alone.

The Texas Indians

Chapter 1

Texas' Earliest Peoples

IT IS NOT certain when the first human being set foot in Texas, just as it is not definite when the first person appeared in the Western Hemisphere. If, as scientists now say, humanity began in Africa about 4 million years ago and trekked outward from there, then the Western Hemisphere's isolation from the rest of the world meant that these earliest humans never reached it. No Australopithecus, Homo Erectus, or Neanderthals ever left their mark on America. Instead human beings first reached North America, somewhere between 40,000 and 12,000 years ago. Texas has played its own role in the development of thought about the peopling of the Americas. During the 1950s, the bones of a woman, dubbed "Midland Minnie," were discovered in Midland County. It caused a stir when her age was estimated first at 20,000 years, then later at 37,000 years, making her remains the oldest ever found in the Western Hemisphere. However, most research says she is about 12,000 years old, though arguments still rage over it.[1]

There is also no agreement on from where and how the first peoples arrived in this hemisphere. Most scientists believe they came from northeast Asia. However, increasing evidence points to several different migrations to the Western Hemisphere and from different parts of Asia. Until recently, the most widely held theory has people crossing the Alaskan land bridge, which anthropologists call "Berengia." During the Pleistocene Epoch, which began about 1.6 million years ago, four separate ice ages, each thousands of years long, came and went. In the Western Hemisphere the last ice age, the Wisconsin glaciation, began 90,000 years ago and lasted for about 80,000 years. During the Wisconsin glaciation, much of the oceans' water became trapped in glaciers, some extending far down into the northern United States. The lowering sea levels opened a fifty-five-mile-long, thousand-mile-wide bridge at the Bering Straits, allowing mammoth hunters from Asia to cross from one hemisphere to the other. Some anthropologists believe there may have been several waves of migrations across Berengia. Another theory gaining credibility points to people in small skin-covered boats, island-hopping across the Aleutians then down the Pacific coast.[2]

Peoples other than northeast Asians may well have contributed to the American Indian gene pool. Recent studies point to migrants from Japan, Europe, and Africa. While it is quite possible that some of these groups reached the Western Hemisphere thousands of years ago, it appears that the vast majority of early Americans descended from Asians, who either killed off or absorbed these other strays. No matter when or how people arrived, once in this hemisphere, humans multiplied and rapidly spread across the land, reaching the southern tip of South America about a thousand years or so later. When the ice age ended about 10,000 years ago and refilled the oceans, Berengia slipped back beneath the waves, essentially isolating the peoples of the Western and Eastern Hemispheres from each other.[3]

Many Indian peoples point to their own oral traditions to explain their presence on the continent. Almost all Indian origin stories say they were created right here in this hemisphere. The Caddo farmers of East Texas say they emerged from underground near present-day Cross Lake and moved west into Texas' Angelina and Trinity river valleys. The Tonkawas, people of North and Central Texas, say they also lived underground until wolves uncovered them and brought them into the Texas daylight. Ever since, the Tonkawas have revered the Great Wolf. The Atakapas of the upper Texas coast believe they came from the sea, later surviving a great deluge that covered all but the highest hills.[4]

In any event, the earliest evidence of humans in Texas so far is about 12,000 B.P. (before the present day), though some archaeologists think this date could be pushed back several thousand years. No matter what the date, Texas was different then from what it is in the early twenty-first century. Much of it was cool, wet, and green, with vast forests growing tall under regular rainfall. Grasslands covered the high plains of the Llano Estacado in West Texas. The climate was a pleasant ten degrees cooler than now, with mammoths, giant bison, tiny horses, and other herd animals grazing alongside hundreds of streams and rivers that flowed across the region.[5] While we will never know what these earliest Texans called themselves, anthropologists and ethnohistorians refer to them as Paleoindians.

Paleoindians (ca. 12,000 B.P.–ca. 8,000 B.P.)

These first peoples of Texas lived by hunting the large herd animals, particularly mammoths and giant bison. They also gathered a variety of local plants. Though Paleoindians may have descended from early Asian hunters, and most shared Type O blood, once they got here they quickly began diversifying in physical appearance. Some were tall, some short, some big, others small. Some had narrow heads and faces; others rounded, broad faces. And of course over time these groups intermarried and had children and so changed even more.[6]

By 11,500 B.P. maybe a few hundred people lived in Texas. Men mainly hunted big animals, as their bulky thrusting spears worked better on them than on smaller game. In much of Texas, that meant bison, mammoth, camels, and horses; the horses then were much smaller than those the Spanish brought with them. Of course, when the opportunity presented itself, hunters took deer, rabbits, squirrels, gophers, prairie dogs, turtles, lizards, and fish as well. In Texas, the giant bison seemed to be preferred over mammoth, possibly because there were more bison than mammoths on the Southern Plains. Women were no less important than men to the survival of the Paleoindian band. They might help the men on the hunt, butchering the animals and dressing the hides. They also gathered seeds, roots, nuts, berries, and firewood, and snared small game.[7]

Since they followed the herds, Paleoindian peoples lived in small bands of upward of forty people. The band formed the basic social and political unit of these hunter-gatherers and essentially was one big extended family. Often on the move, Paleoindians lived in caves and under rock overhangs where available and in small man-made shelters and places safe from wild animals when natural cover was not present. Always on the move meant traveling light, so it was useless for a person to acquire too many possessions. There could be no classes or even any true specializations. While one individual may have been better at making tools than someone else and another a superior game tracker, all men were equal in that all men, as long as they were able, had to hunt to provide for themselves and their family.[8]

Paleoindians followed the herds, moving where the game was most abundant, usually setting up their camps overlooking a watercourse. Teams of fathers, sons, brothers and other male relatives might go out daily or weekly to hunt in the area around their camp. Women might assist in these local hunts. Periodically, longer hunts were made, usually during the fall or spring. During these long hunts, teams trekked out a hundred miles or more and might be gone for several days or weeks. Women usually remained behind at a secure base camp, protected by a few older men. Staking out a water hole, hunters tried to ambush their prey as it came to drink. Sometimes they stampeded mammoths or bison over a cliff then leisurely killed off the wounded. At other times they built an artificial barrier to trap bison. Of course, some days consisted of long, tiring marches with little to show for the effort. No matter which method they used, it often took six or eight spear thrusts to take down a single mammoth or bison and several might be killed at one time. Skeletons have been found with numerous spear points still inside them. Because mammoths and bison were so difficult to bring down, Paleoindians depended to a considerable extent on the plants and small game acquired by the women. However, once the big game had moved on, so did the Paleoindians.[9]

Whatever game they hunted, Texas Paleoindians utilized an efficient set of stone tools. They chipped and pressure-flaked beautiful but deadly flint points. Some of these points had notches in the base, making it easier to bind them to the spear. Others had blood gutters, which quickly bled the wounded animal to death. These spears, some with detachable shafts, they either stabbed or hurled into the animal. After the kill, they used flint knives and scrapers to dress the meat and hides. Animal bones could then be made into spear-point shafts, shaft straighteners, awls, and needles. Ribs might be used as shelter supports.[10]

Hunting shaped all aspects of Paleoindian life. The people became great walkers. A hunting territory was normally about two hundred miles in diameter, and some bands returned to the same area time and again. Sometimes they traveled hundreds of miles to gather a favorite type of flint. Often on the move, the band relocated its camp by an average of sixteen miles a year, and when a person died, she might find herself five hundred miles away from the place of her birth.[11]

This dependence on hunting also gave rise to Paleoindian religious beliefs. Like later hunter-gatherers, each Paleoindian band probably had a medicine man who tried to harness spiritual power for the benefit of the band. This might mean using rituals to draw a herd of bison over a cliff or to areas nearer the band's hunters. The medicine man, who could have been a woman, also tried to cure the sick, heal the wounded, change the weather, and predict the future. He or she also sent off the dead, who were typically covered in red ochre and buried along with stone projectile points, bone and shell beads, maybe even with turtle shells, antler pieces, and bird claws.[12]

Though limited to rocks, wood, and bones, Paleoindians in Texas made important technological advances that propelled their societies into new directions. About 11,500 years ago, Paleoindians throughout North America began creating a rather distinct and efficient spear point. Archaeologists call it the Clovis point because these shapes were first found embedded in mammoth bones at Blackwater Draw near the town of Clovis, New Mexico, on the Texas border. These spear points predominated in Texas between 11,500 and 11,000 years ago, and the people who used them relied heavily on mammoths for food. Clovis people wandered throughout Texas, occupying sites near present-day San Marcos; at Miami in the Panhandle; in Denton County; at an oft-used butchering site near Lubbock; at the "original" Clovis kill site at Blackwater Draw; and in various places around East Texas. Nevertheless, most Clovis sites in Texas are on the Llano Estacado. Clovis people also migrated out of Texas, carrying their tools with them. Clovis points made out of flint from Texas' Hill Country have been found in eastern Louisiana.[13]

Then, between 10,000 and 11,000 years ago, the Paleoindians in the western part of North America made another technological leap, one that made them even better hunters. They created a more efficient spear point, smaller but wider and with a deep blood gutter running from base to tip. At the same time, the climate of Texas' high plains began drying, with many running streams giving way to standing ponds and marshes. During this time, mammoths became extinct in Texas. Whether climate change or human hunters that led to their extinction is still debated. With mammoths gone, Paleoindians in Texas, utilizing these new spear points, now turned on the giant bison. These points were first found near Folsom, New Mexico, embedded in the bones of a giant bison. Because of this, they are called Folsom points, and the people who used them are part of the Folsom culture. Though bison were important to Folsom cultures, those in the forests of East Texas relied to a greater extent on smaller game and foraging.[14]

Though Clovis and Folsom points have not been found mixed together at archaeological sites, one should not think of this as the "dying out" of the Clovis people and the birth of the Folsom, but rather a technological and cultural evolution. Like the people who used Clovis points five hundred years before them, Folsom people, at least those in West Texas, lived in rock shelters and caves, often the same ones previously used by Clovis people, such as at the Lubbock Lake site. Evidence of Folsom culture has also been found in East Texas, the Llano Estacado, the Central Prairies, and in the lower Pecos River valley. These camp sites usually overlooked water sources where bison came to drink. Still, hunting could be a haz-ardous job, so like all human beings, Folsom people tried to make a hard job easier. At Bonfire Shelter near the Rio Grande, Folsom Paleoindians regularly ran herds of bison over a seventy-foot cliff. The bones of about 120 of the huge animals eventually collected at the cliff's base.[15]

Since hunting was their life, Folsom people in Texas possessed a tremendous understanding of stone and its properties. Paleoindians from both the Clovis and Folsom periods knew what type of flint was best for tool-making and where to find it. One of the best places was at Alibates quarries in present-day Potter County, north of Amarillo. Tools made from this particular flint have been found all over North America and as far south as central Mexico. Paleoindian toolmakers dug tons of stone from the Alibates quarries, which continued to attract Indian peoples until the mid-nineteenth century. Now with a quality projectile point, Folsom peo-ple became choosy consumers, as the Lake Theo site near Quitaque in the Panhandle shows. At Lake Theo, Folsom peoples erected a base camp. From there, they drove bison into nearby canyons and killed them. They quickly butchered the youngest, most delectable bison and carried the ribs, legs, and hindquarters back to the base camp. Near the butchering site, the hunters set up a small shrine of bison bones arranged into a circle, then covered it with bones from the butchered animals.[16]

Always looking to improve their tools, Paleoindians in Texas began experimenting with various point designs. Both the Clovis and Folsom points had deep notches in the sides of the point's base. About 10,000 years ago, toolmakers began making points without these notches, while finish-ing them with pressure flaking. Generally called Plano points, such differ-ent styles in Texas as Midland, Plainview, Lerma, Golondrina, Angostura, San Patrice, and Firstview have been identified by archaeologists. While Paleoindians still relied on the giant bison, they also hunted the small horses and the smaller, modern buffalo. And when these large animals were not available, they went after deer, rabbits, and rodents, which they supplemented by gathering and grinding seeds. The variety of point styles from this period seems to indicate that Paleoindians used different points for different animals. For example, Plainview points may have been used to bring down bison, while Golondrina points may have been for smaller game, such as deer, and may even have doubled as butchering knives.[17]

During this time, between 10,000 and 11,000 years ago, the ice age be-gan coming to an end. The same climate changes that first killed off the mammoths in Texas began to alter all North America. Over the next sev-eral thousand years these climatic changes helped bring about the extinc-tion of most giant mammals in the Western Hemisphere. The climate in

Texas warmed in some areas, cooled in others. Rainfall fluctuated, bringing more and longer wet and dry cycles. Ponds evaporated. The tree line retreated east. Deserts formed in Southwest Texas, while on the Southern Plains grasslands appeared, attracting deer as well as the smaller American bison. Texas began to take on much of the geographic and climatic look it has today, though it was probably a little moister then.

Over time, these changes took a toll on the large mammals. Some could not adapt as their habitats grew smaller and water became scarcer. Others could not adjust their reproductive cycles to the changing climate. Mothers might now give birth when there was no food for their young. New parasites and diseases killed their share, while there were always packs of wolves and coyotes ready to take out the young or feeble. Helping this kill-off were the Paleoindians who staked out water holes, ran herds over cliffs, and deliberately preyed on the young female animals. By about 6,000 years ago, all these pressures resulted in the extinction of the mammoths, giant bisons, horses, camels, and giant armadillos, leaving the American buffalos and the members of the deer family as the largest animals in North America. Long droughts continued on and off for the next few thousand years, killing off the big animals and periodically driving the American buffalo north out of the Texas plains.[18]

The disappearance of the large animals forced the Paleoindians to diversify their economy, making them more dependent on foraging and smaller game. In turn, this brought about a flourishing of ancient Native American culture. Anthropologists call this the Archaic Period, in which a rather common hunter-gatherer culture could be seen across the United States. Nonetheless, regions developed certain distinctions based on geography and climate. East of the ninety-fifth meridian, where lush forests grew and deep rivers ran, the peoples of East Texas had access to a wider variety of foods and materials and so developed a denser population than the Western Archaic, or Desert Culture, peoples of Central and West Texas.[19]

Archaic Indians (ca. 8,000 B.P.–ca. A.D. 800)

The Archaic Period covered thousands of years. It was so long that archaeologists divide it into early, middle, and late periods, during which time culture changed gradually but dramatically. Now early Indians became true hunter-gatherers, and their diets diversified accordingly. They tended to stay in one place longer, seasonally cycling through a distinct territory. Men hunted the smaller animals that proliferated as the ice age came to an end. Where a band lived determined much of what they ate. Cultures near the coast took fish, shellfish, and water birds, often creating mounds of discarded oyster shells. In East and South Texas, Archaic peoples hunted deer, rabbits, turkeys, raccoons, even mice and snakes. Plains bands still relied heavily on buffalo, often making long autumn and winter hunts complete with butchering camps. But buffalo could not always be relied upon, as a very bad drought hit Texas about seven thousand years ago and lasted on and off for three thousand years.[20]

During the Archaic Period, women became ever more important to the band's economy. Women gathered seeds, roots, nuts, berries, insects, and shellfish, and snared small game, which provided most of the food eaten by Archaic Indians. Among the plants women gathered were wild grapes and plums, a variety of berries, even wild onions and turnips. Using mortar holes cut in rock, women ground to a pulp such plants as agave, mesquite beans, prickly pear tunas, persimmons, acorns, walnuts, hackberries, and *huajillo* beans. Women and girls gathered firewood and lined campfires with rocks to help conserve heat. They used rock ovens to bake roots and cacti.[21]

To exploit these new resources, Archaic Indians brought about amazing technological innovations. Though still limited mainly to stone, shell, bone, and wood, the number and variety of new tools was truly astounding. Rather than just thrusting spears, Archaic men now used spear throwers, which provided greater leverage and velocity. Along with special darts, these spear-throwers—atlatls anthropologists call them—could bring down deer and buffalo. Other hunting improvements included bolos for taking birds; flat, curved throwing sticks for killing rabbits; snares for mice, squirrels, raccoons, coyotes, and foxes; and an assortment of hooks, nets, and tackle for fishing. Archaic peoples used stone in many more ways, as well. In addition to projectile points, flint knappers made axes, knives, scrapers, wedges, manos and metates, spear-thrower weights, and drills. From bone, ivory, or shells they made awls, pressure flakers, needles, beads, and pendants. Women twisted *sotol* or *olechuguilla* fibers into ropes, twine, sandals, mats, nets, and above all, baskets, and they sewed animal hides into a variety of clothes and bags.[22]

Along with these technological innovations and the increased, surer supply of food came a population explosion. Archaic sites, much more numerous than those of Paleoindians, have been found throughout Texas, including the lower Pecos River and Rio Grande valleys, the Hill Country, the high plains of the Llano Estacado and Panhandle, and the forests of East Texas. Like Paleoindians, the Archaic peoples lived in small family bands, though now the size of bands were getting larger and larger.

Archaic Indians still made their homes in caves and rock shelters, though some built small huts of brush and mud.[23]

Most of the year, bands remained isolated in their own territory. To move into another band's territory without permission could bring violence. On the other hand, some bands were related to others or alliances might be formed. Periodically bands joined each other for a rabbit hunt, a prickly pear harvest, or a shellfish gathering. During these joint ventures, bands shared technology, news, and ideas, but more importantly, men and women from different bands courted and married. After the event was over, the bands returned to their own territory with their brides who brought new ideas and skills with them. And with more food, these women produced more children than Paleoindians ever had.[24]

Neither Paleoindian nor Archaic Indians suffered epidemic-type diseases such as measles, cholera, diphtheria, mumps, or smallpox. Bands were just too small and too isolated for epidemics to occur. This did not mean people had no aches and pains. Evidence indicates that tuberculosis stalked these early Americans, and they may have had an early form of syphilis, though debate on that continues to this day. They also may have been bedeviled by parasites, such as hookworms and flatworms, and by parasitic ailments, such as trichinosis and Rocky Mountain Spotted Fever. Skin ailments such as ringworm may have been common. Besides illnesses, Archaic Indians, like all active people, suffered fractures, sprains, twists, cuts, scrapes, ruptures, and tears. Sometimes these became so severe that a person might lose the use of an arm, a leg, or an eye. Since forty years of age was considered old, cancer and heart disease, usually associated with old age, may not have been the scourge they are today.[25]

Probably one of the worst things for Archaic people in Texas was tooth decay. As plant foods became an increasing part of their diet, particularly such sticky, sweet foods as the prickly pear cactus, Indians began to get cavities and rotten teeth. Heavy wear inflamed teeth and brought on painful abscesses. While some teeth might rot out, it would not have been uncommon for many people of the Texas Archaic culture to live with constant toothache.[26]

Still, it was not a bad time to be alive. With a more diverse food supply, feeding the band became easier and surer. Archaic people did not need as much time to fulfill their needs, and they used their new leisure time to develop specialized talents and attributes. While all people in the band were involved in providing food, some now devoted themselves to making better points or beads or tools. Others became masters of basket weaving and hide work. And sometimes, when the work was done and friends and family gathered around the fire, pieces of carved, painted bones might be tossed, as games of chance began.[27]

Some bands found they could acquire more things through trade than from their own hands. While exchange, particularly as gift-giving between kinspeople, had long been part of the lives of these early Indians, the first stirrings of actual trade came about during the Archaic period. People realized that their area might be rich in some resources, say in bison, and poor in others, such as flint, and they began to go beyond just gift-giving. As folks from different bands met in the forests, prairies, and plains of Texas, they began to exchange goods. This was probably not large-scale trade at first, but it laid the foundation for extensive trade and information networks that eventually spanned Texas and incorporated all the peoples of the Southern Plains and its margins.[28]

Archaic people tried to learn all they could of the world about them. Savvy hunters studied the animals, and as their hunting successes grew, so did their status. This allowed the hunter to exert some measure of authority in the ever-enlarging band. He was not yet a "chief," but he could be considered something of a headman or band leader. Other men and women turned their attention to learning about plants: which were harmful, which could be eaten, and which had medicinal properties, especially those, such as prickly ash, which could dull a toothache. At some point, healers who worked with plants began to believe there was a close relationship between their medicinal and spiritual properties.[29]

Even the earliest Paleoindians seemed to have a sense of spirits and deities, as demonstrated by the shrine at Lake Theo. Through prayer and ritual, these deities could be appealed to, maybe even manipulated. If no bison were to be found, then the building of a simple shrine and an appeal to the "master of animals" might bring them. If so, then, of course, the deity would be thanked for the help. Archaic peoples built upon these religious beliefs. It probably did not take long before an herbalist connected healing an injury with manipulating spirits and deities. Healing a person came to consist of using not only plants but also rituals, chants, and prayer. And if he or she could soothe a toothache then it might be possible to use similar powers to bring rain, attract animals for the hunt, or even foretell the future. In Texas, rituals might incorporate mescal beans, peyote, toasted yaupon leaves, and tobacco. A religious cult centering on the mescal bean seems to have developed in Archaic South Texas. If successful in both the medicinal and spiritual realm, a priest-healer might gain tremendous power and become a "shaman."[30]

This belief in a world filled with both helpful and malevolent gods and spirits who could be prodded and manipulated by prayer, chants, and rituals, infused all aspects of their lives. Since these early Indians relied mainly on animals for food, religion and ritual went hand in hand with hunting. On the lower Pecos River at Seminole Canyon in Val Verde County, Archaic peoples hunted white-tailed deer. However, the best deer hunters in the area were not human beings but cougars, which silently stalked their prey, chased it down, then crushed it with powerful jaws. Hoping to acquire these same characteristics, Indians on the lower Pecos created Cougar Societies in which hunters received instructions from this animal spirit. On rock shelters in the area, they painted huge pictographs in brilliant reds, deep blacks, and bright yellows of shamans, cougars, and of hunters throwing spears at running deer. These rock shelter pictographs and petroglyphs—pictures carved into rock rather than just painted—located near the confluence of the Pecos River and the Rio Grande are found at such places as Parida Cave, Seminole Canyon, Slick Trail Shelter, and Lewis Canyon. These paintings distinguish this area from most other Archaic sites in North America. While rock art, particularly that made at a later date, has been found in a few other places in West Texas, W. W. Newcomb, who studied these Southwest Texas pictographs, believed that "nowhere was this art form cultivated more assiduously or did it develop further than in the Lower Pecos River country."[31]

How heavy religion weighed on the minds of the average Archaic individual is not known. Probably no more than it does on ours today, but they certainly accepted a world in which spirits, animals, and humans lived side by side. However, for the most part, life was not much different for thousands of years. Men hunted, made tools, and defended the band. Women gathered food, made household utensils, bore and reared children. Families were probably close and loving and they spent time and energy caring for the sick and feeble. When a person grew too old to fend for herself, members of her family and band provided food and nursed her injuries. When toothaches became so bad as to make it too painful to chew, then a loved one would pulverize the food, maybe even chew it for her first.[32]

And this world and the spirit world intertwined when loved ones laid their kinspeople to rest. As with Paleoindians, not many Archaic burials have been found, but the arid climate of Southwest Texas has preserved a few. Peoples of the Late Archaic period buried their dead in various ways: in the ground; under the floors of rock shelters; in small, rather inaccessible caves; in small niches in the walls of caves; under a carefully arranged pile of stones. And in some instances they cremated them. Small cemeteries containing scores, even hundreds, of burials have been found.[33]

Common to virtually all these burials was the loving care bestowed upon the dead. Bodies of adults and children, male and female alike were tenderly cared for. Stone dart points, beads made of shell, bone, and stone, even baskets and other utensils might be placed inside their graves. One common form of Archaic burial in Southwest Texas was a "bundle burial." An excellent example of this is the "Skiles mummy" found in a small rock shelter near the confluence of the Pecos River and the Rio Grande. This man was about forty years old when he died sometime around A.D. 700, an old man for that time. He stood five feet, seven inches; he was slender with a broad face, broad nose, and a mouth filled with rotted, abscessed teeth. He wore a shaggy mane of dark hair over his ears and cropped it at about midneck. When he died, his kinspeople dressed him in a rabbit-fur cape and hung a string of stone and bone beads around his neck. His body was then tightly bound into the fetal position. This human "bundle" was then wrapped in a deer hide, hair inside against the body, wrapped again in a series of woven fiber mats, then tied together by a very long length of hair rope. They buried him in a sitting position in the floor of the rock shelter.[34]

The care given to the dead shows a belief in an afterlife. That they were often buried in the floor of the rock shelter or the wall of a cave still used and occupied by their band indicates that Archaic peoples did not fear their dead, but rather loved and missed them and seemed to consider them still a part of the family. It must have been a sad parting when the family of the Skiles mummy said their good-byes to him and trudged off on their seasonal rounds, leaving his body under the floor of the rock shelter, its home for the next thousand-plus years.[35]

The Archaic Period in Texas slowly came to an end during the first thousand years A.D., though some Indians would enjoy a lifestyle similar to the Archaic well into the eighteenth century. A new technological innovation, the bow and arrow, made its way into Texas around A.D. 600 and by 900 it had replaced the spear thrower. The bow and arrow made men more efficient hunters, ensuring greater supplies of game, which in turn brought about a larger population. For people living in the forests and prairies east of the ninety-fifth meridian, the end of the Archaic and a change to the Woodland Period came a little quicker than to those peoples on the lower Texas coast, the Rio Grande, and the central and high plains.[36]

Woodland Indians (ca. 100 B.C.–ca. A.D. 800)

Just as the shift from big game hunting to hunting and gathering denoted the end of the Paleoindian period and the advent of the Archaic, the domestication of plants and animals marked the end of the Archaic and the rise of the Woodland Period. Essentially, a village way of life began, which included the use of the bow and arrow, the appearance of pottery, more permanent houses, the creation of earthen burial mounds in some places, and participation in long-distance trade networks. Exchange and trade may well have brought these other characteristics, or at least news of them, to the peoples of Texas.

Northeast Texas seemed to be the place where many of these innovations first appeared in the state. The Tchefuncte culture arose in South Louisiana about 500 B.C. and lasted until about A.D. 200. Tchefuncte was the first Louisiana culture to use pottery in any great quantity and the first to domesticate crops, in this case squash and bottle gourds. One of the oldest pieces of pottery uncovered in Texas is a small Tchefuncte clay pot found near Marshall. Whether a Louisiana Indian brought this with him on a visit to Texas and left it, a Texas Indian carried it back with him from a visit to Louisiana, or a Texas potter merely copied something he or she saw is not known. Not many Tchefuncte potsherds have been found in Northeast Texas, and that they seem to be limited mainly to this area indicates trade rather than reproductions. This is bolstered by Marksville pottery, the culture that succeeded Tchefuncte in Louisiana, which also showed up in East Texas about A.D. 1. Then, by A.D. 500, East Texas Indians were making their own pottery, a rather plain type, held together and tempered with crushed bone. Some of this pottery eventually found its way into other regions of Texas.[37]

That Northeast Texas formed a link in a vast Woodlands trade network seems evident. While the Tchefuncte and Marksville cultures were creating beautiful pottery in Louisiana, other Woodland cultures were forming throughout the eastern part of the United States. One of these, the Adena, arose in the Ohio River Valley, and from about 500 B.C. to A.D. 500 exerted a tremendous influence on all the peoples then living in eastern America. Like most groups of the Woodland Period, but probably more so than others, the Adena lived in small villages of round, thatch-roofed houses. They planted gardens of squash, sunflowers, goosefoot, and sumpweed; baked pottery; built small burial mounds over their dead; and participated in long-distance trade. Then, about 200 B.C., a religious movement took hold among the Adena and spread to virtually all Woodland peoples of the eastern United States. Archaeologists refer to this as the Hopewell Complex.[38]

The Hopewell Complex, which lasted until about A.D. 500, was characterized by the honoring of the dead. Burial mounds became larger, but more important was the variety, amount, and beauty of items now interred with the dead. These exquisite grave goods, actually objets d'art often made from such exotic materials as beaten copper, became integral to this Hopewell "honored dead" religion. While the Adena area of southern Ohio may have been the religious center of the eastern United States, lesser regional centers certainly existed and all these were connected in a well-established trade network. Mica from North Carolina, copper from the Great Lakes, galena from Missouri, obsidian from the upper Rockies, flint from the Dakotas, and seashells from the Gulf Coast all made their to Adena towns by way of the trade networks. There, craftsmen and artists shaped these raw materials into copper birds and fish, stone platform pipes, beads, gorgets, celts, jewelry, and other works of art, and then often sent then back along the trails to the regional centers, there to be buried among their own dead.[39]

That Indians in Northeast Texas participated in the Hopewell Complex can be seen in a scattering of small burial mounds along the Angelina, Neches, Sabine, and Red Rivers. The Coral Snake Mound, which now sits beneath the waters of Toledo Bend Reservoir on the Texas-Louisiana border, was representative of this regional Hopewell Complex. About A.D. 1, give or take a hundred years or so, these people along the Sabine River dug a pit four feet deep and twenty feet wide. In it they placed a body, cremated it, covered it with dirt, then filled in the pit. The bones of other cremations were placed in the fill, which eventually created a mound about three feet high and fifty feet in diameter. Over the years, additional cremated remains were interred in the mound. Accompanying these were copper beads and ear spools, spear-thrower weights, and stone projectile points, along with some Marksville pottery from Louisiana. Similar remains and grave goods have been found at the other mounds in the area. This Hopewell Complex in Northeast Texas did not last long and did not spread to any other areas of Texas. Nevertheless, for awhile, some early Texas Indians found themselves part of a very cosmopolitan eastern United States and an important link in a long trade chain.[40]

Though late Archaic and Woodland Indians participated in a far-flung trade network, not all of their interactions with other people were peaceful. Raids, possibly even full offensive warfare, took place. In southern Oklahoma, skeletons dated to between A.D. 400 and 600 have been found with arrow points still embedded in their bones. And the types of flint used to make the points indicate that their attackers traveled several hundred miles to make the raid. Several skeletons have been found in Texas that show death came through injuries inflicted by other humans. What sparked these conflicts remains unclear. Possibly, as these people settled into one area, they clashed with others living at their territorial margins. An increase in raids may have helped bring about the rise of a powerful chiefdom political system. Villages most successful in defending themselves from raiders soon attracted other villages willing to put themselves under that chief's protection.[41]

While pottery and warfare are rather easy to pinpoint, when the Indians of Texas began cultivating plants poses a thornier problem. The domestication of plants probably began in Northeast Texas before any other place in the state, but even then the plants the Indians cultivated were some of the same ones they had long foraged. By A.D. 700, women in Northeast Texas were tending small gardens of sunflowers, goosefoot, sumpweed, squash, little barley, and such. These only supplemented their diets. Not until about A.D. 900 did they take more food from farming than from foraging and hunting.[42]

Northeast Texas was an anomaly, as the rest of Texas lingered in the Archaic Period until about A.D. 1100. Pottery slowly spread throughout Texas during this time, with a thick, cord-marked style spreading west out of East Texas and a plain brown style spreading east out of New Mexico. Near the coast, a sandy paste pottery predominated for hundreds of years. Horticulture and village life took equally as long to spread. However, vast changes were on the way as the Indians of Texas diverged between hunter-gatherers living on the coast, the plains, and in the south, and farmers in the east. The coming of corn horticulture would truly revolutionize many of the Indian cultures of Texas.[43]

An Agricultural Revolution

Over the years, some of these early domesticated plants, such as sumpweed, goosefoot, and sunflowers fell out of use or became of only marginal significance. Others, such as bottle gourds and squash, steadily gained in importance. Indians turned bottle gourds into dippers and spoons, but also waterproof containers, which were lighter and sturdier than pottery. Summer squash added a prolific and delicious food to their larders. Then, two new foods—corn and beans—made their way into Texas. A tropical flint corn had been used by American Woodland peoples from about 200 B.C. to A.D. 400 but had disappeared as the weather cooled over the next few centuries. A new variety of corn, along with beans, made their appearance in Texas about A.D. 700, maybe even a bit earlier. However it would take several hundred more years before these would make a truly significant impact.[44]

Corn was first domesticated in Mexico almost six thousand years ago. Beans followed a couple millennia later. But not until about 2000 B.C. did Mesoamerican farmers make any significant use of either. Tropical flint corn made its way into the area north of Mexico but died out about A.D. 400. Around 300 B.C., its hardier successor, maiz de ocho, a small eight-rowed flour corn, began to be grown by the early Puebloan peoples who would come to occupy northern Mexico, New Mexico, Arizona, and far

West Texas. It was maiz de ocho that crossed the plains and arrived in Northeast Texas around A.D. 700. Beans followed a few hundred years later. When corn first arrived in North America is still debated by scholars, but not until about A.D. 900 did it become an important food to the people living along the Sabine, Angelina, Neches, Trinity, and Red Rivers. However, by 1200, the "three sisters"—corn, beans, and squash, sometimes called the "American triad"—were the lifeblood of the peoples of Northeast Texas. By 1500 virtually all Indian communities in Texas either grew corn or wished they could.[45]

Texas Indians did not suddenly drop their bows and arrows, pick up digging sticks, and begin farming corn, beans, and squash. It was a long, slow process. They had been gradually cultivating plants over the last thousand years, and initially corn was just another one of these domesticated weeds. But as Indian women planted seeds from only the most robust and healthiest plants, maize got bigger and produced larger yields. Nevertheless, by the mid-1500s, even when a village might be surrounded by thousands of acres of corn, women still added a variety of roots, berries, nuts, and seeds to their family's diet, while men continued tramping the forests hunting deer.

That said, women began spending more and more time in their gardens, planting, tending, and harvesting. By the seventeenth and eighteenth centuries, probably even earlier, horticulture was providing more food to the Indians of some parts of Texas, particularly in the northeast, than did hunting. As corn slowly improved, so did beans, and Indian women grew a wide variety of them, including pole beans, pintos, snaps, navys, and kidneys. They also developed an ingenious method of planting. A woman would pile up a small mound of dirt, just a few inches high. In it, she planted a few kernels of corn. Once the corn sprouted, she then planted beans and squash. As the corn grew tall, the beans used the cornstalk as a pole, while the spreading squash covered the mound, keeping down weeds and erosion. It was truly a fortuitous match. Corn, by itself, is hard to digest, but adding beans, which are high in lysine acid, allows for the efficient digestion of corn proteins. Also, where corn depletes the nutrients from the soil, beans, rich in nitrogen, replace them.[46]

At first, farming would have been done on any naturally clear and well-watered land, but as Northeast Texas Indians increased their production, men found they had to clear land using controlled burning to get rid of underbrush and open up the forest canopy. Men "girdled trees," meaning they scraped off one or two feet of the bark all the way around the tree. This killed the trees and when they were dead the men piled logs against them and set them on fire. Women then planted their fields amid the blackened stumps. The resulting ash, rich in potash, was mixed in as fertilizer. The fields and new grass that sprouted also attracted deer, a boon to the hunter.[47]

Now agriculture brought an incredible influence to the village's women. Foraging had always been part of the woman's world, and so agriculture, originally an adjunct to foraging, also became part of their domain. While men might clear the land and turn the soil, women planted the seeds, watered the shoots, weeded the mounds, shooed away crows and deer, then gathered the harvest. Women controlled the fields, and as agriculture swelled in importance, so did women's status. For those cultures, such as the Caddos in East Texas, that came to rely mainly on agriculture, their whole society began tilting toward women. People began to trace their descent through their mothers, rather than through their fathers as most hunter-gatherers did.[48]

This is not to say that women took control of agricultural societies. Though women might sometimes attend a council meeting, women were usually excluded from political power, as men controlled most leadership and political positions. But a few women did become chiefs. And when most of the men were out hunting or raiding, it fell to the women to take care of the daily affairs of the village. For the most part, women wielded influence rather than actual power and usually worked behind the scenes to get what they wanted. Among most Texas Indian societies, women manipulated political power by demanding war or insisting on peace. When enemy captives were taken, the women normally decided who would be tortured to death and who would be spared and enslaved or adopted. Women descended from leadership families or married to important men wielded a good deal of influence. And a wife's pillow talk often swayed her husband's mind in one direction or another.[49]

Women also played important roles in the religious life of most societies. They were essential to almost every ceremony, no matter whether they were hunter-gatherers or agriculturalists. In fact, some dances could only be initiated, even performed by women, such as the Turkey Dance, the Caddo's national dance. Men readily acknowledged the spiritual power of women. In most societies, during their menstrual period, women physically separated themselves from the community, often living apart from their families and with other women also then having their period. They were forbidden to cook food or even bathe upstream from the community. This was done not because a menstruating woman was considered unclean but because during her menses a woman was most spiritually powerful. And her power was so strong it could overshadow the normal daily prayers, rituals, and ceremonies. While physical separation might seem harsh, in reality it could be a nice weeklong break each month from the husband, the children, and the drudgery of camp life, with time to spend with other female friends. So while women may not have held the reins of political power, they certainly wielded tremendous influence.[50]

As farming grew in importance, the question arises as to why these peoples of Texas adopted horticulture in the first place? Hunting and gathering takes much less work. A hunter-gatherer works about two days a week, while a farmer works five or six. So why would anyone choose to farm if they did not have to? One reason may be that the flush times of the Late Archaic and Woodland periods brought an explosion in population and diversity. Surer food supplies brought more children, lower infant mortality, and a longer life for elders. Now there were more mouths to feed, and one or two farmers could provide much more food than twice that number of hunters and gatherers. The Archaic and Woodland periods also allowed bands to splinter, move, and over time develop their own cultural and political identity, often tying them to a certain area. Hunters and foragers from different bands and villages met each other in the forests or prairies and fought over resources. The land itself, such as on the plains or in the deserts, may have limited the availability of some resources. Finding their mobility and access to certain foods restricted at a time they needed more and more food, people turned to horticulture.[51]

This increasing reliance on agriculture meant more than just a larger population and new food sources. As Indian peoples, particularly those of Northeast Texas, turned to agriculture they found their economies, beliefs, and whole way of life diverging from those Texas Indians who continued to rely mainly on hunting and gathering.

Mississippian Cultural Tradition (ca. A.D. 700–ca. 1550)

As corn, beans, and squash spread throughout the eastern United States, economics, religion, trade, and politics all contributed to bring about the rise of the Mississippian cultural tradition. After 700, with surer food supplies, large populations coalesced along the major river systems, particularly the Mississippi and its tributaries. By 1200 large cities holding thousands of people, complete with houses, markets, plazas, earthen mounds, workshops, temples, and cemeteries, had arisen at Spiro, Oklahoma; Cahokia, Illinois; Moundville, Alabama; and Etowah, Georgia. At the same time, from Texas to North Carolina, Florida to Wisconsin, medium-size towns of several hundred people also grew up along smaller rivers and streams. These towns might also have ceremonial mounds, plazas, and temples. Around these towns, just a short distance away, clustered villages, with hamlets branching off the villages, and farmsteads, the most isolated of all and consisting of only a family or two, surrounding a hamlet. In East Texas, between 750 and 1300 several medium-size towns and their attendant villages, hamlets, and farmsteads appeared along the Angelina, Neches, Trinity, and Red Rivers. The people of these cities, towns, and villages intensely cultivated corn and other plants, while the people of hamlets and farmsteads may have relied on foraged foods to a greater extent.[52]

While successful hunting usually depended on the skill of the hunter, agriculture required extra special abilities and interactions. Theoretically, in hunting, if animals were scarce, then the band could move to where the animals were. Agriculturalists could not just pick up their fields and move them. And as any farmer quickly realizes, it is not so much their skill that brings bountiful harvests but the cooperation of the natural elements. Indian farmers of the thirteenth-century American South understood that no matter how tenderly they cared for their crops, drought, floods, frosts, insects, or animals could destroy it all and thereby leave their people starving. The sun, the moon, the rain, the river, the wind, the earth, even the corn itself, all essential to bountiful harvests, had to be propitiated, manipulated, and enlisted for the people's survival. Those individuals who could control the elements through prayer, magic, ritual, and ceremony wielded tremendous power and so were people to be reckoned with.[53]

After A.D. 700 a theocratic form of government arose among the corn-growing societies of the American Southeast, including Northeast Texas. Priests, rather than shamans, now performed the necessary rituals to ensure good crops. As as their prestige, status, and power increased, they became priest-chiefs, wielding religious and political power, governing their people, deciding on peace or war. Over the generations, the mystery and awe around them grew, and some priest-chiefs claimed their family possessed a direct kinship with the Sun or the Moon or some other deity. In turn, this affected the people's social organization by creating a ranked society. The priest-chief and his family now sat at the top of the social pyramid. Other families in his lineage and members of other lineages closely connected to his were seen as nobles. People from lineages more distant became the mass of commoners, and as in Europe, there were many more commoners than nobles. These divisions might be most apparent and strictest in the major cities and larger towns and almost nonexistent in the hamlets and farmsteads. Still, regardless of whether class lines were obvious, throughout agricultural societies, some families seem to be singled out as producing leaders. These priest-chiefs tended to be men, but every so often a remarkable woman of skill and ability might rise up to lead her people.[54]

As the relationship between the priest-chief and the sun, the moon, the stars, and the rain solidified, placing the priest-chief physically closer to his celestial kinfolk became desirable. So people throughout the eastern part of the United States began building huge, earthen, flat-topped, temple mounds. In the major cities, these mounds usually reached anywhere from forty to fifty feet in height. In the many towns throughout the Southeast, they might be a more moderate fifteen to thirty feet high; others might be only a foot or two high and barely discernible from the land around them. But some, such as Monks Mound at Cahokia, Illinois, topped out at almost a hundred feet and took scores of years to build. Agricultural Indians not only built large temple mounds but also continued constructing burial mounds over their dead priest-chief and his kin and retainers. In other instances, they might bury important people under the floor of a temple or house. They would then burn the structure, cover the charred remnants with fresh dirt, and build a new temple or house atop the grave. Over the years, a large burial mound might grow. And in the burials Indian people placed breathtakingly beautiful pieces of pottery, jewelry, and sculpture made of clay, stone, shells, bone, and copper. Many of these pieces of art might have originally been made by someone hundreds of miles away and delivered over the trade routes that linked virtually every city and town in the American South, including those in Texas.[55]

The Mississippian cultural tradition reached its peak of sophistication and opulence during the late thirteenth and early fourteenth centuries as the veneration of these agricultural priest-chiefs reached its height. Shells, pieces of copper, and a variety of pottery, etched with figures of spiders, rattlesnakes, cougars, or human figures, passed along the trade routes, and acted like gospel tracts, pulling all peoples of the South into a religious movement archaeologists call the Southeastern Ceremonial Complex. However, by about 1350—earlier in some places, later in others—the cities began to decline. By 1400 Cahokia, which held thirty-five thousand people at its peak, had been abandoned. The great ceremonial center at Spiro, Oklahoma, was gone by 1450. Mound building throughout the South tapered off. Why this came about is vigorously debated. A dramatic climate change, which brought long droughts, seems to be the most likely reason. Or was it an increase in warfare among the various chiefdoms of the South? An invasion of other groups? A breakdown of exchange and trade relations? Maybe it was one of these, maybe all, or maybe something entirely different.[56]

Not all vestiges of the Mississippian cultural tradition disappeared. While the opulence of the Southeastern Ceremonial Complex and the great cities may have declined, the mid-sixteenth and seventeenth centuries still saw many places in the American South, including Northeast Texas, with priest-chiefs, agriculturally oriented ceremonies, a ranked society, their people living in towns, villages, hamlets, and farmsteads, being fed by corn agriculture and participating in trade. But we are getting ahead of ourselves.[57]

Pueblo Cultural Tradition

While the Mississippian cultural tradition was reaching prominence on the eastern side of the Southern Plains, so too were sophisticated corn-based cultures rising on the western side. These were the Pueblo peoples of the Rio Grande and the Pecos River of present-day New Mexico, and they would exert significant influence on the Indians of Texas.

The Archaic Period, from 7,000 to 1,000 B.C., saw the growth of a large population in the rather arid regions of New Mexico, Arizona, and far West Texas. Archaeologists call this the Cochise culture. Like all Archaic peoples, they hunted and foraged for a variety of foods, such as deer, rabbits, birds, prairie dogs, yucca, juniper, and piñon, and used a wide assortment of tools. At some point, maybe around 1000 B.C., the people of the Cochise culture acquired corn from Mesoamerica. Just as it did with the later Mississippians, corn brought a population explosion and a cultural complexity to the Southwest. Out of the Archaic Cochise culture came the corn-growing Mogollon people of southern New Mexico, which in turn influenced the later Anasazis of northern New Mexico.[58]

By A.D. 500, the Mogollons along the Rio Grande were growing corn, beans, squash, tobacco, and cotton. But the arid climate made horticulture precarious, and the Mogollons, with their newly acquired bow and arrow, still depended heavily on hunting and gathering. Nonetheless they turned more and more toward horticulture, and to escape the climate extremes, the Mogollons began building partially underground pit houses, which kept them cool in summer and warm in winter. Their search for reliable water led some to Hueco Tanks near El Paso, where they built a small village of pit houses that lasted from 1150 to about 1350. Eventually, the Mogollons acquired a reputation as fantastic potters, creating beautiful clay pots and jars painted with their distinctive black-on-white designs. These ceramics became valuable trade items and found their way among the Indians of Texas. Though the Mogollons were some of the first to acquire corn and pottery in the Southwest, by about 1200 they found their culture absorbed by the expanding Anasazi to the north.[59]

The Anasazis of the upper reaches of the Rio Grande of northern New Mexico blossomed late, about 100 B.C., but their culture grew with amazing speed and sophistication. Like the Mogollons, the Anasazi grew corn, beans, and squash; wove baskets and sandals out of yucca, leaves, and vines; and lived in partially underground pit houses. Then about A.D. 750, the Anasazi moved aboveground and began building elaborate stone houses. This characteristic would eventually earn them the name Pueblo, in Spanish meaning both "town" and "people." The pit house, abandoned as a living area, now became the kiva, the center of the town's religious ceremonies.[60]

Between A.D. 900 and 1300, when the Mississippian cultural tradition was hitting its stride on the eastern side of the Plains, the Anasazi Pueblo culture was achieving its own golden age in the west. At places such as Chaco Canyon and Mesa Verde, the Anasazis built towns of huge multi-leveled apartment buildings. At Pueblo Bonito in Chaco Canyon, they built a five-story apartment building with eight hundred rooms, the largest living area in North America until the advent of the skyscraper in the late nineteenth century. The Anasazis became renowned for their bread made of corn, their beautiful pottery, turquoise jewelry, and clothing made of cotton and feathers. Some of these goods made their way into Texas by way of exchange, and Anasazi pottery and turquoise have been found scattered across the Southern Plains and into East Texas.[61]

Then, during the fourteenth century, at the same time the Mississippian cultural tradition declined in the east, the Anasazis began abandoning their large towns and villages. The same questions about the Mississippian decline are asked about the Anasazis. Drought? Warfare? Religious change? Internal conflict? Whatever the reason, within the course of a century, the great towns were abandoned and the Anasazi had scattered. Along the Rio Grande and the Pecos River they built smaller towns complete with many-roomed adobe mud houses surrounded by irrigated fields of corn. They also continued making distinctive pottery and turquoise jewelry, a tradition that lasts to this day. Though all of the same culture, these small, densely populated towns—pueblos—in northern New Mexico and Arizona became virtual nations in themselves. Language dialects proliferated and each pueblo directed its own politics and diplomacy.[62]

The Southern Plains proved a barrier to extensive Anasazi and Pueblo eastward expansion. In the Texas Panhandle, some Indians lived in stone slab houses that were influenced by the Pueblos. Other Puebloans migrated down the Rio Grande and formed clusters of hamlets and villages stretching from the Paso del Norte, where El Paso sits today, to a group of several large Puebloan-style towns at the juncture of the Rio Grande and the Conchos River, a place the Spaniards called La Junta de los Rios. Some Pueblo hunters from the Rio Grande and Pecos River towns doubtless migrated to the plains to hunt buffalo. These Puebloans at La Junta and their cousins hunting buffalo on the Southern Plains may have been the ancestors of the sixteenth- and seventeenth-century Jumanos. But what makes the Pueblo cultures along the Pecos and Rio Grande especially important in Texas history is that their corn, blankets, pottery, jewelry, and ideas acted as magnets, attracting a variety of people to them: some to trade, some to raid, and some to conquer.[63]

In modern society, where some new technology arrives almost daily, a mere ten or twenty years bring vast changes. So one of the hardest things to grasp are these extraordinarily long periods of time where change and innovation seemed to crawl across the landscape. For thousands of years, Paleoindians hunted big game with thrusting spears tipped with flint points. Then for an even longer period of time, Archaic peoples hunted, fished, and foraged with a larger assortment of tools. A truly revolutionary innovation came with the production of pottery about A.D. 500. And some Indians in Texas would become master potters, creating works of art that would find their way throughout the southern half of the United States. But when compared to the technology of Europe of A.D. 1500, or even A.D. 500, the Indians of Texas lagged far behind. They did not possess an alphabet, and whereas Europeans had already gone through their Bronze and Iron Ages, the Texas Indians of A.D. 1500 still relied upon the same stone and bone that their Paleoindian ancestors had.

Technology, though, is not the whole measure of a people. And the Indians of Texas underwent tremendous cultural and social changes over the millennia. Men and women learned the land and all it contained. They often migrated to other areas in order to better their conditions. They studied the habits of animals and the properties of plants. Some developed reputations as healers, and some felt they had found ways, through prayer and ritual, to influence the spirits who gave meaning to the universe. Texas Indians also interacted with others both inside and outside the region until a web of worn trails connected them to all areas of the continent. Of even greater importance was the coming of agriculture. To those people who came to rely on it, this new economy brought about a new religion, new relations between men and women, and a golden age of sophistication and power. By 1500 the Indian peoples of Texas, though they had developed distinct cultural characteristics that set them apart from each other, still had many things in common, no matter whether they were hunter-gatherers or agriculturalists.

Chapter 2

The Blossoming of Texas Cultures

W HEN DID any group of Indian people become a recognizable culture? When did the Caddo Indians of Northeast Texas actually come into being? How did the Tonkawas of Central Texas appear? At what point did the coastal Karankawas become Karankawas and the Rio Grande Coahuiltecans Coahuiltecans? Anthropologists and archaeologists would say this happened when the people developed a language, religion, belief systems, and above all, a sense of themselves as a special, distinct people. It might also include the style of pottery they made, how they adorned themselves, how they married, how they went about hundreds of daily activities, from cooking breakfast to the lullabies they sing their children. While dates are rather nebulous, between A.D. 900 and 1500, most, but not all, the Indians living in Texas had developed the distinct cultures that Europeans and Americans encountered and would write about.

With this comes a word of warning. Archaeological digs can provide lots of information, particularly about the physical culture of a people: the tools they used, what they ate, how they designed their pottery, how they built their homes and laid out their villages. But archaeology cannot tell what the Indians of Texas called themselves, how they conducted their religious ceremonies, how they arranged marriages, why they did certain things, and what they felt was important and what was not. Not until

Europeans arrived in Texas during the sixteenth century and recorded their interactions did these blank spaces begin to be filled in.

Even here we must be careful, or at least be aware of several things. First, these Europeans, when they described the Indians they met, were taking a snapshot of them frozen in time. It does not show the changes Indian culture underwent previously, nor how it was to change in the future. Indian cultures were not static. The people migrated, united with other groups, and adopted outsiders. Communities might split apart, and through it all they constantly changed the way they did things. In fact, the word "ethnogenesis"—the creation of a people—is applicable, as most Indian peoples of Texas made and remade themselves over and over again.

Second, reading only European accounts gives the false impression that the Indians of Texas had no history until Europeans arrived. Archaeologists refer to these centuries prior to the coming of Europeans as "prehistoric" or "pre-Columbian"—before Columbus. These are unfortunate terms as they give the impression that only when Europeans arrived did the Indians of Texas spring to life. In reality, Texas Indians had a long history that shaped the way they reacted to Europeans.

The third point leads us to the question of how accurate these European observations were. Europeans had wholly different ways of looking at the universe, and they interpreted what they saw through the lenses of their own culture. They may have stressed things the Indians did not and overlooked what the Indians felt was important. Fortunately, anthropological models can help and suppositions can be made by studying similar peoples.

Fourth, we must realize that the moment Columbus set foot in the Bahamas, the Indian societies of the Western Hemisphere began to undergo tremendous, rapid change. In many instances, long before Texas Indians ever saw a European, their cultures were already being affected by them. Some of this was change the Indians actively accepted and adopted; other times it was change forced upon them. So with the help of archaeology, anthropology, and history, we will try to lay a cultural baseline for these Indians of Texas, but with the understanding that Texas Indian cultures had been changing for thousands of years, were still changing, and were often affected by forces outside their region.

Texas in 1500

By 1500 a variety of distinct Indian cultures had developed in Texas. Some, such as those in East Texas and along the middle reaches of the Rio Grande, depended heavily on corn horticulture but supplemented it with hunting and gathering. Others along the Gulf Coast and in far South Texas were mainly hunters and gatherers. They used corn little, if at all, maybe growing small gardens when they could. Still, at the beginning of the sixteenth century, Indians lived in virtually every part of Texas. Exactly how many is not certain. There is no reliable way to calculate the past populations of people who did not write, took no censuses, and kept no written records; so counts given by scholars have varied widely. Some merely added up the numbers given by the earliest Spanish and French explorers. This method is inaccurate and probably gives low numbers as the Europeans did not take exhaustive or systematic censuses and often merely guessed at populations. Also, from the moment Europeans set foot in Texas, Indian populations rapidly dwindled.

Other scholars use a method called "carrying capacity," meaning they calculate how many people lived in a certain area by how many people the land could support. This might give rather high figures, as just because the land *could* support a large number of people does not mean it actually did. Another method is to take the lowest population figures for a given region, then multiply it by a fixed number. Again, this may give us high counts in some areas and low counts in others. Years ago, when scholars tried to calculate the number of Indians living in the whole of North American, that is, the United States and Canada, they gave a figure somewhere between 1 and 2 million people. Now scholars believe North America held maybe 7 million, some say 9 million people, others say as many as 18 million, and some may go even higher than that. So when it comes to Texas in 1500, there may have been anywhere from 50,000 to several hundred thousand to maybe a million living there. The more agricultural eastern part of Texas, the coasts, and the Rio Grande Valley held the highest populations, while the plains and the deserts certainly held fewer. But Texas was not empty and a person could not travel far before they encountered Indians and often a considerable number of them.[1]

Let us take a snapshot of Texas Indians in 1500, listing the peoples and where they lived. The names by which we call them are certainly not what they called themselves, but were usually European misnomers. In the forests and prairies of Northeast Texas, along the Neches, Angelina, upper Sabine and Red Rivers, lived the Caddos, who were the most agricultural of all the Indians of Texas. Strongly influenced by the Mississippian cultural tradition, the Caddos had been mound builders and by 1500 lived in numerous towns and villages scattered across Northeast Texas, Northwest Louisiana, Southwest Arkansas, and Southeast Oklahoma. They were governed by powerful priest-chiefs.[2]

South of them, in the dense forests of Southeast Texas and Southwest

Louisiana, along the slow-moving Sabine, San Jacinto, and Trinity Rivers and around the eastern part of Galveston Bay, lived the Atakapas. While the Atakapas may have planted a few small gardens, they relied mainly on hunting and gathering, stalking deer and other animals, but also taking advantage of what the rivers and the Gulf Coast offered.[3]

Southwest of the Atakapas, along the central Texas coast, stretching from the western part of Galveston Bay to Corpus Christi Bay, lived the Karankawas. Using their dugout canoes, the Karankawas fished the Gulf estuaries, bays, and the rivers emptying into it. They also hunted deer, bear, and other animals on the barrier islands and on the grassy coastal prairies. The women dug roots and harvested berries, nuts, and others plants among the coastal marshes and forests.[4]

North of the Karankawas, in Central Texas, between the Brazos and the San Antonio Rivers lived numerous small autonomous bands and villages. These groups, bearing such European recorded names, as Tohaha, Eba-hamo, and Spichehat, to name just a few, would eventually merge with other Indian bands coming from the north and south to form the Ton-kawas. While the Tonkawas planted some small gardens of corn, they re-lied to a much greater extent on hunting buffalo and deer.[5]

Southwest of the Tonkawas and Karankawas lived a huge scattering of Coahuiltecans. Stretching across South Texas and northern Mexico, inland from the coast and as far north as the Nueces River, the Coahuiltecans lived in numerous, small, autonomous bands. Because of the rough, arid land-scape they depended heavily on hunting and gathering, but there were not enough animals to feed large populations. So while some Coahuiltecans might have planted a garden of corn along a sure water source, they relied much more on gathering cacti, mesquite beans, various nuts, plants, and roots for their sustenance.[6]

Up the Rio Grande, northwest of the Coahuiltecans, lived the Ju-manos. Originally a Pueblo people who had migrated southeast, by 1500 they had divided between those who farmed and those who hunted and gathered. Farming Jumanos lived in large towns composed of flat-roofed adobe homes and tended enormous fields of corn, beans, and squash. These towns lay scattered along the Rio Grande from its confluence with the Conchos River all the way to where El Paso sits today. Other bands of Jumanos roamed between the Rio Grande and the Pecos River hunting buffalo.[7]

Far north of the Coahuiltecans and Karankawas and northwest of the Caddos, on the eastern margins of the Southern Plains, along the upper-most reaches of the Colorado, Brazos, Red, and Trinity Rivers and stretch-ing as far north as the Arkansas River in Oklahoma and Kansas, were the

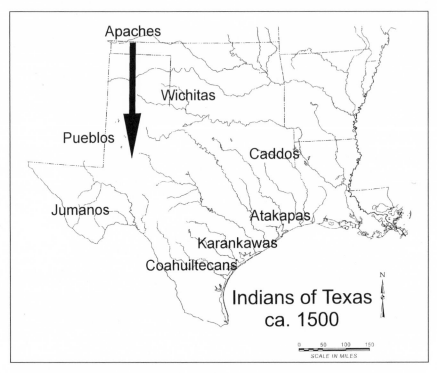

Map 1. Indians of Texas, ca. 1500.

Wichitas. The Wichitas lived in large permanent villages where they grew enormous quantities of corn, but they also hunted buffalos on the plains. In 1500 the most southwesterly of the Wichitas were the Yscanis in the Texas Panhandle, who were early on known as the Teyas. Out on the streams and rivers of the Panhandle, these Plains Wichitas lived in much smaller villages than did their more northerly cousins. In the late 1600s the Kansas and Oklahoma Wichitas began a migration south into Texas. By the mid-eighteenth century they would have villages ranging from Waco north to the Wichita Mountains in Oklahoma. Many of the Yscani Wichitas would eventually join with their southward-migrating kinspeople, but some would be absorbed by other cultures also moving into Texas.[8]

By 1500 the Plains Wichitas and the Pueblos to their west were already facing pressure from Athapaskans streaming down the west side of the Great Plains from Canada. Some of these Athapaskans would move west and become the Navajos. Others would continue south to the rugged mountains of southern New Mexico and Arizona to become the Apaches of Geronimo fame. A third group remained on the Southern Plains of Texas and came to be called Lipans or Plains Apaches. A fourth, the Kiowa-

Apaches, would arrive in Texas much later. These early Apaches hunted buffalo afoot and developed a complex set of relations with the Pueblos to their west. As the Apaches expanded onto the Texas plains, they began to absorb small communities of Plains Wichitas and Coahuiltecans.[9]

Three Indian peoples who have come to be most associated with Texas—Comanches, Kiowas, and Kiowa-Apaches—did not live in Texas in 1500. Another two to three hundred years would pass and several major developments occur before these powerful horse-mounted hunter-gatherers would make their way onto the Southern Plains that they would claim as their own.

The influx of Indians into Texas did not stop there. The late seventeenth century saw the Pueblo Tiguas migrate south to their present-day homes at El Paso, and during the nineteenth century bands of wholly different Indians, mainly from the eastern part of the United States, made their way into Texas. Bands of Cherokees, Chickasaws, Choctaws, Creeks, Alabamas, Coushattas, Seminoles, Kickapoos, Delawares, and Shawnees all briefly called Texas home and some still do.

All these peoples existed as separate cultures. They had their own identity, spoke their own language or dialect, had their own deities, rituals, clans, and families. Nevertheless, people are flexible, sometimes consciously adopting another group's culture. Other times cultural change may come slowly and unconsciously. In the span of a single person's life, certainly over one or two generations, a person, or even a whole band or village, might move from one type of existence and embrace something entirely new. Panhandle Wichitas often found themselves absorbed by Apaches. So while we can talk of cultural differences, it is also correct to talk of cultural similarities. Naturally, some groups may have had much in common. Wichitas, Caddos, and to a degree, the Atakapas, certainly possessed similar agricultural societies. Lipans, Coahuiltecans, and Tonkawas had comparable hunter-gatherer cultures. Coastal Karankawas and Atakapas were not all that different economically. Nevertheless, what really shaped Indian societies was how they made their living—through farming or through hunting and gathering.

Societies and Descent Systems

Essentially all the Indians of Texas could be divided into those who lived primarily by farming and those who lived mainly by hunting and gathering. Farmers usually lived in grass or adobe houses in villages and stayed tied to one place for long periods of time. Hunter-gatherers migrated with their food sources, living in camps of hide-covered shelters. Some of these might be the classic conical-shaped tepees, others just a hide stretched over a few bent branches. Farmers tended to have more earth-based and crop deities, such as the Corn Mother, while hunter-gatherers had more animal deities, such as the Tonkawa's Great Wolf. Farming tended to create larger populations and therefore, one would think, more powerful nations, while hunter-gatherers normally had smaller populations. However, diseases hit settled populations harder. And the coming of Spanish horses to Texas during the seventeenth century added a new dynamic to Indian cultures and helped create potent horse-mounted buffalo-hunting societies.

Whether one was a hunter-gatherer or a farmer also shaped how one acted in society and even whom one considered as relatives. Hunter-gatherers tended to live in small bands, often migrating over a huge territory. Though women provided a large measure of food through foraging, hunter-gatherers depended heavily on meat, and since men did most of the hunting, it paid for fathers, sons, and brothers to hunt together. As they learned the terrain and the habits of the animals and as each hunter honed his own particular skills, these men formed an organized and efficient hunting team. Therefore, many hunter-gatherer societies were patrilocal, meaning that when it came time for a man to marry, he took a wife from outside his band and she moved in with his family. This way new blood came into the family while leaving the hunting team intact. Wives brought with them their own special skills in food, clothing, and tool preparation. Because of the importance placed on male hunters and since women married into a man's family, most, but certainly not all, hunter-gatherer societies tended to be patrilineal, meaning that children traced their descent through their father and his family. They became members of their father's clan, if their societies possessed clans, and might have only weak relations to their mother's often-faraway family.[10]

Once agriculture eclipsed hunting among some Indian peoples and women provided more food than men, the rules of descent shifted toward women. Since women worked the fields, it profited mothers, daughters, and sisters to work together, forming a highly productive gang of farmers. The fields became part of the woman's domain, and so did the household. With the fields providing most sustenance and the farm too productive to break up, agricultural societies tended to become matrilocal, meaning that when men married, they left their families and moved into the homes of their wives. Essentially "guests" in their wives' homes, men had little say in the actual running of the household, which was dominated by a matriarch. Most, but not all, farming societies became matrilineal, meaning that children became members of their mother's clan, were closely connected to the mother's family, and had only tenuous connections with their father and his family.[11]

No matter what type of descent system a child lived in, she was surrounded by loving, caring people, often with several generations living in the same tepee or house. She lived not only among her own brothers and sisters but also among a host of cousins, referring to all of them as "older brother" or "younger brother" and "older sister" or "younger sister." In farming societies, her "aunts" might live in the same household, so she would refer to all her mother's sisters as "mother." Similarly, in a patrilineal household, her father was the most important male in her young life, but she would also call all her father's brothers "father." In matrilineal societies, the most important man in the child's life would be "mother's brother," her maternal uncle, who would be of the same clan as her and her mother. Her father, who was from another clan and who often spent time with his own sister's children, took on something of the role of an older brother or an uncle whose main job was to spoil, not discipline, the child. While this sounds complicated, children knew who their parents were and quickly learned the proper conduct among people older and younger than themselves.[12]

Subsistence

All Indian peoples of Texas, whether farmers or hunter-gatherers, divided labor various ways. At the most basic, a division existed between women and men. There were things women did and things men did and rarely did these lines cross. A second division was that between seniors and juniors. Older men and women held certain offices and had certain duties and privileges that were not available to younger men and women. A division also existed between people with more prestige and status and those with less. Some men and women, whether through their own abilities, their family's reputation and connections, or the wealth they controlled, possessed a high degree of status, rank, and esteem. The more status one had, the more power one could wield. So all people thirsted for status, which usually only came through practicing the cardinal virtues of bravery, fortitude, generosity, and wisdom, though connections to a prestigious family might give one a leg up. Normally, though, acquiring prestige and power took a long time. So older men and women possessed it, while younger men and women strove to acquire it.[13]

The World of Women

Regardless of whether a woman lived among agriculturalists or hunter-gatherers, her world revolved around hearth and home. In all early Texas Indian societies and on any given day, women spent much of their time gathering. They gathered firewood; clay for making pottery; cane, grass, or straw for weaving baskets and mats. They collected foods such as nuts, berries, roots, seeds, prickly pear tunas, grasses, whatever was in season. Much of this food was dried and stored. If her people were farmers, then during the warm growing season, she tilled the fields with digging sticks or hoes made of walnut or buffalo shoulder blades and then planted the seeds. Once the corn and beans were high enough, she watched over them, often building small platforms where she sat to scare off birds, deer, and other hungry pests. When the corn was ripe, she and her sisters and daughters harvested their household's gardens and fields, often getting two crops of corn each season, and then stored it in baskets or on lines to dry. At home she scraped the dried corn off the cob, making it either into hominy for soups and stews, or grinding it into meal with a mortar and pestle, or a mano and metate. Corn meal might then be fried, baked, or boiled into small loaves of bread. While small game—birds, squirrels, rac-coons, and terrapins—might be dressed and eaten at the day's meal, ex-cess meat from buffalo and deer would be cut into long strips a few inches wide, dried over a slow fire, and preserved for months. Coastal Indians prepared fish in similar ways. Bears were rendered for the great quantities of fat, which was then used for cooking or as a lotion for body and hair.[14]

No matter the season, a woman always had to cook for her family. In cold weather, this might be done inside; in warm weather she moved out-side to an open campfire or maybe to a small shaded brush arbor. Roasting meat and corn might be the easiest and most common way of cooking, but boiling was also prevalent. In fact, the Indians of Texas had an affinity for soups and stews. Depending on the people and what they had access to, these dishes might consist of a variety of meats, fish, nuts, seeds, berries, or corn, simmering all day in large clay pots. If a people lacked fireproof pottery, stews might be cooked in buffalo stomachs, heated by dropping hot stones into the mix. Indian women of all nations could be culinarily creative, cooking a wide variety of delicious meals. Indians were hos-pitable hosts, and visitors rarely went away hungry. Of course, as in all so-cieties, there were women who were considered bad cooks, and others whom everybody wanted to visit at mealtime.[15]

Women also made most of the utensils used by the family. Probably the most tiresome, backbreaking duty was processing buffalo, deer, and bear hides. Once a woman had cut the hide from the carcass using a flint knife, in later years replaced with one of metal, she pegged the hide to the ground and laboriously scraped away any remaining bits of flesh. If the hide was to be used for housing or warm-weather clothing, then she would also scrape off the hair. Hair would be left on for bedding or winter clothing.

After scraping the hide, she periodically soaked it, pounded it, and worked in a concoction of animal brains, which preserved the hide and made it supple. Once finished, the hide might be left as it was or maybe meticulously decorated with paint and beads in order to be used in trade. It might also be cut into pieces for tepees or ropes, or sewn into clothing, moccasins, containers, or any number of other useful things. Besides processing hides and making and decorating clothes and shoes, women also threw pottery, wove baskets and mats, made beads and other decorations, and did all the small jobs that allowed a household to run efficiently. The cold season, when the family spent most of its time indoors, was an excellent time for doing this work.[16]

Although a woman was supposed to be demure and retiring, she could be just as sexual as any man and make her wishes known without too much trouble. In fact, particularly in farming societies, women could initiate divorce and as a general rule throughout Texas, divorce was not too difficult to obtain by either sex. As a mother she could be both indulgent and practical. She made cradleboards to carry her babies, often using a wad of soft moss for a diaper and usually breast-feeding her children for the first few years. She taught her children what they needed to know to become good members of the community, and usually did so without resorting to spankings. She sang to them, played with them, worried about them, and took pride in their accomplishments. She loved her husband, comforted him, and sometimes squabbled with him. She gossiped with neighbors, joked with friends, honored her kinfolk, and prayed for a plentiful and secure future. She could cry with sadness, grieve for the dead, and become furious with her people's enemies, inflicting horrible torture on captives without so much as a second thought. As Indians attested, women held up one half of the sky.[17]

The World of Men

A man's life revolved around politics, hunting, diplomacy, warfare, religion, and games. On any given day, a man might gather with his friends or other members of the camp or village to discuss issues facing the community. But just as often it was to loaf, smoke, eat, gamble, joke, and gossip. Nothing happened in the village or camp that was not soon known by almost everyone. Marital discord, extramarital affairs, and the failures and successes of any given individual were always of interest and might elicit admiration, jealousy, a wry comment, or an off-color joke. Tobacco smoking was ubiquitous among Texas Indian men. Virtually every man carried a pipe and a pouch of tobacco, sometimes mixed with sumac leaves, willow bark, or other herbs. This he smoked among friends or when alone and pensive. More than just a pastime, smoking, seen as an aspect of purification, was involved in virtually every ritual. So a man might have a larger, highly decorated pipe he kept at home and used when important visitors arrived and for serious ritual occasions. Communities might even have one or more special ritual pipes that were used in ceremonies, for greeting official visitors, in declaring war, or in making peace.[18]

All men were essentially hunters and what they hunted depended on where they lived. In the forests, deer, bear, squirrels, raccoons, and a variety of birds predominated. The prairies and plains provided buffalo and antelope; on Texas' coast and estuaries, fish and shellfish were added to the diet. In East Texas, deer provided the main source of protein. A man might stalk his prey individually or in groups and often used various hunting methods. Hunters might form an open-ended corral of brush, then beat the bushes so the deer would run into the corral where the men could easily kill them. Sometimes they used fire in a similar way, burning the woods to run the deer into a brush corral. A hunter might disguise himself with the head, horns, and hide of a deer, imitate its movements and noises, and when a deer became too curious, take it down with an arrow, or in later years, with a musket shot. Of course, this could be dangerous as other hunters might mistake him for a deer.[19]

Buffalo was a delicacy as well as a source of tools and utensils. While a few forest buffalo could be found as late as the eighteenth century, most lived far out on the prairies and plains. In the late autumn and early winter, whole villages of men, women, and children would journey to the plains where the men hunted, often using some of the same techniques they used in taking deer. The women then skinned the buffalo, dried the meat, and tanned the hides. In later years, once horses had been reintroduced to Texas, buffalo hunting, rather than a community project, became more of an individual task. In fact some Indian peoples' whole lives and existence revolved around the buffalo. However buffalo hunting was fraught with danger, not so much from the animal itself, but because it attracted many different peoples to the plains, including one's enemies.[20]

Texas Indian men were very competitive. Whether hunter-gatherer or farmer, each man wanted to be considered the bravest warrior, most skillful hunter, or best shot. Men wrestled, ran races, and challenged each other to a variety of contests, using the outcomes as a way of attracting a woman's eye or of acquiring prestige. Indian men were also inveterate gamblers, often wagering everything they owned. Besides wagering on physical contests, men threw a crude sort of dice and played the "hand game," a sleight-of-hand game in which a person guessed who held a small object.[21]

While men and women lived in two separate worlds, some people managed to blur the lines between the two. Homosexuality existed in all Texas Indian societies. There were some men and women who performed all the duties of their own gender but secretly found themselves sexually attracted to people of the same sex. There were also male transvestites, who might dress as a woman and perform the work of a woman, but who remained heterosexual. Some homosexuals were very open about their lives. Some women took on the attributes of men, became hunters, even warriors; and some men became women, dressing as a woman, doing woman's work, refusing to take part in a man's world, maybe even becoming a man's "wife." The term *berdache* has been applied to these openly gay and lesbian Indians. Rather than being persecuted, berdaches were viewed as being spiritually powerful. They were allowed, even encouraged, to participate in rituals and ceremonies and accepted in Indian societies. In some instances, since warriors on a raid were prohibited from consorting with women, berdaches went along to serve the men. This indicates that it was not celibacy that the men of a war party sought, but that a woman's spiritual power might overshadow and negate that of the war party.[22]

Kinship

All Indians were surrounded by a host of kin. How they interacted with their kin was determined by many things, including the person's gender, age, whether they lived in a patrilineal or matrilineal society, clan membership, family connections, and certain well-known demands and taboos. For example, it was taboo to have sex with one's kin. Naturally, members of a person's immediate family—fathers, mothers, brothers, sisters, aunts, uncles, cousins, and grandparents—were all taboo. For modern Anglo-Americans this taboo may extend to fourth, fifth, or sixth cousins, or may not extend beyond one's immediate nuclear family. For Indians of Texas, this taboo would include the immediate family but also extend to anyone associated with their mother's or father's family no matter how distantly related, and since everyone in a person's clan was considered kin, that meant there was a whole range of people a person was forbidden to marry. At the same time, virtually every Indian society in Texas demanded that kin take care of kin. Conversely, it was perfectly fine to cheat, rob, or even kill a stranger with no kin relationship to you or your people. So for a Texas Indian, determining who was and who was not kin was essential. However, Indian peoples of Texas often recognized a much larger circle of relatives than did Europeans and Americans.

Among Indians three types of kin might be counted. Blood kin were those people connected by biology, such as parents and children, brothers and sisters, grandparents and grandchildren. Affinal kin were people connected by marriage: husbands, wives, and in-laws. A third category, fictive kin, incorporated people who possessed no relation by blood or marriage but were so close as to be considered kin, such as people adopted into a family. These fictive kinships might last permanently, if adoptees remained with or near their new family. Or it could be of short duration if the adoptee did not act like kin or left the family. Still, Indian peoples throughout Texas were quick to adopt outsiders; after all, the more kin one had, the more access one had to assistance and commodities, and therefore power.[23]

Kinship anchored every person in his or her society. At the most basic level, every person was a member of a family, essentially a gathering of sons and daughters, brothers and sisters, a father and mother, husband or wife, grandparents or grandchildren, nieces, nephews, cousins, aunts and uncles, and any adoptees. For Texas Indians, the family remained the most basic and most important connection, but there could be other levels to society. For example, in many societies, after family, a person found himself part of a lineage, essentially a group of related families who traced their descent from a common ancestor. A modern-day family reunion is really just a gathering of a single lineage. After lineage, many, but not all Texas Indians, considered themselves members of a clan. A clan is a group of related lineages that trace their descent from a common ancestor, but this ancestor, a vestige of Archaic traditions, might well be a mythological being such as a bear, wolf, or eagle, or even an element such as thunder or lightning. A person was born into his or her clan and never changed it. All members of a person's clan were considered kin no matter how distant in blood or geography, and it was taboo to marry a clan member. Clans spanned any given society, and clan members, who could be found at all levels and locations of that society, would be welcomed by other clan members no matter where they traveled. His own clan members would revenge any injury an individual suffered at the hands of a person from another clan. Not all Texas Indians had clans. They were more common among the farmers of East Texas, and even these lost them as time went on.

Beyond a clan, a person might sometimes be part of a moiety, essentially a group of related clans. With a moiety, which comes from the French word for "half," a society is split in two: half are one moiety and half the other. These are often associated with colors, usually a white moiety and a red one. A person is born into one or the other and cannot marry someone from his or her own moiety. Moieties were rare in Texas, but there is some indication that a few peoples of East Texas possessed them. After moiety, came people, such as Caddos, Atakapas, Comanches, or Tiguas. The word "tribe" is often substituted for "people," but tribe is so inexact and non-specific that scholars tend to avoid it now. Theoretically, a "people" should be composed of persons who spoke the same language, possessed the same customs, shared the same clans, and saw themselves as separate and distinct from their neighbors. However, this was not always so. The Indians of Texas often remade themselves and did so with people who had different languages, customs, and families.[24]

Reciprocity

Most modern Americans rarely give it much thought, but when it comes to kin, all are bound by certain obligations. There are just some things we *expect* our kin to do for us and things they expect us to do for them. We insist parents take care of their children; husbands and wives provide for their families; children assist their parents; older children look after the younger; uncles give good counsel; and all look after the old folks. How heavy these obligations weigh on a person would be determined by the society and time in which one lived. Among Texas Indians, these reciprocal kinship obligations were extremely important because they could mean the difference between poverty and prosperity, even life and death. As with the early hunter-gatherers, each band hunted a certain territory, which was normally respected by other bands. Because of this, some bands might have access to more types of resources than did other bands. By forging kinships through marriages, obligations of reciprocity provided each band with a form of insurance. Since kin helped kin, when a band fell upon hard times, say during a drought that drove away the buffalo, they could turn for support to their kin in another band, in an area where the deer might still be plentiful.[25]

A similar system worked within the hunter-gatherer band itself. Being so often on the move meant traveling light, therefore it was useless for a person to have too many possessions. Even among setled peoples, basic personal items such as clothing, tools, weapons, and ornaments were considered a person's private property, anything more would be given away as gifts or shared with family or friends. By generously giving gifts, a person stored up favors owed to him. In hard times, he called on those who owed him, and remembering their own obligations of reciprocity, they would then return the favors, helping their kin through a rough patch. Or he might call them in and ask his kinspeople for help in preparing a great feast, going on a raid, or some other such project. Sharing and gift-giving became the mainstay of hunter-gatherers and of farmers. Even more, it provided an economic and social structure for how people should live. People gave gifts because it was the thing to do; it was expected; it created obligations that redounded to a person's favor; and it gained a person prestige and status.[26]

The role and power of kinship among Texas Indian peoples cannot be overstated. And much of what Indians said and did cannot be understood unless the rules and obligations of kinship are taken into account. Looking after kin obligated people to a vast number of commitments and strictures, obligations that non-Indian people often had difficulty understanding. A kinsperson might be called upon to provide food, shelter, assistance, protection, goods and commodities, physical and moral support, or give sage advice. In some instances, a man might even share his wife with his brother and a woman her husband with her sister. All this should be done willingly and with generosity. To refuse the request might break the relationship and even bring about violence. Conversely, the giving of these "gifts" created reciprocal obligations of their own.[27]

In Indian societies, the welfare of the community took precedence over individual rights. Unlike capitalism, which stresses that an individual should accumulate as much personal capital as possible, reciprocity and kinship emphasized sharing, family, and community. A hunter shared his kill with his kin. A woman did not grow corn to sell on the open market but shared it with her family. A trader returning from a far-off place was expected to give some of his commodities to his kin. Rather than monetary profit, the sharer, or gift-giver, earned a favor, an obligation to reciprocate from the person who received the gift. Gift-givers also earned esteem through their generosity. This was essential if one wanted to acquire power in Indian societies. Though kinship and its reciprocal obligations formed the heart of Indian societies in Texas, as in all cultures, some people scrupulously adhered to the rules of kinship and some did so to a lesser degree; some tried to manipulate the obligations to their benefit; and others violated them with impunity. Often non-Indians who had been adopted into Indian families enjoyed all the hospitality and assistance given to them but blanched when their Indian kin made demands on them.[28]

Political Authority

In many ways, Indian political authority was also kin based. For lack of a better term, we use the word "chief," imprecise as it is, to designate just about any Indian leader. Some societies, such as the Comanches, had two chiefs, one who led during times of peace, another who took over during wartime. How much authority chiefs possessed differed from one society to another. Among smaller bands, the chief, "head man" might be a better term, would normally be a family patriarch, probably an older, wiser man who solved the petty squabbles that took place in any family. Band members turned to him for guidance and leadership. This was no formal government, but more like a strong father who provided for his wife, children, sisters, and parents. In larger bands or villages composed of several different families, one family might have a tradition of providing chiefs, or there might be several rivals who aspired to the position. In large agricultural chiefdoms, the position might well be hereditary, passing from father to son or to sister's son. Even then rivals might exert a claim. Since Indians had all the vices and virtues all humans have, there may have been attempts to gain power through scheming or force, but leadership was still bound by technology and economics. In small communities, most decisions affecting it were made by consensus, and any leader had to take this into account. As bands and villages got larger and larger, chiefly authority increased and government became more formal, with councils of warriors and older men to give advice.[29]

In agricultural societies, such as those of Mississippian cultural tradition, chiefs might have more power and would often base their authority on their kinship with the sun or moon or stars. Some priest-chiefs might rule over several different communities and their attendant villages. They could order earthen mounds to be built and have wrongdoers punished. The Caddo priest-chief, called the *xinesí*, did not work in his own field; it was tilled, planted, and harvested by the people. In return, he gave gifts, sponsored feasts, provisioned war parties and construction details, and doled out food to subjects hit by hard times. This generosity helped maintain the xinesí's great status and power, and when he died he was often interred in a burial mound, surrounded by sumptuous grave goods. Still, the chief's authority was not automatic, and he was expected to listen to the advice of his council of wise men. Of course, not all chiefs of farming societies wielded this much authority. Many lesser chiefs, leaders of villages, hamlets, and small farmsteads, held their positions in much the same way that hunter-gatherer band chiefs did.[30]

With few exceptions, and regardless of whether they were agriculturalists or hunter-gatherers, men occupied most leadership positions. Chiefs, important advisers and councilors, aide-de- camps, town criers, war leaders, lineage heads, priests, and shamans were usually men. Some of these positions, more so among agriculturalists, were hereditary, at least in theory. And even among hunter-gatherers, some families were seen as leadership families and expected to produce the nation's chiefs and principal men. This was not automatic, however, and even the son of a chief had to show bravery, fortitude, generosity, and wisdom. He must also have the honor and esteem of his people and possess good "medicine," meaning spiritual power. With no written laws, the power of the chief came from the consent of his people. Without these virtues no man could have their confidence, and without that, he could not lead.[31]

Since these virtues are not bestowed upon all men equally, this opened the door for a certain egalitarianism in Indian society. If the heir could not or would not lead, then there was always a rival nearby who would. And this could be almost anyone, commoners, even captives, as long as they possessed the requisite virtues, prestige, and medicine. This gave Indian society a dangerous democracy, because a chief had to be almost always correct and always successful. Too many bad decisions, too many times when he could not provide his people with adequate food or protection, too many dead on a raid, and he risked losing the people's confidence and therefore his power. Unlike a European ruler who could command no matter what those under him thought, an Indian chief possessed no real coercive power. He led only as long as his people followed him. As a result he had to constantly test his community's political waters and then ride whatever wave his people wanted. This often brought about a whipsaw effect in Indian politics and diplomacy. Indian leaders, in their effort to keep power, might advocate one thing one month, then something else the next.[32]

Since all members of the band or village had to be looked after, and since the chief could not risk alienating too many members of the community, important and controversial decisions could not be made arbitrarily. Consensus was vital. To do what was best for his community and his own political life, a chief relied on a council of important wise men for advice. In very important matters, he might convene a meeting of the respected men of the community. During these councils, men with prestige and status got a chance to speak. Often these speeches were very long and flowery, but everyone sat patiently, never interrupting. Younger men, without status, were expected to sit silently, or they might even be excluded. Therefore younger men ached to acquire prestige so their voices could be heard. Achieving consensus was not easy, and it often took a long time for agreements to be reached. If the question was particularly divisive or controversial, then no decision might ever be made. This often meant that Indian leaders could not adequately respond to fast-breaking developments that required their attention and immediate action.[33]

One of the paradoxes of early Texas Indian society was that for all their need for consensus and community welfare, Texas Indians tended to be some of the most individualistic people on the face of the earth. Though guided by mores and traditions, individuals had tremendous freedom. While the chiefs of some more structured agricultural societies might have been able to utilize corporal punishment, in most instances, even if a person broke traditional laws, they risked little more than the contempt and reproach of their people. Other than expressing their disapproval, there was little a chief or the community could do to rein in a person's bad behavior. Since written laws, court systems, and jail cells would not come about until the late nineteenth century, disputes among Texas Indians were usually on an individual level and were resolved on an individual basis. Nevertheless, a person was also a member of a family and lineage, so if a dispute was serious enough, whole families, in an effort to support their kinsperson, might be drawn into it.[34]

This individuality and kinship loyalty also played itself out in the community's political arena. One of the great myths about Indians was that they lived in a sort of paradise where everybody got along peaceably. However, as with all people, Indian men and women often held different opinions on numerous subjects, particularly about the direction their society might be taking. Some advocated one thing, others something else, and consequently factions appeared. Factions are common to societies the world over. Every Indian society in Texas was riven by factions, some minor, others serious enough to threaten the unity of the people. Unlike European and American factions, which usually formed over economic or political ideas, in Indian society, kinship often determined factions. Rarely was there a chief powerful enough to unite all of them. Since the chief led by consent of the people and had no coercive power, he could do nothing if people disregarded his advice.

This problem was particularly vexing with young men, who needed to acquire prestige in order to spark their own rise to power. While a chief might strongly advise against making a raid, young men were free to ignore the chief's advice, and frequently did. The chief also had to beware of rivals who differed with his opinions and were always ready to take over if his decision turned out bad. Still, once a consensual decision had been made, people either accepted it or if they could not, then they separated themselves from that community and went to live with another or formed their own band. Until the mid-nineteenth century, Texas was filled with various politically independent bands and villages of people who spoke for themselves and recognized no higher political authority. Europeans and Americans found this particularly disconcerting when a chief could not compel the obedience of his own people nor speak for any others except his own small band.[35]

Religion

Religions practiced by Texas Indians could be just as vast and complex as Christianity, Judaism, or Islam. Whether a people were hunter-gatherers or farmers also shaped their religion. Hunter-gatherers such as the Comanches, Kiowas, Coahuiltecans, Tonkawas, and Karankawas, since their lives depended on hunting, tended to have deities and ceremonies revolving around animals, such as the wolf, buffalo, or bear. Tonkawas venerated the Great Wolf; the Kiowas held a summer Sun Dance, which ensured the regeneration of the buffalo and thus the survival of the Kiowa people. Individuals sought power from animal guardians, whereas shamans conducted ceremonies, interpreted dreams, and tried to appease and manipulate powerful animal spirits. This hunting religion is the world's first religion and dates back to Paleoindian days. Conversely, farming cultures tended to revere the earth, the corn, the rain, and the sun, and developed beliefs based on fertility and the cycle of the crops. Deities tended to be oriented toward agriculture, such as Earth Goddess and Corn Maiden, with permanent temples or shrines erected to them. Fertility rituals, such as the Green Corn Ceremony, in which the sacred fire was extinguished and then relit, both celebrated and guaranteed the new crop. A brotherhood of priests, rather than individual shamans, directed the many rituals and ceremonies needed to ensure the people's survival.[36]

Nevertheless, there were some commonalities and a Wichita would not have too much trouble understanding the religious beliefs and practices of Comanches or Coahuiltecans. Essentially, the Indians of Texas, along with most Indian peoples in North America, shared a worldview in which everything possessed a spirit that could interact with humans. Along with this, they believed that power and instruction could come through dreams and visions and that there was a harmony to the universe. Problems arose when life went out of balance and so harmony had to be maintained or returned. They also believed in cycles of life and death.[37]

Virtually every Indian of Texas knew that she lived in a world filled not only with physical objects, but also with spirit powers. Anthropologists and historians call this animism, but no Indian ever used the term or had even heard of it. For Indians, every physical thing possessed a spirit or essence. Mountains, plains, wind, forests, rivers all had spirits, as did every animal in the world. Each river and mountain and animal had its own individual spirit, and there was also a collective spirit of the rivers and mountains, as well as one of owls, sparrows, wolves, raccoons, and so on. Indians also might recognize a chief spirit, a sort of "master of animals," who regulated the animals as a whole. Celestial objects, such as the sun, the stars, thunder, rain, and lightning, all possessed spirits as did some man-made items like bows and arrows, and pottery cups. Many Indians also believed in underworld spirits, such as ghosts, monsters, witches, and elf-type people. These spirits or powers were everywhere and had the potential to do both bad and good. Some were strong and one had to be careful around them. Some could be helpful; others, mischievous or downright deadly. And some were weak and could be safely ignored. That is not to say that Indians walked in constant fear of these spirits, but there was an awareness that powers were all around. There was an appropriate way to behave in their presence, but these spirits could also be appealed to or manipulated.[38]

Most Indians believed in a Creator, a very old entity that made the earth and universe. For the Apaches, it was Ussen, a power who lived before the universe came into being and who created two other important deities, White Painted Woman and Child of Water. White Painted Woman and Child of Water created the world, and it was Child of Water who created the Apaches. Child of Water is what anthropologists call a "culture hero," a spiritual being, often associated with the Creator, who helps bring about the creation of the people. The Kiowas viewed Sun Boy as their culture hero who rid the world of monsters and made it livable for the Kiowas. It was Neesh, also known as Moon, who led the Caddos from their underground world into this world. The Comanches have a similar hero, Kawus, made by the Creator, who brought the Comanches into being and taught them how to live. Sometimes this supernatural culture hero has a dual nature, a trickster side, often represented by Coyote, who not only helps but also bedevils his people. The Comanches say it was the trickster Coyote, the other side of the supernatural hero Kawus, who helped bring the buffalo to them. The culture hero, unlike the Creator, is not worshiped as such, but appears mainly as a powerful mythological figure in the people's ancient past.[39]

Beneath the Creator came the world of spirits. Ake Hultkrantz, a professor of Native American religion, explained the hierarchy succinctly. "There is usually a heavenly god who rules over the sky, a host of spirits who control the atmospheric powers, an innumerable crowd of spirits who influence human life on earth, and also some beings, including Mother Earth, who roam the nether world."[40] While the Apaches might appeal to Ussen to provide them with power, it was these many spirits beneath the Creator that most Indians turned to for help. Since all animal spirits had power, an intelligent person tried to harness that power or at least appease the spirit so it would not harm him or her. The spirit of the buffalo could show the Comanches where to find food. A Comanche imbued with the spirit of the coyote could see the future. Eagle spirit helped a man in war, while deer spirit could both cause and cure disease. As seen among the painted caves along the Rio Grande, cougars were the best hunters, so if humans could curry the favor of the cougar spirit, they could become better hunters. Wolves could give a person the power to walk barefoot in the snow. Even small animals might have great power. Skunks gave men prowess in war, while mice imparted the ability to slip in and out of narrow places. Owls, seen as harbingers of death, were to be avoided. These traits applied to animal spirits were not universal and might change from people to people. Nevertheless, the kinship between humans and animals is seen in Indian dances, which often imitate the movements of animals.[41]

Humans hoped to appropriate the power of animal spirits for themselves. To do so would give them, what we call for lack of a better term, great medicine, which indicates the close relationship between physical healing and spiritual power. A person with great medicine was a person with great spiritual power. Acquiring such medicine usually came during visions or dreams. Some men went on vision quests, which often involved privation and fasting in hopes of having a vision in which a guardian spirit, usually in the form of an animal, appeared and imparted its power to them. Quests were not always necessary. Sometimes visions came on unannounced, or spirits might make themselves known in dreams. Once a person had a vision or a dream, he went to the shaman or medicine man to have it interpreted. The guardian spirit might teach him a song to sing when he needed to call upon the guardian's power. Or he might be given a special power object to carry in a special medicine bundle, such as a distinctive pebble or even a stuffed animal. He might be ordered to perform a certain ritual or paint a unique design on himself or his shield when going to war. A Comanche warrior's shield was imbued with powerful medicine.[42]

All men craved a spirit guardian, but some never experienced a vision nor had a guardian spirit. Others might have several guardians they could call on for different purposes. Besides meeting spirit guardians, visions, particularly dreams, might foretell the future or provide a person with instruction. The Karankawas and Coahuiltecans put tremendous emphasis on dreams. Knowing this and fearing what it meant, a Spanish prisoner of the Karankawas tried to escape when a woman dreamed that her son would kill him. During his escape, the dream was fulfilled as the Spaniard was overtaken and killed, presumably by the son. Another Karankawa prisoner recounted that the Karankawas "take life, destroying even their small children on account of dreams."[43]

For hunter-gatherers, the spiritual leader was a shaman, again a name that was not originally used by Indians themselves. For farmers, it was a priest. Another term often associated with spiritual power is medicine man. In Texas, the name the Spanish gave to all these people was *pujajante*, as *puja* was the Comanche word for spiritual power. All shamans were medicine men, but not all medicine men were shamans. Essentially, medicine men tried to cure sickness not only by using plant medicine but also by relying upon instruction received from spirit helpers. While shamans also did this, they, unlike medicine men, went into a trance to visit the land of the dead, where they gathered information on the sickness, sometimes even returning the soul of the dying patient to his body. Shamans were more than just doctors as they could foretell the future, find lost people, interpret dreams, and even determine where game might be found. Any of various plants, such as tobacco, mushrooms, peyote, and jimson weed, and later, alcohol, might help the shaman make his way to the place of the dead.[44]

Priests of agricultural societies were somewhat different from shamans. In farming communities the medicine man, or medicine woman, healed the sick and acted more like the shaman, even going into trances for healing help. Priests, however, were normally powerful men, religious specialists, who underwent a long period of instruction and were valued not because they could fall into a trance or heal the sick but because they knew the proper rituals and ceremonies to ensure bountiful harvests and healthy, happy people. Besides shamans, priests, and medicine men, there were also people who used their spirit connection for doing evil. These were witches, and the Indians of Texas, who deemed them very dangerous to society, believed they must be killed. Witches could change their appearance, becoming animals, even sparks from a fire. They stole people's lives and souls. Unusual incidents or a person's strange, wild behavior could be attributed to witchcraft. For an Indian, recurring misfortune or illness might be caused by a witch, and it took a medicine man or shaman to reveal this.[45]

One thing that made witches so dangerous was that they threw life out of balance. For the Indians of Texas, there was a cosmic harmony to the universe. Most saw the universe divided into three levels: an upper level of predictability, a lower level of chaos, and the level where humans lived, which was a mixture of both. The world was divided into six regions: north, south, east, west, up, and down. During the year there was a cold period and a hot period. Camps were laid out in circles, a sacred shape. Doorways of tepees and houses often faced the east, the direction of the sunrise and life itself. There were roles for women and men and for seniors and juniors. Each Texas Indian society had rules, mores, and traditions that had to be upheld to maintain harmony. Problems arose for a person or a community when these rules were not upheld or taboos were violated. A menstruating woman's power was very great; if she took part in a ceremony or even bathed upstream from her people, her power would overshadow the other powers and bring disharmony. If a person was killed by another, then his blood cried out for vengeance, no matter whether the killing was accidental or purposeful. If a death was not avenged, then life was thrown out of balance as that person's soul prowled the camp causing problems. This gave rise to the idea of blood revenge. Vengeance did not have to be taken on the killer; it was enough to take revenge on one of his relatives, clan members, or people. Only by giving gifts to the dead person's family could a cycle of violence be avoided and life be brought back into balance.[46]

Of course, the best way to maintain harmony and balance was by living a correct life in which one did what was expected in relation to other people and to spirits. Honor was at the heart of this. Honor one's kin by upholding obligations of reciprocity. Honor animals killed by asking to take their lives and thanking them for allowing it. Honor the spirits, recognizing their power and thanking them for assistance. Honor one's people by fighting their enemies. Conduct oneself in an honorable way and perform the correct ceremony at the appropriate time. Nonetheless, Texas Indians were not surprised when disharmony happened, so they developed safeguards to ward it off or return balance. Virtually every ceremony or ritual was an aspect of maintaining or returning harmony, whether it was the Green Corn Ceremony, the Sun Dance, or merely a hunter singing a song under his breath to thank the deer for providing food for his family.

In the course of a day, a person might come into contact with various things that might plant the seed of disharmony: encountering dead things, going to war, visiting strangers, and the like. Purification became a method of maintaining harmony, and people might purify themselves many ways. Bathing and rubbing oneself with aromatic plants, such as sage, were aspects of purification, as was sweating. Indians got rid of impurities by piling into sweat lodges, essentially saunas made by throwing buffalo hides over bent saplings and creating steam by dousing hot rocks with water. East Texas farming Indians also relied on the black drink, an emetic tea, sometimes concocted of toasted yaupon leaves, other times by mescal beans, which they drank in copious amounts until they purged themselves by vomiting. Smoking also purified the body. Sometimes smoke might be wafted over a person, but most times a man ingested smoke through a pipe. Pipe smoking was ubiquitous among Texas Indians: no business could get done until men shared a pipe and no ceremony or council could begin without it. There was even a ritual to ceremonial pipe smoking. Puffs were blown in various directions. Some blew the first puff toward the east, while others directed it up toward the heavens. After the first puffs, some people blew a puff toward the earth, others to the four cardinal points, while others blew smoke up to the heavens and down to the earth. The pipe was then passed to the right and went around the circle, each man holding the pipe in the correct manner, taking a puff, and then passing it on until it came back to first, who received it on his left.[47]

This sense of cosmic harmony can also be seen in the Indians' concept of cycles of life. Just as a year was a circle of time, so was life. The buffalo ate the grass, people ate the buffalo, and when a person died he went back to the grass, to be eaten by the buffalo. Texas Indians certainly believed in an afterlife, even afterlives, but what that actually entailed might differ from people to people. After a person died, his or her soul walked a road to the west, the direction of death. At its most basic, good people went to warm, happy places where there were no wants; bad people went to cold, dark, wanting places. Jean Louis Berlandier, a French scientist who spent much time among Texas Indians in 1828, reported there were three possible afterlives. For good hunters and warriors who died in battle, a land of eternal springtime, with no hunger or pain. For women, old men, and the man who died peacefully at home, a place much like earth, sorrowful and cold, but rich in furs and hides. Suicides and the bewitched walked a never-ending road of hunger and thirst. Even then it was not so cut and dried as some souls were reincarnated as animals, while others trudged the earth as ghosts. Nevertheless, once dead a person was gone and could not come back in his human form. Because to openly long for the dead might bring disharmony or even malevolent spirits, most Texas Indians had strict observances and taboos regarding the dead. Funeral services could be elaborate, often with all the possessions of the dead buried with them or destroyed, as if the very sight of them only prolonged the grieving. Mourning was loud and long. Europeans commented on the loud keening Indian men and women did over their dead. A period of grieving, in which mourners often cut their hair and remained unkempt, might last up to a year. However, when that period was over, it was over. The survivors went on about their business and rarely, if ever, again mentioned the name of the dead.[48]

Indians always danced in a circle, as dance was the outward manifestation of the circle of life. And it was through dance that ceremonies were celebrated, deities honored, harmony preserved, war entered into, even the history of a nation recorded. The Indians of Texas had dances for most occasions. The Comanches, and others Indians as well, had a Hunting Dance before going on buffalo hunts and a Buffalo Tongue Dance when the hunt was over. There was a War Dance before going on a raid and afterward a Scalp Dance, which celebrated a Comanche victory and the taking of an enemy's scalp. A Spanish visitor to the Karankawas in the 1760s reported that the Indians were much given to dances. Using tortoise shell tambourines and gourd rattles, the Karankawa dances could be happy or sad, with dancers circling a large fire for as many as three days. They dance, the Spaniard said, "for liberty and triumph over their enemies, or good success in their campaigns, or abundant harvests in their plantings, or abundance of deer, buffalo, or bear." The Caddos have the Drum Dance, which tells of their origins; the Turkey Dance, which is a record of their people's history; the Bear Dance for hunting and the Corn Dance for a plentiful harvest. Men and women danced at important times of their lives, such as at an Apache girl's Puberty Ceremony or when a Comanche boy returned from his first raid.[49]

The Indians of Texas knew they lived in a world of spirits and powers, some beneficial, some harmful. Through ritual and ceremony they tried to harness and manipulate this power. A ritual, essentially a solemn act performed at certain times, could be almost anything: a dance the camp did before sending men off to war, the song a hunter sang before firing his arrow at the buffalo, the chant a woman made while planting corn, a pipe shared when visitors arrived, the cutting of one's hair and skin to mourn the death of a kinsperson. These were just some of the many rituals Indians might partake in. But whatever rituals they participated in, they did so in hopes of achieving a certain outcome. Success with few casualties for the warriors, a venison dinner for the hunter, a healed patient for the medicine man, generous visitors bearing good news for the smokers, and the passing of one's kin to the warm, wonderful lands of the afterlife. Religion permeated Indian life but did not oppress it.

Warfare

Just as virtually all able-bodied Indian men were hunters, so were they warriors; and as with hunting, some men who were better at it than others. Some groups, such as the Kiowas and Comanches, possessed soldier societies, which attracted men who steadily applied themselves to the art of war. People might go to war for a variety of reasons, such as to expand their territory in order to acquire more resources or to prevent other people from having access to them. Hunting ranges of deer or buffalo, good fishing spots, or prime foraging areas, such as groves of pecan trees or prickly pears, might be fought over. Once Europeans arrived in Texas, new resources to fight over included horses, captives, hides, and manufactured goods. This might mean pushing another people wholly out of an area, maybe conquering them and forcing them to pay tribute or absorbing them into one's own society. Battling for control of resources was only one reason Indians went to war. The most common motive by far was revenge, to pay back another people for an earlier insult, wrong, or attack and thus restore harmony. This falls into the category blood revenge and may well account for the majority of the Indian raids that took place in Texas. Naturally, if attacked, men were expected to defend their people's territory, camp, or village. While warfare was normally conducted against strangers and nonkin, mainly other peoples or nations, sometimes feuding between people of the same band or division might reach something approaching warfare.[50]

Unlike European societies, rarely did Texas Indians mobilize a huge army, carry out chess-piece campaigns, and wage a prolonged all-out war, though these were not necessarily out of the question. During the mid-sixteenth century the Caddos and Wichitas were able to put hundreds of warriors into the field, all divided into regiments and battalions. But most warfare consisted of small-unit raids. Raiding parties could be composed of one or two men to several score, though a party of six to ten was probably the most common. Even then, when the fighting started, it usually devolved into combat between individuals rather than bodies of disciplined troops. Most raids fell into two categories. They could be made to take revenge for an earlier attack or they could be economically motivated, essentially an effort to acquire resources from one's enemies. These motives might also be combined, so a strike for revenge might also gain the raiders hides, captives, and later on, horses.[51]

The quest for prestige was also a motivating factor, especially for younger men, who found raids a way to display those cardinal virtues necessary to gain power. The long march, the attack, the taking of the enemy's property, then escaping with the spoils showed bravery and fortitude. Back at home, the warrior generously gave away much of his booty, creating obligations of reciprocity and earning good will for himself. Continued success would be evidence of his wisdom and medicine. A successful warrior grew in status and power and became a man to be reckoned with as more and more people listened to his advice. Since warfare and raiding became fast tracks for prestige, young men ached to prove themselves in war, often making raids against the advice of their elders and at times when it would only bring trouble down on their people.[52]

While Indian war could be hell, there were strictures and rules to it. In 1500 Indians fought on foot, often in two opposing lines, armed with spears, bows and arrows, war clubs, tomahawks, and knives. By the eighteenth and nineteenth centuries, with the coming of horses and Europeans, Indian cavalry came into being, with metal weapons, lances, and firearms added to their arsenals. No matter what weapons they used, probably the most important rule of warfare was avoiding heavy casualties. The loss of too many men made a raid costly and defeated its purposes. Because camps and villages were not that large, heavy losses could devastate a family or band. To limit casualties, war parties relied on surprise and ambush. If surprise was lost or if the battle went badly, then it made sense to retreat and fight again another day. Surprise and retreat became even more important once firearms and metal weapons made casualties more likely. Gunfire and iron-tipped arrows quickly ended the days of two opposing sides lining up in the open to trade insults and a few arrow shots. However, Indians rarely waged total war. While a war party might take captives and commodities, they seldom leveled villages or destroyed fields of corn. Afterall, enemy villages were renewable resources that could be raided again and again.[53]

Nevertheless, Indian warfare could be terrible and terrifying. Warfare, particularly war for revenge, often resulted in the taking of captives. These captives, for the most part, would be taken back to their captors' villages, which might be a long hard road of several hundred miles or more. War parties often killed infants, the weak, and the feeble, knowing they would slow up the march because they were unable to stand up to the rigors of the journey. And if left alive, they would probably die a slow death of starvation or exposure. Back at the camp, a woman would be put to work, the same sort that all Indian women did, and her captor might or might not force sex on her. She was a captive, a slave, and as in slave-owning societies around the world, her captor had the right to do with his property as he pleased. African American slave women faced similar situations in the Old South. Europeans, Americans, Mexicans, and Texans, as well as Indians, committed what women would consider rape.[54]

Indians also understood the value of terror, so scalping and torture played a role in warfare. Scalping, the taking of a piece of a person's scalp and hair, was done by Indians long before Columbus ever reached the Western Hemisphere. However, Europeans and Americans made it profitable. For Indians, a scalp was a war trophy, proof of their bravery and ability. It might be woven into their own hair, attached to a shield, bow, or lance, or just hung on a wall. Dead enemies were scalped, if possible, but the wounded or captives might be also. While painful, scalping was rarely fatal, and so it was an ever-present badge of a person's inability to defend himself. Europeans and Americans often paid a bounty for Indian scalps.

Nevertheless, captives who did make it back to their captor's village, might be enslaved or eventually adopted into families to replace members who had been killed in raids. Some, men and women alike, might undergo hours, even days of beatings, stabbings, cuttings, and burning before finally being put to death. Torturing enemy captives was common to all Indians of Texas. The French scientist Berlandier reported that when he was in Texas in 1828 some Wichitas captured seven or eight Tonkawas and put them to death "by the slow and gradual tearing of the skin, first of their arms and legs, and finally of their trunks, while burning coals were pressed into the deep wounds cut in their flesh." On one level, torture was an act of revenge done to return balance and harmony; on another, it was pure retaliation. Indian life could be hard and children were taught to withstand pain, so it was just a short jump to inflicting pain. Virtually all Indians in Texas realized that if they were captured, they were going to suffer torture. Of course, torture was also an aspect of terror, and nineteenth-century Texans were certainly terrified of being captured by Indians.[55]

In warfare, men did most of the actual fighting, though some extraordinary women served as warriors. Lozen, sister of the late nineteenth-century Chihenne Apache chief Victorio, was a fearsome warrior with "great medicine" which gave her the ability to detect the direction of approaching enemies. In 1880 she ranged over West Texas stealing horses and killing cavalrymen. But most women played a more indirect role in warfare. They might urge their men to wage a war of retaliation if too many of their people had been lost in raids. Conversely, women might also agitate for peace if they felt the war had gone on long enough and sufficient revenge had been taken. During war, women sometimes served as diplomats and intermediaries. With captives, it was often the women who did the torturing, and they were creative when it came to devising ways of inflicting pain.[56]

Exchange and Trade

It would be wrong to assume that the Indians of Texas spent most of their time raiding one another. They also participated in a dynamic regional trade. Caddo pottery made its way northeast to the great Mississippian cities of Spiro and Cahokia and west to the Pueblo towns. Pueblo pottery has been found throughout western Texas and even into Northeast Texas. Jumano traders from La Junta on the Rio Grande visited people in East Texas each spring and summer. Wichita traders went south and west.

Karankawas went north to the Tonkawas, while Pueblo traders ranged down the Rio Grande and the Pecos River and visited Apache camps on the Southern Plains.[57]

Texas Indians also found themselves firmly linked to all parts of the continent by well-traveled trade routes. From the Atlantic coast near Saint Augustine, Florida, a major highway skirted the Gulf of Mexico, crossed the Mississippi at Natchez, continued to the Red River near Natchitoches, Louisiana, then proceeded west into East Texas. In East Texas it crossed the Angelina and Neches Rivers, then went on to San Antonio, where it angled southwest to the great Pueblo cities at the Casas Grandes in north-western Mexico. From there, it turned due south to the Mesoamerican cities in the Valley of Mexico. The Galisteo Pass at the Pecos Pueblo opened many of the Pueblo cities to the Southern Plains. Rivers acted as trade conduits and some of the most important and busiest were the Red, Canadian, Pecos, and Rio Grande. A trader could visit the cities along the Mississippi, then travel up the Red and across the plains to the Pueblo cities near Santa Fe, New Mexico. The Rio Grande was also an important highway, especially where it connected with the Rio Conchos flowing northward from Mexico and where the Paso del Norte crossed it at El Paso. In East Texas a southwest-northeast route, the Hasinai Trace, con-nected the Caddos and Wichitas with the Mississippian cultures of Cen-tral Arkansas and then to Cahokia. In Central and West Texas, several north-south routes on the plains, used by both traders and war parties, connected the peoples of the Great Plains with northern Mexico.[58]

In Texas Indian societies kinship regulated exchange and trade. Most Indian people lived in an "us-and-them" world. There were their family and their people and then there was the rest of the world, which was filled with strangers. To family one owed all the obligations of reciproc-ity. To strangers one owed nothing, so they were legitimate targets not only of raids but also of swindles and hard bargains. To steal something from a kinsperson or a member of one's own people was considered theft; it was disapproved of and would result in some type of rebuke. However, to steal from a stranger was praised and encouraged. So as dif-ferent cultures came into contact with each other throughout Texas, most tried to create some form of kinship with the other. Essentially they adopted each other. This usually began with the parties sitting down and smoking together. Then they exchanged a few gifts, which was not only a form of exchange, in that it transferred goods from one person to an-other, but also instrumental in creating valuable fictive kinships. If this new fictive kinship were to remain strong, then the parties had to con-tinue exchanging gifts for the remainder of the relationship. To stop would signify a break in the relationship and return the parties to the status of nonkin.[59]

This is not to say that all exchanges were done between kinspeople, though this would have been preferable. Sometimes a person came into contact with someone who did not want to make kin relationships, or if they did, they did not maintain them. These people remained strangers. However, not all encounters with strangers resulted in violence. Indian people often exchanged goods and commodities with people who never became kin. In this case, rather than gift-exchange, it was straight trade. Each party tried to drive as hard as bargain as possible, even resorting to cheating and thievery if need be. Simply put, exchange was done with family, trade was done with strangers.[60]

Goods that were exchanged and traded fell into two categories, "commodity goods" and "status goods." Commodity goods might also be called "subsistence goods" as these were items that all people had access to and used, such as food, animal hides, most pottery, and utensils. They would be part of the many petty exchanges that all people participated in throughout their camp or village. Much of this was gift-giving as the fulfillment of normal reciprocal kinship obligations. Sometimes gift-giving of this sort could be used as a strategy to buffer a person against hard times. At other times commodity goods were exchanged with people outside one's own village or band, usually when it would be mutually beneficial to both parties. In this case, one group usually had access to things the people wanted but did not have. For example, Lipan Apaches exchanged and traded buffalo meat with Pueblo Indians for corn and bread. Though little is known about them, by 1500 some Texas Indians had developed something akin to "professional" traders. If exchange worked best when kinships had been made between the two parties, then it would pay for the same kinspeople to meet year after year to conduct business. While some commodities and status goods were controlled by men, the exchange and trade of food, such as corn, dried meat, cactus tunas, and the like, was usually done by women.[61]

Status goods conferred prestige upon their owners. The need to achieve status drove most Indian men and women, so status goods were valuable and much sought after. Exactly what a status good was might change from people to people, region to region, and over time as well. In 1500 status goods would have been such items as carvings and beads made of seashells, nuggets of turquoise and copper, cloth made of rabbit or buffalo fur, certain forms of pottery, and pipes, all things that if possessed conferred a certain amount of authority. Because status goods conferred power, when traders arrived with status goods, the chiefs immediately took control of the situation. Gifts, trade, and diplomacy all went hand in hand among Indian societies. Upon their arrival, traders met with the chief to smoke and exchange gifts, the traders probably giving more than they got. Once the appropriate welcoming rituals had been completed, the chief and the traders did business, with the chief probably acquiring most, if not all, of the status goods. These he might keep for himself or dole out as gifts calculated to raise his prestige and bring return favors. Once the chief had finished, the rest of the people in the camp or village could make their own deals. Later, the women visited the traders, offering to exchange food, clothing, and utensils. The arrival of Europeans in Texas during the sixteenth century added a whole new type of status goods to the Indian trade networks. Metal goods, guns, and horses came to confer status and were greatly prized by Texas Indians. This would change not only the physical culture of Texas Indians but also their political and social institutions as well.[62]

Texas Indians lived in a world that made perfect sense to them. Preservation of the community, rather than individual rights, sat at the heart of Indian society. Generosity was prized, and a person was expected to take care of his family. And the definition of who was considered family could be extensive. There were places for men and places for women, creatures that inhabited each of the different worlds, but Indians also made room for people and things that did not fit the norm. When a hunter saw a bear, he understood that it might be a bear spirit, a spirit in the form of a bear, or just a bear. It was, in many ways, a logical world for those who lived in it. But this world was about to change.

Chapter 3

The Arrival of Strangers

A S THE SIXTEENTH century dawned in Texas, life was how it should be and as it had been. Whether they were corn-growing Caddos, desert-living Coahuiltecans, coastal Karankawas, or south-migrating Apaches, there was a certain similarity to their societies. While resources might differ from region to region and people to people, for the most part, their societies were not alien to each other. Whether hunter-gatherers or agriculturalists, men hunted, warred, and traded. Women farmed or foraged, and often did both. Weapons, tools, and utensils were all made of stone, bone, clay, wood, or animal hides, and pretty much everyone had access to these raw materials. By no means should these people be considered savages or barbarians. Their societies all possessed complex political, religious, and social frameworks that regulated behavior and tried to assure the survival and advancement of the community. Gods were worshiped, ceremonies conducted, kinships created, obligations upheld, exchanges undertaken, and commodities traded, while families provided structure, and leadership normally gravitated to the bravest and brightest.

However, the sixteenth century would bring the Indians of Texas into first contact with a dynamic and expanding European culture. And, unfortunately, they found themselves woefully unprepared to deal with this new world the Europeans brought. Indian societies possessed certain fatal deficiencies that played into the hands of the Europeans. Technologically, by 1500 Texas Indians lagged far behind Europe. Whereas Europe had gone through its Bronze Age in 4000 B.C. and its Iron Age in 1000 B.C., Texas Indians remained in the Stone Age. While copper nuggets might be hammered into sheets, smelting was unheard of, and Indians possessed no weapons or tools made of iron and no ability to make any. This also meant they had none of the accompanying technological developments, so there were a host of things Indian peoples did not have that Europeans did: firearms, long-range oceangoing vessels, wheeled carts, forges, grain mills, spinning wheels, looms, clocks, paper, and money. In a nutshell, Indians possessed nothing metal or mechanical.

The literary and mathematical skills of Texas Indians also did not measure up to the Europeans, nor with those of the Mayas and Aztecs of Mesoamerica. While pictures on rock, hides, and pottery might convey meaning, the Texas Indians had not developed an alphabet, which meant they had no way to write down their language. Indian people depended on their memory, and priests and shamans kept their people's traditions and history in their heads. Unfortunately, without an alphabet, or paper to record it, important medical, religious, and historical information could be irretrievably lost if a person died before he could pass it on to someone else. How much mathematics Texas Indians knew and used is uncertain. Certainly they developed highly accurate calendars and could navigate across veritably featureless plains without much trouble. Nevertheless, they did not seem to rely on complex numbers, such as thousands or millions, nor did they appear to have concepts of geometry, algebra, or trigonometry. Of course, the average sixteenth-century European had no concept of these either.

Indians also possessed some health deficiencies and ideological differences with Europeans that would not serve them well, but we will touch more on these later. Still, rather than considering the Indians as "inferior" and the Europeans as "superior," it might be better to view the European societies as more ideologically dynamic and technologically advanced than the Indians. Essentially, they were merely developing differently. We have no idea how Texas Indian societies would have turned out had they never met Europeans. Nevertheless, as the Indians of Texas began to encounter these new cultures, new commodities, and new ideas, they tried to incorporate them into their own worldview and social structure. And as they did, each began to change the other. For the Indians of Texas, the world began to change on November 6, 1528.

It was a rather cold autumn day and a band of Coco Karankawas were digging roots around the marshes of Galveston Island. Suddenly they noticed a stranger among their huts, stealing a pottery jar and making off with one of their small dogs and a few fish. The men, armed with bows and arrows, called to the stranger to stop, but he kept walking, gesturing for them to follow him. The Karankawas did and a few yards farther on were astounded to find a bedraggled mass of half-starved men with white skin and long scraggly beards. Their clothes, though torn and threadbare, were unlike any they had ever seen. The Indians hung back, and rightly so, as who knew what powers these strangers wielded. Within half an hour, about a hundred more warriors gathered to stare at the white men. The Karankawas had met Alvar Nuñez Cabeza de Vaca and his shipwrecked castaways, survivors of an ill-fated Spanish invasion.[1]

The Karankawas

The Karankawas were hunter-gatherers of the middle Texas coast. They consisted of five main divisions who shared the same language and culture. The Cocos, or Capoques, were the easternmost, living between Galveston Island and the Colorado River. The Cujanes ranged around the mouth of the Colorado River. The Carancaguases, from which the name "Karankawa" derives, lived around Matagorda Bay and San Antonio Bay, where the Guadalupe and San Antonio Rivers meet. The Coapites were near Aransas Bay and the eastern end of Copano Bay, and the Copanes between Copano Bay and the northern and eastern shores of Corpus Christi Bay. These may just be garbled Spanish attempts at Indian words and not what the Karankawas called themselves. Nevertheless, these are the names given the former five divisions that have traditionally been applied to the Karankawas by anthropologists and historians. Cabeza de Vaca, however, mentions Capoques, Charrucos, Deguenes, Quevenes, Guaycones, Quitoles, Camolas, and numerous other people.[2]

The Karankawas did not practice horticulture and so had little or no corn. Nor were they a maritime people. Though they had dugout canoes made of tree logs, they did not island-hop or go far out to sea. Instead, they lived mainly off what they took from the lagoons, estuaries, shoals, and barrier islands, as well as the coastal marshes and prairies. They ate such fish as the black drum, redfish, speckled sea trout, croaker, sea catfish, flounder, sheepshead, silver perch, and mullet. Oysters, bay scallops, quahog, crossbarred venus, and lightning whelk also made up an important part of their diet. On the islands and mainland, they hunted deer, peccaries, alligators, buffalos, and smaller game, while also gathering a variety of plants, nuts, and berries, including saltwort, acorns, pecans, prickly pear cactus tunas, blackberries, mustang grapes, and cattail roots. The

Karankawas were seasonal hunter-gatherers. In the fall and winter, when the fish were most plentiful, they lived in camps along the shore, depending almost wholly on fish and what plants they could gather in the marshes. In the spring and summer, they moved inland to camps on the coastal prairie. They often ventured as far as forty miles inland to hunt deer and a few seasonal south-ranging buffalo. Karankawa bands made the food circuit, visiting areas where certain plants were ripening at a given time. Even their houses were adapted to this constant movement: small huts, about eighteen feet in diameter, made of woven mats of rushes or animal hides thrown over a dozen long willow poles. All this could be quickly pulled up, stowed in a dugout, or carried by a woman on her back.[3]

It is not certain what language the Karankawas spoke. Some anthropologists believe it was related to Coahuiltecan, spoken by people farther west along the Rio Grande. Another believed it might have been a Caribe dialect. Most anthropologists believe the Karankawas, or at least their Archaic ancestors, had been on the Texas coast for thousands of years. By the time Cabeza de Vaca washed ashore, the Karankawas were masters of their environment, using longbows and arrows tipped with stone for hunting, fishing, and warfare. They wove nets, constructed cane fish weirs, and created baskets and a sandy pottery, both of which they often coated with the natural tar that washes up on the Texas Gulf Coast.[4]

One of the most common things observers mentioned about the Karankawas was their great height. They tended to be much taller than their neighbors, pushing upward of six feet. While their height set them apart, the Karankawas were similar to many other Texas Indians in their clothing and body adornment. Men went naked or wore breechcloths of animal hides. Women wore skirts of woven grass or moss. Men sometimes pierced their nipples and lower lips to wear cane ornaments. Using crushed charcoal and thorns, they tattooed designs on their face, hands, arms, and torso. Men and women used red ochre and other pigments to paint themselves, men particularly when going to war. These piercings and markings may have indicated a person's nationality, rank, lineage, or marital status.[5]

Because they were seasonal hunter-gatherers, migrating from place to place as food sources dictated, the Karankawas lived in small, family-based bands. These bands dispersed over a wide territory when the food was slim. However, when fishing peaked in midwinter or when hunting was at its best in late summer and early fall, bands might congregate in camps and villages of well over a thousand people. At these large gatherings stories were told, items exchanged, and marriages made.

The Karankawas apparently were patrilineal but with marriages arranged by the bride's parents. Since the woman's father lost a valuable, productive family member from his household, the newlyweds temporarily settled into their own home and for an agreed upon time everything the groom caught while fishing or hunting was taken by his wife to her father. Her father then sent food back to the groom. Once the indenture was complete, the couple then moved into the groom's family's house and band. Even then, the groom and his in-laws avoided each other. Neither could enter the other's home, and they turned away from each other if they happened to meet on the trail. Most men had only one wife, and they normally stayed married for life if they had children, if not, then divorce was common and easy. Shamans, by virtue of their prestige, might have several wives. Since a woman went to live with her husband's family, a woman was expected to marry her brother-in-law if her husband died, especially if they had children. Given that a Karankawa woman might, over time, become a wife to a whole family of brothers, it was acceptable for a woman to have sexual relations with her husband's brothers, usually with her husband's consent. Children were very much indulged, particularly male children, as would be normal in a patrilineal hunter-gatherer society. Because the Karankawas often went through cycles of plenty and scarcity, children were often nursed for years, sometimes until they were twelve years old.[6]

The Karankawas did not appear to have clans, and we are unsure about their political structure or how much interaction existed between divisions. In 1500 there was certainly no one chief of all the Karankawas nor even a chief of the Cocos. Respected men led bands, but these men had rivals, and disagreements occurred that split bands even further. Relations with their neighbors ranged from peaceful coexistence, bolstered by exchange and trade, to raids and warfare. Warfare seemed to be common among the Karankawas, even to the point of making long-distance raids against the Caddos far to their north. Karankawa bands not only fought with neighboring people but also sometimes raided one another. In fact, warfare could become so bad that trade was difficult. This opened the door for neutral traders, people without kinship ties to any one band or people, who were welcomed by all and could bring valuable commodities through a dangerous neighborhood. For several years, Cabeza de Vaca successfully played this role among the Karankawas and other Indians of Texas.[7]

Unfortunately, little is known about Karankawa religion. An eighteenth-century Spanish priest recorded that they worshiped two deities named Pichini and Mel. Shamans led the religious worship and used a variety of herbs and plants in their rituals, probably including peyote and mesquite beans. Dances and purification ceremonies using smoke and the "black drink" were held to ensure successful raids, fishing expeditions, and hunts. In some of these rituals, particularly those using the black drink, women were excluded. Ceremonies were also performed to give thanks when these ventures came off well. Death rituals assumed great importance among the Karankawas, particularly if the deceased were a male. The mourning period lasted for a year, with the deceased's closest kin wailing each day before dawn, at noon, and at sunset. For the first three months after a man's death, the members of his household did not hunt or forage, rather food was brought for them by kinfolk and neighbors. When the mourning period ended, the deceased's kin ritually purified themselves and cleansed the year's worth of paint and smoke from their bodies. Most Karankawas were buried in shallow graves, though shamans were cremated.[8]

One charge historically laid at the door of the Karankawas, and of their Tonkawa neighbors to the north as well, has been that of cannibalism. Spanish officials, Catholic clerics, and Anglo-American settlers all insisted the Karankawas were cannibals who dismembered, roasted, and ate their enemies as well as any shipwrecked sailors who fell into their clutches. This accusation was repeated so often over the years that it came to be accepted as conventional wisdom. Little direct evidence bolsters the claim of Karankawa cannibalism. No reliable eyewitness accounts of such behavior exist; nor has archaeology turned up shattered or scraped bones to support it. Most of what has been said is hearsay or came from the mouths of their enemies. To be sure, many American Indians, including Caddos and Atakapas, practiced a form of ritual cannibalism, in which bits of one's enemies were eaten to gain spiritual power, but eating humans for sustenance on a regular basis just does not seem to be the case. In fact, when some of Cabeza de Vaca's colleagues washed ashore at a different location on Galveston Island, in their hunger they began to eat the bodies of their dead. When the Karankawas found them, the Indians were horrified at the Spanish cannibalism. As Cabeza de Vaca wrote, "The Indians were so shocked at this cannibalism that, if they had seen it sometime earlier, they surely would have killed every one of us who had survived."[9]

The Karankawas, though, did not kill Cabeza de Vaca and his fellow survivors. If anything, the Indians saved their lives and the first contact between these two groups was warm and friendly. The Spaniards gave the Karankawas gifts of glass beads and metal bells. The Indians were delighted with such exotic items "and each one of them gave us an arrow in pledge of friendship." Cabeza de Vaca had done the right thing, for giving gifts was the first step in creating kinship. Besides the arrows, the Cocos brought food daily for the Spaniards, mourned with them over their drowned comrades, and finally took Cabeza de Vaca and his survivors to their own village where a hut with a warm fire had been prepared for them.[10]

Then things began to go wrong. Not long after Cabeza de Vaca's group went to live with the Cocos, cholera hit the Indians and killed half of them. Infectious diseases had now arrived among the Indians of Texas. The Cocos, wisely associating humans with the transmission of diseases, immediately blamed the Spaniards. The massive die-off from an illness Karankawa shamans had no experience with, the Spaniard's cannibalism, the hardships and scarcities created by ninety idle Spaniards needing to be fed, and the Spaniards' lack of kinship with the Indians changed the Karankawas' attitude from friendship to suspicion and hostility. Rather than powerful beneficent beings, the Spaniards were now perceived as witches, evil beings who took the lives of others to add to their own. Or if not witches, then certainly evil men who would mutilate and eat their own kinsmen, depriving the dead of a good afterlife.[11]

As the disease swept through the Coco village, the Indians prepared to kill the Spaniards, the usual sentence for witches; only the helplessness of these Europeans prevented them. After all, if they were powerful beings, then why could they not prevent their own deaths from drowning and starvation. Still, the Karankawas recognized the Spanish must possess some extraordinary powers and insisted that they try to cure the sick Indians. Blowing and rubbing on the ill, blessing them, reciting the Pater Noster and singing the Ave Maria seemed to be just successful enough, and similar enough to Karankawa medical practices, that the Spaniards were spared.[12]

While Cabeza de Vaca himself seemed to fair well among the Indians, his comrades were not so fortunate. Of the ninety that washed up on the Texas coast, within days only sixteen remained alive, the rest died of starvation, exposure, disease, and at the hands of other Karankawa bands not so understanding as the Cocos. As the Spanish survivors dispersed among various Karankawa bands, many were manhandled or even executed by their captors. Cabeza de Vaca himself reported being put to hard labor and sometimes beaten by the various Indians he lived with over the years. Essentially, the Spaniards allowed themselves to become slaves. Normally slaves were captives who had been taken in war or on raids. They were not members of any family or clan and so had no kinfolk obligated to protect and support them. Although the Spaniards had not been taken in war, they seemed to seek slavery and did many of the things slaves did. They certainly were not warriors as Cabeza de Vaca never mentions the Spaniards standing up to the Indians or fighting back. They did not hunt and fish as men did, but expected to be fed by their hosts. Eventually the Indians forced them to work, which the Spanish characterized as slavery. In reality, they performed only women's work, usually just foraging and gathering. As Cabeza de Vaca reported of two other survivors, "their constant occupation was bringing wood and water on their backs, or whatever the Indians needed, and dragging canoes over marshy ground in hot weather."[13] In another instance, one of Cabeza de Vaca's companions, frightened by death threats, sought refuge among the women. None of the men that Cabeza de Vaca mentions ever married an Indian woman, which would have created a bond and brought them into the protection of a family. The Spaniards acted like slaves, so they were treated like slaves. Eventually, in 1534, this drove Cabeza de Vaca and three companions to begin an overland journey toward Mexico.[14]

As Cabeza de Vaca and his companions traveled away from the coast and moved southwest into arid South Texas, they encountered innumerable small bands of Indian who differed in appearance and language from the Karankawas. The four Spaniards recorded such names as Mariames, Yguaces, Anagados, Avavares, Cultalchulches, Malicones, Arbadaos, and many, many more as they traveled through southwest Texas. It is difficult to pin down exactly which culture these people were part of or what language they spoke. Cabeza de Vaca reported that the Yguaces were different from the Karankawas in size and appearance, and that the Mariames and the Avavares spoke different languages, but that the Avavares could understand the Mariames. Over the years, anthropologists have come to label these many bands dispersed over South Texas and northern Mexico as Coahuiltecans, a name that derives from the northern Mexican province of Coahuila. "Coahuiltecan" is used here not so much to indicate a single people or culture, but more as handle for the numerous hunter-gatherers living in this hard country of south Texas and northeastern Mexico.[15]

The Coahuiltecans

That South Texas was once populated by numerous bands of people living between the Balcones Escarpment, the Guadalupe River, and the Rio Grande is evident by the tremendous number of arrowheads that have turned up in that area. Anthropologist John Swanton listed 218 South Texas bands, or "nations" as the Spanish referred to them. At one time it was thought that all these bands spoke the same language, but now we believe that many of the people who were labeled Coahuiltecan may well have spoken Coahuiltecan, Tonkawan, Karankawan, Solano, Comecrudo, or Aranama dialects, or even some different, now forgotten, languages. Anthropologist T. N. Campbell listed 55 different bands that probably spoke Coahuiltecan out of more than 300 bands living in the area. In reality, there may have been many more, possibly more than 1,000 different bands. Each band probably had between 100 and 300 individuals in it, though some bands might contain upward of 500 people.[16]

There also does not appear to be as much cultural conformity among the Coahuiltecans as once was thought. Each band considered itself politically autonomous, and there were certainly cultural differences in housing, weapons, clothing, body decoration, even subsistence techniques between Texas Coahuiltecans in the north and those people living far south in the Tamaulipas region of Mexico. So while we still use the term "Coahuiltecans" to designate these many groups, it might be best to think of Coahuiltecans not as a single culture, nation, ethnic group, or language, but more as a wide scattering of bands with a similar hunter-gatherer economy adapted to the arid country of southern Texas and northeastern Mexico.[17]

Among the many Coahuiltecans, several major divisions stand out. In Texas, three bands of Payayas lived where San Antonio is today. Southeast of them, between the Guadalupe and San Antonio Rivers, were the Aranamas and Tamiques. South of them on the lower Nueces lived a dozen or so bands that formed the Orejons. On the Gulf Coast south of Corpus Christi lived the Malaquites, while the Borrados were at the southern tip of Texas, near Brownsville. Inland, between the Frio and the Nueces Rivers, roamed the Pachal; west of them, near the confluence of the Pecos and the Rio Grande, were the Kesale-Terkodams. Downstream from them on the Rio Grande lived the Katuhanos, while farther south, between the Katuhanos and the Borrados, roamed the Carrizos.[18]

The Texas Coahuiltecans were certainly shorter than their Karankawa neighbors, but like them, they also painted, pierced, and tattooed themselves. Most ran a stripe from the hairline to the tip of their nose and tattooed a line around the mouth. Some pierced their lower lip and a nipple. Other markings might also have been used. These tattoos and piercings may have first been applied during a puberty ritual to identify the individual with a certain band or family to indicate his or her status. As most warm-climate peoples did, Coahuiltecan men either went naked or wore a deer hide breechcloth. Some bands used robes of rabbit fur. Women normally wore a grass skirt, sometimes one of animal skins. Shoes and blankets were made of buffalo hides.[19]

This part of Texas is hard country, and it necessitated that people spread over as wide an area as possible. It also meant that virtually everything edible be considered as food. The Coahuiltecans made good use of their territory and the resources available to them. Hunters took south-ranging buffalo, peccaries, rabbits, fish, lizards, snakes, frogs, even insects and insect larvae. Men ran down deer until the animal dropped from exhaustion, or they used fire to drive them into traps. Women foraged for what they could, with pecans, prickly pears, and plant roots being some of the most common foods. Women spent a lot of their time digging dirt ovens and baking roots, which took two days to cook. If Coahuiltecans grew any corn, it would be almost by happenstance, with possibly a few stalks left to fend for themselves as the bands wandered over their territory. They were seasonal hunters, migrating around their territory as plants ripened or animals became plentiful. Cabeza de Vaca's Mariames, who have been identified variously as Coahuiltecans, Karankawas, and Tonkawas, spent the fall, winter, and spring hunting and gathering between the Guadalupe and San Antonio Rivers. Thousands of pecan groves grew in this well-watered area. In the winter they migrated about eighty miles southwest to the area around Corpus Christi to feast on the ripening prickly pears, drinking their juice, drying them like figs, even pounding the peel into an edible powder. Coahuiltecans also used the agave cactus to make an alcoholic drink. Pottery seemed to be rare, whereas flexible baskets and nets proved the most common containers.[20]

Coahuiltecans periodically went through droughts, when there was little food available. Cabeza de Vaca constantly complained of being hungry when he lived among them. While they may have been able to withstand hunger better than the Spaniard, Coahuiltecans nonetheless had to adapt their society to this harsh environment. Since the Indians went where the food was, their houses, consisting of woven grass mats tied over bent saplings, were designed for quick movement. Nevertheless, too many mouths to feed could cause the whole band to starve. To check overpopulation, particularly during hard times, Coahuiltecans sometimes resorted to killing their infant girls. Since a mother could almost never feed two infants at the same time, when twins were born, the least hardy of the two was normally killed. Infanticide may be cold-blooded, but watching a child slowly starve to death is equally so. Being a patrilineal society, and since boys would grow up to be hunters and warriors and bring wives into the band, girls were seen as expendable. Hoping to prevent pregnancies, mothers nursed their children for many years. A man was not supposed to have sexual relations with his wife from the moment she became pregnant until two years after the child was born. Nor was he to have relations during her menstrual period.[21]

As with most hunter-gatherers in the southern half of Texas, Coahuiltecan bands were mainly composed of a large extended family with women marrying into their husband's bands. A chief, usually a lineage head, led the band, but disagreements could arise between principal men and the band could split, with each man taking his closest kinfolk with him. Only when several bands came together during seasons of plenty or to go to war together did a principal chief briefly appear. Some of these camps might have more than fifty dwellings in them. Shamans wielded their own power, serving as doctors and as mediators with the spirit world. And mediators certainly were needed as some Coahuiltecans complained to Cabeza de Vaca of a spirit they called "Evil Thing," who appeared among them, slashing their bodies and leaving visible scars. Coahuiltecans had a host of religious ceremonies, rituals, and dances; many of these lasted for three days and often involved the "black drink," mesquite beans, or peyote. Women were strictly forbidden to participate in some of these, and whole pots of "black drink" were thrown out if a woman passed by while it was uncovered. Dreams played a central role in the spiritual life of an individual.[22]

Warfare seemed to occupy a considerable amount of Coahuiltecan thought and time. Feuds and raids seemed so commonplace that Cabeza de Vaca likened the Coahuiltecan nations to the then-warring city-states of Italy. To protect themselves, the Indians used decoy fires or cleared out sleeping places in the middle of thorn thickets. When danger was anticipated, men stayed awake all night, their bows strung and arrows ready by their side. Raids were often made at night and warriors camouflaged themselves with leaves and brush. Raids could be brief and bloody, while more formal battles might end only when the warriors had exhausted their supply of arrows. Even Cabeza de Vaca realized that most violence was directed against people with whom no kinship relations existed. "All these nations, when they have personal enmities and are not related, assassinate at night, waylay, and inflict gross atrocities on each other." Cabeza de Vaca reported that among the Mariames, warfare, kinship, and the lack of it intersected to create an unusual diplomatic and survival strategy. All members of the Mariames were kin, so it was taboo for men and women from the band to marry each other. They had to take spouses from other nations. However if they allowed their daughters to marry into other nations, it would only make those nations stronger and they would eventually destroy the Mariames. So, said Cabeza de Vaca, the Mariames and Yguaces had rather kill their own daughters than allow them to marry their enemies.[23]

As Cabeza de Vaca and his three comrades crossed into the part of Texas west of the Pecos River, they finally encountered large bands of people different from the Coahuiltecans in both appearance and economics. Taller and larger, some of these people lived along the Rio Grande in houses of adobe and planted corn; others lived on the southern plains in portable hide houses and hunted buffalo afoot. These Indians have usually been referred to as Jumanos.

The Jumanos

Of all the Indians of Texas, the Jumanos are in some ways the hardest to pin down, and the term "Jumano" is just as problematic as "Coahuiltecan." One of the difficulties is that the Spanish applied the name "Jumano" to a tremendous number of groups scattered over a large and diverse territory, often with very different economies. Jumanos have been ascribed to such various places as Arizona; at the Pueblo towns of Gran Quivira and Tompiro in New Mexico; at the pass where El Paso sits today; to a cluster of adobe villages at the confluence of the Rio Grande and the Conchos River; to buffalo-hunting Indians west of the Pecos; to bands in the Panhandle; even to Wichita peoples living as far north as Oklahoma and Kansas. And what language did they speak? Scholars have variously said the Jumanos spoke Tanoan, a main language of the Pueblo Indians; Uto-Aztecan, spoken by such diverse peoples as the Aztecs and the Kiowas; Athapaskan, the language of the Apaches; Coahuiltecan; even Caddoan, spoken by Wichitas and Caddos. Was "Jumano" just a term the Spanish applied to people who tattooed and painted their bodies or did they apply it to all people who mainly lived by hunting buffalo? Was it just a name given to those Indians involved in long distance trade across Texas? Maybe they possessed some of all these traits?[24]

Regardless of name, language, or economics, one thing that is certain: during the sixteenth and seventeenth centuries a large number of corn-growing Indian towns stretched along the Rio Grande from its confluence with the Conchos River northwest to El Paso. At the same time, buffalo-hunting camps of these same people spread into the arid lands west of the Pecos River. These all appear to be our Jumanos. Probably the main town, or nation, of the Jumanos was that cluster of villages at La Junta de los Rios at the confluence of the Rio Grande and the Conchos. The Indians there called themselves Otomoacos. Nearby was another village of people called Abriaches, but together the two villages have come to be known as the Patarabueyes. Up the Rio Grande, about midway between La Junta and El Paso, lived the populous Caguates. At the Paso del Norte, or El Paso, lived the Tanpachoas, who have come to be known as the Mansos. To the west of them were the Sumas. All these river Jumanos lived in houses made of adobe or grass and farmed corn, beans, and squash. North and east of the Rio Grande villages lived the buffalo-hunting Jumanos, the Spanish often referring to them as the Cibolas.[25]

Jumanos certainly seemed different from their Coahuiltecan neighbors. Cabeza de Vaca said they were the "best looking people we saw, the strongest and most energetic."[26] One of the most common things mentioned about the Jumanos was the painted or tattooed stripes on their faces. While women wore their hair long, men cut theirs short up to the middle of their scalp, then, using paint, they curled the remainder over into what looked something like a cap. A lock of hair was left at the crown on which they attached feathers. The men usually went naked, but sometimes covered themselves with buffalo hides. An interesting difference among the Jumanos was that the Mansos at El Paso tied ribbons around their penises, while other Jumanos did not. Women wore ponchos and skirts of deerskin and cloaks of buffalo hides.[27]

The river towns teemed with people. Cabeza de Vaca said the country was "incredibly populous," while Antonio de Espejo, who visited the cluster of villages at La Junta in 1582–83, believed they held ten thousand people who lived in "flat-roofed houses, low and well arranged into pueblos."[28] These houses, apparently large pit houses partially underground and partially above, must have been rather solid, as the Jumanos stood on top of their houses to watch the arrival of a Spanish expedition in the early 1580s. The other Jumano villages up river may not have been as large or have had such permanent structures. Some river Jumanos lived in houses covered with grass. Other houses consisted merely of a frame of sticks plastered over with mud. These towns were governed by chiefs, or caciques as the Spanish called them. Like most Indians, the Jumanos used bows and arrows, gourds, and plenty of buffalo and deer hides and the utensils made from them. Though Cabeza de Vaca reported he saw none, we know the Jumanos used a sort of plain, brown pottery. Cabeza de Vaca reported that the Jumanos dropped hot rocks into gourds filled with water rather than boiling water by setting pots on a campfire.[29]

In good years, the river villages grew large crops of corn, beans, squash, and bottle gourds, but women also gathered mesquite pods and beans to make a sort of flour. They also cooked agave bulbs in earth ovens and harvested prickly pears. River marshes and lagoons provided an abundance of salt. Naturally, men hunted deer, fowl, buffalo, and fished as well. Although the people built granaries, periodic droughts, during which it was useless to plant corn, often caused severe distress among the villages. Cabeza de Vaca, when he and his companions reached one of the Rio Grande villages, was amazed that no corn was growing. The Jumanos explained that they would lose anything they planted because there had been "no rain two years in a row; moles got the seed; must have plenty rain before planting again."[30]

Periodic droughts may have sent some river Jumanos onto the Southern Plains, where they hunted buffalo afoot and lived in hide shelters. Probably at some point in the past, rather than return to the river villages once the drought was over, a few families decided to remain on the plains where they prospered and multiplied by gearing their economy around the buffalo. So arose the Cibola Jumanos. Cabeza de Vaca called them the "Cow People." This move to the plains would not have been unusual as the plains served as a refuge for farming Indians. In what would become a rather common trend over the next few centuries, the Jumanos may well have been some of the earliest horticulturalists to give up farming and migrate to the plains to become hunter-gatherers.[31]

The river Jumanos and the Cibola Jumanos had rather complex, but interdependent, relations. Feuding was common, so the relations were not always peaceful. As Cabeza de Vaca pointed out, "the people who lived along the river route were enemies of the Cow People but spoke the same tongue." However, exchange and trade were common between the two. Cibola Jumanos brought buffalo meat and hides to the river villages, which they exchanged for corn, beans, bows, and a host of other foods and utensils. Both branches of the Jumanos also traded with the Pueblo towns along the upper Pecos and Rio Grande, where they acquired, among other things, cotton blankets and nuggets of turquoise. In fact, during the seventeenth century, the Jumanos would gain a reputation as a nation of traders.[32]

By the early 1600s the Jumanos occupied a very important geographical location. Their villages along the Rio Grande cut directly across the main highway between the Spanish in Mexico and the wealthy, populous Pueblo towns to the north. The Cibola Jumanos formed a wedge between the Pueblos in the west and the Coahuiltecans, Karankawas, Tonkawas, Atakapas, the south-migrating Wichitas, and the Caddos to the east. Though the Jumanos, like most Texas Indians, had long been involved in trade and exchange with their neighbors, the seventeenth century saw them poised to become the Phoenicians of the Southern Plains, exploiting the spiderweb of exchange networks that connected virtually all peoples of Texas. What gave them this ability was the Spaniards moving north out of Mexico. With Hernando Cortez's conquest of the Mexicans in 1521, Spain quickly solidified its hold over New Spain and within just a few years was sending exploring and slave-raiding expeditions into northern Mexico, southern Texas, and New Mexico. However, just as the Spaniards brought about the rise of the Jumanos, so did they help bring about their eventual destruction. For among the many things the Spanish brought with them to Texas and New Mexico during the sixteenth and seventeenth centuries, two had far-reaching impact on the Indians of Texas. These were the introduction of new plants, animals, and germs on one hand, and an infusion of status goods and wealth on the other.

The Great Biological Exchange

The end of the last ice age about twelve thousand years ago essentially cut all contact between the Western and Eastern Hemispheres. Isolated from each other, over the millennia each developed its own unique set of animals, plants, even bacteria. When Europeans arrived in the Western Hemisphere at the end of the fifteenth century, they encountered a world full of things they had never seen before, such as corn, potatoes, beans, squash, peppers, peanuts, tomatoes, pumpkins, tobacco, manioc, and a host of other plants. While the Spanish recognized the Indians' ducks, deer, and dogs when they saw them, buffalos, turkeys, catfish, rattlesnakes, opossums, humming-birds, and armadillos were all new to them. Similarly, the Europeans brought with them things the Indians had never seen: horses, cattle, pigs, sheep, goats, wheat, rice, barley, peaches, melons, coffee, and much more.

These news plants and animals, in some ways, proved a boon to both cultures. Back in the Eastern Hemisphere, corn and potatoes spread across Europe, Asia, and Africa and soon stimulated an agricultural revolution, which in turn produced a population explosion. Africa benefited as corn and manioc quickly became staples. Tobacco, mainly imported from the Americas, became a greatly desired commodity throughout the world. For the Indian peoples of the Western Hemisphere, the Europeans intro-duced whole new sources of food. It was not long after their contact with Spaniards that the Indians of Texas began eating cattle, pigs, and sheep. Peaches and melons were soon growing at many Indian villages and ham-lets throughout the well-watered areas of Texas. Horses were initially hunted for food but eventually altered the lives and culture of virtually every Indian in Texas.[33]

While the Indians of Texas soon had a vast array of new foods available to them, these European-introduced plants and animals could also prove detrimental. As the Spanish pushed out of Mexico and closed in on the In-dian peoples of South and Southwest Texas, their cattle and pigs trampled Indian gardens. In areas where Spaniards consolidated their power, they might forcibly remove Indians from their traditional lands in order to graze cattle or sheep. Spanish cattle and horses often escaped into the wide-open spaces of South and West Texas. Over the next few centuries, large populations of wild horses and feral cattle thrived on the Southern Plains. These cattle wandered north, ate mesquite, and in their wake left droppings filled with mesquite beans, which sprouted, took root, and thrived. As the mesquite line spread steadily northward, essentially turning grasslands into scrub brush, it formed a barrier, limiting the southern range of the buffalo. By the early 1700s the buffalo had disappeared south of the San Antonio River making it harder and harder for the people of South and Southwest Texas to depend on this food source. Making matters worse was that the next couple of centuries saw increasing periods of drought, which only made life more difficult for South Texas Indians.[34]

While new foods might bring good or ill, a variety of new diseases carried by Europeans and Africans brought only devastation and depopulation for the peoples of the Americas. Isolated from the Eastern Hemisphere, Indians had suffered no epidemic diseases. In fact, over the years, any immunities they may have had to Eastern Hemisphere diseases gradually filtered out of their blood. Conversely, Africans, Asians, and Europeans often infected each other with a host of diseases. Some of these periodically swept across the land, as the bubonic plague did in the fourteenth century, killing almost a third of the European population. Other diseases, such as smallpox, cholera, influenza, typhus, and such, often ravaged major parts of the Eastern Hemisphere, but with each outbreak, mortality rates dropped as people developed immunities and passed them on to their children. Some diseases, such as measles and mumps, grew to be so common and so mild that they became known as "childhood diseases," something that children were expected to get, and that came and went without causing too much distress. When the Europeans arrived in the Western Hemisphere, they unwittingly brought these maladies with them.

The Indians of Texas, indeed of the entire Western Hemisphere, were ill prepared for the arrival of these diseases. Because they possessed no immunities, and through their trade route connections, "virgin soil" epidemics of smallpox, dysentery, plague, cholera, measles, whooping cough, influenza, and other diseases passed from one group to another and took a terrible toll. As we have seen, within days of Cabeza de Vaca's shipwreck on the Texas coast, half the Coco Indians of Galveston Island died, probably of cholera. Virtually everywhere Cabeza de Vaca and his comrades went, Indians began dying of mysterious illnesses. Among one group of South Texas Indians, people fell sick almost as soon as the four Spaniards arrived and eight died the next day. As Cabeza de Vaca reported, "they seemed to think they would die at the sight of us. They supplicated us to kill no more of them in our wrath."[35]

With no knowledge of these diseases, Indian shamans and medicine men found themselves powerless to prevent, halt, or cure these epidemics. In fact, traditional Indian cures, such as sweat lodges, often hastened death. The Indians had no concept of quarantining, and ritual dances and ceremonies merely spread the disease. And if the disease did not kill outright, then attendant problems often did. As disease settled among an Indian people, men might be too sick to hunt; women too sick to light the cook fire or feed their families. In their panic, those not stricken might abandon the sick, who were often too weak to care for themselves.

One can only imagine the horror of the Indians as wave after wave of disease broke over them. In many instances, they did not even have to see a European to get sick. Disease was passed through Indian-on-Indian trade and some maladies, such as smallpox, could be carried on hides and various trade goods to strike at unsuspecting recipients. Smallpox this year, then influenza the next, and cholera after that. Measles and mumps, considered mild in Europe, killed hundreds of thousands, if not millions, in the Americas. Smallpox, seemingly the great scourge among American Indians, caused great bloody pustules to erupt on its victims. Not only did it kill, but it also left survivors hideously scarred, some so badly that they committed suicide. According to historian John Ewers, between 1528 and 1890 no fewer than thirty epidemics swept across Texas, killing massive numbers of people, some to extinction.[36]

The impact of epidemics on the Indians of Texas cannot be overestimated. Thousands, maybe hundreds of thousands, of Texas Indians died from diseases and their effects. Between 1492 and 1900, the Indian population of Texas decreased by about 90 percent. This massive die-off weakened Texas nations just as Europeans were beginning to invade their lands. With their populations rapidly dwindling, many Indian nations were unable to field adequate armies to resist European and American incursions and so found themselves defeated, then pushed aside. Depopulation also brought turmoil to Indian societies by taking out important individuals. The village midwife might die, which meant more women and infants died in childbirth. Shamans might succumb to illness before they could pass on valuable spiritual information. The camp's best hunter might be taken, so starvation stalked his kinspeople. The best warrior might be gone and leave a people at the mercy of their enemies. Toolmakers, farmers, linguists, basket makers, and priests might all be taken, and with them died their valuable skills, leaving their people worse off than ever before. Much of the information they might have passed on was lost forever.[37]

An Infusion of Wealth

While Indian societies in Texas were certainly altered by disease, they were also affected by the wealth the Europeans brought with them. Before the coming of Europeans, virtually everything used by Indian peoples was made of stone, bones, hides, wood, clay, seashells, and the like. Everyone had access to such commodity goods as food and raw materials. On the other hand, status goods were often rare, hard to obtain objects, which gave prestige to the owner. When Europeans arrived in Texas, the technological differences between the two groups became immediately apparent. Europeans brought with them a host of manufactured goods made from iron, brass, bronze, tin, glass, flax, and wool, all materials unknown to Indians. Metal knives, axes, tomahawks, hoes, spades, scissors, kettles, bells, barrel hoops, firearms and shot; glass beads, jars, jugs, plates, and mirrors; woolen, linen, and cotton cloth; ribbons, shirts, pants, coats, blouses, and skirts, along with such collateral items as gunpowder, alcohol, and horses soon appeared in Indian villages. Indians immediately saw the value of these items, but unable to make them on their own, they had to acquire them from Europeans as gifts or through exchange. Because of this, though in high demand by the Indians, these very useful items remained relatively rare and so became status goods, raising the prestige of anyone able to possess of them.[38]

The amazement and delight of the Indians of Texas with these manufactured goods was apparent. Durable metal knives and axes made everything easier, from butchering a deer to cutting firewood. Metal hoes and spades made Indian women more efficient farmers. Long-lasting metal kettles began replacing clay jars and pots. Cloth clothing not only immediately displayed the high prestige of its wearer but also was cooler in summer and warmer in winter than clothes made of animal skins. Glass beads, particularly tiny seed beads, and the metal needles needed to sew them, brought about an explosion of ornamentation on Indian clothing. Barrel and wheel hoops became especially sought after as these flat pieces of metal could be fashioned into arrowheads or lance points. Lighter, stronger, more durable, and easier to make, metal projectile points soon edged out stone points, and before too long most Indians quit using stone points altogether.[39]

Indians also recognized the potential of firearms. These early sixteenth- and seventeenth-century matchlocks and wheel lock muskets were highly inaccurate, the smoke and noise they produced doing more to intimidate one's enemies than the ball they shot. Still, musket balls flew unseen, could not be dodged as an arrow could, and caused horrendous wounds if they did happen to hit someone. This, along with their potential in hunting deer and their psychological value, made Indians yearn to get their hands on firearms. Nevertheless, until the development of more reliable bullet cartridges in the mid-1800s, metal-tipped arrows, lances, tomahawks, and war clubs would play a greater role in Indian warfare than would firearms.[40]

Indians often adapted these manufactured goods to their own ideas and did not use them in ways the Europeans did or expected. Broken pieces of glass and mirrors made excellent hide scrapers and tattoo needles, or they could be used to tip arrows. Worn-out metal kettles were cut into arrowheads or rolled into cones to be used as ornaments on clothes. Broken guns served as hammers. European-style clothing was often cut and altered to suit Indian tastes. Women sometimes used mission bells as mortars in which they pounded corn kernels into meal.[41]

As they did with other status goods, chiefs and headmen tried to control the distribution of manufactured goods. When European explorers, missionaries, or traders arrived in Indian villages, they were met by the chief and his principal men, usually with very elaborate welcoming ceremonies. Most Europeans understood the need to give gifts and usually bestowed a quantity of manufactured goods on the chief. In return the chief offered hides and food and the hospitality of his people. Whether the Europeans realized it or not, this gift exchange was the first step in creating kinships. For the chief, this made sense. After all, what person would not want to turn these powerful, wealthy strangers into powerful, wealthy brothers, who if they upheld their obligations of reciprocity, would continue to bring these valuable goods to his new kinsman. Now apparently related to these powerful strangers, the chief's prestige and power skyrocketed, and it only increased as he generously distributed these goods to his people, creating a whole new set of secondary reciprocal obligations. A third set of obligations could come if the chief also exchanged some of these goods with neighboring peoples. He would become a truly wise, generous, and potentially powerful man who was owed obligations by his own people, neighboring peoples, and the Europeans as well.[42]

Prior to the coming of Europeans, prestige and power in Indian societies came through displays of wisdom, skill, and generosity. Even in relatively ranked agricultural societies, any man might be able to show these traits and so advance his status. The advent of manufactured goods began to alter this, as the ability to acquire and control these goods became shortcuts to prestige. Chiefs tried to control all the manufactured goods coming into their bands and villages, often forbidding Europeans from giving gifts to anyone else in the village. They also tried to prevent the Europeans from visiting other Indians. While a chief still redistributed these goods among his own people, he often kept some of the best items for himself. Greater disparities in wealth began to appear in Texas Indian societies, with the chiefs often controlling large quantities of goods, sometimes using Spanish clothing and canes as symbols of prestige. Young men, wanting their own prestige, began trying to find ways to acquire their own goods. Several strategies presented themselves. One might be to receive gifts from Europeans despite the prohibition of the chief. Another would be to acquire manufactured goods through trade. A third would be to raid other Indians, or Europeans themselves, for the goods or for items they could exchange for manufactured goods; and manufactured goods thus brought a whole new cycle of warfare and raids to the Indians of Texas.[43]

One of the biggest problems Texas Indians faced in acquiring manufactured goods during the seventeenth century was that one usually had to get them from the Spanish. And this was fraught with danger. Spaniards were a strange, unpredictable people and not at all alike. Although they gave gifts, they seemed to have no concept of the making of kinship or of obligations of reciprocity. While Indians certainly knew what they wanted from the Spanish—manufactured goods and military alliances—they were not sure what the Spanish wanted from them. Some Spaniards merely passed through, asking for food, clothes, and shelter. Others hoped the Indians would serve as allies and auxiliaries in Spanish wars with other people. Some demanded the Indians give up their religions and their customs, and relocate to missions where they would learn a new religion and labor for the Spanish. Others came spoiling for a fight, were quick to take offense, and would kill or destroy without a second thought. These seemed only to want gold and riches or to take captives as slaves. No matter in which category they fell, few Spaniards, few Europeans for that matter, saw the Indians as equals or possessing a culture and society worth preserving.

For most Indians of Texas, the coming of the Spaniards in the sixteenth century created both good and bad. Diseases swept away whole bands and peoples, but new wealth and labor-saving devices brought new opportunities for status and power. In any case, the Indians of Texas had little choice in the matter. By the mid-sixteenth century the Spanish were advancing north out of Mexico. By 1600 they had created the colony of New Mexico among the Pueblos of the upper Rio Grande and the Pecos River. As the Spanish passed back and forth from Mexico to New Mexico, their routes took them directly through Jumano territory. And the Jumanos were well poised to take advantage of the new wealth the Spanish brought to their villages. Unfortunately, it would be both a blessing and a curse.[44]

Chapter 4

Expansion and Collapse in West Texas

T HE JUMANO PEOPLES of the sixteenth and seventeenth centuries possessed an extraordinarily successful economy. They hunted buffalo, deer, rabbits, and fowl, and took fish from the rivers. Those living along the Rio Grande and Conchos grew corn, beans, squash, and bottle gourds, while women gathered mesquite beans, prickly pears, maguey leaves, and a host of other plants and roots. Nevertheless, droughts periodically withered their crops, so to ensure food during hard times, elders arranged marriages with other Jumano bands and created trade alliances with other groups. And it was as traders that the Jumanos gained their greatest reputation.[1]

An interdependent relationship had developed between the buffalo-hunting Cibola Jumanos on the plains and the farming Jumanos at La Junta. This early Jumano trade network covered a much wider area than just the Rio Grande and the Southern Plains. When Antonio Espejo visited the Jumano villages along the Rio Grande in the 1580s, the Jumano elders who controlled exchanges brought him "many things made of feathers of different colors, and some small cotton *mantas,* striped with blue and white. . . . That another nation that adjoined theirs, towards the west, brought those things to barter with them . . . for dressed hides of cows and deer."[2]

This nation to the west was the Tompiro Pueblos located between the Rio Grande and Pecos River in southern New Mexico. The relationship between the Jumanos and the Tompiros was an ancient one, with the Cibola Jumanos providing the Tompiros with buffalo ribs and buffalo hides in exchange for corn, bread, cotton blankets, turquoise nuggets, and pottery. The river Jumanos also depended on the Tompiros for corn when droughts scorched their own fields. Salt was another commodity in great demand. Great salt flats lay near the Manzano Mountains of southern New Mexico, not far from the Tompiros. Jumano trading bands eventually relocated there in order to control the flow of salt to the east. This would not have been unusual as bands of Indians often relocated to areas where they could acquire important commodities and funnel them back to their own villages. By the late 1500s three, maybe four, Jumano towns existed in the Tompiro area, including one called "the great pueblo of the Humanas," which may have held as many as three thousand residents. The Jumano salt monopoly was short-lived, as the Spanish eventually seized the salt flats for themselves. Nevertheless, events precipitated by the Spanish, along with climatic changes would alter the ethnic makeup of the Jumanos and for a brief while make them the masters of trade and exchange across southern Texas. Ironically, the leaders of this great Jumano trade expansion would come out of the Spanish mission system.[3]

Mission Indians

In the late 1500s and throughout the 1600s, the Spanish tried to establish control of the Indians in northern Mexico and New Mexico. By the early 1600s Spanish Franciscan missionaries had built missions around Monterrey, Mexico, at many of the Pueblo towns in New Mexico, and hoped to create a few in South Texas. But missionization moved slowly and only during the eighteenth century did Spain make any real effort to found missions in Texas. A mission hoped to achieve several goals: control Indians, Christianize them, hispanize them, and then use Indian labor to make the mission self-supporting, even profitable. Backed by the Spanish military, Franciscans rounded up scores, even hundreds, of Indians, often from different nations and bands, and herded them into missions. Here they were not only forced to attend Mass, taught Catholicism as well as the Spanish language and culture, but also compelled to work for the missionaries. Indian men were set to farming or herding while the women spun, wove, and sewed. Early on, the friars essentially tried to eradicate Indian religion and culture and often used whippings, torture, and execution to stamp it out. The same models, ideas, and practices would be used among the missions established in Texas over the next few hundred years.[4]

Despite the harsh measures the Spanish missionaries meted out, some Indian peoples willingly came to live at the missions. Missionaries, understanding reciprocal obligations, drew Indians by giving gifts. Also, disease killed thousands of Indians but rarely touched the relatively immune Spanish. Some Indians acknowledged that the Spanish god was more powerful than their own and made true conversions to Christianity. Others were not interested in Christianity but in acquiring food, iron tools, cloth, cattle, sheep, and of course, horses. At the San Antonio mission of San José during the 1700s, every Sunday the missionary gave "each Indian a peck of corn, some meat and tobacco. He distributes beans, corn, and brown sugar bars to those who need them on Thursdays. During the week, nothing is lacking to them that is needed for living."[5] Others sought the missions as refuges from starvation caused by droughts, from raids made by other Indians, and from the work levies and roundups made by Spanish officials and slave catchers. Many Indians used the missions as temporary safety valves, coming to the mission during bad times and then leaving when things returned to normal. Sometimes "permanent" mission Indians might run off when crops failed there or things got too bad.[6]

Whether in Mexico, New Mexico, or Texas, the missions dramatically affected the Indians who went to live at them. One of the great tragedies of the missions was the tremendous number of Indians who died there. Some Spanish missionaries were compassionate men truly interested in saving the Indians, while others were sadists only wanting to use their power for evil. No matter, both the good and bad saw little of value in Indian culture and certainly viewed Indian religion as nothing more than devil worship. Rapes and murders happened. Indians often died from being overworked and underfed. At other times, the missions themselves became targets of Indian raiders who killed or captured the mission Indians while running off with the horses and cattle. By far the biggest cause of death in the missions was disease. The concentration of people at the missions proved fertile ground for smallpox, plague, and venereal diseases. The death rate in some later Texas missions became so high that the missions had to be restocked with Indians virtually every ten years. One did not grow old in a Spanish mission.[7]

While the missions tried to Christianize and acculturate, Indians often found ways to resist this. Because the friars depended on Indian labor, they usually relied on Indian leaders and caciques to help motivate their people. Among larger bands of the same culture the old social mores prevailed. Status still made leaders, and seniors distributed gifts to juniors and decided who and when people would marry. Not all Indians adopted Christianity or learned Spanish. In fact, an Indian lingua franca of various languages developed among the mission Indians at San Antonio. Of course, the best way to resist indoctrination was to run away and many Indians did just that, abandoning the missions in droves.[8]

Nevertheless, the missions also tended to blur the ethnic identities and thereby created whole "new" Indian peoples. Inside the missions, Indians from one band often found themselves working side by side with Indians from other bands, even other nations. Over the years they exchanged aspects of their culture. At the same time, the missionaries attempted to extinguish Indian culture and replace it with a Spanish one. Women and men from different Indian nations, as well as Spanish men and Indian women, now married each other and the children from these unions were heavily indoctrinated with Spanish culture. The Spanish called these children of Spanish men and Indian women mestizos and this cultural mixing gave them a choice: they could live in Indian society, live in Spanish society, or move back and forth between the two and thereby act as "cultural brokers," helping the Indians understand the Spanish and vice versa. Almost any Indian who spent time at a mission became somewhat acculturated to Spanish ways. Many spoke Spanish, understood Catholicism, became familiar with manufactured goods, horses, and cattle, and developed an intimate knowledge of the workings of Spanish colonial society. Hispanizing the Indians had been a goal of the missionaries, but acculturated Indians could prove dangerous to Spanish interests. Knowing what the Spanish wanted to hear, they could not only manipulate them but also pass on valuable information to other Indians about how to deal with the Spanish. Many Spaniards realized that missionization created only an even more powerful and wily opponent.[9]

Spanish fears soon became reality. By the mid-seventeenth century, many Indians and Indian bands, unwilling to endure harsh treatment, ran away from the missions. The Spanish referred to these runaway Indians as "ladinos," which translated as "cunning" and indicated these people had learned how to use Spanish culture to their advantage. They were also called "apostates," people who had turned their back on Christianity. Spanish authorities desperately tried to return these Indians to the missions before they could "corrupt" other Indians and turn them against the Spaniards. But the genie was out of the bottle.[10]

The Jumano Trade Network

Anti-Spanish feelings among the Indians of northern Mexico, New Mexico, and South Texas increased as Spanish cattle ranching, mining, and slave raids expanded. Wealthy *encomenderos* were authorized by Spanish officials to tax Indians in a certain area, forcing them to provide labor, food, and commodities. Cattle-raising *hacendados* appropriated Indian lands and compelled the Indians to work for them. So did silver miners in northern Mexico who needed a cheap workforce. Slave raiders, wanting to profit from the labor needs of the Spanish, increasingly struck north out of Mexico and, despite orders to the contrary, attacked Indian villages and enslaved hundreds of men, women, and children. Some Indians in northern Mexico, such as the Guachichles, Coahuilas, Quamoquanes, Tobosos, and Gavilanes, fought back and warfare convulsed that region for decades. Even the Jumano Sumas, Mansos, and those around La Junta often became angry and attacked isolated Spanish ranches and traveling parties. So during much of the seventeenth century, refugee Indians, such as Tobosos, Conchos, and Julimes from along Mexico's Conchos River; the Tompiros and other Pueblo Indians from New Mexico; and ladinos, such as the Yrvipiames from northern Mexico, all tried to escape the missions, warfare, drought, starvation, and enslavement. To do this, many fled north of the Rio Grande.[11]

Throughout the seventeenth century the Coahuiltecan and Jumano country of Southwest Texas roiled with ethnicities as bands and peoples disappeared and new ones were created. Diseases swept through Indian communities, overwhelmed them, and sent their survivors seeking refuge with other nations. Drought and starvation seemed to run in ten- to twenty-year cycles, and those of the 1650s and 1660s, the worst ever in Texas, shattered Indian communities. With the establishment of missions around El Paso, La Junta, and in northern Mexico in the latter 1600s, thousands of Indians were sucked into them never to reemerge. Or if they did, they often came out as multiethnic, composite Indian bands or as Spanish-acculturated Indians. From these displaced nations, village fragments, composite bands, starving stragglers seeking refuge, and acculturated Indians on the run came a new, multiethnic Jumano people.[12]

By the 1680s even the Spanish referred to the "extended nation of the Humanas," which consisted of more than ten thousand people and was composed of anywhere between thirty and sixty different bands. The influx of these new groups, particularly Spanish-acculturated Indians, altered traditional Jumano society. With so many "original" Jumanos dead or displaced and with new and different people flooding into Jumano society, the traditional leadership families declined, old kinship bonds snapped, and long-standing obligations of reciprocity faded. Vacant Jumano leadership positions now went to those men who could best deal with the Spanish, provide their band with a steady supply of food and manufactured goods, and protect their people from Indian raiders. And the perfect men to grab these positions were ladinos who knew both Spanish and Indian cultures. One of the greatest of these new Jumano chiefs was Juan Sabeata, a ladino Christian from San José de Parral in Mexico. In the 1680s he led about two hundred Jumano followers. Sabeata and six companions visited the Spanish at El Paso in 1683 and reported that they had been sent by other Jumano "captains" at La Junta. That these other Jumano captains were also ladinos is evident by the Christian names Sabeata ticked off: Don Juan, Alonso, Bartolome, Luis, Don Francisco, and José. What these Jumano leaders wanted, Sabeata announced, was for the Spanish to create missions among them and protect them from the Apaches. While the Jumanos definitely wanted Spanish support in their battles with the Apaches, they did not desire Christianity so much as the goods and horses that the padres would bring with them.[13]

Sabeata and the other chiefs depended on manufactured goods and the trade surrounding them for their individual political survival. With kinship ties weak, Sabeata and the new Jumano chiefs used their knowledge of Spanish customs and their ability to distribute manufactured goods to gain followers and shore up their power. As their power increased and they attracted more followers, the chiefs could offer refuge and safety to other bands and peoples. This increased their personal status and prestige. And with Apache raids on the rise, Sabeata's Jumanos began absorbing all sorts of other groups, including refugees from northern Mexico and South Texas.[14]

Now the Jumanos were able to take advantage of their geographical position to become the primary traders across southern Texas. The old Jumano town of La Junta became a gateway community, a funnel in which goods came and went in all directions. People from East Texas, the Gulf Coast, northern Mexico, and the pueblos all gathered at La Junta to exchange goods and pass on information. Toboso raiders took horses and manufactured goods from Spanish haciendas in northern Mexico and brought them to La Junta. Jumano trading bands then carried them out to other Texas Indians, who, if they possessed something of value, could exchange it for these horses or other goods. Naturally, the Spanish had their own needs and so found a place in the Jumano trade network. Indian-produced commodities such as corn, salt, buffalo meat and hides, pottery, bows and arrows, feathers, seashells, projectile points, chunks of flint, river pearls, nuggets of turquoise and other minerals, even Indian captives all made their way into this cross-Texas Jumano trade. So did such Spanish items as horses, firearms, metalware, beads, cloth, and clothing. Horses and firearms were particularly in demand. No less important was information, essentially news and gossip that told people what was going on where and with whom. It would be the Jumanos who pointed the Spanish toward East Texas and the great kingdom of the Hasinai Caddos. And in the 1680s it would also be the Jumanos who told the Spanish of Robert Cavelier de la Salle's French colony at Lavaca Bay. The Jumanos had, if not created, at least maintained a highly efficient distribution and information system that spanned the southern half of Texas.[15]

Jumano traders like Juan Sabeata usually spent the winter at La Junta in preparation for the upcoming trading season. In the spring Jumano trading bands fanned out in all directions: west to the Pueblos and the Spanish settlements along the Rio Grande and upper Pecos; south to the Spanish settlements in northern Mexico; and east toward the Coahuiltecans, Karankawas, and Caddos. For those heading east, one of the first stops was a large trade fair held among the great pecan groves on the Colorado River, near present-day Ballinger, Texas. At the 1684 trading fair Spanish explorer Juan Mendoza reported that attending were Indian traders from the Jumanos, Ororosos, Beitonijures, Achubales, Cujalos, Toremes, Gediondos, Siacuchas, Suajos, Isuchos, Cujacos, Caulas, Hinehis, Ylames, Cunquebacos, Quitacas, Quicuchabes, Los que asen Arcos, and Hanasines. And these were still waiting for the Tejas, Huicasique, Aielis, Aguidas, Flechas Chiquitas, Ecahancotes, Anchimos, Bobidas, Injames, Dijus, Colabrotes, Unojitas, Juanas, Yoyehis, Acanis, Humez, Bibis, Conchumuchas, Teandas, Hinsas, Pojues, Quisabas, Paiabunas, Papanes, Puchas, Puguahianes, Isconis, Tojumas, Pagaiames, Abas, Bajuners, Nobraches, Pylchas, Dteobits, Puchames, Abau, and Oranchos.[16]

All who showed up hoped to exchange their own goods for Jumano horses, guns, and metalware. Horses were probably the most sought after item and the Jumanos seemed to have a large supply. By 1691 even the Spanish were impressed with the huge Jumano horse herds and worried about the number of firearms they owned. However, not everyone could afford horses or afford to keep them if they got them. Coahuiltecans did not have much to exchange and even when they did acquire horses, they often died during droughts. Karankawas also wanted horses, and were willing to fight the Spanish when refused them, but they too had a difficult time acquiring and keeping them.[17]

From the trade fair on the Colorado, eastward-bound Jumano trading bands might visit the Coahuiltecans and Karankawas just to see what they might have. Nevertheless, poorer nations who could not supply what the Jumanos wanted were usually bypassed in favor of more lucrative customers such as the Caddos in East Texas who exchanged corn, bows and arrows, and other goods for Jumano horses. Jumano traders were welcome visitors in the Caddo villages. It was during one of their trips to East Texas that the Jumanos discovered La Salle's French colony on Garcitas Creek, at the north end of Lavaca Bay. After a summer of trading across Texas, when the leaves began to turn, the Jumano traders made their way back to La Junta carrying their profits with them.[18]

The Jumanos seemed poised to become one of the most powerful Indian peoples in Texas. They occupied strategic regions along the Rio Grande and acted as intermediaries between the Spanish in New Mexico and the Indians east of the Pecos. They had developed methods of incorporating outsiders into their societies and so replenished their population and re-created their bands. They were seen as the consummate traders throughout southern Texas and desired by all as economic partners and military allies. However, Jumano expansion was at the same time being rivaled by the expansion of another people streaming down the Southern Plains from the north—the Apaches. And the Jumanos would be hard pressed to stand against this dynamic Indian people.

The Plains Apaches

The Apache peoples of the American Southwest speak Athapaskan dialects, a language mainly associated with subarctic Canada. Anthropologists believe that Apache ancestors originated there and at some point began migrating down the Great Plains into Texas. These southward-migrating Athapaskans called themselves Indé—"the people"—and there is much debate over how and when they arrived on the Southern Plains. Some anthropologists say they came down to the Southwest out of the Great Basin west of the Rockies; others say they came down the plains east of the Rockies. At some point these Athapaskans began banding into divisions, such as the Chiricahuas, Jicarillas, Mescaleros, Navajos, Kiowa-Apaches, a host of smaller Apache bands in Arizona, and for our purposes, the easternmost Lipans, or Plains Apaches. The name Apache itself came from the Zuni Pueblo word for "enemy." As for when Apaches arrived in the Southwest, some have said as early as the thirteenth century, others put it as late as the mid-sixteenth century, but the mid-1400s seems to be the most accepted. Certainly by 1540 Spanish conquistador Francisco Coronado encountered an Apache people on the Southern Plains called Querechos. Coronado's Querechos were apparently Lipans, and from 1540 on Lipan Apaches, and to a degree the Mescaleros and Kiowa-Apaches, came to play an increasing role in Texas history.[19]

Querechos, Escanjaques, Vaqueros, Llaneros, Natagés, and eventually Lipan are all names that the Spanish gave to these Plains Apaches of the sixteenth and seventeenth centuries. Whether these are just various names for the eastern Apaches—"Apaches de Oriente" as the Spanish termed those on the Texas plains—or whether they were the names of different subdivisions and bands is unclear. Certainly by the early 1700s the Spanish saw two major Apache divisions in Texas: the Lipans who roamed northwest of San Antonio on the upper Colorado, Brazos, and Red Rivers, and the Mescaleros, who lived farther southwest around the Pecos River and the Rio Grande. How much contact, cooperation, and kinship relations these two divisions had with each other is not certain. Though a host of names and spellings would be applied to these two Texas divisions, the Spanish pretty much referred to both of them merely as "Apaches."[20]

Unlike their neighbors, the Apaches did not tattoo themselves, though men and women did paint their bodies, particularly around their eyes. Naturally, clothing depended on the weather, but what clothes they used were made from buffalo hides. During hot weather, men went virtually naked, maybe wearing a breechcloth, while women wore skirts only. Both sexes added leggings and moccasins, with buffalo-hide shirts and ponchos during colder weather. One of the most characteristic pieces of Apache clothing was a moccasin-boot with a turned-up toe. From this, the Comanches often referred to Apaches as Tá-ashi, which means "turned up." Buffalo hides also served as blankets, which the Apaches wrapped around themselves in very cold weather. As European goods made their way into Apache society, some clothing became virtual works of art with beaded designs and metal ornaments. When they could, Apaches also added European cloth and clothing to their wardrobe, so it would not have been unusual to see a man wearing a breechcloth of cloth, a linen shirt, or even wool socks. Besides painting their bodies, men and women also wore earrings, necklaces, and bracelets. Men usually plucked out all their facial hair also cutting their hair short on one side of their head but leaving it very long on the other, then folding it until it was above their shoulder. Women normally wore their hair long and plaited in the back. Of course, hair and clothing styles changed over the years and Apache men eventually wore shoulder-length hair.[21]

Buffalo remained the mainstay of Plains Apache bands. In 1542 Coronado provided a classic description of the Apaches, saying he met some "people who lived like Arabs and who are called Querechos in that region. . . . These folks live in tents made of the tanned skins of the cows [buffalos]. They travel around near the cows, killing them for food."[22] Juan de Oñate, who visited the Apaches in 1601, acknowledged they "were not a people who sowed or reaped, but they lived solely on the cattle."[23] Prior to acquiring horses, Apaches hunted afoot. According to one of Oñate's lieutenants, they used weapons "of flint and very large bows. . . . They kill [buffalos] at the first show with the greatest skill, while ambushed in brush blinds made at the watering places."[24] Once the buffalo was down, they expertly butchered it with flint tools. They saved the hides for clothes and utensils, drying the meat into long strips of jerky, some of which would be ground into a powder and then added to soups. Like many plains people, they ate some of the internal organs of the buffalo as delicacies.

As corn spread across the Texas, some Apache bands tried planting a few patches at campsites they frequented, usually leaving it to fend for itself and then harvesting what they could when they returned. Though horticulture would become more common among some Apaches over the next few centuries, most Apaches relied mainly on the buffalo and on the plants and roots the women gathered. To supplement their diet, Apaches often visited various Pueblo towns, such as Pecos, to exchange buffalo meat, hides, and fat for corn, bread, pottery, and salt. Because the Plains Apaches followed the buffalo herds and so had to move quickly, their hide-covered tepees were easily broken down by the women, and in the days before the acquisition of the horse, loaded onto travois to be pulled along by dogs. "They travel like the Arabs, with their tents and troops of dogs loaded with poles and having Moorish pack-saddles with girths," Coronado observed. "When the load gets disarranged, the dogs howl, calling some one to fix them right."[25] Women usually managed the dogs, holding the animal's head between their knees while they adjusted its load.[26]

One of the curious things about the Apaches was that though they were hunter-gatherers, they were matrilineal. A wife, husband, and children tended to live in one lodge, but lodges of related families clustered together. Women remained part of this family group for the rest of their lives; men married into it and were obligated to protect and provide for it. A man was to listen to what his in-laws said and show them tremendous respect. Marriages were easy to arrange, with the groom's parents contacting those of the bride. Once arranged, the marriage was done with very little ceremony. It was just as easy to dissolve if both parties agreed. An adult brother looked out for his sister, almost to the point of supervising her, while mother's brother was very much involved in the lives of his sister's children, especially in teaching them the Apache way. A particularly strong bond existed between children and maternal grandparents. Women possessed significant esteem among the Apaches. Their most important ritual, the one that virtually defined them as a people, was a girl's puberty ceremony. The ceremony was so important that even in the midst of hard warfare, Apaches tried to stop and make time for it.[27]

Plains Apache political organization appeared relatively loose, much more so than their mountain cousins to the west. The head of an extended family exerted leadership over his kinfolk, but sometimes a man, through his wisdom, skill, and ability to acquire status, became a chief of many. Some families were expected to produce chiefs but there was no one main chief of the Lipan Apaches. When Juan de Oñate met up with an encampment of Apaches on the Texas plains in 1601, he reported a "large *ranchería*, with more than five thousand souls."[28] Others reported similarly large encampments, though smaller bands did exist. Still, an encampment with five thousand people, or even half that number, had to possess some kind of political organization. Someone, either a person or a council, designated when it was time to move, the order of march, when they would stop and where, how buffalo would be distributed, and the like. Early Spanish accounts report that Apaches sought Spanish assistance in their wars against the Jumanos. So Plains Apache leadership may well have been more complex than Europeans imagined. Certainly seniors exercised some measure of leadership over juniors and used the giving and withholding of status goods as a means of bringing about compliance.[29]

As with all Indians, the Apaches saw natural forces, such as lightning and thunder, as manifestations of various deities. Shamans, as well as individuals who had a successful vision quest, might periodically be able to tap into the spiritual forces for beneficent means through ritual and ceremony. Opposing shamans were witches, and witches crowded the minds of Apaches, who attributed prolonged illness and bad luck to witchcraft. They also feared that witches were constantly trying to arrange encounters between them and bad, contaminated animals, such as owls, coyotes, snakes, and bears. Merely the sight, smell, or touch of any of these animals could bring disaster. Even more worrisome to Apaches were ghosts. When a person died, her ghost was supposed to travel to an afterworld, guided by a deceased relative. But some ghosts did not want to leave their familiar surroundings or did not make the trip to the afterworld because of botched funeral rituals. Other times, ghosts returned from the afterworld to take vengeance. Regardless of why, ghosts were dangerous beings who often brought death to those who saw them. Ghosts, lonely in their afterworld, might appear in dreams, taking the form of owls, coyotes, even black misty objects, in order to recruit more ghosts. To see a ghost was to portend one's own death at the worst; to begin a cycle of trouble and bad luck at best. Because of this, Apaches took great pains with death rituals, usually burying or destroying the deceased's possessions and leaving food out for the ghost to eat on its journey to the afterworld. Apaches avoided things that might attract ghosts, such as speaking the dead person's name or whistling at night. They also moved their homes in the opposite direction of the grave to mislead any ghosts that might return. Their fear of ghosts also stopped many Apaches from taking the scalps of those they killed in battle.[30]

And it was in battle where Apaches earned a fearsome reputation. Boys were trained for warfare early on with almost constant tests of their stamina and strength. They ran; they wrestled; they fought mock battles and learned the intricacies of raiding and warfare. Until the mid-nineteenth century the cry "Apache!" sent a shiver through Indians and whites alike in Texas. To be captured by Apaches, particularly for adult males, meant hours of torture and a slow, painful death. Ironically, when the Apaches and Spanish first met each other on the Texas plains, the Spaniards noted their friendliness. When the Apaches saw Francisco Coronado for the first time in 1542, they "did nothing unusual . . . except to come out of their tents to look at us."[31] Coronado's lieutenant later described them as "a kind people and not cruel. They are faithful friends."[32] Juan de Oñate met them almost sixty years later, and when he did, the Apaches "came out with signs of peace" and eventually all the Apache men, women, and children in the large band raised "their hands to the sun, which is the ceremony they use as a sign of friendship, and brought to us some small black and yellow fruit."[33]

Good relations would not last as the western half of Texas, the markets therein, and essentially the whole Southern Plains economy was quickly becoming contested by three major powers: Apaches from the north, Spanish from the south, and the Jumanos already living there. Adding to this confusion were the tremendous numbers of Indian refugees flooding into South Texas from Mexico ahead of the Spanish invasion. However, the Apaches were in the midst of a tremendous expansion and this would serve them well. By the late 1400s or early 1500s they had already attacked some of the Pueblos of New Mexico and gained a toehold on the Llano Estacado in Northwest Texas. And like virtually all other peoples who came to the area, they were attracted by the plains economy.[34]

By the 1500s two major east-west exchange networks crossed Texas. In the south, Jumano traders could leave Tompiro Pueblo and head east to their villages on the Rio Grande and then on to the Coahuiltecans, Karankawas, Atakapas, and finally the Caddos in far East Texas. A second major trade network ran farther north, out of Pecos pueblo and then east along the Red and Canadian Rivers. From here, traders could diverge north to the Wichita villages or continue east to the Caddo communities along the Red. The trade in both traditional Indian commodities and European manufactured goods could be particularly profitable for the geographical middlemen, at this time the Jumanos on the southern network and the Plains Wichitas on the northern. With the greatest access to the all-important buffalo, they could make exchanges with both the Pueblos to the west and the Caddos to the east. At the same time, large quantities of commodities and status goods passed through their hands. It was no wonder the Jumanos, in their attempts to remain strong enough to control the regional network, were more than willing to adopt outsiders into their societies. It also explains why the refugee Indians fleeing Mexico, needing the economy to survive, were so willing to become a part of the Jumano people. The Coahuiltecans, themselves being inundated with refugee Indians, dreamed of dominating the network but did not have sure enough access to the buffalo herds nor enough women laborers in their bands to provide the number of hides needed to do so. On the other hand, the Wichitas, and the Caddos as well, certainly seemed to be prospering. Then came the Apaches.[35]

The Apaches were drawn to this plains economy like ants to sugar. However, the existing networks were old and over the years kinships and partnerships had been established between its various peoples. The Apaches were outsiders, and rather than take a junior partner role within the trade, they instituted what today would be called a hostile takeover. Essentially, the Apaches decided to corner the market on the buffalo hide trade. This meant they would sweep down the Southern Plains, drive off the Plains Wichitas and Jumanos, then usurp their positions in the plains economy by keeping other Indians away from the buffalo. The Apaches would then be able to control the distribution of buffalo goods east and west, as well as the status goods passing through their hands. It was a truly bold move on a magnificent scale, but it would earn the Apaches the hatred of most Indian peoples in Texas. The Jumanos and Wichitas refused to go peacefully, while the Caddos, Wichitas, Comanches, Kiowas, Osages, Spanish, and French had their own designs on the Southern Plains economy. The Apache grab now initiated cycles of war across Texas that would not end until 1881.

The first people the Apaches muscled out of the way were the Yscani Wichitas, those whom the Spanish initially called Teyas, who lived around the headwaters of the Brazos River. In his trip across the plains, Coronado reported visiting the Querechos and Teyas. While both hunted buffalos with bows and arrows and both used dogs to move their baggage, they seemed to be different peoples and not just different Apache bands. Teyas were Wichitas who lived in huge settlements that extended for miles along the riverbanks and grew beans "and prunes like those of Castile, and tall vineyards."[36] The Teyas even dressed differently from the Apache Querechos, with women covering their entire bodies with buffalo hide skirts, ponchos, and cloaks, gathering the sleeves at the shoulders. And the Teyas may have been only one of several Wichita settlements on the Texas plains during the sixteenth century.[37]

The Plains Wichitas were no strangers to warfare. In 1525 the Teyas had besieged the Pecos Pueblo and destroyed several small surrounding settlements. Unable to conquer Pecos, the Teyas made peace and resumed trade relations. Apparently the attack was a Wichita effort to remind the Pecos who their main trading partners should be. Throughout most of the fifteenth century the Plains Wichitas, such as the Teyas, had supplied Pecos and many eastern pueblos with buffalo meat, hides, and tallow. In the late 1400s and early 1500s the Apaches began making inroads on the Pueblo trade, drawing customers and commodities away from the Wichitas. The attack on Pecos was a futile attempt to realign a trading network that was already shifting away from the Wichitas. By 1599 the Apaches seemed to have the Pueblo trade well in hand. Juan de Oñate met a large Apache trading party returning from the Picuris and Taos pueblos "where they sell meat, hides, tallow, suet, and salt in exchange for cotton blankets, pottery, maize, and some small green stones . . . ."[38]

By 1600 the Teyas were nowhere to be found, whereas the Apaches were attacking other plains peoples, including Wichita villages in what is now Kansas. As the Apaches expanded southward, some Plains Wichita villages were pushed east to be absorbed by their more northern Wichita cousins then also migrating south into Texas. Other plains settlements were destroyed by the Apaches and their people assimilated into Apache bands and families. After displacing the Wichitas in the Pecos trade, the Apaches turned their attention to the southern network. As early as 1590 the Apaches had appeared on the lower Pecos, where the buffalo-hunting Jumanos ranged. There they attacked Gaspar Sosa's party of Spaniards heading to Pueblo country. The seventeenth century would see more Apache attacks on Spaniards, Pueblos, Jumanos, Coahuiltecans, Wichitas, and Caddos.[39]

Just about the time the Apaches were consolidating their middleman status on the northern Pueblo-Wichita-Caddo trade network, the Spanish made their own play at tapping into the plains economy. In 1601 Juan de Oñate established the Spanish colony of New Mexico and over the next few decades gradually brought virtually all Pueblo peoples under Spanish authority. On one hand, Spanish New Mexico helped fuel the Apache expansion. On the other, it increased the wars the Apaches fought. The Spanish immediately became a major economic player on the Southern Plains not only by adding new wealth in the form of horses, guns, metalware, and cloth but also by demanding buffalo hides, buffalo meat, and Indian captives, who could be used as slaves in labor-short New Mexico.

By 1617 Apache, Spanish, and Pueblo traders were meeting regularly at Pecos Pueblo, where horses and metal goods were exchanged for hides and Indian captives taken on the eastern side of the plains. Like La Junta on the Rio Grande, Pecos Pueblo became a major western gateway community to the Southern Plains. At Pecos and other pueblos, Apache leaders expressed an interest in Christianity and Spanish missionaries believed they were well on their way to converting the Apaches and having them give up their hunting and gathering ways. The trade brought about close relations between the Pueblos and Apaches. So close that at various times throughout the seventeenth century, Pueblo peoples, frustrated and angry at Spanish abuses, often went to live among the Apaches at a settlement on the Arkansas River that the Spanish called El Cuartelejo. There the Pueblos instructed Apaches in corn horticulture and it was not long before the houses at El Cuartelejo were surrounded by cornfields.[40]

Good relations were not to stay. While some Apache bands made peaceful exchanges with the Pueblos and Spanish, other bands without connections, along with status-hungry young men, raided New Mexican settlements and pueblos for horses, metal goods, and captives. Spanish troops and their Pueblo auxiliaries would march out to the plains to retaliate against Apache camps, where they took Apache captives to serve as slaves in New Mexico or New Spain. Now, with the law of blood revenge set into motion and furious at the enslavement of their people, Apache warriors stepped up their attacks on Spanish settlements and Pueblo villages. The great droughts of the 1660s only made things worse. With the buffalo moving north and with less food on the plains, Apache attacks increased and so cycles of raids and counterraids swept over eastern New Mexico, punctuated by peaceful exchanges between some bands and pueblos.[41]

Apparently the Pueblo peoples suffered most, both from Apache raids and Spanish laws. Over the eighty years since Spain founded the colony of New Mexico, the Pueblos had experienced a worsening relationship with their Spanish conquerors. The Spanish used the *ecomienda*, an institution resembling the old European manorial system, in which Pueblo towns and lands were divided up and "given" to high-ranking Spaniards. In return for his protection and Christianization, the encomendaro taxed "his" Indians, demanding regular payments of corn or cotton blankets. The encomendaro could also conscript Pueblo labor, making them work on his own farm for so many days a month. While not exactly slavery, the ecomienda was not far from it, and New Mexican encomendaros demanded much from their Indians. Missionaries also benefited from

Pueblo urban life. They built churches in virtually every town and stationed a Franciscan padre there to compel the "savages" to accept Roman
Catholic Christianity. For the missionaries, Christianity meant not only
conversion and attendance at Mass but also the eradication of Indian culture. Pueblo religion, deemed satanic, had to be uprooted. Ceremonies
were prohibited, shrines destroyed, Pueblo priests tortured, while missionaries burned every mask, kachina, and prayer stick they could lay
their hands on. Missionaries also demanded that the Indians work for
them. Eventually, this brought the colonial government and its encomendaro supporters into conflict with the missionaries. Like male buffalos,
colonial governors and priests butted heads, while the Pueblo grass got
trampled.[42]

Nevertheless, some Pueblo peoples, such as the Tiwas of Isleta Pueblo
south of Albuquerque, saw benefits with the arrival of the Spanish. Horses,
cattle, pigs, and sheep soon filled Pueblo corrals and Pueblo stomachs.
Certainly the metal tools and weapons proved attractive, especially as the
Pueblos had no way of manufacturing these themselves. And Apache attacks on New Mexico made the Spanish and Pueblos natural allies. Finally,
that the Spaniards seemed immune to the new diseases sweeping through
the towns indicated that their god was very powerful, maybe even more
so than those of the Pueblos. Franciscans reported large number of conversions. While some certainly were forced to convert, many people willingly accepted Christianity and allied with their Spanish neighbors and
overlords.

By 1680 Pueblo towns, many with a long history of feuding with each
other, now found themselves divided between pro-Spanish and anti-
Spanish factions. The anti-Spanish faction was much larger, and most
Pueblo people dreamed of the day when these Europeans would leave
their towns. The harsh Spanish administration, combined with the increasing Apache attacks, contributed to Pueblo anger. Finally, after years
of brooding servitude, the Pueblos exploded in rebellion. Popé, a Tewa
Pueblo priest, managed to unite most of the Pueblos, and on August 10,
1680, they rose up, killing more than 375 Spaniards, including 21 priests.
The surviving Spaniards retreated south and set up a government in exile at El Paso, actually at Ciudad Juárez, as El Paso, north of Rio Grande,
did not then exist. Along with them, whether willingly or by force, went
some 300 Tiwa-speakers from Isleta and other pueblos. In New Mexico,
the Pueblo peoples declared their independence. For fourteen years the
Pueblos ruled themselves, but squabbling between them ended any
chance of unity and by 1694 the Spanish had managed to reconquer the
colony.[43]

The Tiguas

The three hundred or so Tiguas, as they now began calling themselves, for whatever reason, had decided to throw in with the Spanish. When the Spanish withdrew from New Mexico following the Pueblo attack in 1680, the Tiguas went south with them. The descendants of these people, today's Tigua Indians at El Paso, say they did not go willing with the Spanish but were taken as hostages. No matter, at El Paso, they formed a small pueblo, which they called Ysleta del Sur, or Isleta of the South, to differentiate it from their old Isleta Pueblo near Albuquerque. Between 1681 and 1691 the Spanish erected a mission near Ysleta, and over the years, as the Rio Grande meandered over its course, Ysleta del Sur eventually came to sit on Texas soil proper. The Tiguas remained committed to the Spanish, serving as auxiliaries in Spain's fourteen-year campaign to reconquer New Mexico. When Spain declared New Mexico subjugated in 1694, the Tiguas remained at Ysleta del Sur near El Paso, where their descendants live to this day.[44]

The Tiguas of Ysleta del Sur are classic Pueblo peoples. As with all Pueblos, they believe they came to this world from underground. In the case of the Tiguas, badger helped dig a hole from the inner world to this world and the Tiguas used the trunk of a spruce tree to climb out. Though they consider the ancient site of Gran Quivira in New Mexico as their original home, the Tiguas eventually moved several miles to the northwest and prospered. They built their main pueblo at Isleta, but when Francisco Coronado visited them in 1540 and 1541, he reported the Tiguas living in a spacious valley, with twelve pueblos, including Isleta, Pauray, Sandia, Taos, and Picuris, composing the province of Tiguex. Though the Tiguas would later ally with the Spanish, the first meeting of the two was not peaceful. Coronado's Spaniards demanded food and blankets, raped a Tigua woman, and burned one of the pueblos. The Tiguas fought back killing many Spaniards but losing many of their own people. Most Tiguas sought refuge in Pauray and continued their fight. The Spanish besieged Pauray for fifty days. Over the course of the siege, numerous assaults took place in which several hundred Tigua men were killed. Finally, in March, 1542, Coronado's men captured Pauray and quickly subdued the other pueblos of Tiguex. Fortunately, Coronado and his men moved on, but by 1601 the Spanish were back and the colony of New Mexico founded. From then until the Pueblo Revolt of 1680, the Tiguas, probably with old battles still remembered, gradually came under the influence of the Spanish and so followed them south in 1680.[45]

Down at Ysleta del Sur near El Paso, the Tiguas quietly went about their lives as corn farmers. While pretty much left to their own devices, they nevertheless attended Catholic Mass, interacted with their Spanish neighbors, and served as Spanish scouts and auxiliaries. The Tiguas were not mission Indians, as they already lived in a town and so had a church, but similar things happened to them that happened in missions. Essentially, over the years, the Tiguas became hispanized as they adopted Christian ceremonies, Christian names, and all the tools and farm animals that the Spanish brought with them. In a way, the Spanish could consider the Tiguas their greatest success story. Here were Indians who accepted Christianity and Spanish culture and remained loyal to them over the years. From this has arisen questions that bedevil the Tiguas to this day. Can one remain an Indian when one has adopted all the trappings of another culture? If the casual observer could not tell the difference between the Tiguas of Ysleta del Sur and the Mexican peasants who increasingly settled around El Paso, were the Tiguas then, still Indians?[46]

Certainly the Tiguas believed they were Pueblo Indians and still do. Though they may have gone to Mass, taken Spanish names, worn Spanish clothing, and farmed the land with Spanish tools, they brought much of their Pueblo culture with them to Ysleta del Sur. In fact, for years it would have been difficult to differentiate Ysleta del Sur from Isleta in New Mexico. The Tiguas continued to live close together, around a central plaza, in *jacale* houses of wooden branches chinked with mud. They built ramadas, shaded areas for communal dances, and *tuslas*, separate rooms where they stored ceremonial items, just as they had back in Tiguex. They even transplanted their old Pueblo government structure. To this day, a chief, or cacique, who governs the Tiguas also serves as a medicine man. Below the cacique is a governor, essentially a lieutenant cacique. Then comes an *alguacil*, a sort of sergeant-at-arms; a war chief; and finally four principal men called captains. Though the Tiguas accepted Christianity and were baptized as Roman Catholics, they retained many of their dances and songs and combined aspects of their traditional Pueblo religion with Catholicism. This is most obvious at the Tigua's biggest ceremonial celebration—Saint Anthony's Day—held on June 13. Even today, one might see traditional Tigua dances held in the plaza just outside the Catholic church at Ysleta del Sur.[47]

By the early 1700s the Tiguas seemed to be prospering at Ysleta. As one observer reported, they lived in a "spacious valley dotted with farms, where they plant wheat, corn, beans and all kinds of vegetables as well as a quantity of vineyards which yield fruit of superior quality. . . . The natural fertility of the land is improved by the number of irrigation ditches, which carry water from the said Rio del Norte making the farms independent of droughts."[48] Certainly the Spanish considered the Tiguas to be Indians. A 1750 census recorded 500 Indians and 54 Spaniards at Ysleta, while the 1787 census listed 64 Tigua families or 195 persons. The Spanish also tried to guarantee Tigua rights to the land and in 1713 granted them lands stretching one league, about two and a half miles, in all directions from the door of the Ysleta church. In 1751 the Spanish king, hoping to protect Tigua lands from illegal encroachment by Spanish settlers, made the Ysleta Grant, giving the Tiguas 17,712 acres of land. For the next 250 years, the Tiguas lived rather quiet farming lives, following their traditions, which mixed Pueblo and Spanish ways. This is not to say the Tiguas did not have troubles. Settlers often tried to appropriate Tigua lands and prerogatives, with the Tiguas using the courts and only rarely resorting to violence. While other Indians who lived nearby, such as the Jumano Sumas and Mansos, apparently disappeared into the Mexican society that arose around El Paso, the Tiguas remained.[49]

The Impact of Horses

The Apaches certainly encouraged the Pueblo revolt, as with the Spanish out of the way the defenseless Pueblo horse and cattle herds lay at their mercy. It did not take long before they swept clean the corrals of the more easterly Pueblos. Horses, the ultimate status good, were the main prize, and every Indian across Texas wanted as many as he or she could lay their hands on.[50]

Horses had once lived in North America, but these were tiny horses, much smaller than those of today, and they had died out during the great extinctions eight thousand years earlier. Now horses returned with the Spanish. If Indian peoples had ever thought of horses as supernatural beings, this image did not last long. And few Indians in Texas saw horses as stemming from the Spanish. It was not long before horses entered the stories and legends of Indians, and cultures across Texas and the Southwest developed an oral tradition of horses given to them by their own deities. Indians, seeing horses as a gift from the gods, quickly recognized their potential.[51]

When the Francisco Sánchez Chamuscado expedition left a broken-down horse with the Caguate Jumanos in 1582, the Jumanos built it a manger, hand-fed it mesquite, and "talked to it as if it were a person."[52] By the next year, when the Espejo expedition reached La Junta, the Jumanos seemed to have lost all wonder over horses as they attacked the Spanish herd with bows and arrows and killed three horses and wounded seven.[53] However, it did not take long before most Indian peoples realized that it was much better to take horses than merely to kill them or use them for food.

Horses had been streaming northward out of Mexico since the mid-1500s. During the constant wars that ravaged northern Mexico during the sixteenth century, Indians had raided Spanish herds and traded the horses at La Junta. By 1600 most Indians in northern Mexico were mounted and often possessed huge herds. As horses moved into Texas, some escaped to the plains, became feral and thrived. These "mustangs" were small, fast, rather easy to tame, and ideally suited to the plains and prairies of Texas. By the end of the eighteenth century maybe as many as 2 million grazed between the Rio Grande and the Arkansas River. The wild horse herds on the plains should have been easy pickings for Indians who wanted horses, and some Indians did get their horses from them. However, capturing horses required different skills than hunting them, and for most Indians in Texas, it proved easier to raid each other's herds or Spanish corrals.[54]

Whether the coming of horses revolutionized Indian societies or not is still debated. Only a few of the more northerly societies, such as the Cheyennes and Arapahos, gave up horticulture and turned almost exclusively to buffalo hunting. Prairie horticulturalists, such as the Caddos, Wichitas, and Pawnees, remained farmers even with horses. Even the Apaches, some of the first people to acquire horses, ultimately attempted to settle down and raise gardens of corn. Still, horses certainly changed Indian societies. The first horses were seen as food, but this quickly gave way to horses being used for transport. Horses could carry riders farther and faster than ever before, putting things in reach that had once been beyond their grasp. Traveling from one water hole to the next became easier. Buffalo could be followed more quickly and hunted more easily, and more meat and hides could be carried. Horses made men better warriors, creating an excellent light cavalry that could dominate warriors on foot, and allowed raiders to strike farther, get away quicker, and carry off more spoils. Bands could escape their enemies faster, and breaking camp became simpler as horses took much of the load that women and dogs had had to carry on the trail.[55]

As with any innovation, negatives countered positives. Horses also brought more raids and warfare to Indian peoples. Those with horses became the targets of those wanting more horses. Since horses gave their owners almost instant status, bands of young men increasingly raided in hopes of acquiring these hoofed commodities. The concentration of horses on the Southern Plains drew other groups to the area. While nearby Jumanos, Caddos, Wichitas, and Coahuiltecans had their own horse needs, Comanches, Osages, Kiowas, even Chickasaws from east of the Mississippi River, were determined to fight for sure access to horses, buffalo, and a share of the plains economy. The Apaches, who claimed the Southern Plains as their private domain, now found themselves faced by numerous enemies intent on challenging their hegemony. Large horse herds quickly exhausted the grass and forage, meaning the Apaches and other plains Indians found themselves forced to divide into smaller bands. Unfortunately, this came at a time when warfare was on the rise across the Southern Plains. Rarely, if ever, would anyone see plains Indians with an encampment of five thousand people as Juan de Oñate had in 1601.[56]

By the end of the seventeenth century horses became the most prized status good among Indian societies in Texas. Everyone wanted them. Every Indian man wanted as many as he could get. Previously in most Indian societies there had been little difference between rich and poor, if those designations even existed. Now horses created new wealth and increased one's status and power. Unlike most other commodities, horses were rarely parceled out to junior men or to people with less status. When they were given they created tremendous reciprocal obligations. At the same time, they became a sort of currency, with horses usually demanded and given as gifts to the parents of a bride, for the services of a shaman, or for the advice and instructions of a powerful warrior. A man with many horses was a man to be reckoned with. He could afford more wives and create strong bonds of loyalty. A man with no horses was a poor man indeed. So it was no wonder that young men risked death at the hands of their enemies and the anger of their seniors to make horse raids.[57]

Once the Pueblos drove the Spanish out of New Mexico in 1680, horses rapidly spread across Texas. In 1684 a Spanish expedition reported being greeted by a Jumano band riding horses and firing arquebuses in salute. By 1686 the Caddos of East Texas possessed several horses and so valuable were they that the Indians hesitated to give them up in trade. About the same time, the Karankawas raided the Caddos, taking a few horses and herding them back to the coast. However, to acquire large numbers of horses, one had to brave the Apaches. And while this was not impossible, it was dangerous. Increasingly the Apaches seemed to dominate the Southern Plains economy and controlling the flow of goods across Texas, something other Indians were loath to allow.[58]

Collapse of the Jumanos

The Apache expansion south disrupted Indian life in much of Texas and in its significance equaled the coming of the Spanish. Wars between the Apaches and most everybody else over the control of buffalos, horses, and

metalware escalated during the seventeenth and eighteenth centuries.
And all participants sought to make new kin and allies. Even the Spanish
found themselves drawn into these alliances. As early as 1601 the Apaches
used Juan de Oñate's expedition as a screen to sack some Wichita villages
along the Arkansas River. They also asked Oñate to help them attack the
Jumanos. In turn, the Jumanos more than once asked the Spanish for assistance in their wars against the Apaches.[59]

By the 1680s the situation looked bleak for the Jumanos and Coahuiltecans. With the Spanish expelled from New Mexico and retrenched at El
Paso, they had lost not only their main source of horses and weapons but
also important allies, whose absence made the Apaches all the bolder. With
the situation deteriorating and the southern Jumano trade network under
pressure from the Apaches, the Jumano chiefs decided the only solution
was to bring the Spanish back into the game. Jumano delegations visited
the Spanish at El Paso. It is easy to imagine that the Spanish and the Indians were in constant opposition. In reality, many Indians viewed the Spanish as another sort of wealthy and powerful Indian nation, one to ally with
when needed. In this case, the Jumanos and Coahuiltecans needed the
Spanish to counter the Apaches and so shore up the cross-plains trade.
And they knew just what strings to pluck to get the Spanish to return to
Texas.[60]

In October, 1683, the ladino Jumano chief Sabeata and the other six Jumano chiefs visited the Spanish at El Paso and told them a compelling
story of how there were thirty-three Indian nations in Texas begging to
learn of Christianity. Even more, Sabeata related how a cross had appeared
in the sky during a battle with the Apaches and had guided them to victory. Now he urged the Spanish to establish missions among the Indians.
If this were not enough to lure the Spanish back, Sabeata told them that
two ambassadors from the "great kingdom" of the Tejas, another name for
the Hasinai Caddos, were waiting at La Junta as they spoke and were
ready to lead the Spanish back to their chiefdom in far Northeast Texas.[61]

Asking for a mission was an old ploy. The Coahuiltecans, attacked by
Indians from northern Mexico, Spanish slave-raiders, and now Apache
warriors, had been asking for missionary protection in South Texas for
years. It was not so much that they desired to know the word of God,
rather the Indians wanted all the good things that would arrive with the
missions. The coming of Spanish missionaries meant the establishment of
kinship ties between the Spanish and the Indians. Missionaries performed
ceremonies, chanted prayers, and used kinship terms such as "children,"
"father," and "brother," and so the Indians probably assumed that the
Spanish mass and baptism were adoption ceremonies and now they would

become family with these powerful Europeans. And while the Spanish may or may not have realized it, the Indians certainly expected their new wealthy brothers to be generous with food and manufactured goods and to help protect them from their enemies.[62]

The Jumanos also knew that Spanish soldiers normally accompanied missionary expeditions and presidios—Spanish forts—were usually established in the same vicinity as missions. Sabeata's plan seemed viable if the Spanish would take the bait. The missionary expedition, accompanied by soldiers, would escort the Tejas ambassadors home through Apache territory and there see the wealthy Hasinai chiefdom. If suitably impressed, the Spanish, Sabeata imagined, would create missions across South Texas, protected by presidios. The Jumanos and their trade allies would acquire food, horses, weapons, and metalware from the missions and presidios, which would also screen the Jumano trade network from the Apaches. At least that was the plan.[63]

Unfortunately for the hard-pressed Jumanos and Coahuiltecans, the Spanish dawdled in mission building and then miscalculated. Mission Corpus Christi de la Isleta had been built for Tiguas at El Paso in 1682, but it was too far west to protect anyone from the Apaches. Only the establishment of a French colony on the Texas coast in 1684 by Robert Cavelier Sieur de la Salle spurred the Spanish to take an interest in Texas. Even then the Spanish remained desultory, sending out only a few expeditions mainly to round up the handful of French survivors of La Salle's failed colony. However the wealthy Caddos of East Texas had caught the Spanish eye. Rather than shore up their alliances with the beleaguered Jumanos and Coahuiltecans, the Spanish leaped over them and set up a few missions among the Hasinai Caddos in 1691 and 1692. But the Caddos were not bearing the brunt of Apaches raids and so did not need missions as the Jumanos and Coahuiltecans did. Besides, Caddo country was far from the supply centers of Mexico, so the missions could not provide the Caddos with a steady supply of manufactured goods. With no converts, the Caddo missions failed in 1693 and the Spanish withdrew from East Texas.[64]

While the Spanish fiddled in East Texas, Southwest Texas burned with Apache raids. For every year the Spanish delayed entering Texas, the Apaches grew stronger while the Jumanos and Coahuiltecans grew weaker. Epidemics, drought, and warfare all played roles in the collapse of the Jumano trade network and in the actual numbers of Jumanos and Coahuiltecans. As their populations dwindled, so did their ability to participate in the plains economy. Fewer people meant less ability to farm or tan hides. Severe droughts after 1700 not only withered crops but also made foraging more difficult as acorns, pecans, and other food sources did not produce for several years running. Drought also sent the buffalo herds north, and this, compounded by the expansion of mesquite and scrub brush over much of South Texas, meant fewer buffalo. Competition over dwindling food sources brought increased warfare as hungry bands battled it out on the plains. Things had been bad for a while and only got worse.[65]

By 1694 the Jumanos had quit making their trading trips to the Caddos. A smallpox epidemic that swept across South Texas in 1706 killed so many people and destroyed so many camps and villages that the southern trade network ceased to exist. In 1709 the only groups to show up at the Colorado River trade fairs were a few Yojuanes and some refugee Indians. Eventually, the Yojuanes and other refugees would migrate to the Brazos River and begin the ethnogenesis of the Tonkawa peoples. By 1715 Texas had become a dangerous place, with raiding parties replacing trading parties. For the hard-pressed Jumano and Coahuiltecan survivors, normally only two solutions presented themselves: seek refuge among the Spanish or join the Apaches.[66]

With the failure of the Caddo missions in the early 1690s, Spain turned its attention back to New Mexico and Southwest Texas. In 1694 Spaniards reconquered the Pueblos. With New Mexico back in their hands, Spanish authorities now began a concerted effort to establish missions in Texas. This delighted the Jumanos and Coahuiltecans but came too late for many of them. Throughout the eighteenth century Spain created missions across South and East Texas. Between 1700 and 1703 Spain founded three missions—San Juan Bautista, San Francisco Solano, San Barnardo—and presidio San Juan Bautista del Rio Grande among the Coahuiltecans on the south bank of the Rio Grande near present-day Guerrero, Mexico. For the remainder of the century this mission complex served as a jumping-off point for future missionary and exploration efforts in Texas. Spain reestablished several missions in 1716–17 among the Caddos of East Texas. In 1718 a clutch of five missions and a presidio, eventually referred to as the Alamo, was set up among the Coahuiltecans at San Antonio de Béxar, present-day San Antonio, Texas. In 1722 Spain built Mission Espíritu Santo and its presidio, La Bahía, in Karankawa country, and Mission San Francisco Xavier for the Coahuiltecans a few miles below San Antonio. Of all the missions, those at San Antonio fared best. Over the years, scores of different Indian bands, such as the Coahuiltecan Payayas, Pampopas, Pastias, and Sijames, and thousands of Indians speaking a babel of languages and dialects went to live there in hopes of escaping Apache raids.[67]

Unfortunately for many Coahuiltecans and Jumanos, the missions of South Texas provided little refuge. During the first half of the eighteenth century Apache raids, repressive missionary policies, and droughts that destroyed mission crops and livestock forced many Indians to abandon the missions. By 1734 so many Coahuiltecans had run away from the San Antonio missions that work had to be halted. Troops hunted down many of these "apostates" and returned them to the missions. At other times the Indians fought for their freedom and some managed to evade Spanish soldiers. Since 1700 many ladino bands made their way to an area northeast of San Antonio on the Brazos River, where they united for protection against both the Spanish and the Apaches. Eventually so many former mission Indians, local bands, and refugees from shattered nations gathered on the Brazos that this new "composite" band came to be called "Ranchería Grande." Ladino Indians such as the Ervipiames, Tobosos, and Tripas Blancas, as well as Jumanos, Yojuanes, Deadoses, and Tonkawas, all came to live at Ranchería Grande. It became so prominent that Caddos, Karankawas, and Atakapas often visited Ranchería Grande to trade, and in 1748, on the nearby San Gabriel River, Spain built the short-lived San Xavier mission.[68]

While many Indians in South and West Texas kept their independence, even creating wholly new Indian peoples, others gradually adopted Spanish culture. In 1715, when the Spanish returned to La Junta de los Rios to rebuild a church, they found it a shadow of its former glory. Where once five major towns had clustered at the confluence of the Conchos and the Rio Grande, now there were eight much smaller ones and three more a short distance away. Where there had once been maybe ten thousand people at La Junta in the 1580s, now there were fewer than seventeen hundred in all eleven towns. Still, even without the cross-plains trade, the Jumanos at La Junta seemed to be doing well, with large, irrigated fields of wheat, corn, watermelons, pumpkins, and string beans. However, the Jumanos here were also rapidly adopting Spanish culture.[69] The Spanish reported that many of these Indians spoke Spanish and were "well-dressed, men as well as women, the chiefs and their wives being outstanding with better clothes in the Spanish fashion, with shirts of fine white linen worked in silk. Some had skirts of serge, silk shawls, Cordovan shoes, imported Brussels silk socks."[70] They got these by traveling 340 miles into northern Mexico, "at the risk of their enemies to work on the farm estates of [the] San Bartolomé Valley."[71] Of particular significance was the existence of a friendly Apache camp just north of La Junta. Groups that had once been enemies were now living amicably as neighbors.[72]

This is what happened to many surviving Jumanos, Coahuiltecans, and Indian peoples across South and Southwest Texas. As they sought protection from Spanish officials, missions, and landowners in the face of droughts and Apache raids, they eventually became hispanized Mexican campesinos, the backbone of the Mexican nation.[73] Others found themselves absorbed into the ever-expanding Apaches.

To the Jumanos, Coahuiltecans, Plains Wichitas, and Pueblos of South and West Texas of the seventeenth century, the Apaches and Spanish must have seemed like juggernauts. The Apaches from the north swept the Llano Estacado of Indian bands, either pushing them aside or absorbing them into their own society. Eventually they gained control of the northern cross-plains Pueblo-Caddo trade network. Out of the south came the Spanish, bringing with them horses, cattle, guns, manufactured goods, and a host of other items all the Indian peoples of Texas wanted or needed. While these goods could increase the status and prestige of individuals who were able to acquire or control them, they also made them targets of other Indians. The advance of the Apaches and the Spanish caused tremendous disruptions and movement among the Indians of South and West Texas, which were intensified by warfare, epidemics, droughts, and the advancing mesquite line that limited the buffalo range. As the populations of the Jumanos, Coahuiltecans, and others dwindled, some sought refuge with the Apaches and eventually "became" Apaches, while some joined the Spanish in missions. Others tried to find a safe haven where they could be free of both. By the beginning of the eighteenth century it appeared that the Apaches and Spanish would own just about all Texas, but before they could consolidate their control, opposition rose both in the east and the north.

Chapter 5

Resurgence in East Texas

EAST TEXAS POSED a barrier for both the Apaches and the Spanish. The Plains Apaches wanted little to do with the piney woods. This did not mean the Apaches and the Indians of East Texas got along. While the Caddos had little fear of an Apache attack on their villages, increasingly they found their hunting parties pushed off the buffalo-rich plains and cut out of the lucrative Pueblo trade. Making matters worse, by the end of the seventeenth century the Caddos and other peoples of East Texas found themselves under attack from the Osages, Chickasaws, and Chitimachas farther east. At the same time, the huge corn-growing villages of Northeast Texas caught the Spanish eye and looked perfect for missions. By 1700 the Caddos found themselves hemmed in on the west by Apaches, under attack from people to the east, and with an alien people setting up shop in their midst, demanding they change their culture. Just when the Caddos needed help the most, it came—and from a most unusual quarter.

The Caddos

The Caddo Indians speak Caddoan, a language stock they share with the Wichitas, originally of Oklahoma and Kansas; the Pawnees of Kansas and Nebraska; and the Arikaras of the upper Missouri River. They were an ancient people, descended from the Woodland cultures that lived in the area.

Collectively, the Caddos called themselves Hasinai, meaning "our own folk." In later years "Hasinai" came to refer to those Caddo peoples in East Texas, while "Caddo" mainly denoted people living at the great bend of the Red River, near where Texarkana is today, and in Louisiana. However, by the late nineteenth century "Caddo" became the name for all these related groups who eventually wound up in southwestern Oklahoma.[1]

Some of the first Texas peoples to use corn on a large scale, by 1100 the Caddos had built huge cities, towns, and villages throughout Northeast Texas, southeastern Oklahoma, southwestern Arkansas, and Northwest Louisiana along the Red, Sabine, Angelina, Neches, and Trinity Rivers and their tributaries. Building upon their Woodland past, the Caddos participated in the Mississippian cultural tradition, erecting scores of large towns and ceremonial centers complete with temple and burial mounds. One of the most impressive Caddo ceremonial centers is the Davis Site, a clutch of three mounds near present-day Alto, Texas. This Caddo town, which reached its peak between 1100 and 1300, sat at the nexus where the great east-west road crossed the north-south Hasinai Trace and at the edge of the eastern woodlands where the southern prairies and plains begin. Strategically located, the town was a gateway community controlling much of the trade going east-west and north-south.[2]

In East Texas most Caddos did not live in big ceremonial centers but in the many villages, hamlets, and farmsteads scattered along the rivers and streams. There, Caddo men and women went about their daily lives. They were a warm, friendly people, described as light-complexioned, handsome, swift, strong, robust, and stocky, with Caddo men usually standing between 5 feet, 7 inches and 6 feet, while women stood somewhere between 5 feet to 5 feet, 8 inches. Clothing varied with the seasons. In hot weather a man might wear a breechcloth made of deer hide and very little else. Women usually wore a deerskin skirt but no top. In colder weather, both men and women added decorated buffalo robes. Women usually wore their hair long and sometimes plaited it into braids gathered at the back of their head. Men sometimes wore their hair long about their shoulders but more often shaved their heads into a "Mohawk" style, with a long tuft running down the center of the scalp. All facial hair was plucked out.[3]

The Caddos certainly possessed a sense of fashion. Men and women wore necklaces, earrings, pendants, bracelets, and anklets made of shells, shell beads, deer horns and hooves, even rattlesnake rattles; they adorned their clothes with the same. Warriors sometimes wore the scalps of their dead enemies on a belt around their waists. Body painting was common. Using clays and dyes, they often painted themselves, from shoulders to waist, with varicolored streaks. Caddos also tattooed themselves, using a thorn to puncture the skin and then rubbing charcoal into the cut. Tattoos might range in design from simple lines and circles to complex patterns or detailed pictures of birds and animals. Women tattooed circles around their breasts and lines on their chin. Certain patterns distinguished unmarried girls from married women; other designs may have denoted lineage or clan membership. Strangers adopted into Caddo society usually received a tattoo, a visible announcement and reminder of their kinship with Caddo people. Some Caddos also flattened their foreheads. This was done in infancy, by binding a baby's head between the cradleboard and a flat piece of wood. Never widespread among the Caddos, the fashion seemed to have died out by the early eighteenth century.[4]

Although men hunted deer, bear, buffalo, and other animals, the "Three Sisters"—corn, beans, and squash—made the Caddos unlike most other Indians of Texas. In well-watered East Texas, the Caddos came to rely more on farming than hunting, their villages and hamlets often surrounded by immense cornfields. While such backbreaking work as clearing fields of trees and turning the earth fell to men, women tended the corn. Since women planted the fields year after year until nutrients in the soil were used up, villages became somewhat permanent. The Caddos, similar to their Wichita cousins, lived in large, haystack-shaped lodges of log frames covered with straw and thatch rather than in hide tepees. A man married into a woman's family, went to live in her lodge, and the couple's children entered the world as members of the mother's clan. And Caddos seem to have had many clans, some were Sun, Thunder, Beaver, Eagle, Raccoon, Otter, Wolf, Panther, Bear, and Coyote. Women controlled the fields and the household, and a woman could divorce her husband by simply tossing his belongings out of the lodge.[5]

While women exerted tremendous influence, actual political positions went to men. A single town or large village, with its attendant hamlets and farmsteads, composed a virtually autonomous nation, though "city-state" might be a better term. The governor of a Caddo city-state was called a *caddí*, which is where their name comes from. The caddí certainly came from one of the village's leadership families. Originally, the position was passed down from a man to his sister's son, but by the middle of the eighteenth century, and in a break with the society's matrilineal character, a man's son began to inherit the position. As a governor, he dealt with the day-to-day running of the city-state. Assisted by an advisory council of *canahas*, or wise men, who represented outlying hamlets and farmsteads, the caddí dispensed justice, settled disputes, distributed food during hard times, met with supplicants, entertained important visitors, planned harvests and hunting trips, and coordinated raids and warfare. *Tammas* and *chayas,* minor inherited political positions, assisted the caddí and canahas in spreading news and seeing that their orders were carried out. Although important religious ceremonies were conducted by the caddís and canahas, the village *conna,* or medicine man, handled the curing of the people. The war chief, and warriors themselves, honored for their bravery and accomplishments, also had a say in the city-state's decision-making process.[6]

Sometimes the caddí of a single city-state might, through warfare or personal power, expand his control over several other city-states. Essentially he created a chiefdom in which he governed several city-states and their respective caddís answered to him. Chiefdoms were common in the southeastern United States during the Mississippian cultural tradition and the Caddos were no exception. Called xinesís, these chiefs sat at the pinnacle of Caddo society, ruled several Caddo city-states, claimed descent from the moon, and served not only as the main political officer but also as the chiefdom's top religious leader. Priest-chief of a theocracy, the xinesí, along with his own advisory council, guarded the sacred fire, consecrated the plantings and the harvests, and officiated at the many ceremonies and rituals. He did not hunt or do manual labor but had his fields planted and his house built for him. As the religious leader of his chiefdom, the xinesí spent much of his time in a temple, where a sacred fire burned continually. There he communed with the Supreme Being, whom the Caddos called "Caddí-Ayo," or "leader up above." Not far from the temple sat two even more sacred temples, a sort of inner sanctum in which lived two spiritual beings, described as children sent from the Caddí-Ayo. Called *cononicis,* the xinesí discussed with them the problems his chiefdom faced and asked their advice.[7]

By the 1540s more than a score of autonomous city-states dotted East Texas, northwest Louisiana, southwest Arkansas, and southeast Oklahoma. A growing Caddo chiefdom, encompassing the three city-states of Amaye, Macanac, and Naguatex and governed by the Naguatex xinesí, sat in southwest Arkansas near the great bend of the Red River and just east of present-day Texarkana. Not long after the Karankawas and Coahuiltecans met Cabeza de Vaca and while the Pueblos and Teyas were dealing with the Coronado expedition, the Caddos had their own encounter with the Spanish. In July, 1542, the remnants of Hernando de Soto's gold-hunting expedition, which had been rampaging across the southeastern United States, finally reached the Caddos along Red River. With de Soto dead, the expedition, led by Luis Moscoso, was marching across Texas, making for the Spanish outposts in Mexico. The Spaniards' reputation for theft and destruction preceded them and the Naguatex xinesí ordered a surprise attack. But Moscoso's battle-hardened troops severely defeated the Caddo warriors. The Spanish rested several weeks at Naguatex, while stripping it of food and supplies. Then, taking along many Caddos as slaves, the Spaniards continued their march across Texas, destroying town after town. The Caddo city-states of Nisohone, Nondacao, Guasco, Naquiscoza, and Nazacahoz all fell before the Spanish as did other non-Caddo peoples farther west, whom the Spanish called Lancane, Hais, and Soacatino. Some communities fought, only to be defeated; others surrendered without a fight. If that were not bad enough, when the Spanish realized the futility of marching across Texas they turned around and once again sacked the towns before marching back to Arkansas and out of Caddo territory.[8]

The De Soto-Moscoso Expedition of 1539–43 cut a swath of fire and destruction across the American southeast and proved to be the death blow to the already-declining Mississippian cultural tradition. Having been unable to protect his people from the Spanish storm, the individual chief's power eroded. Internal turmoil resulted as rival families now asserted their own claims to leadership. Political reorganizations resulted as some city-states, long under the heel of a paramount chief, took the opportunity to declare their independence and maintain it if they were strong enough to do so. Compounding this were the diseases left by the Spaniards. As epidemics took their toll on Indians, some communities virtually died out, were split apart, or moved to other areas as survivors sought havens that did not hold the memories of the dead. The Caddos were no exception to any of this. Over the next 150 years, the Caddos underwent tremendous turmoil as chiefdoms collapsed and others took their place, while some city-states declared their independence and dared others to conquer them. Epidemics drastically reduced the Caddo population. Much controversy exists over the size of Caddo population at the beginning of the sixteenth century. Some scholars suggest that the Caddos of the four-state area may have numbered between 200,000 and 250,000 in 1500. Others say not nearly that many. In any case, by the late seventeenth century the Caddo population had dwindled to somewhere between 8,000 and 40,000 and was still falling.[9]

By the 1680s two powerful new Caddo chiefdoms had arisen from the ashes of the Mississippi cultural tradition. At the great bend of the Red River north of Texarkana, the Kadohadacho chiefdom had supplanted the Naguatex. The Kadohadacho comprised four city-states—the Cadodachos, the main town of the chiefdom from which the chiefdom derived its name; the Upper Natchitoches, probably remnants of the once-formidable Naguatex; the Upper Nasonis; and the Nanatsohos. The chief of the Cadodachos ruled over all four. In the turmoil of the previous 150 years, several city-states or parts of them, such as the Petit Caddo, Yatasí, and Lower Natchitoches, had broken away from the old Naguatex chiefdom and moved down the Red River into Louisiana. Southwest of the Kadohada-cho chiefdom and along the middle reaches of the Sabine, Angelina, and Neches Rivers arose the Hasinai chiefdom. The xinesí of the Hainai governed this chiefdom, ruling his own as well as nine other city-states: Nabe-dache, Nacogdoches, Lower Nasoni, Nadaco, Neches, Nacono, Nechauis, Nacao, and Nabiti. Just southeast of the Hasinai, along the Sabine River, were two smaller Caddo city-states, the Adaes and the Ais. These two may at one time have been connected to the Hasinai chiefdom but were not now considered a part of it. Despite their political differences, all these people possessed a similar culture and spoke Caddoan with minor dialectical differences.[10]

That the Hasinai chiefdom, sometimes referred to as the "Tejas," was powerful in the late seventeenth century is beyond doubt. The Davis Site is in Hasinai territory, which sat on the margins between the forest, prairies, and plains and at the crossroads of the great east-west highway that the Spanish named the Camino Real and the north-south Hasinai Trace, later known as Trammell's Trace. Deep rivers and bayous made travel by boat easy. The Hasinai chiefdom formed the eastern terminus of the Jumano trade network. Jumano traders often visited the Hasinai city-states, and Caddo traders made their way to La Junta de los Rios. By the 1680s the Caddos of East Texas boasted horses, as well as some Spanish clothing, a few bells, even a sword blade, all coming by way of the Ju-manos.[11] The Spanish in Mexico had heard about the Caddo city-states from the Jumanos and Coahuiltecans, and in 1676 the bishop of Guadala-jara wrote that the Hasinai chiefdom is

a populous nation of people, and so extensive that those who give detailed reports of them do not know where it ends. These [who give the reports] are many, through having communicated with the people of that nation, which they call Texas, and who, they main-tain, live under an organized government, congregated in their pueblos, and governed by a cacique who is named the Great Lord, as they call the one who rules them all, and who, they say resides in the interior. They have houses made of wood, cultivate the soil, plant maize and other crops, wear clothes and punish misde-meanors, especially theft. The Coahuiles do not give more detailed reports of the Texas because, they say, they are allowed to go only to the first pueblos of the border, since the Great Lord of the Texas does not permit foreign nations to enter the interior of his country.

There are many of these Coahuiles who give these reports, and who say that they got them through having aided the Texas in their wars against the Pauit, another very warlike nation.[12]

And therein lay the problem. While the Hasinai chiefdom was powerful, it also had powerful enemies. To the northwest they frequently warred with Wichita villages, as well as the Caddoan-speaking Canohatinos, possibly the descendants of the Soacatinos met by Moscoso in 1542, and the Yojuanes. The Yojuanes inflicted great harm on the Hasinai Caddos in the early eighteenth century when a Yojuane raiding party burned the main Hasinai temple and the two spiritual children—the cononicis, who advised the xinesí—ascended to heaven in the smoke, never to return. To the south, the Karankawas periodically raided Hasinai villages, taking horses and captives back to the Gulf Coast. To the west, the Apaches formed the greatest threat, as they barred Caddo hunters and traders from the plains and severed the trade network linking the Caddos to the Jumanos, the Spanish, and the Pueblos. And things did not always go smoothly within the chiefdoms themselves. Periodically, a city-state might try for independence, and civil war would erupt. Father Francisco Casañas, who lived among the Hasinai in the early 1690s, reported that the Caddo city-states of Nabiti and Nadaco were enemies of the Hasinai chiefdom. And independent Caddo city-states might make their own moves against other Caddo communities.[13]

The Caddos needed help, especially as the Apache expansion increasingly isolated them from Spanish goods coming out of West Texas. This isolation and the need for goods sent the Tejas ambassadors and Jumano chief Juan Sabeata to the Spanish at El Paso in 1683 to ask for missions. But the Spanish dawdled and things looked bleak for the Caddos, until help came out of the blue. In 1686 French explorer René-Robert Cavelier, better known as Sieur de la Salle, set up a colony among the Karankawas near Matagorda Bay. Actually it was merely a small fort. And just as the Karankawas had initially welcomed Cabeza de Vaca, so they befriended La Salle's colony. However, the French, rather than making kinships, stole canoes and other goods from the Indians and even attacked Karankawa villages. La Salle made several exploratory trips north to the Hasinais, and during one expedition members of his own party murdered him. The survivors, rather than return to Fort Saint Louis on Matagorda Bay, made for New France by way of the Hasinai and Kadohadacho chiefdoms. Back at the fort, disaster occurred. Smallpox ravaged the French inhabitants and undoubtedly the Karankawas as well. Relations between the Karankawas and French worsened, and in late 1688 the Karankawas destroyed the fort, killing many of the colonists, adopting others, and carrying off most of the manufactured goods.[14]

The Hasinais marveled at these goods, particularly the guns. Henrí Joutel, one of the French survivors, recorded that when one of the Frenchmen fired at a buffalo, a Hasinai warrior "went to inspect the bullet hole which had passed through the animal. Much astonished, the Indian remained a while without saying anything, admiring the power of our guns."[15] A party of Frenchmen joined the Hasinais on a raid against the Canohatinos in which their weapons proved decisive. The Hasinais took many captives on this raid. The children were adopted, the adult men and women scalped and tortured to death, with some cut up and eaten in order to add Canohatino power to their own. One woman was scalped alive. A musket ball was put in her hand and she was sent back to her people with a warning that now the Hasinais had guns and they would not hesitate to use them again. Overjoyed at the goods the French brought and their willingness to help them against their enemies, the Caddos went out of their way to establish kinships with the French. Adoption ceremonies were held and marriages offered; every enticement available was made to keep the French among them. A few of the exploration party survivors remained but the majority wanted only to go home. So most Frenchmen rejected these offers as they passed through the Hasinai and Kadohadacho chiefdoms on their way back toward New France.[16]

Jumano traders shocked the Spanish along the Rio Grande with news of La Salle's colony. Fearing a French grab for parts of New Spain, the Spanish moved slowly into East Texas. Several expeditions ventured into Karankawa and Hasinai country and rounded up any remaining French survivors. In 1690 and 1691, intrigued by the huge agricultural towns of the Caddos and hoping to Christianize them and turn them into allies, the Spanish built a couple of missions—San Francisco de los Tejas and Santísimo Nombre de María—near the Neches River. These were pitiful things, poorly manned and poorly supplied. The Caddos were not bearing the brunt of Apache attacks the way the Jumanos and Coahuiltecans were and so did not need the missions for protection. The underequipped missions could not supply goods in the quantities the Caddos wanted, and as for food, the missions needed the Caddos more than the Caddos needed them. No Caddos accepted Christianity or went to live at either of the missions. In fact, the Caddos appropriated the mission's cattle and horses for themselves. Accepting failure, the Spanish friars and soldiers burned the missions in October, 1693, and except for those who deserted to the Caddos, trudged back to New Spain.[17]

Once again a Caddo connection to manufactured goods did not pan out. However, the Caddos were on the map, so to speak. Henrí de Tonty, a French fur trader from New France, visited the Caddos in the 1690s. After France created the colony of Louisiana in 1699, French activity among the Caddos increased. In 1713 the French built Fort Saint Jean Baptiste among the Natchitoches Caddos on Red River in Louisiana, and in 1720 they constructed Fort Saint Louis de Cadodaquioux at the Kadohadacho chiefdom near the great bend of the Red River. Led by their wily commandant at the Natchitoches, Louis Juchereau de St. Denis, French traders quickly made their way to the city-states of both the Hasinai and Kadohadacho chiefdoms, where they exchanged manufactured goods for horses, deer hides, and bear oil. The Caddos heartily welcomed these traders into their communities and families. Unlike La Salle's survivors, these Frenchmen had come to stay and so accepted Caddo offers of kinship. Many of them married Indian women, and soon a half-Indian, half-European population, essentially people with feet in both worlds, grew up around the French posts.[18]

To counter the French, the Spanish once again returned to East Texas. Between 1716 and 1721 they built six missions and two presidios among the Hasinai city-states, even designating one of the presidios—Nuestra Señora de los Dolores—as capital of the entire province of Texas. Disturbingly for the Spanish, they found themselves outgunned by the Hasinais, who sported French trade muskets and shotguns. As before, the missions were disappointments for both the Spanish and the Caddos. Again, no Caddos accepted Christianity. None resettled around the missions to work for the friars, and as before, they raided the Spanish corrals for horses and cattle. With the missions ineffectual and the presidios weak, the Caddos mainly turned to their French kinspeople in Louisiana for goods and assistance. Of course, they were more than willing to accept Spanish gifts or play the French and Spanish against each other when it benefited them.[19]

For the Hasinai Caddos of East Texas, the first decades of the eighteenth century must have seemed like flush times indeed. However, such times came with a price as the Caddos found themselves drawn into the European mercantile system. While the French and Spanish gave gifts, as good kinspeople should, the French, and to a certain degree the Spanish, also depended on regular trade with the Caddos. So many guns or kettles or bolts of cloth for so many deer hides or horses or pots of bear oil. To ensure a steady supply of these valuable commodities, Caddo hunters scoured the forests and prairies for deer, depleting them in some areas. To acquire more hides and horses, the Caddos stepped up their raiding, and at the same time found themselves increasingly under attack. This meant they needed more goods, more guns, and more gunpowder, which increased their dependency on their European kinspeople who supplied them. Nevertheless, times seemed good to the Hasinai. The Kadohadacho chiefdom and the Louisiana Caddos bore the brunt of Osage and Chickasaw raiders who had their own trade connections to the French and English. While the Apaches and Tonkawas might be a threat to others, the Hasinais lived well to the east of them and now had a sure access to manufactured goods. So the Hasinai were prepared to resist any raiders, as well as the Apache expansion.[20]

The French connection also benefited other Indians in Texas, particularly the Atakapas, south of the Caddos on the upper Texas coast.

The Atakapas

The Atakapas spanned the Louisiana-Texas border, living along the Texas coast to about Galveston Bay and as far north as present-day Jasper, Livingston, and Huntsville, Texas. Three, possibly four or five, separate groups comprised the Atakapas. The Atakapas proper, who gave their name to the entire people, lived around the Sabine River, from the coast to about Jasper. West of them were the Akokisas, often referred to as the Orcoquisac, who ranged from Galveston Bay north to about Conroe. The Bidais lived north of the Akokisas, between the Trinity and Brazos Rivers, between Livingston and College Station. Spanish missionaries listed the Patiri as an Atakapa people, but there is no other mention of them and they were probably a subgroup of the Bidai or Akokisa. The Deadoses lived just north of the Bidais, but there is a question as to whether they were also an Atakapa group or a band of Tonkawas.[21]

Just as there are questions about the Deadoses, so are there questions about whether the Akokisas and Bidais were actually Atakapas or completely separate peoples. They all spoke Atakapa dialects, which is part of the Tunican language stock found through much of South Louisiana and different from Karankawan. And they all seem to have made marriages and kinships with each other. Simars de Bellisle, a Frenchman who spent a year and a half as an Akokisa slave in 1718, believed they and the Bidais, though different nations, were all part of the same people.[22]

Economically and culturally, the Atakapa proper and the Akokisas seem to have been very much like the Karankawas. They spent summers along the coast spearfishing and collecting oysters and birds' eggs. They used canoes but only in the bays and streams, not out in the open ocean. By the early eighteenth century they possessed a few horses, which allowed them to travel inland where they spent winters, though farther north than the Karankawas usually went. They also hunted the forests

and prairies for deer and buffalo, while the women foraged for wild potatoes and the like. They did not grow corn, and like the Karankawas,
they lived in bands often on the move, residing in small lodges made of
bent limbs covered with hides. One of the first Indian bands Cabeza de
Vaca met when he landed on Galveston Island were the Han, who
may well have been a band of Akokisas, sharing the island with the
Karankawas.[23]

The Bidais, the northernmost of the Atakapa speakers, at least by 1700,
seemed to be moving in another direction, both literally and figuratively.
Increasingly, the Bidais were being pulled into the Hasinai orbit. In fact, the
name "Bidai" is Caddo for "brushwood" and refers to the brush lining the
Trinity River and Bedias Creek bottoms where the Bidais lived. Unlike
their Akokisa and Atakapa cousins, the Bidais rarely, if ever, went down to
the sea; instead they resided in small villages in the forests and prairies of
East Texas. There they hunted deer and planted goodly quantities of corn
and beans. They also spoke Caddoan as a second language. In fact, just as
the Caddo chiefdoms were the powerhouses in East Texas, Caddoan was
spoken by a wide variety of Indian peoples and was a Southern Plains lingua franca well into the nineteenth century.[24]

Not many descriptions of the Atakapa peoples come down to us, but
we can assume that in appearance and clothing they were much like their
Caddo and Karankawa neighbors. Depending on whether one lived on the
coast or inland and whether it was summer or winter, men wore breechcloths or went naked, while women wore skirts of moss and grasses or animal hides. They all apparently sported tattoos and wore paint. There is
some hint that the Bidais flattened their heads, but if they did, they had
stopped doing it by the early eighteenth century. Sometimes we get mere
bits of hard information, such as that the Akokisas yelled a greeting when
members of their band returned to camp.[25]

Even less is known about their society, politics, and religion. Like most
hunter-gatherers, the Atakapas lived in small bands that often hunted sep-
arately but might join with others at various times. Certainly there was no
paramount chief of the Atakapas, Akokisas, or Bidais, nor were there the
social rankings and political hierarchy found among the Caddos. Nevertheless, seniors took precedence over juniors. Slavery existed, as the
Frenchman De Bellisle, put ashore near Galveston and so an outsider with
no kin relationships, allowed himself to be made into one. Though fed and
given a wife, he did women's work—gathering wood and water and carrying baggage—while being slapped and punched by adults and children
alike. Shamans, using herbs and rituals, handled the religious ceremonies
of the Atakapas, and dances were, as always, integral ceremonies. Ataka-

pas may have also used charnel houses, where the flesh was removed from the dead before the bones were buried.[26]

As with the Karankawas, the charge of cannibalism has been leveled at the Atakapas. In fact, the name "Atakapa" is Choctaw for "man-eater." De Bellisle said he saw it firsthand. His Akokisas attacked a band of Toy-als and killed one of them. "One of them cut his head off and another one cut the arms off, while they skinned him at the same time. Several of them ate the yellow fat, which was still raw, and finally they devoured him completely."[27] While the incident is shocking to read about, we should re-member that the Akokisas were not necessarily hunting down humans for food, but instead, they had killed one of their enemies and were then participating in ritual cannibalism. Of course, world over, when times are hard and hunger stalks the land, as it often did in parts of Texas, people turn to cannibalism. Some of Cabeza de Vaca's Spaniards did so when they washed up on Galveston Island. And this might have been the case in the incident described by De Bellisle. No matter what the cause, the "cannibal" label stuck, and Spanish officials feared sailors shipwrecked on the upper Texas coast would be eaten. In reality, most drowned or died of hunger or exposure.[28]

The Spanish had much more to worry about when it came to the Ataka-pas than whether they were cannibals as these Indians were quick to see and exploit opportunities. By 1720 the Hasinai Caddos were rapidly ex-panding their influence among the Atakapa-speakers. The Bidais had adopted agriculture and every day were becoming more like the Caddos. Even the Akokisas and Atakapa proper feared and respected the Hasinai Caddos. At the behest of Louis de St. Denis, French commandant of Fort Saint Jean Baptiste at Natchitoches, two Hasinai warriors went to rescue De Bellisle from the Akokisas. De Bellisle recalled that when a couple of Akokisas tried to prevent it, the Hasinai "told them that if they dared to do me the least harm, they should count that within a short time they would be all destroyed by the Assinais [Hasinai]. This made them tremble from fear and immediately they let me go, not understanding why these Indi-ans chose my side."[29] So while the Bidais welcomed an alliance with the Caddos, the Akokisas and Atakapas seemingly were not as happy with it. The French traders venturing into Atakapa territory gave the Bidais the ability to try to pursue their own agenda.

While De Bellisle may have been the first Frenchman the Atakapas saw, he certainly was not the last, especially as France hoped to press La Salle's claim to Texas. In the mid-eighteenth century the French established the Atakapas Post on Bayou Teche in Louisiana. From there, French trad-ers ventured overland to Atakapa villages in Southeast Texas. Similarly,

French, and possibly even English, ships plying the Gulf often laid anchor at the mouth of the Neches, Trinity, and Brazos Rivers to trade with the Ataka-pas. As guns, gunpowder, and other manufactured goods flowed into Akok-isa, Atakapa, and Bidai bands, they began to expand their trade networks with the Tonkawas to their west. Eventually, an important Atakapa-Tonkawa-Apache trade network grew up that spanned southern Texas.[30]

The Tonkawas

The Tonkawas of Central Texas, as we think of them today, were some of the most complex and fascinating of all the Indian peoples of Texas. Ethno-genesis took place constantly in Texas as Indian peoples made and remade themselves. Bands split, rejoined, were absorbed by other cultures, or were pulled into Spanish missions where they created kinship with other groups. Rather than a single "racially pure" Indian nation, the Tonkawas were a "composite" people who created themselves from the many Indian bands roaming Central Texas.

By the mid-seventeenth century Central Texas was filled with Indian peoples, some native to the area, others hailing from outside regions. Most, but not all, were hunter-gatherers similar to the Coahuiltecans, living off buffalo, deer, and other animals and plants. Some in the northern part of the region were Plains Wichita corn farmers. The expansion of the Apaches and Spanish only sent more people into Central Texas in search of a refuge. Others were bands of ladino Indians, "apostates" from the Spanish mis-sions trying to return to a traditional life. While ladinos wanted to escape mission life, other bands wanted surer access to European firearms, man-ufactured goods, and the horse herds in Spanish and Hasinai corrals, and Central Texas was closer to these commodities. By 1684 Central Texas was filled with Indian bands. In that year, fifty-seven different Indian nations gathered for the trade fair on the upper Colorado River. Many of these were eventually absorbed by Apaches, Wichitas, Caddos, and Comanches. Others were pulled into Spanish missions or as workers on ranches, where they either died out or became the basis of the Mexican campesinos. More disappeared from disease, warfare, and famine. Some managed to band together and create the Tonkawa people. This was nation-building at its most basic, fueled by the shattering of nations due to disease and warfare and assisted by the tendency of Europeans and Americans to lump differ-ent peoples under one name, such as "Tonkawa."[31]

In the late seventeenth century Spanish missionaries among the Cad-dos mentioned that some of the Hasinai's western enemies included the Apaches, but also the Tancaquay [Tonkawa], Diu-Juan [Yojuane], and a host of others. At the same time, to the southwest, just east of the Guadalupe River, sat a large gathering of Indians who were friends of the Hasinai. These included the Emet, Tohaha, Toho, and Cavas Indians. But there were others in the area, both native and immigrants, including the Mayeyes, Yrvipiames, Cantona, Catqueza, Menanquem, Sana, Sijame, Temu, Tueinzum, and Zorquan. While all of these were independent, autonomous bands, speaking a plethora of different languages, their common need to stave off Apache raids drew them together and over time they created the Tonkawa nation.[32]

Juan de Oñate, during his 1601 trip to the plains, brought a "Tancoa" Indian back to Mexico. If the Tancoas, or Tonkawas proper, were living in north-central Oklahoma then, by 1716 they had moved to the Red River, northwest of the Hasinais, and roamed far south into the heart of Texas. Nearby, on the North Canadian River in Oklahoma lived the Yuhuanica, or Yojuanes, a component of that large village of corn-growing people Oñate encountered on the plains. The Yojuanes and Tonkawas, though living in the same general vicinity, were different peoples, speaking different languages. These large corn-growing villages were part of the Wichita peoples, and the early Yojuanes probably spoke Wichita. It is unclear what language the early Tonkawas spoke. By 1717 the Yojuanes had also moved south into Texas and were making raids on the Hasinai city-states, even burning their main temple in 1716.[33]

While the Tonkawa proper and the Yojuanes apparently came from the north, the Mayeyes came from the south. In 1687 La Salle's survivors reported the "Meghey," or Mayeyes, lived between the lower Colorado and Brazos Rivers. Thirty years later, General Don Martín de Alarcón saw them in pretty much the same location. What language the Mayeyes spoke is unclear, but they seemed to have close relations with the Bidais and Deadoses, both Atakapa speakers, so it is possible the Mayeyes originally spoke that language as well.[34]

The Yrvipiames were a "composite" people, ladino Indians who had run away from the missions to create their own nation. In the early seventeenth century the Yrvipiames were Coahuiltecan peoples of northern Mexico. They often raided Spanish ranches and outposts for horses and traded them to the Jumanos at La Junta. Wars with the Spanish gradually drove them north and in the 1690s they settled into Spanish missions in northern Mexico. There they learned Spanish culture and religion but soon left the missions. As St. Denis described them in 1717, the Yrvipiames had been "settled on the margins of the Rio del Norte in the mission of San Joseph and rebelled, and moved to the banks of the Colorado."[35] About this same time, if not earlier, the Yrvipiames created Ranchería Grande, that huge gathering of Indian peoples on the Brazos River, just northwest of the general Bryan–College Station area. Yrvipiame chief Juan Rodríguez, a ladino mission Indian, governed the two thousand plus Indians of Ranchería Grande, which included the remnants of twenty-two different Indian nations shattered by Apache raids. The Yrvipiames had re-created themselves and would now help create the Tonkawas. The Cantona, Catqueza, Cavas, Emet, Sana, Sijame, Tenu, Tohaha, Toho, Tueinzum, and Zorquan peoples, all relatively small nations and apparently native to the area, lived along the road from Mexico to the Hasinais, around Fayette, Lavaca, and surrounding counties. What language these people spoke is not known, but apparently it was not Coahuiltecan, Karankawan, or Atakapan.[36]

As these cultures converged on the plains and prairies of Central Texas, they began to create close relationships, though not until the late eighteenth century would a true Tonkawa nation or identity be established. Nor until that time would the leaders of these different communities come under the governance of a single Tonkawa chief. But even more impressive was the creation of a distinct Tonkawa culture. Clans developed with such names as Bear, Wolf, Buffalo, Snake, Mouth Open, Acorn, Blinking Eyelids, and Long Genitals. Other clan names included "the real Tonkaways," "Méyei," and "Sánux," which may have hearkened back to the once autonomous nations of Tonkawa proper, Mayeyes, and Sana. Supporting this was that a chief led each clan. There is also some evidence that the Tonkawas divided their society into halves—a moiety—with principal men from the halves meeting in council on separate sides of a great fire. Although the Tonkawas were mainly hunter-gatherers, rarely using agriculture, they tended to be matrilineal, meaning children belonged to the mother's clan. This may have been a carryover from the Yojuanes, who had once been Wichita agriculturalists on the North Canadian River so many years ago.[37]

A Tonkawa religion and a host of ceremonies and dances also developed that incorporated both the hunter-gatherer and farming beliefs of its disparate bands. The Deer Dance and Buffalo Dance were probably introduced by the more northerly bands, while the Wild Hog Dance, probably came from the southerly Yrvipiames, where peccaries were much more abundant. The Wolf Dance could be considered the national dance of the Tonkawas, as they believed a Great Wolf had uncovered them on the plains and so brought the Tonkawa people into the world. The Great Wolf had told them to live always on the move, hunting, killing, and stealing, to never settle down or they would die. The Wolf Dance was a sacred, somber dance. Tonkawas also had complex burial ceremonies in which the dead person's hair was cut, his face painted yellow, and the body wrapped in buffalo skins or blankets, then the body was buried in a grave along with such personal property as guns, saddles, enemy scalps, and beads. Other property might be destroyed, particularly items the person had on him when he died. Ashes from the man's pipe were shaken out and hidden.[38]

Whether considered individual nations or collectively, as the "Tonkawas," these people of Central Texas possessed much in common economically and socially. The small bands ranged over an ever-narrowing territory, hunting and gathering what they needed. Some, such as those at Ranchería Grande, might stay in one area longer and make periodic buffalo hunting trips to the plains where they always had to keep an eye out for Apaches. Most lived in small, conical brush or hide-covered huts. And as with just about all the Indian peoples in Texas at this time, save the Apaches, they tattooed and painted themselves, and sported necklaces and earrings of bone and shell. Men wore hide breechcloths and women deerskin skirts, both adding buffalo robes in winter. It may well have been how they cut their hair, the designs of their tattoos and paintings, and the style of their jewelry that differentiated the many bands that composed the Tonkawas from each other. Horses were always in demand, and the Tonkawas traded and raided for them when they could. Essentially, they were an emerging Southern Plains people, increasingly horse mounted and more and more dependent on the buffalo. Unfortunately for the Tonkawas, the Apaches then controlled the Southern Plains, making it difficult to acquire horses and buffalos.[39]

As these groups congregated in Central Texas, one might well ask how they communicated with each other? While they could create a Tonkawa people, culture, and belief system, could they also create a distinct Tonkawa language? So few written words of Tonkawa exist that there is no way be sure. But since the Tonkawas were an amalgam of many peoples speaking many languages, it might well be that if a Tonkawa language existed, it also was a mixture of languages, dialects, and words. Nevertheless, the Tonkawas, as well as all other Indian peoples in Texas, such as the fifty-eight different nations attending the trade fair on the Colorado River in the late 1600s, needed a way to communicate with each other. So trade languages developed. Mobilian, a derivative of Choctaw, was spoken by the Caddos and probably the Atakapas as well. Some languages, such as Caddo and later Comanche, became very common on the Southern Plains and were spoken as a second language by many groups. But the most common way for different people to communicate was through sign language. The true magnificence and importance of this sign language cannot be overestimated and it was truly one of mankind's great accomplishment.

Using both sweeping gestures and intricate hand movements, all the Indians of Texas could communicate complex thoughts, details, and directions. When Father Gaspar José de Solís spent time among a gathering of Mayeyes, Yojuanes, Tonkawas, Cocos, and others in the mid-eighteenth century, he reported that by using sign language, these people could "talk not only for hours but entire days."[40]

As with the Karankawas and Atakapas, the Tonkawas also gained a reputation as cannibals. Virtually all Texas Indian peoples utilized a ritual cannibalism, where the people of a band or village might eat part of the body of an enemy for revenge, to gain his power, or to deny him a whole body in the afterlife. Anthropologist Kelly Himmel writes that during the eighteenth century the Spanish never mentioned Tonkawa cannibalism and the French only once, but "overwhelming evidence of Tonkawa cannibalism exists for the nineteenth century."[41]

Problems in Central Texas

The sixteenth and seventeenth centuries were good to the Apaches. They expanded into Texas at the same time European diseases and warfare decimated the populations of native Indians. As they moved south, they acquired horses and became some of the finest mounted warriors in the history of the world. Nevertheless, this came at a price. They had to constantly find fresh forage for their mounts, ensure the safety of their herds, and replenish lost horses. They increasingly adopted Spanish manufactured goods and soon tipped their lances and arrows with metal, armored their horses with leather, and used firearms when they could acquire them. Equally as important, as the Apaches expanded into Texas, they integrated a variety of different groups into their bands, essentially creating a "new" Apache people.[42]

The Apaches, like most other Indian peoples, the Iroquois of New York being a good example, incorporated a host of people to replenish population loss and to create valuable kinship and trading relationships. In the mid-seventeenth century Pueblo Indians from Taos abandoned their town and settled among the Apaches at El Cuartelejo, a community on the Arkansas River in southern Colorado. There Apaches and Pueblos intermarried, resided in flat-roofed, pueblo-style adobe houses, and planted small fields of corn and beans. The people of El Cuartelejo and other nearby Apache bands may have been the genesis of the Jicarilla Apaches, who eventually moved into the mountains near Taos and Santa Fe.[43]

As other Apache bands moved south in the late seventeenth and early eighteenth centuries, they also began absorbing bands of Jumanos,

Coahuiltecans, and others. By 1716 Apache bands were living just north of La Junta and were engaged in peaceful relations with the Jumanos there. Jumanos often married Apaches and joined them in attacking the missions at San Antonio in 1731. Pelones and Ypandes, the Pelones certainly coming from Mexico, assimilated with the Apaches, and soon the Spanish referred to them as the Pelone Apaches. The name "Ypande" eventually became "Lipan," the name given to the easternmost Apache division. Another name given to these eastern Apaches—"Cannecy"—may have come from the "Chentis," a southern people absorbed by the Apaches. "Apostate" Indians escaping from the missions might also join with the Apaches, as they did in 1707 when together they battled Mission San Juan Bautista commandant Diego Ramón on the Nueces River. Not all Apaches appreciated the adoption and acculturation of these outsiders into Apache culture. The Natagés, or Mescalero Apaches as they came to be called, lived west of the Lipans, between the Pecos and Rio Grande, and considered themselves as the "true" or "legitimate" Apaches. They sneered at the amalgamated Lipans, sometimes even raiding Lipan camps for horses and slaves. A distinct dialect difference could be found between the Lipan Apaches and the Mescalero Apaches.[44]

Incorporation might be accomplished by force. An Apache band would swoop down on an unsuspecting camp of Pelones or a village of Jumanos and race off with scores of captives. Some would be exchanged among other bands, and most of these would be adopted into Apache families, the women becoming wives of Apache men. But not all assimilations came through violence. Some small nations with few options chose to acculturate and put themselves under the protection of Apache leaders. Other groups came to identify themselves as Apaches in order to tap into the Central Texas trade networks, which the Apaches controlled. As they had for centuries, the Plains Apaches provided buffalo meat, and slaves to the village Indians along the Pecos and Rio Grande in exchange for bread, corn, and Spanish manufactured goods. As more and more small nations came to identify themselves as Apaches, by the first decades of the eighteenth century we have what historian Gary Clayton Anderson has called the "Apacheanization" of the Southern Plains.[45]

As the Apaches expanded south and east, they turned their attention to Ranchería Grande, where numerous Indian peoples had concentrated for protection from these very same Apaches. Now some peoples of Ranchería Grande found themselves pulled into the Apache world, mainly as captives taken in raids. By 1746 even the Spanish had to admit that Ranchería Grande was increasingly becoming a southern Apache enclave. Father Benito de Santa Ana reported that one hundred Natagé

Apaches he knew of came "from the missions on the Conchos River or from a mission called Ana de la Individual of the ranchería grande and river Conchos." So maybe even the Natagés were not as "pure" as they imagined.[46]

Of course, not all Indian peoples of Ranchería Grande, or Central Texas for that matter, were willing to become Apache. These Apache attacks created the crucible from which the Tonkawas were formed. At the same time, the residents of Ranchería Grande tried to ensure additional protection from the Apaches by playing the age-old card of getting the Spanish to build a mission among them. Many of these groups, such as the Yrvipiames, had spent time in the missions and saw that they could be places of refuge, where one was protected from one's enemies while also being fed and acquiring manufactured goods. Of course, the missions could also be abandoned when good times eventually returned. But for now, the people of Ranchería Grande realized they needed help against the ever-pressing Apaches. The interests of the Central Texas Indians intersected with that of the Spanish when four chiefs from Ranchería Grande visited San Antonio in June, 1745, and asked for a mission to be built among them.[47]

By then the Spanish had become worried about Apache raids into the San Antonio area. They were also concerned about possible French expansion into East Texas. French traders seemed to be everywhere, and French guns, flags, and goods could be found in almost every Caddo, Tonkawa, Bidai, and Atakapa village. Even worse, from the Spanish point of view, Apaches, as well as the now south-ranging Comanches and Wichitas, were also getting goods from the French. The appeals of the Tonkawas for a mission in their area, something the Spanish friars had long advocated, spurred Spanish authorities to begin a third round of mission and presidio building. The Spanish had first built missions among the Hasinai Caddos in the 1690s, but these had failed after only a couple of years. Then, between 1716 and 1722, they reestablished five missions and two presidios among the Hasinais; built a clutch of missions and presidios in the San Antonio area for the Coahuiltecans; and constructed a mission and a presidio, commonly called La Bahía, for the Karankawas not far from Matagorda Bay. The Hasinai missions were too far away from Spanish supply centers and too close to the French in Louisiana to be effective. Bad feelings between the Karankawas and the Spanish at La Bahía erupted in warfare and so in 1726 the friars moved the mission complex to the Guadalupe River to work among the Xaranames and Tamiques. Only the missions at San Antonio seemed to have any measure of success in retaining Indians. The third round, which was to be much more comprehensive, would be shored up by settling more Spanish colonists in Texas.[48]

In the thirteen years between 1749 and 1762, Spain built more than a dozen new missions and presidios across Texas. Missions San Francisco Xavier de Horcasitas (1746), San Ildefonso (1749), Nuestra Señora de la Candelaria (1749), and Presidio San Francisco Xavier (1751) were built on the San Gabriel River to serve the Tonkawas of Ranchería Grande as well as any Akokisas, Bidais, Deadoses, and Karankawas who could be convinced to settle there. And scores of each nation did. In 1749 the La Bahía mission of Espíritu Santo de Zúñiga was moved to the lower San Antonio River. Nearby, Spain built Presidio Nuestra Señora de Loreto (1749) and Mission Nuestra Señora del Rosario de los Cujanes (1754) to serve the Karankawas and other peoples in that area. Mission Nuestra Señora de la Luz and Presidio San Agustín de Ahumada were both built on the lower Trinity River in 1756 for the Bidais and Akokisas. This complex was normally referred to as El Orcoquisac, the Spanish spelling of Akokisa. The Spanish also hoped to convince the Apaches to settle at missions and in 1757 built Mission Santa Cruz de San Sabá and Presidio San Luis de las Amarillas on the San Sabá River. Also for the Apaches, they later built Missions San Lorenzo de la Santa Cruz and Nuestra Señora de la Candelaria del Cañon in 1762 on the Nueces River.[49]

The San Gabriel River missions provided few benefits for the Tonkawas and their allies. Tonkawas of Ranchería Grande, as well as Akokisas, Bidais, and even Karankawas from the Gulf Coast, showed up at the mission when it opened only to be told there was not enough food. The missions never seemed to work out as the Spanish or the Indians hoped. Though the Spanish eventually set up three missions and assigned the Mayeyes, Yrvipiames, and Yojuanes to one; the Bidais, Deadoses, and Akokisas to another; and the Coco Karankawas to a third, the Indians found little food and even less protection and so came and went pretty much as they pleased. The missionaries might wake up one morning, as those as Mission San Ildefonso did, to find all the Indians had disappeared. And they might not return for months.[50]

Besides the periodic epidemics that swept through the missions' Indian population, the missions attracted Apaches, which made the Tonkawas more than willing to abandon the San Gabriel River missions. During its first year of operation, the San Xavier mission was raided by Apaches four times. Never having more than five hundred Indians at any one time and usually many fewer, in 1755, with the Tonkawas, Bidais, Akokisas, and Cocos rarely visiting the missions and resisting any attempts at permanent settlement, the San Xavier missions closed. Similar relationships existed between the Karankawas and the La Bahía missions on the San Antonio River and the Atakapas with the El Orcoquisac missions on the lower Trinity. While some Indians settled around the missions, most came and went as they pleased. The older missions among the Caddos in East Texas and West Louisiana proved absolutely useless in either attracting Indian converts or stopping French activities among them.[51]

While the Indians of Central and East Texas were not succumbing to missions, they were succumbing to diseases. The vast depopulation of Indians throughout Texas cannot be overstated. Epidemics swept through missions, villages, and bands, carrying off scores if not hundreds of people. Even worse, they took out crucial members of society—chiefs, warriors, shamans, midwives, potters—often before they could pass on their knowledge. Three thousand East Texas Caddos died from some unknown disease in 1691. Smallpox virtually wiped out the Coahuiltecan Indians living in the Rio Grande missions in 1706. The Caddos got hit again in 1718 when more than a hundred people died. Smallpox and measles killed off most of the Indians in the five San Antonio missions in 1739. Sometime before 1746 smallpox and measles devastated the Tonkawas and Atakapas. Smallpox hit them again in 1750, as well as those Indians living in the San Xavier missions. And the list goes on and on. An epidemic swept through the San Antonio missions in 1751. Malaria and dysentery got the San Xavier missions and the Tonkawas and Atakapas in 1753. Smallpox and measles hit the Hasinais in 1759. "Half the population" of the San Antonio missions died in 1763. Smallpox caught up with the Lipan Apaches in 1763–64. The Karankawas caught smallpox in 1766, and in 1777–78, cholera, possibly the bubonic plague, followed by smallpox hit East Texas and destroyed large numbers of Caddos, Tonkawas, Atakapas, and Wichitas.[52]

As disease, raids, and famine shattered bands, survivors coalesced into fewer and fewer communities. In 1691 the Hasinai Caddos of East Texas counted ten city-states: Hainai, Nadaco, Nasoni, Nabedache, Nacogdoches, Neches, Nacono, Nabiti, Nechauis, and Nacao. By the latter part of the eighteenth century only four remained—Hainai, or Tejas; the Nadaco, or Anadarko; the Nabedache; and the Nacogdoches. By mid-nineteenth century only the Tejas and Anadarko remained, and they would join with the Cadodachos, the only remaining community out of the four at the Great Bend of the Red River, to constitute the Caddos. Similarly, by the nineteenth century the many nations of Ranchería Grande as well as the Yojuanes and Yrvipiames would be lumped together as the Tonkawas. Names such as Mayeye and Deadose, as well as scores, if not hundreds, of Coahuiltecan nations disappeared from the written records. It was all part of the constant roiling of Indian peoples throughout Texas as they made and remade themselves in a constant search for protection and continuity.[53]

Ethnogenesis was one strategy for dealing with disease, depopulation, raids, and the constant need for horses, buffalo, and manufactured goods. However, Indian people devised a host of others. Inviting the Spanish to set up a mission was one, but it was not always successful, as the Tonkawas and Atakapas discovered. Adopting French traders who would supply their Indian kin with manufactured goods was another and was heavily pursued by the Caddos. Straight trade and accepting diplomatic gifts from the French and Spanish was a strategy adopted by just about every Indian people. But dire circumstances could create strange bedfellows. By the 1740s a trade network had formed that linked the Lipan Apaches to the Tonkawas to the Atakapas and finally to the French outposts in south-western Louisiana. The network was a tribute to the power of kinship. The Atakapas proper, Bidais, Mayeyes, and Deadoses certainly intermarried with each other and then intermarried with the Yojuanes, Yrvipiames, and other Tonkawa people in the San Xavier missions. Apache raids on Ranchería Grande and the missions in which Tonkawas and Ata-kapas were captured and adopted meant that kinship links now existed among all those peoples. Gift-giving and trade sent manufactured goods, hides, horses, and captives passing back and forth among the Apaches, Tonkawas, Atakapas, and French. This is not to say that all Tonkawas or Atakapas suddenly made peace with the Apaches, but some bands did and trade took place, particularly between the Bidais and Apaches. Also making this trade network possible was the dire straits the Apaches found themselves in at mid-eighteenth century.[54]

Since 1540 the Apaches had been an expanding force on the Southern Plains, and by the early seventeenth century they had become its masters. They had managed to snap the Caddo-Jumano-Pueblo trade networks and barred many bands of people from the plains. Their raids, along with the Spanish push northward, had churned Central Texas, bringing together a host of refugees who eventually coalesced to create the Tonkawa peoples. But by 1740 the Apache expansion had reached its zenith and they found themselves on the defensive. The Caddos, backed by their connection to the French in Louisiana, now proved formidable adversaries. Comanche peoples from the north and Wichita peoples from the northeast were them-selves migrating to the Southern Plains and they battled the Apaches for control of the region. Apaches found themselves pushed farther south. This southward move brought them into Central Texas and the Ranchería Grande area. It also brought them into contact with the Spanish settle-ments and missions in South Texas, which the Apaches raided to replenish the herds lost to Comanches, Wichitas, and Caddos. As raids by Apaches increased, the Spanish decided to make a concerted effort to neutralize them, through missions, if possible, or warfare if need be. Hammered by Comanches, Wichitas, Caddos, and some Tonkawas from the North and East; opposed by the Spanish and their Indian allies in the South; pushed off the bountiful Southern Plains into the more arid regions of South Texas, the Apaches found themselves in a desperate situation by 1750. Altogether this would force a major readjustment among the Indians of Texas.

Mississippian cultural tradition burial mound (ca. A.D. 1200) at Caddo Mounds, near Alto, Texas. Photo by the author.

Interior of a Caddo grass lodge. Courtesy Archives and Manuscripts Division of the Oklahoma Historical Society.

Tonkawa branch house along with an outdoor arbor and sweat lodge. Courtesy Archives and Manuscripts Division of the Oklahoma Historical Society.

Wichita grass lodge. Caddos lived in similar structures. Courtesy Western History Collections, University of Oklahoma Libraries.

A Kickapoo village. Courtesy Western History Collections, University of Oklahoma Libraries.

Cynthia Ann Parker and her child Prairie Flower. Cynthia was captured by
Comanches in Texas in 1836 and spent most of her life with them. She was
the mother of Comanche chief Quanah Parker. Courtesy Western History
Collections, University of Oklahoma Libraries.

A Comanche winter camp. Courtesy Western History Collections, University of Oklahoma Libraries.

Comanche women erecting a tepee. Courtesy Archives and Manuscripts Division of the Oklahoma Historical Society.

A Comanche baby in a raccoon skin–lined cradle. Courtesy Western History Collections, University of Oklahoma Libraries.

Comanche chief Quanah Parker and his family, Fort Sill, Oklahoma, 1892.
Courtesy Western History Collections, University of Oklahoma Libraries.

Comanche women and children on the Comanche reservation, probably daughters and
other family members of Chief Quanah Parker. Courtesy Western History Collections,
University of Oklahoma Libraries.

A Kiowa Indian village about 1872,
probably that of Lone Wolf. Courtesy Archives
and Manuscripts Division of the Oklahoma
Historical Society.

Kiowas watering their ponies
in the Washita River. Courtesy
Archives and Manuscripts
Division of the Oklahoma
Historical Society.

Kiowas drying meat. Courtesy Western History Collections, University of Oklahoma Libraries.

On reservations lifeways began to change. Here, Caddo Indians skin a beef, ca. 1895. Courtesy Archives and Manuscripts Division of the Oklahoma Historical Society.

Wichita Indians playing "monte" in the late nineteenth century. Courtesy Archives and Manuscripts Division of the Oklahoma Historical Society.

Caddo village in the late nineteenth century. Courtesy Western History Collections, University of Oklahoma Libraries.

Wichita sweat house on the Wichita dance grounds, March 3, 1900. Tepee may be Cheyenne or Arapaho. Courtesy Western History Collections, University of Oklahoma Libraries.

Kiowa Indians receiving rations on their reservation in Indian Territory. Courtesy Archives and Manuscripts Division of the Oklahoma Historical Society.

An aged Apache woman is visited by two Presbyterian missionaries, November 3, 1898. Courtesy Western History Collections, University of Oklahoma Libraries.

Christianity became a force on Texas Indian life. Here, Kiowas are at prayer in the late nineteenth century. Courtesy Archives and Manuscripts Division of the Oklahoma Historical Society.

Apache women with gifts for Comanche guests. Government officials tried to prevent what they called "give-aways." Courtesy Archives and Manuscripts Division of the Oklahoma Historical Society.

Mexican Kickapoo village in Coahuila. Courtesy Archives and Manuscripts Division of the Oklahoma Historical Society.

Walking the white man's road. The Caddo Business Committee and friends on the steps of the Oklahoma State Capitol, January 25, 1929. Courtesy Archives and Manuscripts Division of the Oklahoma Historical Society.

Indian girls, whose people once called Texas home, at the Riverside Indian school in Anadarko, Oklahoma. Courtesy Western History Collections, University of Oklahoma Libraries.

Nine members of the Caddo-Wichita baseball club, June 20, 1901. Courtesy Archives and Manuscripts Division of the Oklahoma Historical Society.

The old and the young. A gathering of Caddo women in the mid-twentieth century. Courtesy Archives and Manuscripts Division of the Oklahoma Historical Society.

The Turkey Dance, the Caddo national dance, performed by members of the Caddo Tribe at their headquarters in Binger, Oklahoma, summer, 1996. Photo by the author.

A gathering of Indian nations. The annual Red Earth Native American Cultural Festival, Oklahoma City, June, 1996. Photo by the author.

Chapter 6

The Nations of the North

THE SIXTEENTH and seventeenth centuries were times of unparalleled Apache expansion. The Apaches swept the Wichita, Jumano, and Caddo trading parties off the Southern Plains and set themselves up as the masters of the area. There they conquered and absorbed smaller Indian nations or sent them scurrying for protection. Still, the Apaches would not be the last Indians to journey into Texas. By the end of the seventeenth century two other groups were migrating south into Texas. Sliding down the eastern side of the plains came the Wichitas, being pushed by the expansion of Pawnees, Osages, and Comanches. At the same time, those very same Comanches were expanding on the western side of the plains. Originally a Shoshone people from the Great Basin region of Wyoming, the Comanches were moving into Texas to put themselves nearer the horses and buffalo herds. The Wichitas and Comanches initially battled each other, but in their efforts to tap into the Southern Plains economy, they soon turned their combined fury on the Apaches. Together, the Comanches and Wichitas, along with the Hasinai Caddos, gradually pushed the Apaches farther south into the heart of Spanish Texas.

The Wichitas

When first met by Spanish conquistador Francisco Coronado in 1541, the Wichitas lived in towns and villages along the rivers of the Texas Panhandle,

Oklahoma, and Central Kansas. They spoke Caddoan, making them linguistic, economic, and cultural cousins to the Caddos, the Pawnees, and the Arikaras of Kansas, Nebraska, and South Dakota. Scholars, using Wichita oral tradition, believe the Wichitas and Pawnees were at one time united and that they migrated from the southwest to the Central Plains where the two peoples separated. In later years the Wichitas would claim the Wichita Mountains of southwestern Oklahoma as their ancestral homeland.[1]

Economically, the Wichitas were farmers and during the sixteenth century lived in large villages of beehive-shaped grass houses surrounded by immense fields of corn, beans, and squash. But their location on the eastern margins of the Great Plains also meant they hunted buffalo, deer, and other smaller game. The Wichitas were matrilineal, tracing their descent through their mothers. A man married a woman from his own village or town and then went to live with his wife and her family, where he provided food for his in-laws. Unfortunately, very little is known about Wichita clans, or even if clans existed among them.[2]

When Coronado visited the Wichitas in the mid-sixteenth century, he found numerous autonomous towns, some stretching for miles along the riverbanks. Over the years, some of the villages expanded, others contracted, until the Wichita people could be divided into five main divisions. Up near the Great Bend of the Arkansas River in Kansas lived three Wichita divisions: the Taovayas, sometimes called the Tawehash, which was the largest division; the Guichitas, who gave the name "Wichita" to the people as a whole; and the Tawakonis. These three comprised the famed cities of Quivira reported by Coronado. Farther down the Arkansas River, near the convergence of the Neosho and Verdigris Rivers, lived the Kichais, who spoke a different Wichita dialect from the others and often moved back and forth between the Wichitas and the Caddos. Far to the southwest on Texas' Llano Estacado lived the Teyas. As the Teyas were pushed off the plains by the Apaches, those who were not absorbed into Apache bands merged with their Wichita cousins and became the Yscani division. In later years, the Iscani were often called Wacos. The Canohatinos, quite possibly the same "Soacatino" met by the Moscoso expedition in 1542, were also a Wichita peoples living northwest of the Hasinai city-states and often at war with them. Eventually, the Canohatinos were absorbed by the Tawakonis and Yscanis. Other Wichita peoples such as the Yojuanes moved farther south to help form the Tonkawa peoples. For the purposes of this history, the Wichitas include the Wichitas proper, Taovayas, Tawakonis, Yscanis, and Kichais. In the mid-sixteenth century they were seen as a very numerous people, with a total population that might have reached more than two hundred thousand.[3]

In appearance, the Wichitas were short and stocky and darker complexioned than many of their neighbors. Both the men and women tattooed themselves. Men put lines about their eyes, face, and arms, while crosses and triangles might decorate their chests. Women tattooed lines along their nose, chin, and lips, and circles around their breasts. These tattoos may have been marks signifying family membership as well as marks of distinction. They may also have differentiated Wichitas from the captives they took. Since the Spanish often used the term "Jumano" to designate those Indians who tattooed themselves, the Wichitas may have been confused with the Jumanos who lived down on the Rio Grande at La Junta. Certainly it was the Taovayas' intricate tattooing that earned them the nickname of "Panis Piques"—Pricked Pawnees—from the early French explorers. And their dark skin gave them the additional French sobriquet of "Black Pawnee." Tattooing also gave them the name they called themselves—Kidikides—meaning "Raccoon Eyes." The Wichitas often wore earrings and other jewelry and clothed themselves with deer hide breechcloths and skirts as did many other Texas Indians. Members of Coronado's party described the Teyas women as "well made and modest. They cover their whole body. They wear shoes and buskins made of tanned skin. The women wear cloaks over their small under petticoats, with sleeves gathered up at the shoulders, all of skin, and some wore something like *sanbenitos* with fringe, which reached halfway down the thigh over the petticoat."[4] As the Wichitas began trading with Europeans, these hide clothes gradually gave way to clothes made of cloth.[5]

In their religion, the Wichitas developed a cosmology around both farming and hunting. According to their traditions, their chief deity, Man-Never-Known-on-Earth, created the universe and the earth. He also created the first woman, to whom he gave an ear of corn, and the first man, who received a bow and arrows. Stars represented many other Wichita deities. After Man-Never-Known-on-Earth came the Sun, which helped things grow and constantly renewed the earth. Then came Morning Star, chief of the stars and herald of daylight; South Star, who protected warriors and chiefs; North Star, the protector of medicine men; the stars of the Great Bear, which warriors prayed to when they went to battle; Ghost Star for healing; and Flint-Stone-Lying-Down-Above, which could only be seen overhead on moonless nights and was prayed to for good luck. Besides stars, the moon was the special helper of women, assisting them during their menses, pregnancies, and births, and bringing growth to the Wichitas, as well as to animals, birds, and plants. Mother Earth was seen as giving birth to everything; while Woman-Having-Powers-in-the-Water was similar to the moon. As her name indicated she brought water for the

Wichitas to drink and with which to purify themselves. She was also the protector of women whose husbands had gone off to war. The Wind was also a deity and carried the breath of life.[6]

In general ways, the Wichitas' religion was not all that different from Christianity. They recognized a creator who lived above and who directed everything on earth including life and death. The Wichitas called upon him for success in war and just about every other enterprise and provided the first fruits of their harvest and their hunts as offerings. They kept a sacred fire burning, which represented this deity. Wichitas certainly believed in an afterlife, where the good would be rewarded with eternal youth, strength, clear water, fine foods, and delicacies. Evil people would be sent to a country filled with thorns, stones, wild animals, disease, hunger, and thirst. As one eighteenth-century Frenchman reported, from these beliefs sprang such Wichita characteristics as "the observance of promises, respect for elders, gentleness toward women, indulgence toward children, charity for the sick, generosity toward strangers, and obedience to the chiefs."[7]

Similar to the Caddos, each major Wichita town, or division, had its own chief, while subchiefs governed nearby villages and hamlets under the authority of the town chief. Some archaeologists believe the Wichitas had been part of the great Mississippian cultural tradition through an association with the great chiefdom at Spiro. If so, then, as with the early Caddos, leadership fell to powerful hereditary chiefs who linked their kinship to celestial deities. With the decline of the Mississippian cultural tradition and as Wichitas moved west and south, heredity played a less important role in the selection of a chief, while bravery, fortitude, generosity, and wisdom became increasingly important. In time, the principal warriors selected the chief. Nevertheless, as with many Indian peoples, some families were seen as the mainstay of the chiefly line, but not all leaders necessarily descended from this lineage.[8] Early Wichita chiefs, who certainly possessed high status and power, often carried symbols of their high office. Coronado noted that the "lord" of Quivira wore a copper gorget around his neck and "prized it highly."[9] Juan de Oñate, visiting the Wichitas on the Arkansas River in 1601, marveled at their chief named Catarax and how the Indians "obeyed him and served him, like a people more united, peaceful, and settled." Though the Spaniards took Catarax hostage and so feared an attack by the Wichitas, the Indians "did not do so, merely because he signaled to them that they should withdraw."[10] Over time, as some Wichita divisions and bands became more oriented toward a plains hunter-gatherer lifestyle, chiefs lost some of their power and had the same problems controlling their young men as did Apache, Comanche, and Kiowa chiefs.

Oñate witnessed firsthand the problems Wichitas were beginning to have with the Apaches. Following essentially the same route as Coronado had sixty years earlier, Oñate found no Teyas on the plains, only Apaches and Escanjaques, who seemed to be another division of Apaches. Escanjaques led Oñate to the Wichita villages on the Arkansas River and urged the Spanish to attack the settlements. They became enraged when Oñate refused, attacking the Spanish troops for not supporting them on their Wichita campaign. Oñate and his men made their way back to New Mexico, leaving the Wichitas and Apaches to fight their own battles.[11] As a result, over the next 150 years, the Wichitas steadily migrated south into Texas and southern Oklahoma. As they did so, they acquired horses. Now, Wichitas, who had once been mainly farmers, began to hunt buffalo in greater numbers. This not only changed their economy but also began a sort of leveling process in Wichita society. Gone were the massed ranks of warriors that Oñate saw. Increasingly, smaller war parties were led by men who held status not so much through heredity or their families but by the wealth gained through successful raids. Horses allowed the Wichita to counter the Apache expansion onto the Southern Plains as well as put themselves closer to the Spanish trade networks.

On the other hand, the Wichitas also found themselves pushed south by the Osages coming from the east. During the middle part of the seventeenth century the Iroquois nations of New York and southeastern Canada began a tremendous expansion fueled by their attempts to gain access to beaver lands and to take captives in order to bolster their sagging populations. Other groups tried to escape these northeastern wars. Lakotas and Cheyennes from the western Great Lakes region migrated into Minnesota and the Dakotas, wresting territory from earlier occupants. The Dhegian Siouan-speaking Osages, also pushed west, now stumbled upon the Wichitas. As French traders from Canada moved into the upper Mississippi Valley, they brought firearms to the Osages, Pawnees, and others, who used them to raid Wichita villages. Adding to Wichita troubles were disease, which caused tremendous depopulation and the loss of people essential to the village's survival. To escape, the Wichitas moved south, not only to put some distance between them and the Osages but also in hopes of finding their own sure access to manufactured goods.

By the early years of the eighteenth century Taovaya villages had moved near the juncture of the Verdigris and Fall Rivers. The Tawakonis had moved east of the confluence of the Arkansas and Cimarron. The Kichais were already on the Red River, while the Yscanis had joined the Wichita proper on Deer Creek in Kay County, Oklahoma. The Wichitas had also changed the setup of their villages from long, loose rambles along streams to ones that were more compact and therefore easier to defend. The southward migration did not stop there, and by the 1770s the Taovayas could be found on Red River and the Wichita proper on the upper Brazos; the Tawakonis had several villages stretching between the middle Brazos and the middle Trinity; the Yscanis were on the upper Neches; and the Kichais had divided, with one village on the middle Trinity and another on the Red River in Louisiana.[12]

The Wichitas' move south proved to be a good strategy at the time. It not only put them closer to Spanish missions and outposts in Texas but also anchored them to the French expanding out of Louisiana. The Wichitas had long been awaiting the day when French traders would arrive. They happily greeted Bénard de la Harpe when he visited their villages on the Arkansas River in 1719. Quickly establishing both diplomatic and kin relations with the French, the Wichitas made it clear to la Harpe that they expected the French to provide them with "arms in order to defend themselves against their enemies, [and] several sorts of merchandise proper and advantageous for their usages."[13] The French were more than willing to do so. Over the next few decades, French traders and gunsmiths out of Fort Saint Jean-Baptiste at Natchitoches, Louisiana, and Fort Saint Louis de Caddoquiox at the Great Bend of the Red River, visited Wichita, Caddo, and Tonkawa villages. Some Frenchmen became virtually permanent residents, often taking Indian wives and producing children who could easily pass back and forth between the Indian and the colonial worlds. Such quantities of goods and hides eventually flowed into the Taovaya villages on the Red River not far from present-day Spanish Fort, Texas, that the villages became a major trading center on the Southern Plains, attracting Wichitas, Caddos, Tonkawas, Comanches, Frenchmen, and a host of other people.[14]

Osage raids on the Wichitas along the Arkansas River continued to drive them south, but Caddo villages farther east suffered the brunt of these attacks. However, the weapons the Wichitas received from the French allowed them to better defend themselves. While braving Osage attacks, the Wichitas, along with their Caddo and Tonkawa allies, now armed with French muskets and metal weapons, managed to turn the Apache tide. Apaches might still make an occasional successful raid on a Wichita village, increasingly it was the Apaches who limped away wounded. As Wichita and Caddo warriors gave chase, the Apaches found themselves driven farther and farther south. But credit for Apache defeats in the mid-eighteenth century cannot be handed to the Wichitas alone. The Comanches played an equal, if not greater, role in driving the Apaches off the plains and into the mountains of New Mexico or south into Old Mexico.

The Comanches

Originally, the Comanches lived west of the Rocky Mountains, in the northern Great Basin area of Wyoming and Colorado. They called themselves Nim-ma—the people. They spoke a Shoshonean dialect and so were linguistic and cultural cousins to the Shoshones and Utes. In about 1500 they drifted east of the Rockies and began a buffalo-hunting lifestyle north of the Arkansas River. It proved to be the perfect time, as 1500 marked the beginning of the Little Ice Age, bringing increased rainfall to the plains and a tremendous expansion of the buffalo herds. Over the next two centuries the Comanches prospered, and during that time they acquired horses. Wanting more and pushed a little by the Pawnees and Cheyennes moving onto the plains during the mid-1600s, the more southerly Comanche bands began migrating toward Texas.[15]

As with all Indian peoples, the Comanches were not a homogenous people but consisted of different divisions, bands, and families. Exactly how many divisions and what their names were has been hotly debated. The earliest Comanche divisions may have been Cuchanecs and Jupes, which were actually lineages or clans. These later split into other divisions. Contributing to the problem of delineating Comanche divisions was the Comanches' rather loose social organization in which individuals could cross not only between bands but divisions as well. The many different names applied to Comanche divisions by the Spanish, French, Mexicans, and Americans only added to the confusion. Some Comanche division names, Cuchanec, Jupe, Pibian, first identified by the Spanish, and Ietan, used by early Americans in Texas, have long since disappeared from the records. Nevertheless, there seem to have been two main Comanche groupings. One was a southeasterly one that roamed much of North and Central Texas, essentially the Penetaka division, which the Spanish called "Comanche Orientales" or "Eastern Comanches." The other was a more northwesterly one nearer the Arkansas River, usually called "Comanche Occidentals" or "Western Comanches" and often referred to as the "Yamparikas".[16]

Beyond these, the Comanches can basically be divided into five major divisions and several minor ones. The Penetakas became the largest and southernmost, establishing themselves across Central Texas from the Cross Timbers to the Llano Estacado. North of them along the Red River ranged the Noconis. North of the Red River and the Noconis roamed the Kotsotekas, while the Kwahadis lived north and west of them in the Texas and Oklahoma panhandles. The Yamparikas, the northernmost Comanche division, lived around the Cimarron River in southern Kansas. Smaller divisions might include the Tanima and Tenewa. All these divisions, great and small, particularly the Penetakas, would have a direct influence on Texas.[17]

Divisions were composed of numerous smaller bands linked by kinship and common interests when it came to war, trade, and subsistence. These may have arisen from clans, if clans existed in Comanche society. There also may have been minor cultural differences between them, but political leadership seemed to play a greater role in creating Comanche divisions.[18] Out of the many bands arose a principal chief, who possessed medicine, bravery, and generosity. Sort of a first among equals, he became the division leader. Lesser band chiefs hoped to become division chiefs, while warriors tried to acquire status and power to become band chiefs. As for Comanche political leadership, Pedro Vial, who spent time among the Comanches in 1785, wrote: "Their rancherías are organized by captains, who each [one] endeavoring to have his own [ranchería], they do not have a fixed number of subjects, but only those who can adjust to the spirit of each captain. The two most famous in that nation, the one named Camisa de Hierro, and the other Cabeza Rapada, to whom they listen with much respect and attention from their respect among them as the most valiant of all. There are another ten little captains who govern and order their respective rancherías. They are nevertheless, subject to the two greatest."[19] Assisting the chiefs were the *tlatoleros,* essentially town criers who went around the camp explaining the decisions made by the chief and principal men. While the Comanches as a whole never gathered together at any one place, divisions might congregate at various times, particularly to discuss important political topics, such as war and peace. When they did, several thousand people might form a large village of hundreds of beautifully decorated buffalo-hide tepees.[20]

In many ways the Comanches were similar to almost all the hunter-gatherer horse peoples of the Great Plains. They hunted the buffalo, following its migrations, and used almost every part of it for food or tools. Prior to the introduction of the horse, they used dogs for transporting household goods and may have used them even after they began acquiring horses in the mid-1600s. As with the Apaches, the Comanches expertly used lances, tomahawks, and bows and arrows, which they tipped with metal once manufactured goods made their way into Comanche society. Even the acquisition of firearms never fully displaced lances and bows. Once horse mounted, the Comanches became truly formidable warriors. Similar to the Lakotas and Cheyennes, the Comanches had soldier societies: the Big Horse people, the Little Ponies, and the Black Knife people. The most elite was the Lobos, who could not retreat from a battle, even if outnumbered. Members of these societies acted not only as camp police but also as enforcers, ensuring compliance on hunts, on raids, and during warfare. For example, when one warrior violated war party rules by hunting buffalo, the Little Ponies attempted to confiscate his meat but were prevented from doing so by the warrior's high status. One of the singular characteristics of a Comanche warrior was a round, hide-covered shield of about one to two feet in diameter. The shield possessed great power for its holder and its tough leather could deflect arrows and lances, but not musket balls or bullets. The shield was so important to the Comanche warrior as a source of power that it was stored inside a fine hide envelope and normally kept in its own special shelter facing the door of the warrior's tepee. The shield, along with its cover, was painted and often bedecked with bird feathers or animal hide amulets. It was never to touch the ground.[21]

The quest for medicine power, or *puha* as the Comanches referred to it, shaped Comanche religion. No man could become a great warrior or achieve high status without great medicine. One might acquire puha in a vision quest. Powers might include the ability to find lost objects, doctor pregnant women, discover enemies, be protected from harm, or provide food. Some men possessed no power at all, whereas others might avoid or refuse it because of the burden it placed on them. Those people who shared the same power might form a medicine society where they sang medicine songs attributed to their particular power. Shields and medicine bundles possessed puha. Dances also contained power and were a major part of Comanche society, with the Sun Dance being the primary ceremony celebrated during the summer. There has been much controversy over whether the Comanches had a long tradition of the Sun Dance or acquired it during the mid-nineteenth century from other plains peoples. As with so much about Comanche religion and beliefs we will never know for sure, but that the Comanches had numerous dances, ceremonies, and rituals in which they tried to harness puha for their own benefit is certain. Puha could also be found in certain geographic locations throughout the *comanchería*, that area of the Southern Plains claimed by the Comanches. As the Comanches expanded across much of Texas they found power spots, such as a great meteor in eastern Texas, Enchanted Rock north of Fredericksburg, and Comanche Peak southwest of Fort Worth.[22]

The Comanches tended to be of medium height—men about five feet, six inches and women about five feet—but seemed almost square and stocky, with barrel chests and broad shoulders. The painter George Catlin visited the Comanches in 1834 and wrote that in "their movements, they are heavy and ungraceful; and on their feet, one of the most unattractive . . . races of Indians that I have ever seen; but the moment they mount their horses, they seem at once metamorphosed, and surprise the spectator with the ease and elegance of their movements."[23] While the Comanches used jewelry, particularly earrings, and decorated their clothing and tepees with beads and paints, they did not tattoo themselves the way most other Texas Indians did. Naturally, they clothed themselves with hides, the men wearing breechcloths and moccasins in summer, and buffalo robes, leggings, and hide boots in winter. The women wore buckskin skirts and blouses and added robes and clothing during cold weather. While such backbreaking work as tanning buffalo and deer hides and sewing and decorating clothing fell to Comanche women, they often elevated it to a higher level. They spent much time and attention on their blouses, which could become veritable works of art complete with fringes, painted designs, beads, and medallions.[24]

As Catlin and others noted, a Comanche became a different person once he mounted his horse. As a whole, once the Comanches began acquiring horses in the late 1600s, their warriors formed an excellent light cavalry. Because the Comanches could move rapidly on horseback, their migration south was fast. When they burst onto the Southern Plains of Texas about 1700, they found themselves in a well-populated area with complex economic and diplomatic alliances and agendas. Stumbling into a land rich in trade goods, exchange networks, and markets, the Comanches determined to dominate these trade networks, just as the Apaches had before them. This meant supplanting those same Apaches, taking control of the buffalo herds, and acquiring horses and captives. It also meant restricting outsider access to the grass, streams, and canyons needed for the Comanches' own horse herds. Naturally, the Apaches were reluctant to give up the lucrative trade alliance they had made with the Pueblos and Jumanos, and they needed the grasslands and water holes for their herds.[25]

This meant war between the Comanches and Apaches; a war that would rage for almost 150 years. By the 1720s the Comanches had driven the Jicarilla and other Apache divisions of eastern Colorado off the plains and into New Mexico. At the Jicarilla's request, the Spanish resettled them among the Pueblos in the Valley of La Jicarilla in north-central New Mexico. The old Apache-Pueblo town of El Cuartelejo disintegrated under Comanche attacks. With the Jicarilla and Cuartelejo Apaches no longer a barrier, the Pueblo towns and Spanish corrals of New Mexico lay naked before the Comanches.[26]

The timing of the Comanches' move into Texas proved to be ideal, allowing them to exploit Pueblo and Wichita needs and Spanish and Apache fears. The Comanches needed not only firearms, metalware, and cloth goods but also pottery, salt, tobacco, corn, bread, and gourds, all things the Pueblos and Spanish of New Mexico could provide. The Comanches, having driven the Apaches from the more northerly parts of the Southern Plains, had the buffalo meat, hides, and Indian slaves the Pueblos and Spanish desired. Over the next few decades Comanche trading parties visited Pueblo villages and Spanish outposts, and even attended Spanish-sponsored trade fairs. The problem was that the Spanish could not provide the Comanches with the volume of manufactured goods they wanted. New Mexico, and Texas as well, were backwaters of the Spanish empire and far from the distribution centers of Mexico. To get and keep a supply of manufactured goods in New Mexico was difficult, particularly since not only the Comanches but also Pueblos, Apaches, Navajos, Utes, Jumanos, numerous smaller nations, and the mission Indians needed them. Adding to the Comanches' frustration was the Spanish refusal to provide firearms to Indians. However, with the French to the east the Comanches had an alternative source.[27]

After 1720 French traders from Louisiana made extensive trade relations with the Atakapas, Tonkawas, Caddos, Wichitas, Osages, and Pawnees. When the Comanches first moved into Texas, they often raided the Wichitas for commodities to trade to New Mexico, and the Wichitas complained bitterly to both the French and the Spanish about Comanche attacks. When the Comanches received their first French traders in the 1720s, they soon realized they could acquire many more commodities from the French if they had good relations with the Indians to their east. So during the 1740s the Comanches made peace with the Wichitas and the Hasinai Caddos. The alliance proved strong and the Spanish often referred to these three nations as the Norteños, or nations of the North. Soon, a major Comanche trading center began operating along the Upper Arkansas River, attracting French traders as well as Wichitas, Caddos, Pawnees, and even Comancheros, a name given to Spanish-Pueblo traders out of New Mexico who visited the Comanches.[28]

All this brought about complex relations between the Comanches and the Spanish. On one hand, Comanche trading parties often showed up at New Mexico pueblos to exchange hides and captives. On the other hand, when the Spanish in New Mexico could not provide the quantities of manufactured goods the Comanches needed, and with the demands of French and Indian traders to the east for Comanche goods, the same Pueblos and Spanish outposts became targets of opportunity. Between 1716 and 1786, except for a brief period of peace in the early 1750s, Comanche warriors raided New Mexico villages and outposts with virtual impunity, driving off thousands of horses. Taos, Pecos, and Galisteo Pueblos time and again suffered raids in which scores of Pueblo villagers and Spanish settlers were killed, wounded, or taken captive. Spanish troops, along with Pueblo and Apache auxiliaries counterattacked. While they might punish a few Comanche bands, they did not score many lasting results. A few Comanches might be killed or taken captive but the attacks caused no real hardship. In fact, the Spanish could not be too harsh on the Comanches. To prohibit them from trading in New Mexico or to wage a major war against them, even if that were possible, would only drive the Comanches firmly into the arms of the French. It made the Comanches virtually fearless and they would dominate the Southern Plains until the mid-nineteenth century. When Comanches made peace with the Spanish, Mexicans, or other Indian peoples, it was not because they feared military reprisals but because they wanted trade goods.[29]

The Comanche-Apache Wars

Comanche bands, to say nothing of young Comanche warriors hungering for status, needed a constant supply of horses and captives to replenish those lost in battle and to pay their Pueblo, French, and Wichita trade partners. Therefore Apaches found themselves in the bull's-eye and their expansion came to a halt. By the 1740s Comanche, Wichita, and Caddo raiding parties were driving deep into Central Texas, making heavy attacks on Apache camps. With their trade connections to the Pueblos usurped, the Apaches found themselves with no sure source of horses and manufactured goods, a disastrous situation as they constantly needed to replace the weapons, goods, and mounts they lost in Norteño raids. Just as bad, the Apaches found themselves politically isolated. Indian nations that had long suffered under Apaches attacks, now bolstered by the Comanches and the French, took the opportunity to make raids of their own. Adding to Apache misery was that the Spanish also waged war against them. Surrounded by enemies and on the defensive, the overall Apache picture looked bleak. To escape the Comanches and Wichitas, they moved deeper and deeper into South Texas and northern Mexico, areas beginning to fill with Spanish settlements. By 1732 Lipan Apaches were roaming Central Texas, north of San Antonio, along the San Saba, Llano, and Pedernales Rivers. By 1750 the same Lipans lived farther south between the Medina and Nueces Rivers. The Natagés roamed along the Rio Grande and Pecos, while the Mescaleros moved to the mountains of southern New Mexico.[30]

The Apaches found themselves with only a few options and none of them very good. They could open trade with the French, but this proved difficult as the French were already allied with their enemies who would not condone French traders visiting the Apaches. In addition the Apaches lived far from French Louisiana and many Indian nations stood between them and the colony. To get around these difficulties, the Apaches sent out peace feelers to Indian peoples of East Texas who had a French connection. In 1750 a large band of Lipan and Natagé Apaches visited the presidio at La Bahía where they made peace with the Coco Karankawas, Akokisas, Mayeyes, and Bidais. The peace seems to have held, as in a few years the Bidais, Tonkawas, and even some Hasinai villages began supplying the Apaches with French goods. But this network grew slowly, remained rather tenuous, and never provided anywhere near the quantity of merchandise the Apaches needed.[31]

A second possibility for the Apaches was to make peace with the Spanish and ask them for protection and goods, maybe even have a mission built for them. Here the Apaches faced the same problems the Comanches had in New Mexico—Spain just could not provide the quantity of goods the Apaches needed. And Spain's prohibition against providing Indians with firearms left the Apaches at a severe disadvantage when faced with Comanches and Wichitas armed with French muskets. They also realized that the Spanish military in Texas was too small and too inept to protect them. They had often given Spanish troops a run for their money and the Comanches did the same. While the Apaches were open to the idea of a Spanish mission and, in fact, had requested a mission as early as 1748, they certainly had a different idea of what a mission should do than did the Spanish. Spanish authorities envisioned a place where all the Apaches could be permanently settled to become Christianized farmers and herders and thus cease raiding ranches and villages. Unfortunately for the Spanish, there was no way the Apaches were going to settle down permanently at a mission. The Jicarillas, Cuartelejos, and even some Lipan had tried settling down, even planting crops of corn at their camps, but they soon found that being tied to their gardens made them an easy target for their enemies. Instead, the Apaches saw the mission as more of a way station, a place where they might receive goods and food and stay when conditions on the plains were bad, and maybe a place to use as protection from prowling Comanches or as a refuge in case they were ambushed. The mission would serve as a barrier between them and the Norteños.[32]

With all these difficulties and desperate to replenish their supplies of goods and horses, the Apaches were forced to turn to their last option—raiding Spanish outposts while simultaneously trying to forge a Spanish alliance. Spanish documents from this time are filled with words like "treacherous" and "perfidious" in relation to the Apaches. Spaniards were disgusted that Apaches could ask for peace or visit San Antonio to trade

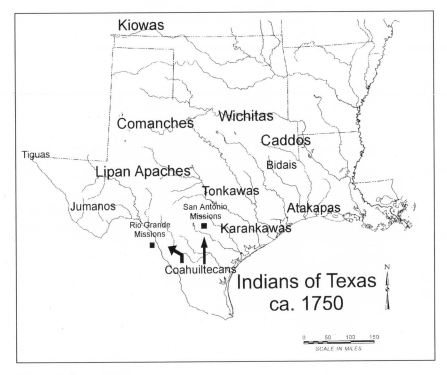

Map 2. Indians of Texas, ca. 1750.

and then turn around and raid a nearby ranch or mission. Just as bad, it seemed that the Apaches made most of their attacks when the Comanches were making their own raids on the Spanish.[33]

Certainly the Spanish did nothing to prevent Comanche attacks on the Apaches and in fact encouraged warfare between Indian nations as a means of breaking their power. If Spain were going to follow a policy of sponsoring intertribal warfare, then she had no right to cry foul when the Indians raided her outposts. So Apache attacks on Spanish outposts were not so much treachery as an attempt to protect themselves from the Norteños. Peace with Spain provided no relief nor did it provide the quantities of merchandise the Apaches needed. The Apaches eventually realized that it was better to have the Spanish angry at them than to leave themselves defenseless in the face of the Comanches. Therefore throughout the first half of the eighteenth century Apaches raided not only Indian villages and camps but also Spanish missions, settlements, and ranches in the provinces of Texas, New Mexico, Sonora, Chihuahua, Coahuila, Nueva Leon, and Nueva Vizcaya.[34]

These raids are what wreaked so much havoc among the Indian peoples in Central Texas. As Apache raids on Tonkawa, Yojuane, Yrvipiame, Karankawa, and Coahuiltecan villages increased, the people scrambled to protect themselves, creating Ranchería Grande and the Tonkawa nation as well. Many Indians, their villages shattered by Apache attacks, called on the Spanish for protection. The Tonkawas seemed especially hard hit and the short-lived San Gabriel missions built in the late 1740s and early 1750s for them, and for the Akokisas, Bidais, Deadoses, and Karankawas, were an attempt to protect them from the Apaches. The same went for the other Spanish missions built about this time on the San Antonio and lower Trinity Rivers. Spanish outposts in Texas suffered as well, and by the 1730s the San Antonio missions found themselves targeted by Apache raiders. Prior to the 1730s most raids had been quick hit-and-run affairs in which a mission horse herd would be driven off. Few people were killed and maybe only a captive or two taken. However, as the Norteño-Apache war grew hotter and the Apaches found themselves virtually cut off from supplies of manufactured goods, the raids became more lethal. Lone Indians and Spaniards, such as herd guards, were killed for their guns, clothes, and any other goods they might possess. The increased raiding and the blood spilled terrified and angered both the Indians and Spaniards of Central Texas.[35]

The Apache raids galvanized Spain on the idea of a mission to pacify the Apaches. Spanish Indian policy had been to encourage peace, but to punish raids and killings. Red tape, the need for approval from a slow-moving chain of command, and the Spanish government's hesitancy to wage war on the Indians made punitive expeditions difficult to mount. Authorities at San Antonio did manage to make peace with some Apache bands, and the number of raids often rose and fell in relation to supplies of goods and the intensity of Indian wars. Raids around San Antonio slackened after 1726, started up again after 1731, and then waxed and waned over the next few decades. Encouraged by times of peace and by Apache requests for a mission, authorities finally created Mission Santa Cruz de San Sabá and Presidio San Luis de las Amarillas in 1757 on the San Sabá River in present-day Menard County. They chose the site because it was well watered, and they may have imagined that the Apaches would flock to it. In reality, the mission was in a bad location. It was too far north, putting the Apaches directly in the line of Comanche attacks. So no Apaches greeted the missionaries when they arrived and few, if any, stayed at the mission once it became operational. In fact, the mission soon became a target of raiders, not only of Comanches and Wichitas but also of Hasinais, Tonkawas, Yojuanes, and Bidais.[36]

The San Sabá mission complex was a serious diplomatic blunder by the Spanish. They unwittingly inserted themselves into the Norteño-Apache wars and, even worse, onto the losing side. If the Spanish thought that they could build a mission and presidio for Apache protection and that there would not be any repercussions, they were sadly mistaken. For decades the Tonkawas, Yojuanes, Bidais, Karankawas, and Yrvipiames had suffered Apache raids and appealed to the Spanish for protection, and now the Spanish appeared to be siding with their enemies. Similarly, when the Norteños saw the Spanish ally with their Apache enemy, San Sabá, in their minds, became a sort of declaration of war against them by the Spanish. Any friend of my enemy is my enemy too. The Spanish alliance with the Apaches managed to unite the Indian peoples of East, Central, and North Texas against them both. The Norteños and others decided to teach the Spanish a lesson in Indian diplomacy. On March 16, 1758, maybe as many as two thousand Norteño and Tonkawa warriors attacked the San Sabá mission. They managed to get inside the compound, where they sacked the buildings and killed eight people, including two priests.[37]

Spain decided to teach the Norteños their own lesson. The next year, in August, 1759, Colonel Diego Ortiz Parilla, along with 139 soldiers, 241 militiamen, 254 Apache, Tlaxcaltecan, and mission Indian auxiliaries marched out of San Antonio, hauling two cannons, and headed north toward the big Wichita village on the Red River. Along the way, his men attacked a band of Tonkawas who had been at San Sabá, killing scores and taking 149 captive. If the victory over the Tonkawas buoyed Parilla's confidence, the reality of Norteño power deflated it just as quickly. Reaching the Red River in early October, Parilla found the Wichita village enclosed within a wooden stockade complete with firing ports and surrounded by a moat. Hundreds of well-armed Norteños manned the walls, while a 70-man detachment of Indian cavalry protected its flanks. The Battle of the Wichita Fort on October 7, 1759, often overlooked in history books, was one of the most spectacular battles of the American West. While the Indians in the fort kept up a harassing fire, the cavalry constantly probed Parilla's flanks, never letting him get his cannons into position. While a few French traders were in the fort, this was a Norteño battle and their disciplined battle tactics, along with their large supply of ammunition, carried the day. During the night, Parilla and his men declared themselves satisfied that they had taught the Indians a lesson, and taking their Tonkawa captives with them, they retreated to San Antonio, abandoning the two cannons to the Wichitas.[38]

Incredibly, the Spanish remained committed to their Apache alliance, even strengthening it by sending soldiers to guard the Apaches when they made their buffalo hunts. In response, the Norteños, emboldened by their victories, stepped up their attacks on the Apaches and the Spanish in the San Sabá and San Antonio areas. For the Apaches, Central Texas became untenable and they moved south. Refusing to settle at the San Sabá missions, the Apaches again hectored the Spanish for protection, demanding another mission farther south. Again the Spanish agreed, and in 1762 they built Missions San Lorenzo de la Santa Cruz and Nuestra Señora de la Candelaria del Cañon on the Nueces River near present-day Camp Wood. These missions would last only a few years and provide scant relief for the beleaguered Apaches. So the Apaches found themselves pushed to the Rio Grande and beyond, into lands once occupied by Coahuiltecans, who had long since died, gone to the missions, been assimilated, or become Mexican peasants. Certainly there were far fewer Coahuiltecans, as well as fewer Karankawas, Jumanos, and Atakapas in the 1760s than ever before.[39]

For the Apaches, the old problem of securing a sure access to manufactured goods remained. And the dictates of blood revenge demanded they strike back against their Comanche and Wichita enemies. This brought Comanche and Wichita raiders down on them and their Spanish allies to exact their own vengeance. The decades of the 1760s through the 1780s saw heavy warfare between the Norteños and the Apaches in Central Texas. Both sides lost horses, and captives became a major trade commodity. Apaches often showed up at Spanish outposts to exchange Comanche, Wichita, and Caddo captives for merchandise, while Wichita and Caddo traders appeared at French Natchitoches with Apache captives of their own. In fact, so many captives made their way into Louisiana that a large Apache community grew up around Natchitoches, Louisiana. Their descendants still live there, near the town of Zwolle, at the turn of the twenty-first century.[40]

With no overarching Apache leadership, band chiefs tried various strategies to solve their problems. Some bands put themselves under the protection of the Spanish and hoped to settle safely around the missions. Others professed peace and hoped to trade. While others, badly needing goods, struck at Indians and Spanish alike. Sometimes bands fell apart; at other times they grew large. Some disappeared altogether; others reappeared around more promising chiefs. It was all very confusing and frustrating for the Spanish who never seemed to grasp that Indians made peace and kinship with people not nations. If one Apache band made peace with the commandant at San Antonio, then essentially it was an agreement between two chiefs. Even then the Apache chief could not guarantee that his young men would listen to him. And it was perfectly within the Apache code to raid a mission down in Nueva Leon, where no agreement had been made. While the Apaches viewed this merely as taking what they needed from strangers, the Spanish called it "treachery."[41]

The Norteños' anger at the Spanish, which was never very deep-seated, was mainly the result of the Spanish alliance with the Apaches. After all, the Spanish were a major supplier of goods, something all the Indians needed. The smoke had barely cleared from the Wichita Fort battle when some Caddo and Wichita divisions reached out to the Spanish in East Texas. Tawakoni and Taovaya Wichitas even asked for a mission to be established in their territories. While no mission was ever founded among the Wichitas, their overtures began to reshape Spanish thinking on their Apache alliance. Even more, the Spanish acquisition of French Louisiana in 1762 portended greater changes, not only for the Indians of Texas, but for Spanish Indian policy as well.[42]

The acquisition of Louisiana by the Spanish after the French and Indian War brought tremendous confusion to the Indians of East Texas. Spain did not actually occupy the French outposts at Natchitoches and Atakapas in western Louisiana until the late 1760s. Even then she did not replace French soldiers and officials, instead keeping them in place but now as citizens of Spain sworn to uphold her policies. For the Indians, their French traders, commandants, and kinspeople virtually overnight became Spanish traders and commandants, the same as their enemies in San Antonio and points farther south. Fortunately for the Spanish, this move also brought to the fore such capable Frenchmen as Athanase de Mézières, commandant at Natchitoches, who firmly understood the nuances of Indian diplomacy. De Mézières had married the daughter of St. Denis, the French officer who had made such close alliances with the Caddos and Wichitas. As heir to St. Denis and with his own ability to work within Indian society, De Mézières had prospered in the hide trade.

Now, as a Spanish official, De Mézières advocated a pro-Norteño policy, which was not surprising considering his strong ties to the Caddos and Wichitas. The Norteños, he pointed out, were much the stronger Indians and had the greatest potential for destruction of Spanish missions and settlements. If peace could be made with them, the Norteños could provide a formidable barrier against possible English expansion into Texas. Conversely, De Mézières pointed out, the Apaches could not be trusted to honor any peace. Other officers recommended a similar diplomatic change and the Spanish government finally agreed, cutting its alliance with the Apaches. The new Spanish Indian policy for the remainder of the eighteenth century was to make peace with the Norteños, wage war on the Apaches, and encourage the Comanches, Wichitas, and others to make war on them as well. With the French out the way and thinking the Indians had no other alternative, the Spanish imagined they could accomplish this new policy by providing the Norteños with just enough guns to make their hunts and raids successful, while still severely limiting the quantity of goods they received in order to make them dependent on the Spanish.[43]

Peace and War in East Texas

The Caddos of northeast Texas quickly recognized the potential of Spain's new pro-Norteño, anti-Apache diplomacy. Tinhiouen the Elder, great chief of the Cadodacho Caddos, and Cocay of the Yatasí Caddos on the lower Red River, offered to broker a peace between the Wichitas, Comanches, and Spanish. The Cadodachos wielded considerable political leverage on the Southern Plains, not only with the Spanish in Louisiana but also with the Hasinai Caddos and Wichitas in East Texas who "look up to [the Cado-dachos] as their fathers, visit and intermarry among them, and join them in all their wars."[44] In September, 1770, Tinhiouen arranged a meeting at his village between Spanish officials and chiefs from the Taovayas, Tawako-nis, Yscanis, Kichais, Tonkawas, and Eastern Comanches. He and Cocay urged peace, and their diplomatic efforts paid off the next year when a treaty was signed. While it did not mean that all bands quit raiding, this treaty was the first between the Wichitas, Comanches, and Spanish and from the Indian point of view, tied them more securely to Spanish goods out of Louisiana and Texas. Fifteen years later, in 1785, with the Co-manches interested in securing even more trade goods, a more substantial treaty would be signed between the Comanches and the Spanish. For the most part, this peace between the Comanches and the Spanish in Texas would hold until the turn of the nineteenth century.[45]

The main reason the Caddos and Wichitas were so anxious to make peace with the Spanish was because of the raids the Osages were then making on their villages. Similar to the Caddos and Wichitas in econom-ics, the Osages lived in settled villages in western Arkansas and Missouri and eastern Oklahoma and Kansas. There they planted crops in the spring and hunted buffalo on the prairies during the summer and fall. Like the Caddos, the Osages also acquired horses about the same time and made exchange relationships with the French traders on the Arkansas River. The Osages and Caddos now became trade rivals, competing for the horses and hides, and linked to different trading outposts: the Caddos to Natchi-toches, the Osages to the Arkansas Post and Saint Louis.[46]

The Osages needed horses, hides, and captives to acquire their own manufactured goods, so by the early years of the eighteenth century they began raiding the Caddos and Wichitas. These raids proved quite successful. By 1720 terrified Caddos and Wichitas hesitated to venture too far out onto the plains for fear of meeting up with an Osage war party. Any sign of the Osages was enough to send hunting parties scurrying for cover. Caddos and Wichitas fought back as best they could, but the Osages seemed to have the upper hand. It was Osage raids that eventually drove the Wichitas out of the Arkansas River Valley and into Texas. They also forced the Caddos at the great bend of the Red River to move their own villages farther south. In the early 1750s the Wichitas appealed to the Comanches for assistance, and together they attacked an Osage village in which they killed numerous chiefs and warriors. Rather than stopping Osage attacks, it escalated hostilities.[47]

By the 1770s Northeast Texas had become, as one Spanish official described it, a "pitiful theater of outrageous robberies and bloody encounters" between the Osages and the Norteños.[48] The Wichitas, now pushed farther and farther into Texas, had to raid Spanish villages and outposts to replenish the horses and goods lost in Osage raids. The Norteños struck back as best they could. In 1770 a large force of Taovayas, Tawakonis, Skidi Pawnees, Comanches, Tonkawas, Mayeyes, and "apostate" Xaranames from the La Bahía mission attacked the Osages, but with little effect. When the Spanish changed their pro-Apache alliance and offered a treaty in 1770, the Wichitas and Caddos jumped at the chance so they could be assured of receiving guns and merchandise from Spanish Louisiana. The Norteños also demanded that the Spanish live up to their promise of punishing the Osages for their attacks. However, the Spanish feared that if they honored their treaty with the Norteños and attacked the Osages, it would push the Osages into an alliance with Britain, who sat just across the Mississippi River and whose traders secretly visited Osage villages. So the Spanish did nothing while Osage raids continued and the Norteños could only seethe in frustration about broken Spanish promises.[49]

By the mid-1780s Osage raids had been so successful that they found themselves as masters of a territory stretching from the Missouri River to the Red, from the Mississippi in the east to the margins of the Southern Plains. By the late 1780s the Osages were poised to actually break out onto the plains, where they could secure unhampered access to the buffalo and horse herds and so usurp the increasingly Comanche-dominated trade networks. But in late 1789 a force of seven hundred Comanche and Wichita warriors defeated a major Osage attack and blocked Osage westward expansion. To solidify their control of the Southern Plains, beginning in 1790, the Comanches initiated an ever-strengthening alliance with the Kiowas and Kiowa-Apaches, who were then migrating south from Yellowstone country. Unable to break out onto the Southern Plains, the Osages stepped

up their raiding of Caddo villages in Texas and Louisiana. This war between the Caddos and Osages would continue into the nineteenth century,
but by then both would be facing new pressures arriving from the east.[50]

With the Osage attacks, the Apache wars, and the constant need for
goods, the Comanches recognized the benefits of making peace with Spanish New Mexico. For a brief time this situation brought about an astonishing
change in Comanche politics in which one man rose to become chief of all
Comanches. The Comanches, as with most hunter-gatherers, had never
been a unified nation, but a collection of autonomous bands each led by its
own chief. Spanish officials in New Mexico found this confusing, as one
band might come to Pecos pueblo to trade, while another might come to raid
it. With Spain's shift to an anti-Apache policy, New Mexico held out an olive
branch to the Comanches, promising unlimited trade but urging them to se-
lect a single man who could speak for the entire Comanche people. Kotsoteka Comanche chief Ecueracapa, sometimes known both as Cota de
Mallo (Mail Coat) and Camisa de Fierro (Iron Shirt), seized the moment.
Known and respected in both Texas and New Mexico, Ecueracapa, through
his own power and force of personality, rose to become spokesman for virtually all Comanches. In 1786 Ecueracapa forged a peace with New Mexico
governor Juan Bautista de Anza and displayed his newly acquired power by
executing a band chief who refused to abide by the agreement. The single
leader position went against the autonomy stressed by Comanche society
and would die with Ecueracapa in 1793.[51]

As Apache raiding shifted farther south, Karankawas, Atakapas, and
Coahuiltecans peoples often sought refuge in the missions at San Antonio,
La Bahía, Rosario, and Orcoquisac. This was not always a satisfactory
strategy as lack of food and strict rules by Spanish officials often made the
Indians abandon their missions, as the Xaranames did in the 1760s and
the Karankawas in the 1770s. Having left the missions, the Xaranames,
Tonkawas, Karankawas, and Bidais targeted San Antonio and La Bahía, as
did the Tawakonis, Taovayas, and Comanches. Apache raids around San
Antonio and points farther south, which had been going on for years, continued almost unabated. Nevertheless, the Apaches, fearful of the treaties
signed between the Spanish and the Norteños, hoped to arrange one of
their own. In an effort to end their political isolation, they again reached
out to the Bidais, the Tonkawas, even their old Hasinai Caddo enemies.
The Apaches encouraged the Bidais to arrange a peace between them and
the Spanish. At the same time, El Mocho, an Apache who had been captured and adopted by the Tonkawas, had risen to become their chief. No
friend of Spain, El Mocho advocated a Tonkawa alliance with the Apaches,
and soon firearms and merchandise trickled through the Tonkawas to the

Apaches. Distrusting the Apaches, fearing the wrath of their new Norteño allies should they make peace, and worrying that this Apache-Tonkawa friendship might presage an Apache-Norteño alliance, the Spanish rejected the Apache peace overtures and arranged for El Mocho to be assassinated by a rival in 1784. They replaced El Mocho with a more anti-Apache chief while continuing to encourage the Comanches and Wichitas in their wars against the Apaches.[52]

Spain at the end of the eighteenth century was long past her prime. While she may have been more secure in New Mexico, in Texas, Spain was just as weak as ever. Stagnation had set in and this, along with lack of money and problems resulting from involvement in the Napoleonic Wars, forced a Spanish retrenchment in Texas. Some missions and presidios were closed or moved to other areas, while fewer and fewer troops manned the Texas outposts. The end of the century saw the Spanish with a weak presence in East Texas at Nacogdoches, a few missions and presidios along the Gulf Coast at Orcoquisac and La Bahía, the larger mission complex at San Antonio, and a string of missions and presidios along the Rio Grande. These were seemingly under constant attack from the Apaches, Comanches, Wichitas, Bidais, and Tonkawas. Spain's pro-Norteño policy provided no end to hostilities. Even limiting the number of guns provided to the Indians was undercut by French Creole traders, who, upholding their long-standing kinship obligations to the Indians in Texas, continued providing them with guns and merchandise. Adding to this were English and American traders who made their way into Texas despite Spain's attempt to keep them out.[53]

The real power in Texas at the end of the eighteenth century was the Comanches. The comanchería extended from Central Texas to the Arkansas River, from the Pueblo villages in New Mexico to the Cross Timbers of East Texas. The Comanches had driven the Apaches south to the Rio Grande and beyond and were the senior partners in a cross-plains trade network, with one leg anchored in Spanish Louisiana and the other in New Mexico. Even the Spanish had a healthy respect, even fear, of the Comanches. They signed a treaty with the Eastern Comanches in Texas in 1785 and with the Western Comanches in New Mexico in 1786. This marked a time of greater cooperation between the two cultures, even to the point of joint campaigns against the Apaches. Nevertheless, Spanish missions, outposts, soldiers, and settlers, even normally friendly Wichita and Pawnee villages, remained potential targets of Comanche raiders, particularly young men in search of status. More importantly, the Comanches were an expanding nation with a growing population in Texas despite the epidemics that periodically swept across the Southern Plains, decimating the more sedentary Wichitas and Caddos.[54]

The once powerful Apaches found themselves hounded into the far-thest reaches of South Texas and the mountains of New Mexico, Arizona, and northern Mexico. The Lipans, most closely associated with Texas, roamed along the Rio Grande, their southernmost bands alternately attacking and trading with the Karankawas and Coahuiltecans, while those on the upper Rio Grande tended to be involved in battling the Comanches. The Natagés, Mescaleros, and Jicarillas lived in the mountains between the Rio Grande and the Pecos River and often fought the Comanches to their east. West of these four Apache bands and into northern Mexico lived the Mimbreños, Gileños, Chiricahuas, and Coyoteros Apaches; north of them were the Navajos. The Apaches were the enemy of all nations, and the Comanches, Wichitas, Caddos, Tonkawas, and Spanish made war on them, particularly the Lipans. The Lipans counterattacked, making their own raids on Comanche and Tonkawa camps when they could. Some Apache bands tried to make peace with the Spanish and asked for protection, while others, always in need of horses and manufactured goods, raided Spanish outposts and missions. For the Apaches, it was a life of war, raid and counterraid.[55]

The Wichitas also continued as a power in Texas, but junior to their Comanche allies. The Osages had hammered them down into Texas and southern Oklahoma, and most of the villages of the five Wichita divisions lay scattered along the Red, Brazos, and Trinity Rivers, squeezed between the Comanches to the west, Caddos to the east, and Tonkawas to the south. Actually, the turn of the nineteenth century found the Wichitas rather prosperous. Most Wichita villages lay beyond the reach of Apache raiders, while Osage raids also slackened about this time. Peaceful relations with the Spanish gave the Wichitas one less thing to worry about. In fact, their only real worries were the onset of an epidemic or a stray band of Comanches, Tonkawas, or Osages ready to take off with the village horse herd. Their villages produced large quantities of corn, beans, squash, melons, and tobacco, supplemented by buffalo meat. The Taovaya village on Red River served as a gateway community, attracting numerous Indian, European, and American traders.[56]

The Caddos of the Red, Sabine, Angelina, and Neches Rivers of East Texas suffered mightily over the decades. What had once been numerous city-states comprising the great chiefdoms of the Kadohadacho at the great bend of the Red River and the Hasinai chiefdom in East Texas had dwindled under disease and Osage attacks to four main divisions. These were the Cadodachos, or Caddos proper, the only surviving city-state of the old Kadohadacho chiefdom; the Nadacos, now sometimes called the Anadarko; the Hainai, sometimes called either Tejas or Ioni; and the

Nabedaches, these last three all that remained of the old Hasinai chiefdom. Nevertheless, because of their proximity to commercial centers of Spanish Louisiana and their kinship with French Creole traders, the Caddos, particularly the "great chief" of the Cadodachos, exerted considerable political influence in the eastern half of Texas.[57]

The Tonkawas were still in the process of nation building. Tonkawas proper, Yojuanes, Yvripiames, some Mayeye and Bidai bands, even a few Coco Karankawa families had intermingled at Ranchería Grande and then at the short-lived missions on the San Gabriel River. A great epidemic that swept through the Tonkawas in 1777–78 further blurred the distinctions between these groups. Just how much of a composite people the Tonkawas were can be seen in the rise of El Mocho, the Lipan Apache who became the principal chief of the Tonkawas in the early 1780s. After his assassination in 1784 by a pro-Spanish rival, the Tonkawas abandoned their Apache alliance and tried to ally with the Wichitas to the north. By the end of the nineteenth century the Tonkawas, who also suffered periodic Osage attacks, were again at war with the Apaches. As one Spanish soldier reported, Tonkawa country was "perilous due to the frequent raids and invasions of the Apaches, and they are always on the alert against ambushes by them and by their other enemies."[58]

Similar events were taking place for the Karankawas on the Texas coast, which resulted in a more cohesive and identifiable Karankawa nation. Karankawa bands had always been quite autonomous, but in the 1770s an "apostate" Karankawa leader, José María, rose to become principal chief of the Karankawas as a whole. As spokesman for the Karankawas, José María established a tradition of powerful chiefs who led through their own personal status and generosity toward their people. The Karankawas had hot and cold relations with the Spanish during the second half of the eighteenth century. They usually looked to the Spanish for protection against the Apaches and Comanches, and sometimes settled in missions. But they were quick to abandon the missions and raid them for resources. Always in need of manufactured goods, the Karankawas increasingly took to plundering Spanish ships and sailors wrecked on the upper Texas coast. In 1771 José María and his Karankawas managed to capture a Spanish ship in the eastern part of San Antonio Bay, killing the sailors and soldiers and making off with six swivel guns, two barrels of gunpowder, three crates of shot, eleven guns, and all the food and goods. Spain considered attacking the Karankawas or resettling them in some distant country, but nothing came of this plan. Periodic raids by Comanches in the 1780s forced the Karankawas to sue for peace and ask for protection from the Spanish. Even then they tended to leave the mission when it suited them.[59]

By the turn of the century Coahuiltecans, who had once lived in hundreds of bands in South Texas, seemed on the verge of disappearance. Similarly, the name "Jumano" had long vanished from the historical record. Disease, drought, famine, and warfare had killed many of these people. A great many were pulled into the missions of northern Mexico and South Texas to die or become Mexican peasants; others were absorbed into Apache bands during their drive south. The Coahuiltecan Yvripiames joined the Tonkawas, while the Xaranames had moved eastward to live around Mission La Bahía. In Southeast Texas, the Atakapas also declined. The Bidais moved toward the Caddos; the Mayeyes, and Deadoses gravitated toward the Tonkawas; the few families who composed the Atakapas proper either lived scattered in the woods or moved back into Southwest Louisiana, where the majority of their people lived. The mission Indians were a dwindling lot. Disease, raids, and natural attrition took their toll. Most became hispanized farmers and herders, but when they died, there were fewer and fewer Indians able or willing to take their place.[60]

The century-long Apache wars were the most significant feature of Texas during the 1700s. As the Comanches and Wichitas migrated south, they allied and together battled the Apaches for control of the Southern Plains trade networks. This meant they needed to increase their own raiding in order to replenish supplies of horses, captives, and manufactured goods. The turmoil created by these wars had a dramatic impact on the peoples of Texas. They decimated the Coahuiltecans and Jumanos and destroyed Spanish missions and settlements. They created the Tonkawa nation, made the Karankawas more dependent on a principal chief, bolstered the political power of the "great chief" of the Caddos, brought wealth to the Wichita villages, and made the Comanches the primary power on the Southern Plains. As the nineteenth century dawned, the Indians of Texas would face new challenges as invaders from the east began settling on their lands.

Chapter 7

Immigrants from the East

Texas never sat in isolation. Events in the eastern half of the continent could produce dire consequences for Indians in the West. As England colonized the eastern seaboard, France the Mississippi Valley and Canada, and Spain the Southwest and Florida, a rivalry developed among the three empires. Colonial wars broke out and Indians found themselves drawn into the conflicts as allies, auxiliaries, and enemies. The deer and beaver hide trade remained the main economic activity connecting the eastern Indians and Europeans. As manufactured goods changed the daily lives of Indians, it also sent them fanning out into the forests, where they overhunted the animals and then invaded their neighbors' territories to find more. The expanding English plantation system made the need for fresh lands, Indian lands, essential. The constant demand for labor on these plantations sent slave raiders smashing into Indian villages throughout the Southeast.

All this disrupted the lives of the eastern Indians and sent many streaming west to escape. By the end of the eighteenth century the Caddos, then the Wichitas, and finally the Comanches and other Texas Indians found their lands being invaded by Indians from the east. First came the Choctaws and Chickasaws, then the Cherokees and Creeks, and on their heels came the Delawares, Shawnees, and Kickapoos. Along with these Indian immigrants came the Anglo-Americans who would call themselves

"Texans." These invasions initiated a complex set of relations between Texas Indians and the newcomers, ranging from warfare to peace, trade to intermarriage.

As early as the 1680s Caddo villages near present-day Texarkana suffered raids by Chickasaw warriors out of western Tennessee and Mississippi. In South Carolina, English traders paid high prices for Indian slaves they could ship off to Britain's sugar islands in the Caribbean. Supply rose to meet demand, and the Chickasaws, firm allies of the English, struck into Texas to hunt down captives and march them back to Charleston. Though the Indian slave trade in the east died out during the 1730s as Africans became the slaves of choice, competition for deer hides meant Chickasaw and Choctaw hunters continued to prowl through Northeast Texas. During most of the eighteenth century these raids remained minor in comparison to the hammer blows stuck by the Osages, but all this changed after the end of the French and Indian War in 1763 when Spain tried to build an Indian buffer against English and American encroachment. Realizing just how fast the Anglo-Americans could spread across the land, the Spanish, determined to hang onto their southwest colonies, now initiated a policy of welcoming, even inviting, eastern Indians to settle in Louisiana and Texas. The most significant of these were the Choctaws of Alabama and Mississippi.[1]

Choctaws and Chickasaws

Both these nations spoke Muskhogean, the dominant Indian language of the American Southeast. They also represented two of the four largest and most important Indian nations of the Southeast, the other two being the Cherokees and the Creeks. The Choctaws and Chickasaws were a united people at one time, but their oral tradition tells of their migrating from the Southwest into Mississippi where they split, the Chickasaws going one way and the Choctaws the other. The Choctaws remained the much larger nation, with more than twenty thousand people by 1800 and growing rapidly. They spread over a wide swath of Central Mississippi and Alabama. The Chickasaws, numbering about five thousand, but growing too, lived around where Memphis, Tennessee, is today.[2]

Culturally and economically, the two groups were much like the Caddos. Farming Indians, they lived in large, highly organized towns surrounded by huge cornfields controlled by the women. Children were born into their mothers' clans and all clan members were seen as kin. Both the Choctaws and Chickasaws had been major participants in the Mississippian cultural tradition of the thirteenth and fourteenth centuries, and some of the paramount ceremonial centers in the Southeast—Nanih Wayah in Mississippi and Moundville in Alabama—were in Choctaw territory. Both had histories of theocratic governments, powerful priest-chiefs, ranked societies, and mound building. But as with the Caddos, by the eighteenth century much of this had tapered off as the Choctaws and Chickasaws had to deal with the affects of European colonization. Developing their own thirst for manufactured goods, they made alliances with the European powers and became heavily involved in both the Indian slave trade and the deer hide trade. This not only changed their societies but also brought them into conflict with each other and other Indian peoples.[3]

Though the Choctaws and Chickasaws may have been related, they were often at odds diplomatically. Early on, the Chickasaws allied with the British and remained firm in their loyalty. That the Chickasaws emerged victorious in several wars with the French enhanced their military power. The Choctaws, though they might have factions pulling one way or another, generally remained friendly toward the French but were not averse to dealing with the English or Spanish when it suited them. With the ouster of the French after the French and Indian War, British traders began showing up in Choctaw and Chickasaw villages in greater numbers. Bringing goods and alcohol to trade for deer hides, the traders sometimes married Indian women, and the children from these unions were citizens of their respective nations through their mothers but connected to the Anglo-American world through their fathers. Fearing the close ties developing between the Choctaws and the British, Spain began inviting Choctaw and Chickasaw villages to resettle in Spanish Louisiana, particularly on lands claimed by the Caddos.[4]

The Caddos took a dim view of these Choctaw families invading their territory, hunting their deer, and trying to appropriate their trade connections with the Spanish. Hunting parties clashed in the woods, and warriors plundered each other's villages for hides, horses, cattle, and crops. Counterraids, revenge killings, and warfare spiraled out of control in Northwest Louisiana and Northeast Texas. The tiny Adaes and Ais Caddo bands appealed to Spanish Texas for protection without success. The Bidais lost a chief during a Choctaw raid. Even the Hainais, Nadacos, and Wichitas complained. Osages also felt the sting of Choctaw raids and increased their attacks on the Caddos and Wichitas to replace lost goods. Eventually, the Texas Caddos, Bidais, and even some of the Wichita Kichais turned for protection to Dehahuit, the great chief of the Caddos. The great chief prevailed upon the Spanish in New Orleans to broker a peace, and in 1797 the Caddos and Choctaws in Louisiana and Texas agreed to end the raiding, which more or less held up for the next few years. One group of Choctaws, known as the Yowanis, eventually tied itself to the Caddos by intermarriage and soon became known as the Yowani band of Caddos. In the mid-1790s bands of Choctaws, Chickasaws, and other Indians petitioned the Spanish government to settle in Texas. Over Caddo protests, Spain agreed, and by the early years of the nineteenth century several Choctaw villages, including the Yowanis, had sprung up along the Sabine and Neches Rivers; a Chickasaw village sat at the confluence of the Neches and Angelina. The Choctaws and Chickasaws were only the vanguard of this eastern Indian invasion of Texas, others, such as the Cherokees and the Creeks, soon followed.[5]

Cherokees

The traditional lands of the Cherokees lay in the mountains and piedmont of western North Carolina, eastern Tennessee, northern Georgia, the northeastern tip of Alabama, and the westernmost bit of South Carolina. They spoke Cherokee, an Iroquoian dialect, and were distantly related to the Iroquois peoples of New York and Canada. Like their Muskhogean-speaking neighbors, the Choctaws, Chickasaw, and Creeks, the Cherokees were matrilineal farmers with a rigid clan system and a religion that emphasized agriculture. They honored the mythical hero woman Selu, who gave her life so the Cherokees could have corn. Good-size towns and villages dotted their country, and as they lay astride important East Coast trade routes, the Cherokees also became very prosperous. By 1800 the Cherokee population had been diminished by the colonial wars of the eighteenth century to around ten thousand, but was rapidly rebounding. And like their neighbors, cultural fault lines were beginning to divide Cherokee society.[6]

The Cherokees in their southern Appalachian towns were the first major Indian nation British traders and settlers out of Virginia, the Carolinas, and Georgia encountered as they moved west. Their interactions with the British brought not only wealth and influence but also change to Cherokee society. The English government set up forts in Cherokee territory and gradually swayed Cherokee politics. British traders brought manufactured goods to villages, married Cherokee women and produced children. Able to live in both worlds, many Cherokee British offspring went to English schools and returned home to urge the Cherokees to adopt the trappings of English culture. As missionaries set up shop, they begged the Cherokees to give up their "heathen" ways and accept Christianity and an American style of "civilization." Pressures increased during the first decades of the nineteenth century as the U.S. government appropriated money for "civilizing" the Indians of the Southeast. Essentially, the United States hoped to turn the Southeastern Indians into American-style small farmers, who spoke English, attended Christian churches, and would be willing to give up their surplus land to American settlers. Soon, as with their Creek, Choctaw, Chickasaw, and Seminole neighbors, Cherokee society found itself split between progressives who advocated the adoption of American culture and traditionalists who wanted to preserve old Cherokee values.[7]

By the early nineteenth century Cherokee traditionalists faced a difficult choice. They could remain in the Southeast but see the ancient ways corrupted and their influence diminished as English-speaking progressives grabbed the reins of political power. Or they could move west, away from the grasping American government where they could practice the old ways as they wanted. By 1807 two large Cherokee villages had been established in Missouri while several Cherokee, Choctaw, Chickasaw, Creek, Appalachee, Biloxi, and Pascagoula communities lay scattered along the lower Red River in Louisiana. In that same year, bands of Cherokees, Chickasaws, and Shawnees approached the Spanish commandant at Nacogdoches about settling in Texas. The Spanish government approved their request. In 1810 traditionalist Cherokee chiefs Duwali, Saulowee, and Talontuskee moved their towns to northern Arkansas. Within a decade, several thousand Cherokees, maybe a third of their entire nation lived in Arkansas and Missouri and came to be known as the "Cherokee Nation West." However, this was Osage land, and a bitter war broke out between the two peoples, providing some respite to the Caddos and Wichitas in Texas.[8]

The Osage war divided the leadership of the Cherokee Nation West. Some wanted a negotiated peace and an end to the revenge killings that escalated the bloodshed. Traditionalist chief Duwali, sometimes known as Chief Bowl or Bowles, insisted on blood revenge, but his sentiments ran against the tide then rising in the Cherokee Nation West. The concept of a "loyal opposition" was unknown among most Indian nations. Consensus was a characteristic of Indian politics, and people or factions who disagreed with the prevailing view were expected to withdraw rather than publicly oppose it. Since Duwali could not accept the prohibition of blood revenge, in 1819 he and his followers moved southwest to the Great Bend of the Red River, lands once occupied by the Caddos. Pressed by American settlers moving into the same area, by 1822 Duwali and his Cherokees were in Texas, living northwest of Nacogdoches.[9]

Welcomed by the newly established Mexican government, Duwali's Cherokees re-created their towns and society, began growing large crops of corn, and sporadically battled Caddos and Wichitas over land, resources, and access to the trade networks. A Mexican official in 1828 numbered their Texas population at about six hundred and described them as wrapping their heads "in a sort of turban. A short frock coat, ornamented with fringe, covers the body. Red stockings, with a kind of short, tight-fitting trousers, and slippers of deerskin complete their costume. Almost all of them also wear a red sash, from which they hang a small axe. They are tall in stature and relatively light-skinned." On the heels of the Cherokees followed the Creeks, Delawares, Shawnees, Kickapoos, and other immigrant Indians.[10]

Alabama-Coushattas (Creeks)

The Alabama-Coushattas, more properly known as the Alibamu and Koasati, originally lived in east-central Alabama and were two of many powerful Muskhogean-speaking city-states. The Muskogees, Alabamas, Coushattas, Hitchitis, Yuchis, and other peoples came to be collectively known as "Creeks," or "Muscogees." They occupied a vast country, stretching from eastern Mississippi to central Georgia, and encompassed some of the most fertile land in the United States. The Creeks were some of the most urban Indian peoples of the United States, and large cities, as well as small towns and villages, all supported by enormous cornfields, became their signature. During the Mississippian cultural tradition, great theocratic chiefdoms arose, sometimes expanding to conquer neighboring city-states. Some of the greatest temple mounds of the Southeast, such as Etowah and Okmulgee in Georgia, could be found in Creek territory, while Moundville, near Tuscaloosa, Alabama, was on their western edge. When Hernando de Soto and his conquistadors cut their way through the Southeast in 1540, powerful Creek armies opposed them. The Spanish beat back the Creeks, but not without suffering high casualties of their own, and they limped out of Creek territory on their way toward the Mississippi River and the Caddos. The destruction of Creek towns, along with the diseases the Spanish left in their wake, toppled many of the Creek Mississippian chiefdoms. The great cities split up, their residents dispersing up and down the rivers and streams to create much smaller villages and hamlets. The smaller towns regained their autonomy but remained bound together both politically and culturally in what the seventeenth-century English termed the "Creek Confederacy."[11]

Culturally, the Creeks were similar to the other agricultural Indians of the Southeast. They were matrilineal, with people tracing their descent through their mother and her clan. The Creeks counted up to nine clans:

Wind, Bear, Panther, Bird, Polecat, Fox, Potato, Red Paint, and Isfanna, this last a collection of many tiny clans. Like other farming Indians of the Southeast, the Creeks worshiped agricultural deities and celebrated the Green Corn Ceremony every summer, in which all the fires in the confederacy were extinguished and new fires lit from the one sacred fire.[12]

Several things differentiated the Creeks from their Cherokee, Choctaw, and Chickasaw neighbors. First, the Creeks were quite urban and town government was the norm. A town council headed by a *mikko,* who served as the town's spokesman, governed each town. Members of each Creek clan could be found in every town. Second, Creek society also divided itself into two parts: a white division and a red division. The white division was seen as the "peace" division and the red was the "war." During times of peace, mikkos from the white division led, while members of the red division took over during hostilities. In every town, the various clans separated themselves into either the red or white division. Towns also considered themselves red towns or white towns. In white towns, white mikkos led; in red towns, red mikkos did. Dividing the society even more was that the Upper Creek towns in Central Alabama between the Coosa and Tallapoosa Rivers tended to be red towns, whereas Lower Creek towns on the Chattahoochee River near the Alabama-Georgia border were white towns. The Alabamas and Coushattas lived nearer the Upper Creek red towns. Finally, the Creeks possessed the largest population of all Indians of the Southeast, more than twenty-six thousand by the turn of the nineteenth century.[13]

British men who visited the Lower Creek towns for the deer hide trade exacerbated these divisions in Creek society. Many Lower Creeks were impressed with the goods and institutions of British society and began adopting its trappings. British traders, many of whom spent a considerable part of the year among the Indians, took Creek wives and raised families who were both Creek and British. The children of these families, usually because they could speak English and understood English ways, became Creek leaders. Many became "progressives" and advocated even more acculturation of European ways. Conversely, the Upper Creeks, of whom the Alabamas and Coushattas were part, were farther away from the English and remained more "traditional." By the second half of the eighteenth century the Creeks found themselves divided between the "progressive" Lower Creek white towns and the "traditional" Upper Creek red towns. The Alabamas and Coushattas, upset at the progressive direction Creek society seemed to be taking and encouraged by Spanish officials to relocate, decided to move west into Spanish Louisiana. By the late 1700s bands of Alabamas and Coushattas lived along the Mississippi and lower Red Rivers.[14]

Soon the Alabamas and Coushattas were in Texas. By 1820 three main Alabama towns and three Coushatta towns, together totaling well over a thousand people, dotted the Big Thicket region of present-day Polk and Tyler Counties. It was a good place, an isolated, densely wooded country between the lower Neches and Trinity Rivers, but sitting astride several important highways, such as Long Tom's Trace and Long King's Trace. Here the Alabamas and Coushattas settled down to farming and trading. In 1828 a Mexican official described the Alabamas, as numbering about six hundred and being involved in the deer hide trade with the people of Nacogdoches. Though "liberal and industrious . . . [t]hey use firewater, and paint their faces. They are kind, and their customs and inclinations are not barbarous." The Coushattas, who numbered five hundred, "are found to be more given to the use of firewater. Some of them are seen to be gaily adorned with the plumage of birds on their heads, dressed in flowered chintz shirts, their faces painted with vermillion, and with silver pendants hanging from their noses. They have considerable trade and are great hunters without neglecting to cultivate the soil."[15]

Repopulation of East Texas

In addition to the Choctaws, Cherokees, Chickasaws, and Creeks, other eastern Indians also began arriving in East Texas during the early years of the nineteenth century. The War of 1812 displaced many Indian peoples, particularly those who had sided with the British, such as the Shawnees and "Redstick" Creeks, sending them west, many into Texas. In the 1824 Treaty of Prairie du Chien, the United States managed to persuade virtually all Indian nations living north of the Ohio River to cede their lands and move west of the Mississippi. In that same year, Congress created Indian Territory, just north of Texas and stretching from the Red River north to the Great Bend of the Missouri River, and from the western boundaries of Arkansas and Missouri as far west as the hundredth meridian. Here, the U.S. government planned to resettle Indians removed from the East. Along with the Shawnees, some bands, such as the Delawares and Kickapoos, not liking Indian Territory, moved farther south into Texas.[16]

By 1830 a large number of immigrant Indians lived in East Texas. More than 600 Shawnees, Delawares, Kickapoos, and Pottawatomies resided along the upper Sabine and Trinity Rivers in present-day Rusk, Henderson, and Anderson Counties. About 150 Quapaw families lived south of the Red River on Sulphur Creek. Six hundred Cherokees, led by chiefs Duwali, Gatunwali, and Richard Fields, farmed a large territory north of the old San Antonio Road, bounded by the Sabine and Trinity Rivers in present-day

Rusk, Cherokee, and Smith Counties. They were considered some of the most prosperous Indians, with well-tended, fenced-in fields and comfortable log cabins. A few bands of Chickasaws and Choctaws, along with the Yowanis who had intermarried with various Caddo peoples, lived just west of the Sabine River, on the lower Angelina and Neches Rivers. Farthest south were the thousand-plus Alabama and Coushatta farmers in and around the Big Thicket of Southeast Texas. Nearby lived a few score families of Biloxis and Creeks. As the United States sent more and more eastern Indians to Indian Territory, many crossed the Red River international boundary and entered Texas to visit kinspeople or Mexican officials, to hunt, trade, settle down, or just sightsee. To the indigenous Indians of East Texas, these easterners were not just immigrants but invaders, and the Caddos and Wichitas bore the brunt of their incursions as peace with one did not necessarily put an end to raids by others.[17]

Making matters worse for the Caddos, Bidais, and Wichitas was that the second decade of the nineteenth century brought turmoil to Texas. The Hidalgo Revolt of 1810 initiated years of hard, bloody warfare in Texas in which Mexican criollos and American adventurers fought Spanish royalists. Filibustering expeditions from American Louisiana periodically invaded Texas in hopes of liberating the colony from Spain and making a profit in the process. In August, 1812, José Bernardo Maximiliano Gutiérrez de Lara and American soldier Augustus Magee led a force of several hundred men into Texas, defeating the Spanish army at San Antonio in the spring of 1813. Gutiérrez appealed to the Indians of East Texas to join his rebels. Though Caddo great chief Dehahuit refused, many of his young men and some Wichitas did join. More than a hundred Alabama, Coushatta, and Choctaw warriors also joined Gutiérrez and fought alongside him at San Antonio. Whether the Indians were with Gutiérrez when Spanish troops defeated his army at the Medina River in August 1813 is not known. Though Spanish authority returned to Texas in 1813, filibustering expeditions remained common, and the revolution virtually stripped the colony of Spanish settlers and officials. With political unrest continuing in Mexico itself, for all intents and purposes Texas had been abandoned by the Spanish. This power vacuum attracted many eastern Indians to East Texas, and during these years of turmoil the majority of immigrant Indians, such as Duwali's Cherokees, made their way into Texas.[18]

The problem for the Indians of Texas was that Texas attracted not only other Indians but also Americans. As early as the 1770s Spain believed that the Anglo-Americans who sat across the Mississippi River from Spanish Louisiana were a greedy and rapacious people who would stop at nothing until they controlled the entire continent. Her fears seemed justified in

1803 when Napoleon, who had pressured Spain to return Louisiana to France, turned around and sold it at a bargain-basement price to the United States. Suddenly, with a stroke of the pen, land-hungry Americans sat just across the Sabine River and cast covetous eyes at Texas. And the Sabine was nowhere near as wide as the Mississippi.

Actions by the U.S. government in Louisiana did nothing to allay Spanish suspicions. John Sibley, the U.S. Indian agent at Natchitoches, went out of his way to upset relations between Spain and the Indians of Texas. At the same time, Sibley tried to convince the Indians to abandon the Spanish and ally with the United States. He disrupted the activities of the Natchitoches trading house of William Barr, Samuel Davenport, and Edward Murphy, which had been contracted by Spain to provide the annual gifts of merchandise to the Indians of East Texas. Sibley also encouraged American entrepreneurs, such as Philip Nolan and Anthony Glass, to slip into Texas and begin trading with the Caddos, Wichitas, and Comanches. He gave these men American flags to be distributed among the villages and had them tell the Indians to visit him at Natchitoches. To pull the Indians toward American Louisiana, Sibley established a government trading post at Natchitoches and invited Indians from across Texas to come do business. Many did and were delighted with the quantities of high-quality manufactured goods they received.[19]

If the United States wanted alliances from the Indians of Texas, Sibley and other American officials realized that the person to turn to was Dehahuit, a truly remarkable man who was the great chief of the Caddos. Dehahuit came out of the Cadodacho division, which had always produced the great chiefs, and he could probably trace his lineage back to the Mississippian priest-chiefs and the two Tinhiouens of the 1770s as well. He seemed to have an uncanny ability to play the Spanish against the Americans and vice versa while keeping trade goods flowing and his alliances to the Wichitas and Comanches strong. Both the Spanish and Americans recognized that he possessed great influence not only with his Cadodachos but also with the Nadacos, Nabedaches, Ais, and Hainais of the old Hasinai Caddo chiefdom, as well as the Bidais, Kichais, Tawakonis, and Yscanis. When the Hidalgo Revolt broke out, Spanish officials quickly approached Dehahuit. They commissioned him a colonel in the Spanish army and showered gifts of horses and merchandise on him and his Caddos until he agreed to try to protect Texas' eastern border from bandits who might want to take advantage of the confusion.[20]

The Americans also recognized Dehahuit's influence. The governor of Louisiana instructed Sibley to curry Dehahuit's favor as the "Caddo nation manifested a decided influence over the various tribes of Indians with whom our frontiers can have connection."[21] Sibley needed no urging and presented the great chief with gifts, but not nearly as many as the chief expected. Nevertheless, Dehahuit saw potential in the Americans as a foil to play against the Spanish, thus increasing his supply of goods and his own personal power. He urged Sibley to send American traders to his villages, and men like Anthony Glass became some of the first Americans to enter Texas. Dehahuit's influence with both the Norteños and Americans can be seen in his orchestration of the 1807 Grand Council at Natchitoches in which hundreds of Comanches, Wichitas, and Caddos left the prairies and plains of Texas and rode into the piney woods of western Louisiana to meet Sibley and receive gifts. Spain complained about the great chief's actions, but dared not touch him.[22]

Still, the Hidalgo Revolt was the beginning of Dehahuit's undoing. With gifts of manufactured goods no longer arriving from Spanish officials, Dehahuit and the Indians of Texas increasingly looked to American traders. Americans happily filled the void, and soon East Texas was awash with American traders, many of them, unfortunately, whiskey peddlers. Within a short time, the Caddos and other Indians of East Texas had an alcohol problem. French and Spanish traders, understanding their relationship with the Indians was to be a long one, rarely used alcohol in their exchanges. Conversely, the English had found whiskey to be an excellent trade item; it was a commodity that was quickly used up and when gone, its users, now often addicted, would trade away almost anything—hides, clothes, horses, even land—to acquire more. American whiskey peddlers thought the same way. They had no desire to create kinships with the Indians as this was slash-and-burn capitalism—get in, get the goods, and get out.[23]

For many Indians, the inebriating quality of whiskey made it seem a part of their spiritual world, therefore many sought out whiskey for its ability to bring on visions and voices. Not all Indians drank; those that did drank for many reasons: spirituality, boredom, despair, addiction, courage, forgetfulness, essentially the same reasons people anywhere drink. The effect of drunkenness on Indian society could be devastating. Men sold off their winter's hunt of hides for a barrel of ol' bursthead rather than the kettles, needles, gunpowder, and muskets they needed for the coming year. Men ran up huge debts with American traders, often so high that only a cession of Indian land could extinguish them. Men and women brawled, injuring or killing each other. Parents neglected their duties. Those who did not drink had to deal with the wreckage whiskey left behind in families and villages. Many preached against it, and Dehahuit demanded that the United States restrain the traders, but even Sibley and the American army in Louisiana could not stop the influx of whiskey.[24]

On the heels of whiskey peddlers came a host of other people who developed a keen interest in Texas. Some were members of filibustering expeditions out of Louisiana on their way into Texas to fight for Mexican independence. Others were American entrepreneurs who began claiming land up the Red River and into East Texas, often infringing on long-held Caddo and Bidai lands. Others were the immigrant Indians from the East. Dehahuit saw his lands swamped with wandering parties of Americans, Cherokees, Choctaws, Creeks, Shawnees, Delawares, Kickapoos, Miamis, Biloxis, and Pascagoulas. Despite his complaints, the United States did nothing to stop the whiskey peddlers, the Osage raids out of American Arkansas, or the invasion by American settlers and immigrant Indians. It was no wonder that by 1820 Dehahuit had hardened his attitude toward the United States. The situation got so bad that a few American settlers turned up dead in Caddo country.[25]

In order to stand up to the encroaching Americans, Dehahuit decided on a bold plan of building a pan-Indian confederacy, with himself as its leader. Other Indians in the East had tried to build a political alliance among all Indians of a given area, such as Blue Jacket and Tecumseh of the Shawnees, but all had failed. Since Dehahuit could not prevent the immigrant Indians from settling in his territory, he drew on the Caddos' ancient tradition of powerful Mississippian chiefs and tried to make peace with all the immigrant Indian bands hoping they would place themselves under his authority. If all worked out, he would be able to call on 150 Nadaco warriors, 60 Nabedaches, 100 Hainais, 200 Kichais, probably an equal number of Tawakonis, Yscanis, and Bidais, and who knew how many immigrant Indian warriors. Unfortunately for Dehahuit, he was not able to build his alliance into a real Indian barrier. The Americans were not going to be stopped by an Indian confederacy, especially as Mexico, once it gained its independence from Spain in 1821, began inviting Americans into Texas. Also, many immigrant Indians had no desire to put themselves under the leadership of Dehahuit. Bands of Osages, Choctaws, and others still periodically raided Caddo villages. The worst problem for Dehahuit came from the immigrant Cherokees, who wanted to build their own confederacy.[26]

As Chief Duwali's Cherokees migrated into northeast Texas in 1819, they settled on lands long claimed by the Caddos and Wichitas. By 1821 they lived down on the Three Forks of the Trinity River near present-day Dallas and almost immediately clashed with the Taovaya Wichitas as their men hunted over the same territory. In 1822 Taovaya raids forced Duwali to move his Cherokees eastward to the region north of Nacogdoches. Soon more Cherokees were on the way to bolster Duwali's numbers. Back in the

Southeast and in Arkansas, the Cherokees had learned the difficulty of keeping their land in the face of white encroachment. Soon after Mexico gained its independence, the Cherokees approached the new government to grant them clear title to their lands in East Texas, which lay within the bounds of the land grants given to American empresarios Haden Edwards and Frost Thorn. To encourage the Mexicans, Cherokee chief Richard Fields pointed out that his people commanded all the Indian nations of East Texas, including the Comanches and Wichitas. This was certainly wishful thinking on the Cherokees' part and it put them in direct opposition to Dehahuit, who considered himself the spokesman for all East Texas Indians. Over the next decade, horse thefts and revenge killings strained the relations between the Caddos and Texas Cherokees, and the two bands always seemed just on the verge of all-out war.[27] As Manuel de Mier y Terán, a Mexican census taker, reported in 1821, the Caddos "formed a powerful nation, respected by all the savages. . . . They remember with pride their antiquity and power, and pretend to have rights superior to all other tribes, considering themselves the owners of the land. . . . They are rivals of the Cherokees; they were jealous of the influence that these were going to acquire; and in all their conversation with the Mexicans, they manifest their disgust at the introduction of foreign savages."[28]

Dehahuit and his Caddos soon found power slipping from their grasp. In 1542 when De Soto's men cut through their territory, the Caddos had consisted of several paramount Mississippian chiefdoms and many minor ones, altogether comprising almost twenty city-states stretching across northeast Texas, northwest Louisiana, southwest Arkansas, and southeast Oklahoma. By the 1830s, while a few bands of Ais, Nacogdoches, and Nabe-daches might still be found, disease and warfare had reduced the Caddos to three main divisions: the Cadodachos, which was often shortened to "Caddo" and was the name given to the entire people; the Hainai, sometimes referred to as the Ionies; and the Nadacos, also called the Anadarkos. For Dehahuit, the nominal leader of these Caddo divisions, the biggest problem was that most Cadodachos lived in American Louisiana and Arkansas, while the Hainai and Nadacos lived in Mexican Texas. As American settlers and land speculators began carving up Louisiana and Arkansas, the Cadodachos and other Indians peoples, both immigrant and native, found their lands being taken from them. Most of these "Louisiana" Indians now moved into Texas, which made both the Texas Cherokees and the Mexican government nervous. Nevertheless, the Mexican government, viewing most immigrant Indians as a potential barrier against Comanche and Apache raids, invited some Cadodachos into Texas and settled more than eighty Caddo men, women, and children on the Guadalupe River.[29]

Any chance of the Caddos remaining a major power in either Texas or Louisiana ended in 1833 when Great Chief Dehahuit died. His successor, Tarshar, possessed little of Dehahuit's power and charisma and had little influence with the Hainai and Nadacos. Within two years, the United States managed to strong-arm the Caddos into signing a treaty in which they agreed to give up all claims to land in Louisiana and Arkansas for eighty thousand dollars, much of which they never received, and to leave the boundaries of the United States. Unlike removal treaties the government was then signing with Indians in the Southeast, this treaty did not guarantee the Caddos lands in the West. Now homeless, most Louisiana Caddos moved into Texas to live among their Hainai and Nadaco cousins. Some went to Indian Territory, and one band briefly went to live in Mexico. Overall leadership of the Caddos now passed from the Cadodachos to the Nadacos. By the early 1840s Nadaco chief Iesh, known as José María to Texans and Americans, began to expand his influence. Soon the chiefs of other communities and the leaders of other Caddo factions deferred to him. Until his death in 1862, Iesh remained the most influential Caddo chief and spokesman for his people.[30]

The death of Dehahuit left the Cherokees as the most powerful Indian nation in East Texas. It also made them targets of Comanche, Wichita, and Tonkawa raiders. The law of blood vengeance demanded a Cherokee counterstrike, but this was easier said than done. Not wanting warfare to spiral out of control as it had done with the Osages, the Cherokees hoped to make peace agreements with the Norteños. This desire for peace and to demonstrate to the Mexican government that the Cherokees could bring tranquility to Texas was at the heart of Chief Richard Field's attempt to form a Cherokee confederacy. As early as 1824 the Cherokees had made some agreements with a few Comanche bands, but they had been unable to get the Comanches, the Tonkawas, or the Lipans to meet with Fields at the Sabine River in August of that year. In reality, the proposed Cherokee confederacy made the Mexican government apprehensive. Fearing it could be used against them, authorities in Mexico City ordered their officials in Texas to prevent this alliance from taking place, even if that meant using force. Cherokee diplomatic machinations also made the steadily arriving American settlers suspicious.[31]

Americans had long been interested in Texas. The filibustering expeditions during the Hidalgo Revolt intensified that interest. The revolution had stripped Texas of its Hispanic settlers and essentially left Texas undefended. So when Mexico gained its independence from Spain in 1821, she grew concerned that the U.S. government might make a grab for this northern province. At the same time, as had the Spanish before them, Mexican authorities worried about Comanche and Wichita warriors sacking Mexican towns. To combat these threats, Mexico hoped to repopulate Texas with settlers who would serve as a barrier to both Plains Indian incursions and U.S. expansion. Since few Mexicans wanted to migrate north to Texas, the government now opened the province to immigrant Indians and American settlers on the condition they swear loyalty to Mexico, keep the peace, and uphold Mexican law. But Mexican authorities did not view the immigrant Indians in the same way they viewed the American settlers. Despite numerous attempts by the Cherokees to receive written guaranteed title to the lands they occupied in Texas, the Mexican government never gave it to them. Only the Shawnees received a contract in 1824, giving them about 250 square miles of land in East Texas, but even here there was some dispute as to whether they possessed actual title to the land or just user rights. Conversely, American empresarios, such as Stephen F. Austin, Haden Edwards, and Frost Thorn received written title to thousands of acres in East Texas. Other American settlers were able to acquire title to more than four thousands acres by paying a small fee, declaring loyalty to Mexico, and not openly practicing Protestantism.[32]

These new Anglo settlers were much different from the Spanish and French before them. For one thing, there were many more Americans in Texas than there had ever been Spaniards. They outnumbered Indians as well. By 1834 there were more than 15,000 Anglos and close to 5,000 African American slaves as compared to 4,500 Indians in East Texas. And the number of Anglos and slaves grew daily. Most of these incoming American settlers brought with them a racial ideology that put white men at the top of the social pyramid and Indians and blacks at the bottom. They had a rapacious desire for land, which they saw as the basis of all wealth. American settlers hoped to own vast tracts of territory from which they could make money, some of it through cotton plantations, some through farming or grazing, and some through land speculation. Since Indians lived on some of the best lands in all of Texas, many settlers naturally saw them as impediments to their own economic progress. Another thing that set many Texans apart from their Spanish and French predecessors was that many were more than willing to acquire their riches by raiding Indian and Tejano (Mexican Texan) villages for horses and hides. If Texas settlers feared Indian raids, many Indians came to fear Texans just as much.[33]

Few Texans supported giving the Indians title to their lands, while many saw the Indians as threats. The Cherokees, with their demands for land titles and their claim of being the "elder brothers" of all the Indians of Texas, came under particular scrutiny. In 1825, when Comanches, Wichitas, and Tonkawas made heavy raids on East Texas settlements, many

Americans believed the Cherokees were behind it. Though he had no proof, Stephen F. Austin thought the Cherokees instigated the raids to blackmail the Mexican government into granting them title to the lands the Cherokees claimed. Still, Austin was quick to turn to the Cherokees for help when he contemplated an attack on the Wichitas. This tendency to be seen as both friend and foe would bring the eventual downfall of the Texas Cherokees. As more and more Americans arrived in Texas, they not only wanted Cherokee lands but also believed the Cherokees were too easily swayed one way and then another. If, as Austin believed, the Cherokees could side with Americans one day and Comanches the next, then what was to prevent them from siding with a hostile Mexican government against the Anglo-Texans? In the end, the Cherokees, in fact all the Indians of Texas, and the Mexican government as well, had much to fear from the ever-expanding American population in Texas.[34]

Unfortunately, Cherokee attempts to acquire guaranteed title to their Texas lands seemed to confirm Austin's and the Mexican government's suspicions that the Cherokees were dangerous, could not be trusted, and were too easily pulled into the machinations of others. When Haden Edwards began the Fredonian Rebellion in late 1826, he appealed to the Cherokees for support, claiming that if they would back him in creating the independent nation of Fredonia in East Texas, he would guarantee title to Cherokee lands. Though Duwali and others doubted the wisdom of joining the rebellion, Cherokee chief Richard Fields and special envoy John Dunn Hunter managed to convince most Cherokees to support Edwards. Before the Cherokees ever got involved the rebellion collapsed in late January, 1827, when Mexican troops supported by Stephen F. Austin and other American settlers marched on Nacogdoches, forcing the rebels to flee to Louisiana. Realizing the situation the two men had gotten them into, Cherokee leaders executed Fields and Hunter. Even more damaging for the Cherokees and other Indians was that by the early 1830s, Mexico itself was in political turmoil as various factions vied for control of the government. In 1832 Duwali and his Cherokees supported the Mexican Centralist faction, which put them at odds with most American settlers who supported the Federalists. The Cherokees' backing of Haden Edwards and now their loyalty to Mexico angered many Texans and increased settler distrust of all Indians in Texas.[35]

Still, playing one power against the other had long been a staple of Indian diplomacy and the Indians of East Texas saw the conflict between the Texans and Mexico as an opportunity. By 1835, as revolution seemed imminent, both Texas and Mexico appealed to Indians for support. Mexican Indian agent Peter Ellis Bean hoped to persuade the Cherokees and their

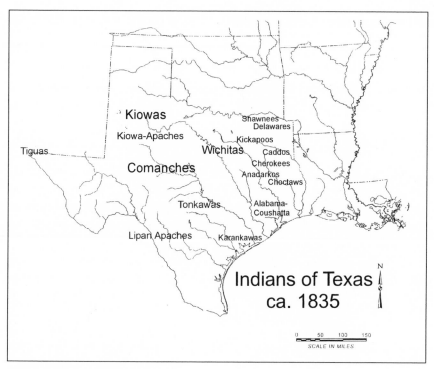

Map 3. Indians of Texas, ca. 1835.

allies to attack the Comanches, who would in turn attack Texas settlements. When that proposal fell through, Mexican officials took a more direct approach and tried to enlist the Cherokees as allies, urging them to attack the Texas militia. Again nothing came of this plan. Conversely, the provisional government of Texas tried to get the Cherokees to attack the Cadodachos and Wichitas, who were viewed as enemies of Texas and potential friends of Mexico. As before, the Cherokees refused to take the bait.[36]

To guarantee Cherokee neutrality during the impending revolution, the provisional government sent Sam Houston to arrange a treaty of friendship. Houston had the right credentials. He had been adopted by John Jolly, chief of the Western Cherokees, and lived with them for a while in Arkansas. He had even married a Cherokee woman, but he abandoned her when he came to Texas in the 1830s. On February 23, 1836, Houston signed a treaty of "firm and lasting peace forever" with the Cherokees "and their associate Bands now residing in Texas . . . to wit: Shawnee, Delaware, Kickapoo, Quapaw, Choctaw, Biloxi, Ioni, Alabama, Coushatta,

Caddo of the Neches, Tahocullake, and Mataquo." The treaty stated that these Indians would "form one community" and that they would all eventually move onto lands promised them north of the old Camino Real, between the upper Sabine, Angelina, and Neches Rivers. This promised land was actually much smaller than what the Cherokees inhabited and certainly much smaller than the areas most East Texas Indians then occupied. According to the treaty, the Indians could live there under their own laws, trade with the Texans, and expect justice from the new government. On March 2, 1836, with the ink barely dry on the treaty, a convention of Texas delegates met at Washington-on-the-Brazos. There they declared their independence from Mexico, refused to discuss, much less approve, the Cherokee treaty, and came out against guaranteeing lands to the Indians.[37]

News of the broken promise soured many Indians on supporting the Texas revolutionaries. And General Antonio López de Santa Anna's invasion of Texas and the "runaway scrape," in which Anglo settlers abandoned their homes and headed for Louisiana in the face of Santa Anna's army, made many East Texas Indians amenable to Mexican overtures. The Cherokees, Shawnees, Delawares, Kickapoos, and Cadodachos welcomed to their villages Mexican agents, who promised them land and plunder if they would attack the Texans. Though Duwali tried to walk a fine diplomatic line between the two powers, a strong pro-Mexico faction arose among the Cherokees. The Caddos seemed even more anti-Texas and in March, 1836, a band of Cadodachos, Nadacos, Hainais, Kichais, and Wichitas raided Northeast Texas settlements, making off with scores of horses. In April several hundred Cadodacho warriors camped on the upper Sabine in hopes of forming an alliance with the Cherokees. Sam Houston's victory over Santa Anna at San Jacinto on April 21 made them rethink their plan and they returned to their villages.[38]

Though Texas won its independence on that day in April, the Indians of East Texas still found themselves caught in the middle. Mexico remained reluctant to give up its former colony and over the next decade continually threatened to reinvade. In fact, she periodically launched sallies into South Texas, even briefly taking San Antonio in 1842. The smoke had hardly cleared from San Jacinto before Mexican agents filtered out among the Indians. They promised that the Mexicans would soon return and tried forming military alliances with the Indians. During the summer of 1836 Duwali sent a delegation of Cherokees to Matamoros to meet with Mexican officials who were promising an immediate reinvasion of Texas. Duwali supported the proposed attack and reported that a large band of Caddos had gathered on the Trinity River to await it. Besides the Caddos and Cherokees, the Choctaws, Alabamas, Biloxis, and several Comanche and Wichita bands seemed open to the Mexican cause. However, the proposed invasion never materialized, and so, except for a few Caddo, Kickapoo, Wichita, and Comanche raids along the Brazos and Navasota Rivers, most East Texas Indians remained at peace with the new Texas government.[39]

When the promised Mexican invasion of late 1836 never came, many chiefs believed the best policy was to come to some kind of accommodation with the Texas government. Fortunately for them, Sam Houston, the new president of the Republic of Texas, was eager to make peace. Houston tried to soothe Duwali's feelings by submitting the Cherokee treaty of February 23, 1836, to the Texas Senate for ratification. Apparently mollified and urged on by Houston, the aged Duwali agreed to visit the Indians of East Texas as well as the Wichitas and the Comanches to persuade them to make peace with Texas. Duwali's diplomatic mission bore fruit, and when he returned in May, 1837, he reported that the Caddos, Wichitas, and the immigrant Indians were all receptive to peace. To follow up, Houston sent commissioners to various Indian nations. He also appointed a three-man committee to investigate and report on the conditions of the Indians of Texas and make recommendations on the 1836 Cherokee treaty. During his first two-year term, Houston's Indian policy bore mixed results. He managed either to pacify or sign peace treaties with various bands of Tonkawas, Lipans, Karankawas, Kichais, Tawakonis, Iscanis (now often referred to as Wacos), Taovayas, Nadacos, Hainais, and Comanches. On the negative side, the three-man committee on Indian Affairs rejected the Cherokee treaty, which would have guaranteed land to the Cherokees. In December, 1837, despite the Cherokees' having kept their promise of remaining neutral during the revolution, the Texas Senate officially rejected the treaty.[40]

Nullification of the treaty angered the Cherokees and other Indians who now believed they would never receive their lands. It also played into the hands of Mexico, which was again talking invasion and wanted the assistance of her Indian and Tejano allies. Notified of the plan by Mexican agents, the Cherokees and Caddos again supported it and in late May, 1838, sent a band of twenty warriors as an escort for Captain Vicente Córdova and his force of more than a hundred soldiers. In July the Cherokees, Shawnees, Delawares, and a few Cadodachos met with Córdova at Duwali's village and tentatively agreed to attack Texas settlements as soon as the Mexican army invaded. The Coushattas and Kickapoos, though not at the council, indicated their support, while the Chickasaws, Hainais, Nadacos, Wacos, Kichais, and Tawakonis welcomed Mexican agents and listened to what they had to say. By the end of the month, more than three hundred warriors and Tejanos had joined Córdova on the Angelina River, northwest of Nacogdoches. President Houston, belatedly learning of the "Córdova Rebellion," tried to assure Duwali that the Indians would get their land, but at the same time he sent the Texas militia into East Texas to search for Córdova and his allies. Once again, Mexico canceled its invasion. This and the approach of the Texas militia undermined threw cold water on Córdova's plans. His Tejano supporters deserted him and went home, while a faction of Cherokees led by Chief Gatunwali met with Texas General Thomas Rusk to declare their peaceful intentions. Even Duwali agreed to meet with the Texans. As his allies melted away, Córdova abandoned his attack plans and took what few allies he had left to the headwaters of the Trinity River, out of reach of the Texas militia.[41]

The appearance of Rusk's militia may have prevented any immediate attacks, but it did nothing to address the Indians' grievances. Over the next two months, Indian anger simmered and pro-Mexican factions among them grew stronger. Córdova, from his hideout on the Trinity, again coordinated his plans. Then, in October, 1838, the raids began. A band of Cherokees, Shawnees, Biloxis, Tejanos, and even a few white outlaws attacked the large Killough family who lived near Neches Saline in present-day Cherokee county, killing eighteen. Another force attacked Fort Houston on the Trinity River just west of present-day Palestine. Cadodachos made their own raids in East Texas. In response, Rusk again mobilized the Texas militia. Cherokee chief Gatunwali, leader of the pro-Texas faction of Cherokees, informed Rusk that Córdova and his allies were then at the Kickapoo village on the Trinity River.[42]

In what has come to be called the Kickapoo War, on October 16, a large force of Kickapoos, Caddos, Biloxis, Coushattas, Cherokees, and Tejanos ambushed Rusk's troops as they neared the village. After a particularly hot battle, the Texans managed to drive off the Indians, but not before each side lost eleven men. A few days later, on October 21, Texas troops under General John H. Dyer attacked the Cadodachos on the Trinity River, killing six warriors. For many Texans, the Cadodachos seemed the most threatening enemy, and in November, Rusk led seventy Texas Rangers across the international border into Shreveport, Louisiana. There Rusk forced a band Cadodachos to surrender their weapons and extracted a promise that they would remain in Shreveport. Returning to Texas, Rusk and four hundred men marched on the three Caddo villages at the forks of the Trinity River, near present-day Dallas. The Caddos, hearing of the army's approach, abandoned their villages and retreated up the Brazos River, leaving most of their supplies to be burned by the Texans. With little food and supplies, the Texas Caddos moved across the Red River to spend the winter of 1838–

39 in Indian Territory. For all intents and purposes the Córdova Rebellion was over.[43]

Even before the October raids, Mirabeau B. Lamar, vice president of the Republic and political rival to Houston, had criticized Houston's peace policy. Many Texans certainly believed it a failure. In their minds, peace had not come and never could come as long as Indians lived in Texas and were susceptible to being recruited by Mexico. Since Houston could not serve a consecutive term, Lamar was easily elected in September, 1838, as the Republic's second president. Almost immediately after taking office, Lamar stated that his policy was to remove all immigrant Indians from Texas. Adding weight to Lamar's pronouncement was that in early 1839 Mexico was again encouraging the Indians of East Texas to join Córdova and attack Texas settlements. Having learned from the previous year's fiascos, the Indians rejected Mexican overtures. During the spring, in separate battles, Texas troops defeated first Córdova's small force and then a small expedition led by Mexican agent Manuel Flores. On Flores's body they found letters from Mexican officials addressed to Duwali, the Caddos, and other Indians in East Texas urging them to begin raiding Texas settlements. Though the Indians had no control over letters being sent to them and probably had no idea of their instructions, Lamar saw this as proof that the Cherokees were siding with Mexico. He was now more determined than ever to remove the immigrant Indians from Texas, particularly the Cherokees.[44]

In late May, 1839, Lamar sent a three-man delegation to deliver his position to Duwali. He wrote that the chief had been "beguiled" by the Mexicans and that he should listen to "the voice of reason and power." He explained that the Cherokee treaty of February, 1836, was "never sanctioned by this Government, and never will be. It is therefore, vain for you to build any hopes upon it." And even if it were ever valid, the Cherokees had forfeited all claims "by leaguing with other Indians and Mexicans, against our peace and safety." As Lamar saw it, "the red man and the white man cannot dwell together," and so he informed Duwali "in the plain language of sincerity, that the Cherokee will never be permitted to establish a permanent and independent jurisdiction within the inhabited limits of this Government . . . and that they are permitted, at present, to remain where they are, only because this government is looking forward to the time, when some peacible [sic] arrangements can be made for their removal." And removal was certain, Lamar said. Therefore the Cherokees should "remain at home quietly and inoffensively, without murdering our people, stealing their property, or giving succor and protection to our enemies" until the Texas Congress could make arrangements for "their return to

their own tribe beyond the Red River." He concluded by telling the Cherokees that their "destiny is involved in the rejection or adoption of this
counsel. If you listen to the voice of reason, you may become a prosperous
and happy nation; but if you follow the dictates of improper passions, your
ruin is inevitable."[45]

Upon receiving the delegation and letter, Duwali protested that his
people had not killed anyone or stolen any property, and blamed the violence on the "wild Indians." And he may have had a point. The old chief
then reiterated his people's right to the land, saying it had been given to
them by Mexico and even the Texans recognized their right to it in 1836.
The Texas delegation remained adamant about removal, so Duwali asked
for a week to consult with his people. When the delegation returned, a very
grave and serious Duwali reported that while he did not want war, his
young men did and believed they could beat the Texans. As Duwali saw it,
"if he fought, the whites would kill him; and if he refused to fight, his own
people would kill him." But he had been his people's leader for many
years and "felt it to be his duty to stand by them, whatever fate might be-
fall him." With that, the delegation withdrew and both sides prepared for
war.[46]

In late June, Lamar appointed a commission of Texans to bring about
"the immediate removal of the Cherokee Indians, and the ultimate removal of all other emigrant Tribes now residing in Texas."[47] Texas troops
marched to Cherokee territory, and on July 9, 1839, the commissioners began a week of negotiations with Duwali of the Cherokees, Spy Buck of the
Shawnees, and Harris of the Delawares in which they tried to convince the
Indians to peacefully remove north of the Red River in return for compensation for the improvements on their lands. Nothing came of the negotiations, and on the evening of July 15, the first battles of the Cherokee War
began when the five-hundred-man Texas army marched on the Cherokee
village located on the Neches River. As the Texans neared the village
around eight hundred Cherokees, Shawnees, Kickapoos, and Delawares
attacked, using guns and bows and arrows. By the next day, the Indian
forces had withdrawn six miles up the Neches and the Texans attacked
again, burning the nearby Delaware village. The battle lasted about two
hours before the Indians were forced to retreat. Despite his age, Duwali led
his Indian troops and was one of the last on the battlefield. As eyewitness
John Reagan reported, Duwali's horse had been wounded and the chief
was shot through the thigh. When his horse could go no farther, Duwali
"dismounted and started to walk off. He was shot in the back . . . walked
forward a little and fell, and then rose to a sitting position facing us. . . .
As I approached him from one direction, my captain, Robert Smith, ap-

proached him from another, with his pistol drawn. As we got to him, I said, 'Captain, don't shoot him,' but as I spoke he fired, shooting the chief in the head, which caused his instant death." That night, the remaining Cherokees and their families moved north and dispersed, "some going to the cross timbers, some to the north of the Red River, and some to Mexico." In the fighting, the Cherokee chief Gatunwali was also killed, as were more than a hundred Cherokees. Texas losses were only about five dead, twenty-eight wounded. Cherokee territory was devastated, their cabins and villages burned.[48]

The Cherokee War ended any chance of the immigrant Indians' remaining in Texas. Most Cherokees fled to Indian Territory. A few others, along with some Shawnees, Delawares, and Choctaws moved to the upper Brazos, beyond the line of Texas settlements, where they built a small village and tried to plant crops. A couple of weeks later, Texas negotiators signed a treaty with the Shawnees in which the Indians would leave Texas in return for a compensation of $7,806 for the improvements on their lands. Most eventually went to Indian Territory. By 1840 while there might be a few isolated families of Choctaws, Chickasaws, Shawnees, Kickapoos, and Delawares living in East or Central Texas, most immigrant Indians, at least as unified nations, had left Texas.[49]

Only the Alabamas and Coushattas received title to lands in Texas. In 1840 Lamar agreed to give the Alabamas and Coushattas two leagues of land each, but their title quickly got snarled in competing claims by nearby whites. Finally, in 1854, the Alabamas received title to 1,280 acres of land in present-day Polk County. In 1855 the Coushattas received 640 acres, also in Polk Country. As before, the Coushatta claim was contested by white settlers, and in 1859 the Alabamas allowed the Coushattas to join them on their reservation. Of of all the Indian peoples to have ever called Texas home, only these Alabama-Coushattas in East Texas, the Tiguas near El Paso, and the Mexican Kickapoos near Eagle Pass continue to occupy lands recognized by Texas and the United States. Of the indigenous Indians of East Texas, only a few families of Bidais remained in the area. The Caddos, most of whom had been forced out of Texas in late 1838, returned in late 1839 and early 1840, settling on the upper Brazos River, far from the Texas settlements.[50]

So by 1840 just about all Indians, both indigenous and immigrant, had been forced out of East Texas. Most had gone north, leaving only a few families or bands roaming beyond the line of settlement in north-central Texas. Some, such as a few families of Bidais and the Alabamas and Coushattas, scratched out a tenuous existence in the woods of East Texas. Similarly, Cadodachos, Hainais, and Nadacos resided in a few villages on the upper Brazos. Down on the coast, only a few dwindling remnants of the Karankawas survived. In south-central Texas, the Tonkawas found themselves pressed by both Texans and Comanches, while most Coahuiltecans had long since disappeared or had become hispanized peasants around San Antonio and towns farther south. The Lipan Apaches, the Wichitas, the Comanches, and the ever-growing Kiowas remained powerful and would pursue their own agenda of controlling the Southern Plains, which included trying to check Texan and American expansion onto them.

Chapter 8

The Wars for Texas

T HE COMING OF Anglo-Americans brought serious challenges to the
Indians of Texas. Prior to the nineteenth century most Texas Indians
could ignore the Spanish if they so desired. Spain's power over the
Indians in Texas was weak, if not nonexistent. If Indians ever obeyed Spanish dictates it was because they saw it was to their own advantage rather
than that they feared Spanish reprisals. However, the Anglo-Americans
who began filling up Texas in the early nineteenth century were very different from the Spaniards and Mexicans before them. They were a touchy,
aggressive lot, certain of their racial superiority, eager to grow wealthy, and
convinced that the entire continent was theirs for the taking. They were also
quick to use force against anything or anyone that stood in their way. Most
saw little worthwhile in Indian culture and unlike the Spanish before them,
few wanted to reach an accommodation with the Indians, much less make
kinships with them. For them, Texas was just not big enough for Indians
and Americans. As the Caddos, Bidais, and most immigrant Indians of East
Texas learned, when settlers moved onto Indian lands, it was not long before Indians were pushed out. The Karankawas soon realized the same.

The Destruction of the Karankawas

Ever since Cabeza de Vaca washed ashore at Galveston Island in 1528, the
Karankawas had been a thorn in Spain's side. They maintained their inde-

pendence despite the ravages of disease, attacks by Apaches, and Spain's attempt to lock them into missions. Their freedom had even attracted the "apostate" Xaranames, who moved in with them on the coast. Though their population had dwindled considerably, by the turn of the nineteenth century most Karankawas lived a life not all that different from when Cabeza de Vaca came ashore. They still hunted, fished, and gathered along the coast and barrier islands, scavenged what they could from shipwrecks, and traded with anyone who was willing. Aside from their independence, the most serious charge laid against the Karankawas was that they were cannibals. Virtually every writer who came into contact with them mentioned it, but not one of the writers ever witnessed it firsthand. Ironically, it was the Karankawas who had been shocked by the cannibalism practiced by the Cabeza de Vaca survivors, not the other way around. As one Mexican official finally admitted in 1834, "They have been accused of being cannibals, but I believe this is merely a fable."[1]

Despite many attempts by the Spanish to subdue them, the Karankawas did not submit. The main thing working in their favor was their location. Hot, humid, sickly, infested with mosquitoes, the upper Texas coast drew few settlers. Even the missions established at the head of Lavaca and San Antonio Bays did not last long and were soon moved to higher, healthier ground at Goliad and Refugio. There the Karankawas came and went as they pleased. However, Karankawa isolation ended in the early nineteenth century with the arrival of Jean Lafitte and his buccaneers. Lafitte's pirates, who had previously operated out of Barataria, Louisiana, south of New Orleans, gained fame and pardon by helping General Andrew Jackson defeat the British at New Orleans in 1815. Joining Mexico in her revolution against Spain, in 1817 Lafitte and his men founded Campeche, an outpost on the eastern end of Galveston Island. It was not long before the cutthroat community numbered about a thousand men and women. Initially, the Karankawas and Lafitte's men got along, but relations soon soured. In an ironic twist, the pirates accused the Karankawas of being thieves. The Karankawas were outraged when the pirates kidnapped and raped several of their women. In revenge, Karankawa warriors began laying ambushes for Lafitte's men. Eventually, in 1821, Lafitte with two hundred men and two cannons attacked a camp of more than three hundred Karankawas, killing thirty. They lost two of their own but succeeded in driving the Karankawas off Galveston Island. Not long afterward, Lafitte and his men were ordered off the island by the U.S. government.[2]

The Karankawas did not have time to resettle Galveston; later in that same year empresario Stephen F. Austin, carrying authorization from the

Mexican government, began colonizing lands between Galveston Bay and the Colorado River. "Austin's Colony", with its capital of San Felipe de Austin on the lower Brazos River about eighty miles from the Gulf of Mexico, sat on the edge of Karankawa territory. As they had so many times before, the Karankawas viewed these strangers as targets of opportunity. Austin's colonists had barely set foot in Texas when Karankawa warriors attacked the colony's supply depot at the mouth of the Colorado River, killing four men and making off with most of the supplies. Over the next few years, Karankawa warriors made several raids on colonists along the lower Colorado and San Bernard Rivers.[3]

The settlers gave as good as they got. Skirmishes became common, with losses mounting on both sides. Colonists developed a shoot-first-ask-questions-later attitude, often ambushing canoes filled with Karankawa families even when no raids had been reported. Austin authorized a virtual war of extermination and most colonists were more than happy to comply. In 1826 colonists gunned down a large contingent of Karankawa men, women, and children as they tried to swim the Colorado River. For many Texans, hunting Karankawas became something of a sport and some unmarried men captured Indian women to serve as unwilling concubines. Under pressure, several Karankawa bands signed a peace treaty with the American and Tejano colonists on May 13, 1827, agreeing to cease their raiding and remain west of the Lavaca River.[4]

Now the Karankawas found themselves in serious difficulties. The more easterly Karankawas had been pushed away from traditional fishing holes, hunting areas, and gathering spots, and onto unfamiliar lands held by the more westerly Coco and Cujane Karankawas. This meant less food for all. As starvation stalked them, many turned to raiding or to stealing cattle. This brought the wrath of the colonists and Tejanos down on them. Hounded on all sides and with bands increasingly shattered and kinship and exchange relations snapped, some Karankawas found they had to beg food and goods from settlers. As a result, many bands developed personal relationships with nearby settlers, often performing menial tasks or field labor in exchange for food and protection. Much depended on the settler. For some Karankawas, this work got them through rough patches, while others found themselves caught up in debt peonage, even enslavement. As revolutionary fever heated up in Texas, these Karankawas normally supported whichever side their patron did. Though Texas urged the Karankawas to remain neutral, a few bands allied with pro-Mexican Tejanos raided some Anglo settlements. However, most Karankawas did not take up arms against either side. Still, this did not save them, but rather made them targets of both sides. The Texans believed all Karankawas supported Mexico, and the Mexicans saw them as traitors because of their close relations with such Anglo patrons as Phillip Dimmitt, the Texas commandant at Goliad in early 1836.[5]

The years after the Texas Revolution proved even worse for the Karankawas as they found themselves caught in the continuing clashes between Mexico and Texas, often attacked by both sides. Disease, alcohol, and raids by Anglo "cowboys" decimated their already dwindling numbers. The expanding ranching economy that developed along the Texas coast after the revolution meant there was little room for the Karankawas. Arguments, brawls, and skirmishes broke out as townspeople accused them of being beggars and thieves, while ranchers, who had appropriated Karankawa lands, saw them as potential rustlers. Things reached a violent conclusion in the winter of 1844–45 when a band of Karankawas killed a rancher on the lower Guadalupe in an argument over a cow. About the same time, a band of citizens from Victoria and a few nearby ranches virtually wiped out a Karankawa band near present-day Tivoli.[6]

Fearing more attacks, most Karankawas abandoned their homes and fled to the mouth of the Rio Grande. What few Karankawas were left on the middle Texas coast were killed in an attack by settlers in 1852, the survivors chased out to join their kin on the Rio Grande and nearby Padre Island. On the Rio Grande, the Karankawas made kinships with nearby Indians and often wandered back and forth across the international border. Ranchers on both sides of the border accused them, and other Indians, of raiding and rustling. Finally, in 1858 Juan Nepomuceno Cortina and other Tejano ranchers in Texas attacked the Karankawas and killed them to a man. For all intents and purposes, the Karankawas now ceased to exist as a people.[7]

Raiding in the Republic

Much of the folklore that goes into creating Texas and Texans rests on the image of nineteenth-century settlers fending off Plains Indian raiders. Seminal Texas books such as James T. DeShields's *Border Wars of Texas,* Noah Smithwick's *Evolution of a State,* and Rip Ford's *Texas* depict in vivid detail the raids Comanches, Kiowas, Wichitas and other Indians made on settlers during the years of the Republic. And there were Indian raids on Texans, plenty of them, which did not end with Texas statehood in 1845. They continued until about 1881 when the U.S. Army pushed Victorio's Chiricahua Apaches out of far West Texas. From the mid-1830s to 1881 just about every Texas community west of Waco experienced some sort of negative interaction with Indians. The raiding of strangers, people who were not of one's own people or kin, was an ancient economic activity. As Texans expanded west and replaced the Spanish as sources of valuable commodities, it was their turn to be raided. But Texans made their own raids, and they were never hesitant about attacking Indian camps, burning tepees, destroying supplies, stealing Indian horses and hides, taking captives, or gunning down warriors. Naturally, both sides believed they could justify their own actions.

No two raids were exactly alike, however each was much the same as any other. Whether Indian or Texan, raiders employed similar tactics. They scouted their targets and then, usually at night with no moon, attacked, relying on the element of surprise. Some raids might be simple thievery, the victim not realizing his horses or equipment were gone until the next morning. Sometimes it might be a show of daring bravado, with a small raiding party swooping down and making off with the horses right in front of the wide eyes of their astonished victims. Other times, raids could be supremely violent, with men, women, and babies killed, captives taken, homes or equipment looted or burned, and horses driven off. Sometimes they were not raids at all, but pitched battles between armed parties. The question was not whether raids took place, but why so many occurred.

In Southern Plains Indian society, a man proved his bravery through raiding and so gained status, which could eventually propel him into a leadership position. Young men craved status and position. This made them particularly susceptible to joining raiding parties, often ignoring the directives of chiefs and elders, and usually not even thinking about potential consequences. A man who continually acquitted himself well on raids eventually began leading raiding parties. Success gained him a following, which translated into political power. He could, if his luck held out, become a noted chief of his own band, maybe even spokesman for his people. And since the number of horses a man owned also contributed to his status, the horse raid became common. A man could gain status both through displaying bravery and acquiring horses.[8]

While many things in an Indian's life were communal, horses were personal property. Men were not expected to share them, though they might give them as gifts or exchange them in trade. Poor men without horses often went on raids afoot in hopes of receiving a few as a share of the spoils. And since Indian life was hard on horses, men always wanted as many as they could get. The constant movement, the long distances, the hard riding meant horses did not live particularly long. So a man, his family, bands in general, tried to keep as many horses as they could. The average Plains Indian household, which consisted of about five adults and maybe an equal number of children, needed a minimum of ten horses: at

least five for hauling the tepee and household goods and another five for
buffalo hunting and raiding.[9]

Since Plains Indians did not breed horses, most were replaced through
raiding, which was far easier than breaking wild mustangs. In 1821 Jacob
Fowler visited a Kiowa camp. He counted seven hundred lodges, which he
reckoned held a minimum population of eighty-four hundred, but numbered their horses at twenty thousand. Twenty thousand horses was a considerable herd. It meant that forage was quickly exhausted and the camp
could never stay in one place too long. Despite the numbers, Fowler noted
that some men did not own any horses at all and so went everywhere
afoot. Also, the huge herd attracted attention. Fowler calculated the Kiowas lost more than four hundred horses a night to Indian raiders. Kiowa
warriors went out almost daily to replenish their losses. And not all raids
were successful. Sometimes, if a horse could not be successfully taken, the
warrior might kill it to prevent it being used to follow him, or maybe because of simple frustration. Valuable guns, metalware, cloth, and hides
would also be taken if possible.[10]

Captives became another important item to be taken in raids, particularly women, but also children past infancy. Over the years, diseases had
depleted Indian populations. Taking captives and adopting them into
one's society was a time-honored method of increasing a band's population. The Apaches, during their great seventeenth-century expansion, had
absorbed large numbers of Jumanos, Coahuiltecans, Wichitas, and Pueblos. Comanches, Wichitas, Caddos, and Tonkawas had done the same.
However, by the 1830s horses and buffalos had brought about a greater
demand for captives. Indian horse herds needed to be watched and protected, and the bigger the herds the more guards one needed. Boys provided the perfect herdsmen, but there were not enough Indian boys to
watch these large herds, so warriors captured young Mexican, Indian,
African American, and Anglo boys and put them to work watching horses.
Many of these children were eventually adopted into Indian society, some
rising to become powerful men. When artist George Catlin visited the Wichitas and Comanches in 1834, he painted the portrait of His-oo-sán-chees,
a Comanche war leader. Catlin was surprised to discover that His-oo-sán-
chees was actually Jesús Sanchez, who had been captured as a boy in Mexico. Female captives were put to work doing the labor all Indian women
did. They assisted a man's wives and bore the brunt of their jealousies, but
often became a man's junior wife. And by the mid-nineteenth century a
successful Plains man believed he needed many wives.[11]

Women were the true laborers of any household, producing the numerous goods and utensils all homes needed. Because so much in Indian

life came from the buffalo, Plains women spent a large part of their time skinning, tanning, and decorating buffalo hides. Since a Plains Indian ate an average of six buffalo a year, just processing these hides provided plenty of work. However, by the 1830s buffalo hides had become a major trade commodity valued by Indians and whites alike. Some hides were made into blankets, robes, moccasins, and such; others were transformed into beautifully painted tepees or robes; many became belts to turn the machines of America's Industrial Revolution. Because of their value, the more buffalo hides a man could trade, the more status and wealth he received. Since women processed the hides, the more wives a man could afford, the more hides his household could produce. Polygamy increased substantially in nineteenth-century Plains Indian societies as successful men acquired more wives for their labor. To meet family needs and the demands of the hide trade, the average Plains hunter killed forty-four buffalo a year, while women processed about one hide a week.[12]

Captive women provided an almost instant labor force. One of the most famous raids in Texas history occurred in 1836, when a band of Comanches and Kiowas attacked Parker's Fort near Groesbeck in Limestone County. The story is that John Parker had gone on a horse raid with the Indians but had cheated them out of their share of the spoils. Determined to teach him a lesson, a band of Noconi Comanches and Kiowas attacked the fort in May, killed most of the inhabitants, and took five captives. One was Mrs. Rachel Plummer, who spent almost two years as a Comanche captive, much of the time processing buffalo hides. Another captive was nine-year-old Cynthia Ann Parker who spent twenty-four years with the Comanches. Cynthia eventually married Peta Nocona, a Comanche chief, and gave birth to Quanah Parker, one of the greatest Comanche chiefs of all time.[13]

Some white men, fearing a long, slow torture, committed suicide rather than be taken alive. Men seemed equally horrified about what might happen to captive women, imagining all sorts of fates. And naturally, a parent or husband wanted to have his family restored. If a band of settlers or a troop of Rangers could not catch up with the raiders, then families might spend hundreds of dollars in rewards or trade goods trying to regain their people, thus actually increasing the incentive for abducting people. Even the U.S. government offered cash for the return of captives. Surplus captives became commodities, and some, such as Texas boy Gillis Doyle, might change hands several times. Delawares, Kickapoos, Shawnees, Caddos, even Cherokees, Chickasaws, and others might visit the Comanches or Kiowas, exchange merchandise for a captive, then return her to her family for the reward. In one incident, a party of Choctaw and

Kickapoo traders found George Wilson, a Texas boy owned by an old Comanche man. To ransom him, the Choctaws and Kickapoos gave the old man forty beads, eight yards of stroud, ten pints of gunpowder, twelve bars of lead, sixteen yards of blue grilling, half a dozen paint pieces, six plugs of tobacco, four butcher knives, six coils of brass wire, and twelve yards of cloth called Choctaw Stripe. Because the band chief helped arrange the trade, the Choctaws and Kickapoos gave him a pony, a rifle, and six plugs of tobacco. In all, this amounted to five hundred dollars' worth of goods. How much they got from the boy's family is not known. Not all captives wanted to be ransomed. Some acculturated to Indian life and willingly spent years, maybe even the rest of their days, as a Comanche or a Kiowa or a Wichita.[14]

Some raids were punitive in nature, either as acts of revenge or as offensive war. In Indian society, if a person was killed on a raid or as a result of an attack, then their blood cried out for vengeance. If the death was left unavenged, then the world was thrown out of balance. Harmony, so essential in Indian society, was lost. Only revenge on the killer or his people could right things. Also, unanswered killings and attacks struck at a leader's status. Lose too many men on a raid too often and a man gained a reputation as unlucky. Allow an attack on one's camp or village to go unanswered and a chief lost prestige. Followers deserted him and his people came to be seen as an easy mark. Any loss had to be challenged; any attack countered. At the same time, it did not take the Comanches, Wichitas, and Kiowas long to realize that their territory was being invaded. They were determined to preserve their lands, resources, and economy. To do this, the Southern Plains Indians sometimes drove hunters away from the buffalo herds, attacked wagon trains of Santa Fe Trail traders, contested the building of roads and forts, and, particularly, tried to disrupt the work of land surveyors.[15]

Texans did not sit idly by; they fought back as well. They often raided Indian camps for the same reasons that Indians raided theirs. Many men saw the economic potential in acquiring horses and hides. Some of these men were outlaws who would prey on anyone, Indian, Anglo, or Mexican. Others might be bands of settlers, often mixing their punitive expedition with economic gain. In 1829 militia commander Abner Kuykendall, along with 100 men and several Lipan Apache scouts, attacked a Tawakoni Wichita camp at the mouth of the San Sabá River. The Tawakonis managed to retreat with only the loss of one man, but the Texans occupied the village for three days, eating the Indians' corn, beans, and meat. When they left, they took with them all the buffalo hides they could manage, about eighty horses, and the Tawakonis' kettles, saddles, and surplus food. Nevertheless, the men prided themselves on sparing the women and children. For other settlers, it was a war of vengeance and extermination. In October, 1840, when John Moore led an expedition of settlers against a Comanche camp on the upper Colorado River, he reported that his troops killed 125 men, women, and children; took 34 Indians captive; made off with more than 500 horses; then looted and burned the camp.[16]

Such a raid would be devastating to the Indians, not only in loss of valuable lives but also because of the destroyed camp utensils. Men would have to hunt more buffalos and women work all that much harder to replace them. It would also enrage the Comanches and certainly bring retribution. Still, most Texans summed it up as did early settler Noah Smithwick: "I really felt mean and almost ashamed of belonging to the superior race when listening to the recital of the wrongs the redmen had suffered at the hands of my people. Nevertheless, when they made hostile incursions into the settlements I joined in the pursuit and hunted them as mercilessly as any one."[17]

Both sides certainly had issues with the other. Texans could not understand why a peace treaty with one Comanche chief did not carry over to other Comanches. And why could a chief not keep his young men under control? Why did the rules of blood revenge mean that an innocent person often died for the killings committed by a different white person? Why did the Indians seem to kill so indiscriminately? Why did they not recognize personal property rights? Why did they insist on taking horses and people, even African American slaves? At the same time, mid-nineteenth-century Texans held Indians to a standard they refused to accept for themselves. Texans ignored Indian land claims while insisting their own claims be respected. They refused to accept that a chief could not control his young men, while at the same time Texans could do little about their own outlaws. While demanding Indians obey every jot and tittle of a law or treaty, Texans, as southerners, also championed the right of a state to ignore laws made by the federal governments in the United States and Mexico. And many individual Americans disregarded their own state laws if they happened to disagree with them.

This confused the Indians and left them with their own questions. Why could the government not live up to its own treaties? Why, if the government promised one thing, such as a land title, did whites violate this promise and settle on Indian lands? How could white juries continually leave white men unpunished for crimes against Indians? Why was one Indian band punished for the crimes of another? Why did white men say one thing and then do something else? Why did the promises made by one administration change when a new one came to power?

It had not always been so. In the early years of the nineteenth century many Anglo-Americans, as individuals, had good relations with the Southern Plains Indians. Men such as Anthony Glass, David Burnet, Jacob Fowler, and Noah Smithwick spent months living peacefully and rather profitably among the Comanches, Kiowas, and Wichitas. A band of Comanches went out of their way to inform Stephen F. Austin of the friendship they had for Americans. Gracious hosts, the Indians accorded their guests every hospitality, even protecting them from other Indians who might have wanted to do them harm. Early on, there was little chance of conflict between the Texas settlers and Comanches because they were so far apart geographically. In fact, most of the raiding was as it had always been: Comanches and Kiowas attacking Lipan Apaches and Tonkawas and raiding the Wichitas, Caddos, Shawnees, Delawares or Kickapoos every now and then.[18]

Also attracting raids were the Cherokees, Choctaws, Creeks, Chickasaws, and Seminoles who had been removed from the Southeast to Indian Territory over the Trail of Tears. These eastern immigrant Indians were not necessarily pushovers. Shawnees, Delawares, Kickapoos, even Sac and Foxes often managed to fend off Comanche and Kiowa attacks, sometimes making raids of their own on the "wild Indians" as they called them. Still, Chickasaw and Seminoles farms and ranches, the farthest west of the "Five Civilized Tribes," bore the brunt of many raids. But because of the Indians' constant need for goods, the growth of the horse and buffalo-hide trade, and the steady westward creep of Texas settlements, by the mid-1830s raiding between Southern Plains Indians and Texans was quickly gathering steam. Raids were also becoming bloodier with the Republic's creation of the Texas Rangers and their charge to protect the settlements from the Indians.[19]

Just as they had with the Spanish and French, the Indians initially viewed the Texans not only as sources of merchandise but also as potential allies to help them in their battles. Texans were just as quick to make allies of friendly Indians. Lipan Apaches under Chief Castro and Tonkawas under Chief Placido, long the victims of Norteño raids, saw the arrival of the Texans as an opportunity to strike back. Both made peace with the Texans, continued their war against the Norteños, and rode with Texas Rangers and later with the U.S. Cavalry as scouts and auxiliaries.[20]

Still, being an ally of Texas was not always easy. The Tonkawas served as a barrier between the Norteños and the early Texas settlements and so suffered their own losses in raids. On the other hand, despite their service to Texas, even providing food and horses for Austin's colony, the Tonkawas came in for a large share of abuse by Texans. Outlaws stole their horses while bands of settlers gunned them down, accusing them of rustling. With no recognized rights, Tonkawas were more often the victim of violence by Texans than the other way around. Misunderstandings and quarrels escalated into killings, and some Anglos killed Tonkawas merely for sport. The charge of cannibalism against the Tonkawas only added to their problems.[21]

Virtually all Indians of Texas had practiced some sort of ritual cannibalism, eating a small part of their enemies to take their strength and gain power over them. By the nineteenth century most Texas Indians had abandoned the practice. Aiding in its demise was the arrival of the Chickasaws, Choctaws, Creeks, and Cherokees who possessed a strong aversion toward cannibalism. Only the Tonkawas retained the practice, with mainly Comanches and Wichitas as their victims. Whether this was merely ritual cannibalism or an actual need for food during hard times is still debated. In any case, Tonkawa cannibalism turned powerful people against them. Texans and "civilized" Indians viewed the Tonkawas with disgust. Comanches and Wichitas, horrified at Tonkawas' eating their people, gave no quarter when it came to battle. With every man's hand against them, Tonkawas led a furtive life. Even as they served as scouts and auxiliaries, their population dwindled.[22]

A major problem for the Indians was that Texans seemed to be divided over how to deal with them. Many men, who either through choice or necessity maintained close relations with Indians, developed sympathy for them. Traders, Indian agents, farmers who might employ a band of Karankawas or Tonkawas, ranchers who had lost stock returned by Caddos or Shawnees, even Ranger captains often came to respect Indians and believed they had certain rights that should be upheld. Others, particularly those who had little if any dealings with Indians, made no attempt to understand Indian culture, believed they had no rights that a white man must respect, and prayed for the day when Indians, even those who were allies, would be pushed from the state.

The question as to whether Indians should have guaranteed title to land split Texans all the more. Some said yes and Indians certainly agreed. As Penetaka Comanche chief Muguara advised, "If the white men would draw a line defining their claims and keep on their side of it the red men would not molest them."[23] Other Texans adamantly disagreed, believing Indians as permanent residents inside of Texas were impediments to progress. As Sam Houston complained, "If I could build a wall from the Red River to the Rio Grande, so high that no Indian could scale it, the white people would go crazy trying to devise means to get beyond it." Adding to the confusion was the whipsawing of the Republic's Indian policy between Sam Houston who advocated peace and Mirabeau Lamar who advocated war.[24]

Though the Republic signed a treaty with Muguara's band of the southernmost Penetaka Comanches in 1838, it meant nothing to other divisions. Bands of Kotsoteka, Kwahadi, Yamparika, and Noconi Comanches, as well as Kiowas and Wichitas, raided along the upper Trinity, Brazos, and Colorado Rivers and as far west as El Paso and New Mexico. Once again, many Texans incorrectly believed that a single chief spoke for the entire Comanche people. Similarly, the Comanches "could not understand why hostility toward the whites in one section necessarily implied hostility toward all, nor why a treaty made with the people of the Colorado [River], for instance, should extend to the whole country."[25]

Nevertheless, in 1840 Muguara and a few other Comanche chiefs who approached Texas officials about strengthening the treaty were invited to San Antonio. On March 19, 1840, twelve Comanche chiefs, along with fifty-three men, women, and children, and a few Texan and Mexican captives, arrived for negotiations. The council did not go well from the start as citizens became enraged at the sorry physical condition of Matilda Lockart, a captive Texas girl the Comanches brought in. The Texans demanded that all captives be returned, but Muguara and the chiefs explained that this was the only one they had, which may well have been true, as other bands held other captives. Muguara's people could only negotiate for themselves; if Texans wanted the other captives then they would have to come up with merchandise to make the Comanche owners part with their property.[26]

What seemed a sensible explanation to Muguara, the Texans saw as extortion. Angry and ignoring the particulars of diplomacy, Texas negotiators ordered the Comanches held hostage until the other captives could be returned. As armed Texas Rangers entered the council house, the surprised Comanches jumped for their own weapons and a firefight broke out. In the battle, all twelve Comanche chiefs were killed as well as eighteen other men, three women, and two children. Only a few escaped; the remaining women and children were taken captive. Seven Texans were killed and eight wounded. The "Council House Fight" was a serious blunder by the Texans. Indians across the Southern Plains saw it as evidence of Texas treachery and a declaration of war. It can be considered the spark that set off the wars of the Southern Plains, which lasted until 1875. From this point on, the Comanches, Kiowas, and Wichitas became implacable foes of Texas and distinguished between Americans, whom they liked, and Texans, whom they hated.[27]

To take revenge for the Council House Fight, large raiding parties

struck deep into Texas. In July and August, 1840, Penetaka chief Pot-
sanaquahip, known as Buffalo Hump, and his Comanche warriors and
Kiowa allies seized the town of Victoria and a few days later sacked Linn-
ville on Lavaca Bay. As Buffalo Hump and his men returned north with
their plunder, Texas Rangers and their Tonkawa scouts ambushed them at
Plum Creek, inflicting heavy casualties. In October, as a follow-up to the
Plum Creek battle, Colonel John Moore's men and his Lipan Apache allies
attacked a Comanche camp on the upper Colorado and killed more than
120 men, women, and children. Though Texas president Lamar supported
the attacks on the Indians, many Texans had grown tired of his bellicose
policy. Attacks caused seemingly endless war, at tremendous expense, calculated at $2.5 million.[28]

In 1841 Texas voters reelected Sam Houston as president of the Republic in hopes of bringing peace. In September, 1843, at Bird's Fort on the upper Trinity River, the small bands of Delawares, Chickasaws, Cherokees,
Biloxis, Cadodachos, Nadacos, Hainais, Wacos, Tawakonis, and Kichais
who had moved there after the Cherokee War signed a peace treaty with
Texas. Then in October, 1844, they did it all over again, signing another
treaty, this time, with three Comanche chiefs, including Buffalo Hump,
putting their mark on the paper. In these treaties, the Indians and the Texans agreed to live in peace. The Indians would quit stealing horses and
give up their captives. The Texans would set up trading houses and prevent "bad men" from crossing onto Indian hunting grounds. Texas would
also periodically give gifts to the Indians and send blacksmiths and teachers among them to instruct them "in a Knowledge of the English language
and Christian Religion, as well as other persons to teach them how to cultivate the soil and raise corn." Though Houston tried to establish a boundary line between Texas settlements and the Comanches and Kiowas, neither side accepted or respected it. Raids by Indians and Texans continued,
while Texans, Rangers and settlers alike, battled the Comanches, and their
Taovaya and Kiowa allies.[29]

The Kiowas and Kiowa-Apaches

Most Kiowas actually lived outside the boundaries of Texas, usually between the Red and Platte Rivers. However, many bands camped in Palo
Duro Canyon in the Panhandle, and Kiowa raiding parties struck deep
into Central and West Texas. The Kiowas were horse-mounted Northern
Plains hunter-gatherers who spoke Tanoan-Kiowa, which is closely related to what the Pueblo peoples speak and is a dialect of the Uto-Aztecan
family. The Kaigwu, as they called themselves, considered their place of

origin as the headwaters of the Yellowstone and Missouri Rivers. There they had been allies of the Crows, the Arikaras, and the Canadian Atha-paskan peoples—the same people who had earlier moved south and be-came the Apaches and Navajos. In fact, one group of these northern Apaches attached themselves to the Kiowa and became the Kiowa-Apaches, a distinct Apache-speaking division of the Kiowa people. Six di-visions comprised the Kiowas: the Kaigwu or Kiowa proper, the Katas, the Kogui, the Kingep, the Kongtalyui, and the Semat or Kiowa-Apaches. During the 1770s the expansion of the Dakota peoples onto the Northern Plains pushed the Kiowas farther south, onto lands claimed by the Co-manches. For a while they battled each other, but between 1790 and 1820 the Kiowas and Comanches gradually made peace, formed an alliance, and created an almost impenetrable barrier to groups wanting to break out onto the Southern Plains, Indian and Texan alike. This Kiowa-Comanche alliance, though not always harmonious, has lasted up to this very day, and the two peoples remain closely associated with each other.[30]

The Kiowas formed one more link in a chain of powerful, highly mo-bile Indians, stretching from the Lipan Apaches and Tonkawas in South Texas up through the Comanches, Kiowas, Cheyennes, and Arapahos, to the Lakotas and Crows on the Northern Plains. With the Kiowa migra-tion south, by the 1840s Texas found itself confronted by three different groups of Apaches: the rapidly dwindling Lipan Apaches along the Rio Grande; the Jicarilla, Mescalero, Chiricahua, and other Apache bands in New Mexico and Arizona; and the Kiowa-Apaches in and about the Texas Panhandle. Economically, the Kiowas and Kiowa-Apaches, like all other Plains Indians, were horse-mounted buffalo hunters. They lived in tepees, kept large numbers of horses, followed the buffalo herds, raided other Indians, and often joined the Comanches in their strikes against Texans, the "civilized" Indians in Indian Territory, and the settlers be-ginning to straggle into Kansas. Not all was warfare, as the Kiowas cele-brated a summer Sun Dance and often traded with the Comancheros out of New Mexico, as well as traders from Indian Territory, Texas, and the United States.[31]

Physically, the Kiowas have been described as dark-skinned, short, stocky, and barrel-chested as well as tall, erect, and graceful. Men wore deer hide breechcloths and moccasins, while women wore deerskin skirts and tall moccasins. In winter, men and women alike changed to cold weather gear made of buffalo hides. By the mid-nineteenth century cotton and woolen clothing was becoming more common among the Plains Indi-ans, so while buckskin was the norm, a man might wear a cotton shirt and a woman a woolen skirt or blouse. Kiowas decorated their clothing and horses, particularly with silver. Men wore their hair long, though some cut the right side to accent the length of the left side. Women braided theirs into pigtails. Kiowa society was certainly slanted toward the men if not outright patrilineal. Men held the band's political positions, and parents showered much time and attention on their sons, much more than on their daughters. The favorite son received the most attention. Fathers spent vast quantities of resources trying to advance the reputations of their sons by giving feasts in their honor or buying powerful names for them from warriors too old to go into battle. As with other Plains Indians, young Kiowa men sought status and power, and one way to do this was through the buffalo hide trade. Polygamy, normally only available to the most prestigious of men, expanded as even common men wanted additional wives to process buffalo robes. A Kiowa man normally married the sisters of his first wife, the thinking being that sisters knew each other, got along better, and so were less inclined to jealousy. When a female captive was thrown into the mix, someone with no kinship ties, then the jealousies were aroused. The sister-wives might bedevil her incessantly with insults and beatings, making her life nearly intolerable.[32]

The best way for a man to make a name for himself was through being a warrior, and Kiowa society was specially geared toward warriors. Men normally belonged to one of six dog soldier societies, which cut across all Kiowa bands. All young men first became a member of the Polanyup, or Rabbits. Some men might remain Rabbits all their lives, and if they did it did not reflect badly on their bravery. But most Kiowas eventually joined one of the five other societies. They usually went next to the Adaltoyuo, or Young Sheep; then the Taupeko, or Skunkberry People. Finally, as they got older, more mature, and more accomplished, they might move on to the others, which were the Tsentanmo, or Horse Headdresses; the Tonkonko, or Black Legs; and finally, the Kaitsenko, or Real Dogs. The Kaitsenko society, the most prestigious of all, was limited to only ten men. Its members were the most notable and bravest of the Kiowas and were distinguished by wearing a red sash of painted deerskin. The Kiowa-Apaches had three soldier societies: the Big Horse, the Raven, and the Swift Fox. While most men gradually earned their way out of the Rabbits and Young Sheep, some powerful fathers gave gifts and provided feasts in order to "buy" their son's entry into the more prestigious societies.[33]

Dog soldiers served in many capacities. They coordinated buffalo hunts and made sure hunters did not prematurely chase the game away. They served as scouts, guards, pickets, and camp police. They not only led raids but also disciplined individuals who had done something detrimental to the well being of the band, such as raiding in an unauthorized area.

Soldier societies made men close, but a Kiowa man might also have a very close personal friend and companion, a sort of "blood brother," with whom he would have a lifelong relationship.[34]

Theoretically, any man, as long as he displayed bravery, fortitude, generosity, and wisdom, might rise to become a member of the Kaitsenko society. He could also aspire to become a band chief, even a principal chief and spokesman for the entire Kiowa people. But Kiowa society was not particularly democratic or egalitarian. It did not possess classes, per se, but ranks. The highest, with the smallest number of members, was the Onde, whose members were seen as the superior rank. It comprised the greatest warriors, important shamans, and often the wealthiest men, though wealth was not a requirement for membership. Men and women could achieve the rank of Onde but membership was also hereditary. Children could be born an Onde, and Onde families were expected to provide most Kiowa political leaders. A person might fall out of this rank by meanness, cruelty, or lying, but never through the loss of wealth. Most Kiowas belonged to the second rank, the Ondegup'a, which might be considered a sort of middle class. These were men and women of secondary honors, including those who might be on the move up toward Onde rank. The Kaan, made up of the poor people with few honors or wealth, was almost as large as the Ondegup'a. The last rank was the Dapom; here were lumped the incorrigibles, outsiders, and misfits. These ranks were not rigid, as a brave and successful warrior strove to become a member of the higher ranks and often did so. For a person to be born a Kaan but end up an Onde or for a high-ranking man to fall from grace and wind up a Dapom was not uncommon.[35]

Counterbalancing their renown as warriors were the Kiowas' strong spiritual and artistic qualities. Ten sacred medicine bundles, handed down from Sun Boy, the creator of the Kiowa people, were entrusted to various families. All together these bundles formed the collective spiritual force and identity of the Kiowas. The bundles were very powerful and wherever one sat was sacred. It was forbidden to commit violence, even argue, in front of one. Bundle-keepers, who could be either men or women, might be called upon to mediate arguments between people, families, or bands. The most important bundle was the *tai-me*, which was used during the Sun Dance, the most sacred ceremony of the Kiowas. Held in late spring or early summer, the Sun Dance brought the Kiowas together, reinforced their identity, and focused on regeneration of the buffalo. A Sun Dance pole in the center of a Sun Dance lodge formed the center of the earth around which the Kiowa danced and performed ceremonies. Sun Dance time was also the time when family members were reunited, old acquaintances were renewed, and young men and women courted. In the early nineteenth century the Kiowas also kept a calendar of years painted on a buffalo hide. It recorded the events most important to the Kiowas that year. Rarely dealing with warfare, it recounted Sun Dances or more ethereal things, such as the meteor shower designating 1833 as "the year of the falling stars." That was also the year the Osages massacred a band of Kiowas and stole the tai-me, which the Kiowas did not get back for a few years. While the calendar is informative, it is also a work of art. Kiowa artists would go on to distinguish themselves in the twentieth century, and some, such as James Auchiah, Spencer Asah, Jack Hokeah, Stephen Mopope, Monroe Tsatoke, and Lois Bougetah Smoky, would achieve international fame.[36]

For the Kiowa, Comanche, and Wichita man, everything—horses, buffalo hide production, status, wealth, additional wives, social rank, political power—stemmed from raiding. And the opportunities for such seemed increasingly endless. While the settlements in Texas and the Chickasaws in Indian Territory were attractive, other targets were also making their way onto the Southern Plains. Bands of fur trappers began crossing the comanchería as early as the 1820s to search for beavers in the mountains of New Mexico. The 1820s also saw long caravans of wagons loaded with rich merchandise squeaking across the Santa Fe Trail, which cut directly through Comanche and Kiowa territory. In 1833 Charles Bent, William Bent, and Ceran St. Vrain built Bent's Fort near the confluence of the Arkansas and Purgatory Rivers in present-day Colorado. Located on one of the legs of the Santa Fe Trail, it drew trappers, traders, and Indians, and sat on the margins of lands claimed by the Comanches, Kiowas, and Cheyennes. The U.S. government sent army expeditions up the Red and Arkansas Rivers to map the area, discover resources, and locate places to lay a transcontinental railroad. The early 1840s also saw the beginning of the great migration of American settlers across the overland trails. The famous Oregon Trail sat at the far northern range of the Kiowas, and the discovery of gold in California in 1848 sent many others across the Southern Plains in an attempt to find a shorter route to wealth. All at a time when the Southern Plains Indians were at their most powerful.

The Indians and these intruders had hundreds, if not thousands, of peaceful encounters in which the parties smoked, talked, exchanged goods, and generally got along just fine. Still, misunderstandings were common. Seeing so much valuable merchandise rolling along before their eyes, young men found it hard to control themselves. Comanches and Kiowas could also be aggressive in their demands for merchandise, frightening greenhorn traders who had never had much experience with Indians. And many traders and settlers, who would not hesitate to pay a toll on a road or ferry, angrily called it extortion when a Comanche band said the traders should give them gifts for traveling through their territory. Many traders and settlers forgot the advice of Josiah Gregg, a Santa Fe Trail trader, who advised that gifts "are an indispensable earnest of friendship from the whites—the essence, the seal of the treaty, without which negotiation is vain." He also pointed out that Indians were "much less hostile to those with whom they trade, than to any other people . . . [and] are generally ready to defend them against every enemy."[37]

Still, violence happened. In 1828, as a band of Comanches peacefully approached a Santa Fe Trail caravan, panicky traders shot first, killing most of the band. From then on, wagon trains increasingly became targets of Comanche and Kiowa attacks, and in 1831 on the Cimarron River, a band of Comanche warriors killed Jedidiah Smith, considered one of the best of the mountain men explorers. While men such as Smith realized the dangers of their work, most of the Santa Fe Trail men were storekeepers, with little Indian experience. As Comanche and Kiowa attacks on their caravans increased, the traders demanded the U.S. government do something to protect them. Texas settlers heartily agreed, and many longed for the day Texas would become a state and be protected by the U.S. Army.[38]

Forts, Reservations, and Indian Removal

Texans got their wish in 1845 when the Lone Star Republic joined the Union. As an independent nation negotiating its own admittance to statehood, Texas retained ownership of all her public lands. This had a direct bearing on the Indians of Texas. Normally the federal government owned all unsold land in its territories and could set aside some tracts for courthouses, schools, military posts, and reservations. At the same time, the United States acknowledged that Indians actually owned land within these territories and used the treaty system to extinguish Indian title and then create smaller reserves for them. Inside the reserves, the Indians supposedly would have guaranteed title to their land and govern themselves as they saw fit as long as they posed no threat to American citizens. Nevertheless, the United States, through treaty clauses, encouraged Indian "civilization" by promising schools, churches, and farming implements. Almost immediately, the federal government found itself caught between Texans' demands to be protected from Indians and their insistence that Indians have no claim to the land. The federal government recognized Indian land ownership and saw treaties as the only legal way to purchase Indian land. As the government viewed it, if Texans wanted peace, then they would have to accept what Sam Houston had long advocated, the right of Indians to claim land in Texas. And Indians would have to accept Texans as Americans, live within certain boundaries, stop raiding, return captives, and gradually settle down and start farming. It was too much to ask of either side.[39]

Nevertheless, the United States sent negotiators to meet with the Indians of North Texas. A decade earlier, in 1835 and 1837, the United States had signed its first treaties with the Comanches, Wichitas, Kiowas, and Kiowa-Apaches in which, the government believed, the Indians recognized the land rights of the Cherokees, Creeks, Choctaws, Chickasaws, and Seminoles in Indian Territory. The few bands of Southern Plains Indians that signed the treaties probably had a different view, and besides, the government had done little to maintain relations with them ever since. Now, in 1846, the federal government hoped to again meet with as many Southern Plains bands as possible. In March at Comanche Peak and then in April at Council Springs near Waco, more than thirty chiefs from the Comanches, Taovayas, Wacos, Kichais, Tonkawas, Caddos, and Kiowa-Apaches met with delegates from the United States and the Cherokees, Creeks, Chickasaws, Seminoles, Delawares, and Kickapoos. In May they finally hammered out a peace treaty in which the Americans believed the Indian chiefs recognized U.S. authority in Texas, promised to stop raiding, and agreed to remain at peace with all Indians who were then at peace with the United States. The Indians were also to give up all their non-Indian captives in exchange for all their people being held captive by Texas. In return, the United States promised to give all the signatory nations ten thousand dollars' worth of presents at some future unnamed date. Blacksmiths, schoolteachers, and preachers would be sent to move them down the white man's road. However, it all came to naught as the U.S. Senate refused to ratify the treaty. And the Southern Plains Indians, not understanding the American ratification process, grew angry over the government's reneging on the promised presents. So the Comanches, along with their Taovaya and Kiowa allies, continued raiding into Texas and along the Santa Fe Trail.[40]

The Mexican-American War, which had broken out while the Council Springs negotiations were under way, brought a bustle of activity to the new state. Army units and volunteer detachments from across the United States flooded into Texas. U.S. troops bivouacked at Bent's Fort in preparation for an attack on Santa Fe, while General Zachary Taylor's men pushed across the Rio Grande and drove the Mexican army south. The State of Texas, wanting to keep the Comanches, Kiowas, and Wichitas out of the war, sent quantities of goods to the Indians who waited impatiently for the promised treaty annuities. And for the most part, except for the normal raids and thefts, the Indians of Texas had little effect on the war. With victory and the acquisition of New Mexico and California, the United States now paid much closer attention to the Southern Plains. Also, Texans now had votes and representatives in Congress. So to protect its constituents, in 1849 the U.S. government began building a barrier of forts across Texas.

By 1854 more than twenty forts guarded the line of settlement, stretching from Fort Belknap and Fort Worth on the upper Brazos and Trinity Rivers in the north to Fort Brown and Ringgold Barracks on the Rio Grande to Fort Davis and Fort Bliss in far West Texas. Over the next forty years, some of the forts were abandoned as the line of settlement moved past them while newer ones were created to provide additional protection. These forts normally held company-size detachments of cavalry, infantry, and artillery. Prior to the Civil War, the government also utilized units of dragoons and mounted rifles, and for a year financed units of Texas Mounted Volunteers. So whenever Indians raided inside of Texas, they might be pursed, at one time or another, by informal posses of citizens, companies of Texas Mounted Volunteers, the Texas Rangers, units of the U.S. Army, and, of course, other Indians, who might be their traditional enemies or serving with the Rangers or army as scouts and auxiliaries.[41]

Between 1849 when government troops were first stationed in Texas and 1881 when the cavalry helped chase Victorio's Apaches into Mexico bringing an end to the Indian Wars on the Southern Plains, army troops in Texas fought 219 engagements with various Indian peoples. In reality, there were many more than 219 Indian attacks during these years; this number only counts actions that involved U.S. troops and does not include Indian raids or engagements between the Indians and the Texas Rangers or civilian volunteers. Nor does it take into account the Civil War years of 1861 to 1865 when U.S. troops were not in Texas. Between 1849 and 1861, the army fought 84 battles with Indians; between 1866 and 1881, it fought 135. The great majority of these battles, 58 percent, were with the Comanches and Kiowas, a third were with Lipan and other Apaches, while just over 10 percent involved Tonkawas, Kickapoos, Cheyennes, Wichitas, and other Indians. In all, the commissioner of Indian Affairs calculated that from 1812 to 1889, the Comanches alone committed 1,031 "depredations," the Apaches 759, and the Kiowas 310 for a total of about $8 million in damages. Of course, not all these raids were made against Texans. Nevertheless, from these Texas forts, detachments numbering from just a few troopers to companies of more than eighty men tried to chase down Indian raiding parties. There were only a few truly major battles in which scores of men on both side slugged it out, and the majority of these came after the Civil War. Most engagements were unorganized running skirmishes in which a few troopers caught up with Indian raiders or encountered them while on patrol.[42]

Along with forts and army patrols, the United States again turned to treaties to help stop the raids. In December, 1850, to make up for the failed 1846 treaty, the government managed to sign a new treaty with the Penetaka Comanches, Lipan Apaches, Caddos, Quapaws, Tawakonis, and Wacos, and reaffirmed it the next year. The Indians promised not to ride south of the Llano River without the army's permission. Essentially these were efforts to bring an end to raids and to ensure the return of captives, runaway slaves, and stolen horses. However, the same recurring problems arose. Hotheaded young men on both sides refused to listen to their leaders. Other Indian bands that had not signed the treaty were not bound by it. And the least violation by either side seemingly negated the whole thing.[43]

While the United States alternately battled and treated with the Southern Plains Indians, it also tried to do something about those Texas Indians without a home to call their own. In 1854 Texas was persuaded to pass the Ysleta Relief Act, which recognized the land claims of the Tigua Indians near El Paso. However, most government attention focused on the remnants of those Indians pushed out of East Texas after the Cherokee War. Also in 1854, after much pressure from the federal government, the State of Texas finally agreed to create two reserves. The Clear Fork, or Upper Reserve, on the Clear Fork of the Brazos in Throckmorton County, would be home for bands of Penetaka Comanches who were willing to try their hand at farming. The Brazos, or Lower Reserve, on the Main Fork of the Brazos in Young County, was for the remnants of the Caddos, Anadarkos, Hainais, Delawares, Shawnees, the handful of remaining Cherokee and Choctaw families in Texas, and a few bands of Tonkawas, Bidais, Tawakonis, and Wacos. Most of these farming communities welcomed the reserves as it would guarantee them land and, they hoped, protect them from Texas settlers and outlaws. They were fortunate that the United States appointed Robert Simpson Neighbors, a capable and sympathetic man, as Indian agent. Still, many Indians avoided the reserves. Several Tonkawa bands moved south to Mexico and joined with the Lipan Apaches there, while a few remained in their haunts across South Central Texas. And thousands of Comanches, Kiowas, Taovayas, Wichitas, Kichais, Wacos, Apaches, and Tonkawas still roamed free across the Southern Plains.[44]

For the farming Indians, the Brazos Reserve proved a boon. Leaders

such as Jim Pockmark and Caddo John of the Cadodachos, José María of
the Anadarkos, Toshaquash of the Wichitas, Tawakoni Jim of the Tawakonis, Jim Linney of the Shawnees, and Jim Ned of the Delawares urged their
people to settle down and return to village life. They did, but now there
was an American flavor to it. Soon, to the delight of Neighbors and other
officials, the Indians of the Brazos Reserve constructed cabins, dressed in
modern American clothing, and rode in wagons and buggies when they
went to town. They sent their children to the reservation school, farmed
huge fields of corn, and raised good-size herds of horses and cattle. To their
American guardians, the Brazos Reserve Indians seemed well on their way
to being "civilized."[45]

The Penetaka Comanches on the Clear Fork Reserve never possessed a
tradition of farming, so reservation life proved more difficult for them. Un-
used to permanent villages and reservation boundaries, many Penetakas
continued hunting buffalo off the reserve. More dangerous was that some
of the young men, just as hungry for status as ever, periodically left to go
live with other Comanche divisions. Once with their off-reservation kin,
they might participate in raids and then return home to Clear Fork, leaving a visible trail behind them. Comanche raiding parties striking deep
into Texas might also rest and regroup among their Clear Fork kin. Nevertheless, things looked promising as most Indian peoples on both reserves
proved to be good, peaceful residents, willing to help Texas ranchers find
lost stock, act as hunting guides, or provide contingents of warriors to
serve with the Rangers or the army as scouts against other Comanche, Wichita, and Kiowa bands.[46]

One of the hardest things for non-Indians to grasp is that Indians
served alongside army and Ranger detachments against other Indians.
Indians were not one homogenous "race," but many different nations,
bands, and peoples, often with different agendas. For the Indians of the
more settled Brazos Reserve, serving as scouts and auxiliaries allowed
them to battle as they once had. Men had always fought, it was almost second nature, and scouting was a way to gain horses, goods, and status. So
while Cadodachos, Anadarkos, Ionies, Delawares, Shawnees, and others
normally had peaceful relations with the Comanches and Kiowas, they
had lost enough horses and goods to Comanche raiders not to feel too
much compunction about striking back. It also allowed them to show their
friendship to the Texans and Americans, proving that they were no threat
but rather loyal allies. They hoped Texans would recognize this and leave
them in peace on their reserves.

A final reason Indians were willing to aid the army was that by the
1850s diplomatic agendas were once again shifting on the Southern Plains.

As the Creeks, Cherokees, Seminoles, Choctaws, and Chickasaws—collectively known as the Five Civilized Tribes—settled into Indian Territory just north of Texas, they brought with them a different cultural consciousness. Over the years, many citizens of the Five Civilized Tribes had adopted those same American traits now being pushed on the two Texas reserves, such as going to school, speaking English, becoming Christians, and running their farms and ranches for profit. Viewing themselves as "civilized" Indians, though Indians nonetheless, they saw the hunter-gatherer Comanches and Kiowas as dangerous "wild Indians" who needed to become civilized. Influenced by the Five Civilized Tribes, the Indians of the Brazos Reserve began to have the same feelings, seeing the Comanches and Kiowas as different from themselves. The Caddos of the Brazos Reserve began to break their century-and-a-half-long coalition with the Comanches and drifted into the diplomatic and cultural orbit of the Chickasaws and Choctaws. Serving as scouts and auxiliaries with the army was a way of ensuring their own peace and farming lifestyle.[47]

During the late 1850s reserve scouts often got the chance to prove their mettle. Comanches, Kiowas, and Taovaya Wichitas had long realized the benefit of Indian Territory. During the years of the Republic, Indian Territory was a different country and the Red River an international border. Raiding parties could leave their families in comparative safety in southwestern Indian Territory, strike into Texas, and then retreat to their villages beyond the reach of Texas forces. Even after Texas became a state, the United States prohibited Texas forces from crossing into Indian Territory. Nevertheless, in mid-May, 1858, in retaliation for a rash of raids in Texas, many actually made by white outlaws, a contingent of 100 Texas Rangers and 112 Caddo, Shawnee, Tonkawa, and Kichai warriors from the Brazos Reserve under the overall command of Ranger Captain John S. "Rip" Ford rode into Indian Territory. They attacked a Comanche camp on the Canadian River, killing Kotsoteka Comanche chief Pohebits Quasho, better known as Iron Jacket, and 75 other Comanches. They also took 300 horses, and captured 18 women and children.[48]

The raid enraged the Comanches, who stepped up their attacks into Texas and Indian Territory to replenish their lost horses. Throughout the summer, government officials in Indian Territory tried to placate the Comanches and bring their counterraids to an end. Peace efforts bore fruit and in late September, 1858, at the behest of the government, a large band of Comanches arrived at the Taovaya village located near present-day Rush Spring, Oklahoma, for a council and to return stolen horses. As the peace council was getting underway, on October 1, the U.S. Second Cavalry, then stationed in Texas under the command of Brevet Major Earl Van

Dorn, along with 135 Tawakoni, Waco, Caddo, Tonkawa, and Delaware scouts attacked the Comanche and the Taovaya village. They killed 56 Comanche warriors, wounded an untold number, captured another 300 horses, burned 120 lodges, and destroyed the Comanches' entire supply of ammunition, cooking utensils, clothing, dressed hides, corn, and other food stores. Once again, this threw the Southern Plains into turmoil. Thinking they had been lured into a trap, Comanches blamed the Taovayas and the raids began all over again, which resulted in another attack by the Second Cavalry on Comanche villages at Crooked Creek in southeastern Kansas in May, 1859.[49]

Though the Brazos Reserve Indians acquitted themselves bravely in all their battles and earned the praise of such notable Rangers as Rip Ford and Sul Ross, nearby settlers would have nothing of it. They cast a suspicious eye on the two reserves, certain that it was the Reserve Indians who had been doing the raiding, no matter what Rip Ford said. Willing to believe the worst about their Indian neighbors and unwilling to accept Indian land ownership, the settlers insisted the Indians be removed. Ignoring the law, some Texas families built farms and ranches inside the reserve boundaries and had to be removed time and again by Agent Neighbors and army troops. Neighbors' assurances that the Indians were good, even useful, citizens fell on deaf ears; Texans blamed the Reserve Indians for any raid, kidnapping, killing, or horse theft committed in the vicinity. Mobs often patrolled the reserve boundaries, stealing Indian stock and murdering individual Caddos, Wichitas, and others caught out alone.[50]

By early May, 1859, the situation had become intolerable as a mob raided the Brazos Reserve and murdered several peaceful Caddos. On May 23 John R. Baylor and a rabble of 250 white settlers again invaded the Brazos Reserve with the intention of exterminating all the Indians. This touched off a skirmish, in which several Caddos were killed, that was only stopped by the intervention of troops from nearby forts. Agent Neighbors realized that Texans would never allow these Indians to live in peace and would, in all probability, eventually massacre them. Fearing for the safety of his charges, in the summer of 1859 Neighbors packed up the Indians of both reserves and led them north across the Red River to Indian Territory. On their own Trail of Tears, the Caddos, Wichitas, Tonkawas, and Peneteka Comanches, all Indians who had called Texas home for hundreds, even thousands of years, found themselves driven from the state. Abandoning farms, tools, and livestock, they took only what they could carry in a few wagons. For the Shawnees and Delawares it was a second exodus. In Indian Territory, the government leased land from the Choctaws and Chickasaws and created the Wichita and Affiliated Tribes Reservation, headquartered at Fort Cobb in the western part of Indian Territory. Agent Neighbors, having successfully completed his rescue mission, returned to Texas where members of a white gang, incensed that he had not allowed them to kill the Indians, murdered him by shooting him in the back with a shotgun.[51]

The removal of the Clear Fork and Brazos Reserve Indians was the culmination of the process begun by Mirabeau Lamar some twenty years earlier. By 1860 Texas found itself virtually denuded of Indian peoples, both native and immigrant. The Coahuiltecans, Jumanos, and Karankawas had been wiped out, absorbed by other Indian cultures, or hispanized to such a point that most observers viewed them as Mexican peasants. The Tiguas at El Paso, at least on the surface, appeared to be moving in the same direction. What few Atakapas remained had been pushed into Louisiana. The Bidais were being pulled into the Caddos, while the Caddos, Wichitas, and Tonkawas, all of whom considered themselves native to Texas, had been driven north to Indian Territory. Virtually all immigrant Indians who had come to Texas in the late eighteenth and early nineteenth century had also been expelled. Most Cherokees, Choctaws, Chickasaws, Shawnees, Delawares, and Kickapoos had been forced out of East Texas after the Cherokee War of 1839; the few individuals who remained left Texas with the Reserve Indians in 1859.

By 1860 the only Indian reserve recognized by the State of Texas was that of the Alabama-Coushatta Indians, who remained despite pressure to remove with the Reserve Indians. While the Alabama-Coushattas and Tiguas constituted the only settled Indian peoples still living in Texas, the Comanches, Kiowas, and Kiowa-Apaches, as well as the Taovaya and Yscani Wichitas still roamed the Llano Estacado and still used Texas trails as thoroughfares on their way to raid into Mexico or strike at the ever westward-moving line of Texas settlement. Some of the removed Indians in Indian Territory, the Kickapoos and Seminoles particularly, often entered Texas on their way to Mexico. Mass migration of settlers to the American West after the Civil War would bring a showdown between the Southern Plains Indians and the U.S. government.

Chapter 9

Conquered

THE INDIANS of the now-defunct Brazos and Clear Fork reserves barely had time to get settled in southwestern Indian Territory before the Civil War thundered to life. The withdrawal of U.S. troops from forts in Texas and Indian Territory left the line of white settlement unprotected. Frightened settlers, who earlier had demanded the extermination of the Reserve Indians, now begged them to ally with Texas and serve as a buffer against both Comanches and Union forces. By late 1861 Texas and Confederate diplomats were fanning out to Indian villages and soon the Indians found themselves just as divided as the United States. Among the Five Civilized Tribes, the Choctaws and Chickasaws, closest to Texas and with many of their leaders slave owners as well, sided almost wholly with the South. The Cherokees, Creeks, and Seminoles split and engaged in their own bloody civil war, with some factions remaining loyal to the Union and others to the Confederacy. Many of the wealthier pro-Confederate Indians moved their families, livestock, and slaves to North Texas, which they hoped would be out of reach of Union raiding parties. Down in Texas, a few Alabama-Coushattas served briefly with the 24th Texas Cavalry but by late 1862 had left the service and returned to their homes in East Texas.[1]

The former Brazos Reserve Indians, now on the Wichita Reservation in Indian Territory, also split. Some Caddo and Wichita bands went to

Union-held Kansas. Others moved farther west, willing to brave the plains, the Comanches, and the Kiowas to get away from the war. A large faction stayed put and sided with the South, especially when their Indian agent, Matthew Leeper, accepted a commission in the Confederate Army. The turmoil of the war years provided an opportunity for old enemies to even old scores. On October 23, 1862, a large band of Indians attacked the Confederate-allied Wichita Agency. They burned the agency headquarters, killed some Confederate officials, but concentrated mainly on the Tonkawas, killing Chief Placido and about a hundred of his people. The Wichitas, Caddos and other Indians at the agency scattered. No one could say exactly what instigated the Tonkawa Massacre, as it has come to be called. Some said it was an attack by pro-Confederate Wichitas, Comanches, Shawnees, and Delawares on the pro-Union Tonkawas. The Wichitas and Comanches blamed the Shawnees and Delawares, saying they were taking revenge for Tonkawa cannibalism. Others said it was a Union attack on the Wichita Reservation and the Tonkawas just happened to be in the way. Whatever the reason for the attack, the few surviving Tonkawas fled back to Texas, settling around Fort Belknap, not far from their old reserve at Clear Fork. There they served as scouts for Confederate Texas forces. Only years after the Civil War, would the government step in and provide a reservation for the Tonkawas in the northern part of Indian Territory, well away from their old Texas Indian neighbors.[2]

In Texas, the Civil War brought more raids and violence. Comanches, Kiowas, Kiowa-Apaches, Kickapoos, and others, their supplies of manufactured goods severely curtailed by the war, stepped up their raids into Texas in hopes of replenishing their supplies. For Texans, this could not have come at a worst time as there were fewer people to give chase. Federal troops had been withdrawn to Union territory, while the Confederacy stripped Texas of many of its fighting men, leaving fewer Ranger companies, most of these undermanned. With raids on the increase, the line of settlement halted its westward march and even backtracked about a 150 miles. Nevertheless, Ranger companies, such as those led by Sul Ross, attacked as they always had. Ross's company had attacked a Comanche camp in December, 1860, and come away with Cynthia Ann Parker, who had been taken by the Comanches in 1836. By this time, Cynthia Ann had become a Comanche. She spoke no English, had a Comanche husband and family, and was the mother of the soon-to-be-famous Comanche chief Quanah Parker. So for the second time in her life, she was stolen away from her family. Brokenhearted, she did not live long after.[3]

Mexican Kickapoos and Seminoles

While Comanches, Kiowas, and Kiowa-Apaches struck from the north, Kickapoos out of Mexico raided across South Texas. Kickapoos were immigrant Indians, a band of which had settled in East Texas in the early nineteenth century. After the Kickapoo War of October, 1838, most Texas Kickapoos moved beyond the line of settlement or to Indian Territory. However, a small band of about eighty immigrated to northern Mexico and settled around the town of Morelos in the State of Coahuila. Mexico warmly welcomed these Kickapoos and soon the men were serving as scouts and auxiliaries for the Mexican army in their pursuit of Comanches, Kiowas, and Apaches.[4]

In 1849 the number of Mexican Kickapoos increased with the arrival of Seminole chief Coacoochee and his band. Coacoochee, better known as Wild Cat, had fought the United States during the Seminole Wars. Forced to move to Indian Territory, he wanted as little to do with Americans as possible and so determined to move to Mexico. Many Kickapoos agreed with Wild Cat's assessment of Americans and about 250 Seminoles, Kickapoos, and African Americans decided to join him. The next year, Wild Cat was again recruiting in Indian Territory and convinced another 250 or so to immigrate to Mexico. About half the Kickapoos returned to Indian Territory the next year, however most Mexican Kickapoos and Seminoles were again serving as auxiliaries, turning back raiding parties that crossed into that part of Mexico. Though most Seminoles would eventually return to Indian Territory, the remaining Mexican Kickapoos became so successful in battling Indian raiders that Comanche and Kiowa attacks in Coahuila dropped off considerably.[5] During the 1850s, while Mexican Kickapoos battled Indians south of the Rio Grande, Kickapoos in Indian Territory joined with their Comanche and Kiowa trade partners and heavily raided Texas settlements along the upper Colorado and Brazos Rivers and as far west as the Pecos. In 1858 even the El Paso mail route was threatened and several California-bound immigrant trains in West Texas were attacked.[6]

Several incidents during the Civil War served to increase Kickapoo raids. As the Civil War divided the Kickapoos and other peoples of Indian Territory, a band of about six hundred Kickapoos under Chief Machemanet decided to immigrate to Mexico in December, 1862. Wanting to avoid Texas settlements, Machemanet's village swung wide into West Texas, but in Tom Green County near present-day Knickerbocker, a Confederate patrol spied the Indian horse herd, shot down three Kickapoo peace emissaries, and attacked the immigrants. The Kickapoos held their ground, retook their horses, and sent the patrol reeling, with sixteen cavalrymen shot out of their saddles. The Kickapoos resumed their journey and joined their kinspeople in Mexico. Word of Machemanet's village's prosperity soon reached the remaining Kickapoos in Kansas and Indian Territory, and in September, 1864, seven hundred Kickapoos under Chiefs Pecan, Papequah, and Nokoaht began their own migration to Mexico. As before, they swung wide to avoid Texas settlements. However, on January 8, 1865, while camping on Dove Creek near present-day Mertzon, they were attacked by a detachment of Confederate scouts and militia. Once again, the well-armed Kickapoos held fast and aimed a devastating fire on the charging Confederates. In an all-day fight, the Texas Confederates had twenty-six men killed, sixty wounded, and sixty-six horses killed. The survivors barely managed to escape during the night, while the victorious Kickapoos, losing a total of fifteen warriors, continued their move into Mexico. Once there and settled, the Kickapoos determined to take revenge on Texas for twice attacking peaceful migration parties.[7]

During the next two decades, the Mexican Kickapoos certainly took their retribution. Over the years, as the Mexican Kickapoos battled Comanche, Kiowa, and Apache raiding parties, a benefit had been the horses, mules, and goods they acquired in battle. These items found ready markets in Mexico and brought prosperity to the Kickapoos. After the Civil War, as raiders struck less frequently into northern Mexico, the Kickapoos were deprived of these commodities. While supplies dwindled, the demand remained; so to acquire the ever-wanted horses and goods, the Kickapoos began raiding ranches and farms on the Texas side of the Rio Grande. A great semicircle, curving from Laredo in the south up to San Antonio and then west to Terrell County, became the Mexico Kickapoos' area of operations. Atacosa County, just south of San Antonio, became a favorite raiding ground. South Texans demanded protection, claiming the Kickapoos were much worse than the Comanches and Kiowas North Texans faced. A government commission investigating the Kickapoo raids in 1872 calculated that between 1865 and 1872, Kickapoo raiders had taken five hundred thousand head of cattle and fourteen thousand horses, most making their way to markets in Mexico. No count was given of the number of women and children taken captive nor the number of ranches burned and men killed.[8]

Finally, in 1873, the government ordered Colonel Ranald S. Mackenzie and the U.S. Fourth Cavalry to deal with the problem. Mackenzie and his four hundred men rode into Mexico without Mexican permission and on May 18, while the Kickapoo warriors were away hunting, attacked their village at Remolina. Though the women, children, and old men fought back as best they could, the Fourth burned the village and supplies and killed an untold number of Indians. They also took forty women and children captives, who were quickly herded up to Fort Gibson, in the northeastern part of Indian Territory.[9]

Mackenzie's raid had the desired effect, rapidly pushing along the Kickapoo removal plan the government had sought. Authorities believed the best way to stop Kickapoo raids was to get them to return to the United States and take a reservation in Indian Territory. Several approaches had been made but each had been rebuffed. With some of their villages destroyed, the realization that the United States would cross into Mexico if need be, and the knowledge that forty of their kinspeople were being held in Indian Territory, many Kickapoos agreed to return to the United States. In August, 1873, 317 Mexican Kickapoos moved back to Indian Territory, reaching Fort Sill in late December. The next year they were assigned a reservation in the central part of Indian Territory, just east of present-day Oklahoma City. In 1875 another 114 Kickapoos returned from Mexico, leaving about 100 Kickapoos along the Mexico-Texas border. Many of their descendants still live in Mexico, but a few crossed the Rio Grande and settled around Eagle Pass, where they became the Texas Band of Kickapoo Indians and remain there to this day. While Mexican and Texas bands of Kickapoos sporadically raided into Texas over the next few years, counterattacks by U.S. cavalry had the desired effect, and by 1880 the Kickapoos had ceased being a threat to Texas.[10]

Raids and Reservations

The Civil War provided opportunities for Kickapoo raids into Texas, and it did the same for the Comanches, Kiowas, and Kiowa-Apaches, who seemed to grow ever more powerful. By 1864 they threatened the Santa Fe Trail, the supply route to Union-held New Mexico. To protect the trail, on November 25, 1864, Union colonel Kit Carson and his New Mexico Volunteers attacked a series of Comanche, Kiowa, and Kiowa-Apache camps near Adobe Walls. These were the ruins of an old Bent–St. Vrain trading post built in 1840 on the Canadian River in the Texas Panhandle. Though Carson's men managed to destroy one Indian camp, unexpectedly strong resistance from the Indians forced the troops to retreat to New Mexico, barely getting away with their lives. Though the battle secured the trail, it did not deter Comanche and Kiowa raids on Texas farms and ranches.[11]

Four days after Kit Carson's attack, not far to the northwest at Sand Creek in southeastern Colorado, the Colorado militia attacked Chief Black

Kettle's peaceful Cheyenne village, killing and scalping well over a hundred Indian men, women, and children. The Sand Creek Massacre shocked both the eastern establishment and Washington officials. When the Civil War ended five months later, Congress turned its attention to the Plains Indians and determined to bring about what they hoped would be a lasting peace. In October, 1865, government representatives met with various Comanche, Kiowa, Kiowa-Apache, Cheyenne, and Arapaho chiefs in Kansas. After several days of negotiations, feasts, exchange of presents, and the restoration of captives, they hammered out the Treaty of the Little Arkansas River. Essentially, the treaty provided for the Comanches and Kiowas to receive virtually all the Texas Panhandle and western Oklahoma as a reservation. Even better, they could hunt outside the reservation boundaries, south of the Arkansas River until the buffalo were gone and the area settled. They would also receive between ten and fifteen dollars per person annually for the next forty years. In return, the Indians were to allow the government to build forts along the Santa Fe Trail and refrain from raiding U.S. citizens and Indians people friendly to them.[12]

While certainly Indian-friendly, the treaty was dead on arrival in Washington. Texans protested bitterly and would have none of it. Similarly, cost-conscious senators severely amended it, making renegotiation virtually impossible. Many individual Kiowas and Comanches also opposed the treaty, refusing to be fenced in or fenced out of lands they had long called home. In the end the treaty was not ratified and raids continued into Texas, with Texans complaining that between May, 1865, and July, 1867, Indians had killed sixty-two people, wounded forty-two, and taken another forty captive.[13]

Help for Texans was not long in coming. With the Civil War over, the U.S. Army now reoccupied Texas forts. Immediately after the war, the United States sent more than fifty thousand troops to Texas, most stationed on the Texas-Mexico border to prevent any spillover from the French invasion of Mexico. Others served on Reconstruction occupation duty. By 1867 their numbers had been reduced to three thousand but with a good number of these now stationed farther west in forts guarding the line of settlement. Texas now hosted the 17th Infantry, 19th (Black) Infantry, 38th (Black) Infantry, 114th (Black) Infantry, 117th (Black) Infantry, 6th Cavalry, and 4th Cavalry. Later would come the famous 9th and 10th (Black) Cavalry. None of these units remained congregated at any one place. They were divided into company-size units, usually of about ninety to one hundred men, and distributed among various forts. For example, the 4th Cavalry was headquartered at Camp Sheridan in San Antonio, where its headquarters and B, C, D, F, L, and M companies remained. But Company A was stationed at Fredericksburg; Company G, at Clinton; Company H, at La Grange; Companies E and P, at Fort Brown; and Company K, at Fort Inge. In time, other units would come and go, but as always, they gave chase whenever raids were made.[14]

Most of these encounters were small unit actions, such as running battles or brief skirmishes, rarely involving more than a score or two of men on either side. And though cavalry troopers and Texas Rangers often served together, there was little love between them. As one soldier believed, the Rangers were far superior to the army in the field but their tendency to "kill every Indian on sight without pardon" made them less civilized than U.S. troops, who "endeavored to kill as few as possible and to capture alive if possible."[15]

As before, the army turned to the reservation Indians for help. Tonkawas from around Fort Griffin, along with Caddos, Wichitas, and Delawares from the Wichita Reservation in southwestern Indian Territory served as scouts and auxiliaries for the Rangers and cavalry. In December, 1866, Toshaway and a few other Penetaka Comanche chiefs, as well as Caddo chiefs George Washington, Tinah, and Jim Pockmark all agreed to serve as scouts. The number and variety of Indian scouts serving with the army grew considerably. By late 1874 one cavalry officer reported his detachment of scouts included Wichitas, Tawakonis, Wacos, Kichais, Caddos, Delawares, Shawnees, Pawnees, Arapahos, and Comanches.[16]

The continued raids, the good example of the Indians of the Wichita Reservation, and the failure of the Little Arkansas treaty made Congress redouble its efforts to get a workable treaty with the Southern Plains Indians. In October, 1867, government negotiators met with various Comanche, Kiowa, Kiowa-Apache, Cheyenne, and Arapaho chiefs at Medicine Lodge Creek in southern Kansas. By this time, many more chiefs were open to the reservation idea. Buffalo on the Southern Plains were fast disappearing, a crippling blow to people for whom it was the staff of life. The attacks and potential attacks by Rangers and cavalry often meant life had to be lived on the run. Hunger, warfare, disease, as well as the steady westward migration by non-Indians made many chiefs realize that times were changing and their people now had to walk a different road. They advocated peace, if at all possible. Twenty Comanche and Kiowa chiefs signed the Treaty of Medicine Lodge Creek, which stipulated peace between their people and the United States. The Indians gave up all claims to lands in Texas and accepted a much smaller reservation between the Red and Washita Rivers in the southwestern part of Indian Territory. They agreed to adopt "civilization" by sending their children to school and becoming farmers. The United States pledged to build the schools and pro-

vide teachers, blacksmiths, carpenters, instructors, clothing, farming implements, and even agricultural instruction. The Comanches, Kiowas, and
Kiowa-Apaches still had the right to hunt on lands south of the Arkansas
River as long as the buffalo ranged there. Their reservation lands were
guaranteed to them, none of which could be taken without approval of
three-fourths of the adult male population. In return, the Indians were to
receive annual clothing distributions as well as twenty-five thousand dollars a year for thirty years, sometimes in cash, sometimes in goods. To ensure the peace, just over a year later in 1868 the government built Fort Sill
almost dead center in the new Comanche-Kiowa reservation.[17]

Just to the north, the former Texas Reserve Indians on the Wichita and
Affiliated Bands' reservation set an example of acculturation. With the end
of the Civil War, scattered bands of Taovayas, Tawakonis, Wacos, Kichais,
Nadacos, Hainais, Cadodachos, and Delawares returned to their reservation and settled down to farming. The Penetaka Comanches of the old
Clear Fork Reserve settled nearby. Now able to live in peace, their lands
guaranteed and their persons protected, the Wichitas and Affiliated Bands,
as they were collectively called, seemed to prosper, growing large crops of
corn and melons, raising small herds of cattle and pigs, even building a
sawmill. Young men might divide their time between hunting, farming,
and scouting for the government. "Progressive" chiefs, such as Guadeloupe and George Washington of the Cadodachos, José Mariá of the Nadacos, Black Beaver of the Delawares, Toshaway and Esahabbe of the Penetaka Comanches, along with Tawakoni Dave and Tawakoni Jim, urged
their people to settle down, send their children to school, and peacefully
walk this white man's road. On the reservation, a curious melding of cultures began taking place. Through proximity and intermarriage, the many
different bands began to form into one. Where there had been Taovayas,
Tawakonis, Yscanis, and Kichais, soon there were only Wichitas. Similarly,
the Cadodachos, Nadacos, and Hainais became collectively known as the
Caddos. While the Indians themselves still recognized traditional bands
and lineages, most non-Indians in Texas and Indian Territory now just saw
Wichitas, Caddos, Delawares, Comanches, Kiowas, and Apaches. Adding
to this melting pot, Wichitas, Delawares, and Caddos sometimes intermarried, as did some whites who settled nearby.[18]

Peace Policy and the Red River War

Of course, not all Comanches, Kiowas, and Kiowa-Apaches wanted to
settle down to farming as the Wichitas and Caddos did. Nor did they accept their "progressive" chiefs' willingness to live on a reservation. Many

chiefs and warriors, particularly younger men, refused to give up the culture and lands they valued. They determined to resist at all costs. The Kwahadi Comanches absolutely refused to settle on the reservation, while other bands might drift on and off at will. Most men still saw raiding as the road to individual status and power. Fueling their fire were failures and missteps by the U.S. government. Despite all its promises of clothes, blankets, and food, government indifference, bureaucratic foul-ups, corrupt contractors, and a primitive transportation system meant that supplies often came late and were usually short and substandard. Food supplies were inadequate, and though the Indians could leave the reservation to hunt for food, the buffalo were quickly disappearing. Already starvation stalked the Comanches and Kiowas. Discontent with the treaty increased as many Indians believed the government only fulfilled those treaty stipulations that worked to its favor. Some chiefs who had signed the treaty, such as the Kiowas Satank and Satanta, now turned against it. By the early 1870s Comanches, Kiowas, even Cheyennes, in search of food, goods, status, and revenge, rode into North Texas, hitting cattle herds, stagecoaches, wagon trains, isolated ranches and farms, and virtually anybody who crossed their path.[19]

President Ulysses S. Grant's "peace policy" did nothing to stop the raids. Looking for scapegoats for the United States' disastrous Indian policy, eastern churchmen pointed to corrupt, spoils-system Indian agents, accusing them of cheating the Indians of their due and so causing much of the conflict. When Grant became president in 1869 he began appointing churchmen and missionaries as Indian agents, which everyone hoped would bring about peace, hence the term "peace policy." The Comanche-Kiowa reservations came under the authority of Quaker missionary Lawrie Tatum. Tatum was honest and his heart was in the right place, but he was naive when it came to Indians. Kiowa chiefs Satank, Satanta, and Big Tree, who had grown up in the rough-and-tumble world of Kiowa politics, easily manipulated Tatum and played to his sensibilities. Comanche and Kiowa raiders found they could strike into Texas and then take refuge back on the reservation in time to receive their share of allotment goods, boasting of their exploits and unpunished by Tatum who wanted to believe the best of everyone. Each successful raid emboldened the young men. They even raided the Fort Sill horse corral as well as that of the agency itself. Army officers fumed over Tatum's reluctance to arrest and punish them. Texans complained loudly, demanding the government do something about the raids stemming from Tatum's slipshod reservation. As one Texan wrote, "Give us Phil Sheridan and send Philanthropy to the devil."[20]

Then, in mid-May, 1871, the Kiowas overplayed their hand. Satanta, old Satank, Big Tree, and more than a hundred other Kiowas rode down into North Texas and set up an ambush on Salt Creek Prairie, along the Fort Richardson road not too far from Jacksboro. A small wagon train appeared that was escorted by a few cavalrymen, but as the Kiowas prepared to attack, the shaman Mamanti urged them to let it go as another, far better wagon train would soon appear. The Kiowas allowed the wagon train to pass. They did not realize that in the train was General William Tecumseh Sherman, general in chief of the United States, who was personally investigating the validity of Texas' complaints. Not long after, as Mamanti predicted, a second train of ten freight wagons loaded with supplies clopped by and the Kiowas attacked. Of the twelve teamsters, five escaped; seven were killed, some tortured to death, all mutilated. The wagons were plundered and burned, and the Kiowa raiding party made off with all the supplies they could carry, as well as forty-one government mules.[21]

Word of the wagon train attack quickly spread. Sherman, now at Fort Sill, was determined to capture the raiders. The Kiowa raiding party returned to the reservation to receive their ration allotments, and when Tatum asked Satanta about the attack, the chief readily admitted it. He had lost three men, so was willing to call it even. Still, he boasted to Tatum, "If any other Indian claims the honor of leading that party he will be lying to you. I led it myself." Tatum now had to forget his Quaker sensitivities. With Satanta's boast as proof, he determined to arrest the leaders of the raiding party. Tatum, Sherman, and Colonel Benjamin Grierson stood on Grierson's porch at Fort Sill; troopers were concealed around the quadrangle and inside the house. When Satanta, Satank, and several other chiefs arrived to "size up" Sherman, the troopers sprang the trap. For a tense moment it was touch and go, but the chiefs surrendered without a shot being fired. Satanta, Satank, and Big Tree were arrested and sent to Texas to stand trial. En route to prison, Satank was killed while trying to escape. But his death seems more like suicide, with the old man not willing to be imprisoned. In Texas, Satanta and Big Tree were tried and sentenced to death. However, public opinion suggested that keeping them in prison might be a better way to end the raids. The idea seemed valid, so Satanta and Big Tree were imprisoned at the Texas State Penitentiary at Huntsville. And it did seem to diminish Kiowa raiding into Texas. Nevertheless, many people, particularly the Five Civilized Tribes in Indian Territory, called for clemency and begged Texas to eventually release the two chiefs.[22]

While the imprisonment of Satanta and Big Tree may have caused the Kiowas to think twice about raiding into Texas, it made little impact on the

Comanches and their strikes continued. Then, on September 29, 1872, up in the Texas Panhandle, Colonel Ranald Mackenzie and his Fourth Cavalry attacked a large village of more than 260 lodges of combined Kwahadis, Kotsotekas, Yamparikas, Noconis, and Penetakas. The Fourth Cavalry killed twenty-four Comanches, burned the village and its utensils, and took 124 women and children captives. These were taken to Fort Sill, essentially hostages to ensure the good behavior of the Comanches. They remained prisoners until June, 1873. During this time, Comanches raids slackened considerably. The women and children were later returned to their families and a few raids took place. Without the women and children in custody, the government tried to tie Comanche behavior to the impending release of Satanta and Big Tree. It demanded that at least five Comanche raiders be turned over for punishment or the Kiowa chiefs would not be released. The Comanches refused and in October, 1873, its bluff called, the government finally released Satanta and Big Tree as it had promised, despite demands from Texans and Sherman himself to keep the two in prison.[23]

The spring of 1874 saw tensions at near breaking points across the Southern Plains. Texans had no illusions about the freeing of Satanta and Big Tree and prepared for more raids. The Comanches and Kiowas were angry. Angry at their chiefs' imprisonment and the short rations; angry about American horse thieves out of Kansas who stole Indian ponies and peddlers selling cheap whiskey to the Indians on credit, often getting them so deeply in debt that they had to forfeit what little cash they received from their annuities. But what really enraged them were the buffalo hunters. In the late 1860s American buffalo hunters armed with high-powered rifles began invading the Great Plains. By 1870 they had wiped out the buffalo on the Central Plains, taking only the hide, maybe the tongue, and leaving the rest to rot. Now they cast greedy eyes toward the few remaining buffalo south of the Arkansas River. By 1874 buffalo were almost impossible for Comanche and Kiowa hunters to find. With government rations often late or short, the reservation Indians began to starve. Ignoring Indian complaints, the government did nothing to stop the buffalo hunters, in fact, some officers encouraged them, realizing that killing off the Plains Indians' main source of food was the best way to defeat them. With the government turning a blind eye, by the summer of 1874, a number of hunters had banded together and were killing off the buffalo in the heart of the Comanche and Kiowa hunting grounds in the Texas Panhandle.[24]

Now many Comanches, Kiowas, and Southern Cheyennes had had enough. On June 27, 1874, about three hundred Comanche and Cheyenne warriors attacked a band of buffalo hunters at Adobe Walls, the site of Kit Carson's fight ten years earlier. And so began the Red River War, the last desperate fight of the Southern Plains Indians to remain free. Not all Comanches, Kiowas, or Southern Cheyennes wanted war or joined it. A good many chiefs and their followers had long recognized that their way of life was changing and so had grudgingly accepted the white man's road. War, they understood, would be a disaster and could not be won. Still, fiery young chiefs, such as Quanah Parker of the Noconi Comanches, who led the attack on the buffalo hunters, and Isatai, a young shaman who urged the war, were determined to try. From the first, the Indians experienced mixed results. The hunters, with their high-powered rifles, held off the Indians for several days, suffering only a few losses, and killing at least fifteen warriors, maybe many more. Nevertheless, the hunters quickly abandoned the area once the Indians withdrew. On July 12, a large party of Kiowas successfully ambushed a troop of Texas Rangers at Lost Valley, west of Jacksboro and not far from where the wagon train had been ambushed three years earlier.[25]

The attacks drove a stake through the heart of President Grant's "peace policy." Those Indians siding with the war factions left the reservation to try to live on the Southern Plains as they once had. Given the okay by Washington, army troops out of Fort Sill marched onto the reservations where they made lists of "friendly" and "hostile" Indians. The friendlies, consisting of a majority of Kiowas, as well as all the Penetaka Comanches and about half the Yamparikas and Noconis, were rounded up and placed on Cache Creek within the reservation boundary. As it always had with Indian peoples, family came first and hostiles were able to take advantage of the confusion. They often slipped in to the friendly area for food and rest. At the same time, hostiles posing as friendlies sometimes left the camp and made raids of their own.[26]

By late August several hostile factions of Comanches and Kiowas, many of whom had participated in the Adobe Walls or Lost Valley fights, settled around the Wichita Agency at Anadarko, using the peaceful Wichitas, Caddos, and Delawares as protection. On August 22, when the army demanded the Comanches and Kiowas give up their weapons, a battle broke out at the Wichita Agency. Over the next two days, a fierce firefight raged. About seven non-Indians were killed; the Comanches and Kiowas lost around fourteen. The agency store was looted, and many of the farms of the peaceful Indians were burned, including that belonging to Delaware chief Black Beaver. Starting a grassfire to cover their retreat, the Comanches and Kiowas made their way to the safety of the breaks of the Red River.[27]

The army was already on the offensive, putting more than five thousand men into the field. Columns out of Kansas, Indian Territory, Texas, and New Mexico all converged on the Texas Panhandle. Once again, the

Wichitas, Caddos, Delawares, and Penetaka Comanches served as scouts and auxiliaries. Though parties of Comanche, Kiowa, and Cheyenne warriors raided ranches and small wagon trains when they could, they soon found themselves on the run, constantly hounded by army detachments and the Indian scouts. On August 30 cavalry under the command of General Nelson Miles defeated a large camp of Cheyennes at the Battle of the Cap Rock on Prairie Town Fork of the Red River. To escape, the Indians burned their lodges, abandoned their camp utensils, and scattered into the scorching Llano Estacado. A month later, on the night of September 28, Colonel Ranald S. Mackenzie's Fourth Cavalry, along with Tonkawa and Seminole scouts, surprised and destroyed a large camp of Comanches, Kiowas, and Cheyennes inside Palo Duro Canyon, just south of present-day Amarillo. Though the Indians only lost three men killed, they were totally routed. Mackenzie captured more than 1,400 Indian horses and the entire camp of tepees and utensils. Understanding the importance of both to the Indians, Mackenzie kept 350 of the horses and mules for his own men and methodically killed the remaining thousand-plus animals. He then destroyed the entire village and its contents.[28]

For the Indians, the loss of so many horses and tepees, as well as winter food and clothing, proved a crushing defeat. Even the elements turned against them. The horrendous 100-plus-degree heat and drought of the summer now gave way to incessant rains and autumn chill. Constantly harried by the army in what has come to be called the "wrinkled hand chase," many cold, wet, hungry, shelterless hostiles opted for reservation life. Slowly, bands of defeated Comanches, Kiowas, and Cheyennes made their way back toward Fort Sill. Blue northers and blizzards of December sent back more until only a few bands remained at war. On February 25, 1875, the last 250 Kiowa holdouts, led by Lone Wolf, surrendered. Finally, on June 2, the last Comanche warriors under Quanah Parker came in, bringing an end not only to the Red River War, but also to the free life the Southern Plains Indians had always known. Seventy-four Comanche, Kiowa, and Cheyenne warriors, some of them not involved in the war at all, were imprisoned for three years at Fort Marion, Florida. Satanta was sent back to the Texas State Penitentiary in Huntsville. Despondent, he committed suicide in March, 1878, by jumping from an upper-story window. Now all Texas Indians were on reservations.[29]

Apache Incursions into West Texas

By the 1870s the Lipan Apaches, whose heyday in Texas had been in the seventeenth century, and the Kiowa-Apaches, who had migrated south with the Kiowas in the late eighteenth century, had largely disappeared from Texas. The Lipans had been pushed ever farther south by the Comanches, and by the 1870s, the Lipans, as a recognized division, had ceased to exist. What few remaining Lipans there were had either integrated with other more numerous Apache bands in New Mexico and Arizona or become hispanized peasants living in northern Mexico. During the latter part of the nineteenth century, when Texans mentioned the name "Apache," most were thinking of the Kiowa-Apaches. The Kiowa-Apaches had been defeated along with the Kiowas and Comanches during the Red River War of 1874–75 and took their place on the reservation around Fort Sill. On the reservation, the Kiowa-Apaches dropped the term "Kiowa" and became known just as the "Apaches," or more specifically, the Apache Tribe of Oklahoma.

Then, in 1881, the very last Indian raids ever made into Texas took place. They came from the Chiricahua Apaches, a band not previously known for venturing into Texas. The Chiricahuas mainly confined their activities to the mountains of southern Arizona, southern New Mexico, and northern Mexico. During the 1870s, as the U.S. government tried to concentrate the many different and often antagonistic divisions of Apaches onto the San Carlos Reservation in Arizona, some Chiricahua leaders, such as Naiche, Geronimo, and Victorio, resisted. Geronimo and Naiche never made it to Texas, at least as warriors, but Victorio and his band of Chiricahuas put a scare in West Texans.

In 1877 the government tried to move Victorio and his band of Chiricahuas and Mescaleros away from Ojo Caliente in central New Mexico to the huge San Carlos Reservation in Arizona. Victorio refused, pointing out that he and his people had been living at Ojo Caliente peacefully for the past decade. When the government insisted, Victorio, an excellent tactician, began raiding into Mexico, New Mexico, and West Texas, mainly in the area between Fort Davis and El Paso. The government ordered two African American cavalry units, the Ninth Cavalry and Tenth Cavalry, to give chase. The Tenth recruited Tigua Indian scouts to lead them. In early 1880 the Tenth Cavalry, which had been moved from Fort Concho to Fort Davis, went after Victorio and found itself being led on a fifteen-hundred–mile wild-goose chase. They returned to Fort Davis in May without ever catching a whiff of Victorio. Sent back on the Apache's trail, the Tenth Cavalry caught up with Victorio's band. On June 11 Tigua scouts and the Tenth Cavalry "buffalo soldiers" slugged it out with the Apaches just west of Valentine. Twenty Apaches and four Tiguas were killed. In August, at Rattlesnake Springs in the Guadeloupe Mountains, the army and Apaches met again in a three-hour battle. Once again, Victorio and his band managed to slip away and headed toward Mexico. In September a detachment of Texas Rangers joined the chase and illegally entered Mexico during their hunt. They also had no luck in catching up with Victorio. As one writer calculated, during fourteen months of raiding in Mexico, New Mexico, and Texas, Victorio's band, "seldom more than seventy-five strong, had taken the lives of more than one thousand whites and Mexicans while eluding three American cavalry regiments, two American infantry regiments, a huge number of Mexican troops, and a contingent of Texas Rangers."[30]

However, Victorio's luck was quickly running out. In October, 1880, he and his people took refuge in a mountainous area of northern Mexico called Tres Castillos. On October 15 a detachment of Chihuahua State Militia managed to surround the band and in an all-day battle defeated the Apaches, killing Victorio and all his warriors. The women and children were taken captive and held in Chihuahua City for the next several years. However, though Victorio was dead, some of his band who had not been at Tres Castillos were roaming far West Texas. In January, 1881, at the Sierra Diablo Mountains of West Texas, the last Indian battle in Texas took place. Tigua Scouts fighting alongside Texas Rangers caught up with the last Apaches and routed them. With this, the Indian wars in Texas came to an end, as did the freedom of any and all Indians who had once called Texas home.[31]

Reservation Life

By 1881 only two small recognized Indian "tribes" remained in Texas: the Alabama-Coushattas, with their tiny reservation in Polk County of East Texas, and the Tiguas near El Paso. In the late 1860s Texas tried to get the federal government to take over administration of the Alabama-Coushattas but nothing came of it and for the next several decades the state virtually ignored the small group of Indians. As for the Tiguas, though Texas had granted them about thirty-six acres of land in 1854, through actions by the Texas legislature and unscrupulous whites, they lost virtually every inch of it. Finally in 1871 the Incorporation Act restored about twenty acres to the Tiguas. The remainder of the nineteenth century saw the Tiguas ignored by the state and federal governments and left to their own devices. None of the other Texas Indians, such as the Comanches, Kiowas, Apaches, Caddos, and Wichitas, lived in Texas anymore. They were on reservations in southwestern Indian Territory.[32]

Defeated and virtually prisoners on their reservations, these Texas Indians in Indian Territory relied on government allotments of cattle, flour,

and clothing, though some did try to plant crops and raise cattle. Many Comanches and Kiowas shrewdly learned how to make do on the white
man's road. The Kiowa-Comanche reservation contained huge expanses
of lush grasslands, excellent for fattening cattle. The Comanches, under
the leadership of Quanah Parker, and the Kiowas to a lesser extent, now
began leasing their lands to Texas cattlemen for cash payments called
"grass money." By 1885 Texas cattlemen were running 75,000 head of cattle
on the Kiowa-Comanche reservation, using 1.5 million acres and paying
only six cents an acre per year. Though less than market value, grass
money did provide about $55,000 a year for the Kiowas, Comanches, and
Apaches. Twice a year the cattlemen distributed the grass money. In the
summer of 1885 the companies paid each Indian on the Kiowa-Comanche
reservation $9.50, all in silver dimes. Many government officials disliked
the idea of the Indians leasing their lands, rather than farming them, so in
1890 the United States declared the cattle leases null and void and ordered
the cattle off the reservation. Making matters worse, whites living near the
reservation often targeted its resources. For example, white settlers often
slipped onto the reservation and stole Indian timber to be used as fence
posts, housing, and firewood. As one settler recalled, a local missionary
had been caught stealing wood by a Kiowa. "White man talk heap Jesus on
Sunday," the Kiowa commented, "and steal Kiowa's wood on Monday." It
got so bad that an Indian police force had to be created to keep white
thieves out of the reservations.[33]

During the twenty-five-odd years of the reservation experience in Indian Territory, the Indians not only had to adjust to farming and ranching but also got "heap Jesus." By the late 1870s Roman Catholic, Presbyterian, Methodist, and Baptist missions had been founded in Anadarko,
Oklahoma, and around Fort Sill, where they experienced varying degrees of success. Although many Indians might have gone to church on
Sunday, most still attended their traditional ceremonies and dances, at
least when they could, as reservation agents normally banned these as
"uncivilized." Quanah Parker, who became the main spokesman for the
Comanche people, and a few Caddo chiefs founded the Native American
Church, which blended traditional Indian beliefs, peyote use, and Christianity. While agents, white churchmen, and even some "progressive" Indians condemned the "peyote road" as mere drug use and a throwback
to tribal days, the adherents advocated a peaceful, harmonious, industrious life, and their ceremonies were always quiet and dignified. The
church spread rapidly and soon had adherents across Indian America. In
1944 the Native American Church received a charter, with its stated pur-
pose to "promote morality, sobriety, industry, charity and right living."

The Native American Church still exists and many American Indian people across the United States are quite active in it. Other religious movements, such as the 1890 Ghost Dance, touched reservation Indians in Indian Territory, but this passed peacefully without causing the bloodshed it brought to the Lakotas at the Battle of Wounded Knee in that year.[34]

Along with religion, the United States also forced American-style education on the Indians. Schools, such as the Riverside Indian School at Anadarko, taught Indian girls and boys domestic and mechanical arts. Besides English, basic reading, writing, and arithmetic, the girls were taught how to sew, cook, and clean. Boys learned how to be farmers or carpenters. Little effort was made to prepare the students for the modern industrial world nor were they given courses that would lead them to universities. Many children were sent to boarding schools far away from their families, such as Rainy Mountain Boarding School near Gotebo, Oklahoma; Chilocco Indian School in northern Oklahoma; Haskell Institute in Lawrence, Kansas; or the most famous of all, Carlisle Indian School in Carlisle, Pennsylvania. At these schools, boys had their hair cut; their old "Indian" clothes were burned; and they were prohibited from speaking their native tongue.[35]

While the government and the churches actively tried to erase traditional Indian culture, the Comanches, Kiowas, Apaches, Wichitas, Caddos, and others also found themselves changing by virtue of the ever-increasing number of Americans around them. White and black storekeepers, teachers, preachers, government officials, cowboys, and ranch hands lived on or around the reservations and came into contact with the Indians in a variety of ways. Many non-Indian men married Indian woman, "squaw men" as they were called. Some of these were loving husbands and from the union came children who lived with a foot in both the Indian and American worlds. Other "squaw men" were opportunists who hoped to get their hands on as much Indian land and resources as they could. Claiming they were now a member of the "tribe," they demanded every benefit they could, but then turned to the U.S. government when tribal governments attempted to control their activities. Indian culture changed rapidly. As Indian women came into contact with white women, dress styles and cooking methods changed. Although some people remained committed to the past, others learned how to walk the white man's road.[36]

Still, by the mid-1880s many government officials and philanthropists believed the Indians were not "civilizing" fast enough. Seeing only reservation poverty and not the community it contained, these "friends of the Indians" felt that communal reservation land was hampering Indian

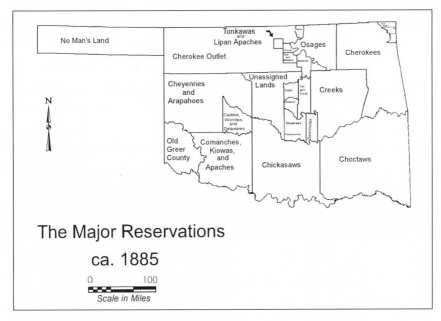

Map 4. The Major Reservations, ca. 1885.

"progress." The key to Indian "civilization" and prosperity, they believed, was to break up the reservations, give each Indian family its own plot of land, teach them to become small farmers, and force them to swim in the ocean of profits and losses. This approach ignored several realities. The Caddos and Wichitas had been successful farmers for hundreds of years and had their own ideas of farming. The Comanches and Kiowas never possessed any form of agriculture nor had any desire to learn how to plow a field. Cattle leasing was rather profitable and more conducive to reservation geography than farming. And finally, small farms in America were on their way out, being replaced by agribusiness, and the United States was fast becoming urban and industrialized. But as Merrill Gates, a "friend of the Indian," saw it: "To bring [the Indian] out of savagery into citizenship we must make the Indian more intelligently selfish before we can make him unselfishly intelligent. We need to awaken in him wants. In his dull savagery he must be touched by the wings of the divine angel of discontent. Then he begins to look forward, to reach out. . . . Discontent . . . is needed to get the Indian out of the blanket and into trousers,—and trousers with a pocket in them, and with a pocket that aches to be filled with dollars!"[37]

So despite almost unanimous protests by the Indians, the U.S. government passed the Dawes Severalty Act of 1887, which would give 160 acres of land to each head of an Indian family and lesser amounts to unmarried or orphaned Indians. Excess land would be sold off by the government, with the proceeds going into Indian accounts to pay for their education and the purchase of stock and farming implements. Most whites, especially land-hungry settlers, small ranchers, railroad companies, and oil companies strongly supported the Dawes Act. Only the big cattle companies of Texas protested, and not because the Dawes Act was bad for the Indians but because they would lose their cattle leases.[38]

Gates said of the Dawes Act, it would be "a mighty pulverizing engine for breaking up the tribal mass."[39] It was. The Dawes Act finally caught up with the Comanches, Kiowas, Apaches, Wichitas, Caddos, and Tonkawas in the 1890s as the Jerome Commission began negotiating the reservation allotment process. In June, 1891, the commission managed to get the Wichitas, Caddos, and Delawares to accept $715,000 for their 574,000-acre reservation, about $1.25 per acre. Congress approved the plan in 1895 and shortly thereafter the reservation was broken up and the Indians began receiving their individual plots of land. In October of that same year, the commission pressured the Tonkawas to give up their 90,000-acre reservation for $30,600 and take individual allotments. In October, 1892, after much arm-twisting, the commission managed to get the Kiowas, Comanches, and Apaches to sell their several-million-acre reservation for $2 million. Congress ratified the agreement in 1900 and the allotment process began soon after. The Tonkawa reservation was thrown open to white settlement first, in September, 1893. A few years later, on August 6, 1901, the surplus land on the Kiowa-Comanche-Apache and the Wichita and Affiliate Bands reservations were sold off to white buyers.[40]

The negotiation and ratification process was not without controversy. According to the 1867 Medicine Lodge Creek Treaty, the government could not take any of the Kiowa-Comanche-Apache reservation without approval of three-fourths of its adult male Indian population. There were grave doubts as to whether three-fourths of the reservation Indians actually approved the Jerome Commission agreement in 1892, but the government ignored these concerns. Showing a shrewd understanding of American society, Kiowa chief Lone Wolf filed suit on this point to prevent the allotment from taking place. Lone Wolf v. Hitchcock wound its way through the court system and in 1903, the U.S. Supreme Court rejected Lone Wolf's arguments, ruling that Congress could make any law it wanted for the Indians and was not bound by previous treaties. If Indians had any doubt that they were conquered, the ruling in Lone Wolf v. Hitchcock put those doubts to rest. Before allotment, many reservation Indians had prospered as ranchers by running their cattle on the communal lands. They now found themselves in bad shape, their allotment too small for ranching and the land too poor for small-scale farming. Within just a few years, many Comanches, Caddos, Kiowas, Wichitas, and Apaches had lost their allotments to whites and sunk even deeper into poverty.[41]

Tiguas around El Paso had their own land problems during the last half of the nineteenth century. In 1871 the State of Texas, with the urging of unscrupulous Anglo land speculators, incorporated the Tigua's town of Ysleta. On paper, the new city was the largest in the state at the time—thirty-six square miles. Suddenly, the Tiguas found their property heavily taxed, and when they could not pay it was confiscated and sold to Anglos. Much of their land had been taken from them by 1874 when the incorporation was declared illegal. Just as bad, in 1877 the Tiguas were barred from using the salt beds near the Guadalupe Mountains that had attracted the Jumanos in years past. For centuries the Tiguas, as well as the Jumanos and Pueblos, had gotten their salt from these dry lakebeds. They were considered communal property. Local speculators at El Paso, including Judge Charles Howard, tried to gain control of the salt beds and prohibited the Indians from using them. This began the El Paso Salt War in which the Tiguas and nearby Hispanic settlers rose up and attacked the Anglos, killing five, including Judge Howard. Troops had to be sent in to stop the violence. In the end, the Tiguas still lost access to the salt beds.[42]

By the turn of the twentieth century the Indians of Texas, both those living in and out of the state, had been defeated. It had not taken long, just under 400 years from the time Cabeza de Vaca washed ashore at Galveston; about 180 since Spain established a firm presence in Texas; only 64 years since the Texas Revolution; and a mere 35 since the end of the Civil War. Despite a valiant defense, people who had once fearlessly roamed the Southern Plains and whose lands had stretched from the piney woods of western Louisiana to the Rocky Mountains of New Mexico found themselves confined to tiny reservations or land allotments. Nor were they free to live their lives as they wanted. Traditional religious ceremonies were banned. Certain types of clothing were too. They could not do with their allotment as they saw fit and were even told how they must slaughter cattle. Government officials forcibly interfered in the lives, politics, and religion of these Indians to a degree that other Americans would never have tolerated. Even the education provided for them was secondrate and did not prepare them for the modern, industrialized twentieth century.

Chapter 10

From One Millennium to the Next

F OR MOST American Indians, not just those of Texas, the first four
decades of the twentieth century were days of poverty and sorrow.
Programs by the U.S. government to speed up the assimilation of Indians into American society often worked at cross-purposes and dissolved
ancient institutions while replacing them with nothing. Government
officials put great hope in the allotment process, but it continued unevenly.
Reservations with good lands or near emerging settlement areas were
usually broken up, while others, with worse lands, never were. The Comanches, Kiowas, Apaches, Wichitas, Caddos, and Delawares had their
reservations allotted in the late nineteenth century, whereas the Alabama-
Coushattas of East Texas never did. The Tiguas were not recognized by the
federal government as "Indians," so they had no agent, no real reservation,
nor any assistance and had to scramble to keep their lands from being
taken by El Paso entrepreneurs.

The Indians as a society also found themselves splintering as never before. Children who had been sent to government boarding schools returned home to find themselves caught between two worlds. They could
not climb the ladder in the white world because they were Indian, but they
were distrusted back in their old communities because they were too acculturated. Not being around their people during their formative years,
these students often missed out on important ceremonies and rites-of-

passage and so had a difficult time working within their communities. At the same time, government officials and missionaries, seeing nothing of value in Indian society, pressed Christianity and the "American way" on them. Progressives might find some measure of prosperity, while traditionalists tried to ignore the new ways, even physically separating their families from whites and progressives as much as they could.

At the same time, Congress was often the Indians' worst enemy. The men who created the Dawes Act feared that once Indians got their own allotment of land, they might easily lose them to speculators, farmers, or ranchers. To prevent this, individual Indian allotments were to be held in trust for twenty-five years. However, as whites clamored for more land, Congress created an unofficial distinction between "competent" and "incompetent" Indians. Competent Indians were able to handle their own affairs and so could get title to their lands before the twenty-five-year period was up. Incompetent Indians were not deemed able to handle their affairs and so were turned over to guardians. Often these guardians were nearby prosperous whites who took the opportunity to cheat the Indians out of their lands. Even worse, the Burke Act of 1906 said that incompetent Indians could get title to their lands by going in front of a judge and being declared competent. Under the Burke Act, some Indians, naive in the workings of the white world, found themselves declared competent by crooked judges and soon had their land swindled from them.[1]

Through such maneuvers, Indians, both individually and as a whole, lost tremendous amounts of acreage. By 1934 almost 50 percent of Indians had lost their allotment and were landless. When the allotment process began in 1887, Indians across America owned a total of 138 million acres of land. When allotment ended in 1934 Indians possessed only 48 million acres, and much of this was inferior land, not good for farming. Just as bad, Congress often tried to balance its budget on the backs of the Indians. Appropriations fell when the cost-cutting impulse hit Congress. Schools, medical facilities, and aid in general were often inferior or nonexistent. In 1928, after a three-year investigation of Indian America, the Brookings Institution issued the Meriam Report, which stated that "an overwhelming majority of the Indians are poor, even extremely poor, and they are not adjusted to the economic and social system of the dominant white civilization." It harshly criticized the Bureau of Indian Affairs for providing deplorable healthcare, substandard education, and failed economic programs.[2]

Not until 1934, after the election of President Franklin D. Roosevelt and his appointment of John Collier as commissioner of Indian Affairs, would the allotment process come to an end. In that year, Collier managed to push through Congress his important yet controversial Indian Reorganization Act (IRA). The IRA ended land allotment, kept the remaining reservations intact, returned unsold allotments to the Indians, and tried to increase the Indian land base by purchasing additional tracts. For the Comanches, Kiowas, Apaches, Wichitas and Caddos, their reservations long allotted and surplus lands sold, there would be no new reservations. The IRA also tried to reinstate Indian self-government. Under its provisions and using Bureau of Indian Affairs guidelines, Indians could write a constitution or corporate charter and create a representative government for the "tribe." While a step in the right direction, this was a controversial move. Most Indian people had never lived under a "tribal" government. Indian government, for the most part, had come through bands, villages, or pueblos with allegiance to a leader through kinship or obligations of reciprocity. Leaders rose and fell depending on their success and on how many people still followed them. A single government, complete with executive and legislative branches serving fixed terms, elected by voters, and governing everyone in the whole tribe was rare. Though Indians adjusted their ways to the new governments, kinship and reciprocity were as important as ever and Indian politics, in general, remained as rough-and-tumble as it had always been.[3]

Just as they had served as scouts in the nineteenth century, Texas Indians eagerly joined the United States in its wars of the twentieth and twenty-first centuries. The hope of assimilating Indians meant that they, unlike African Americans, served in integrated units spread throughout the military. While there was some question as to whether the government could legally draft Indians during World War I because they were not considered citizens, many Indians responded to the draft and even more volunteered. When America entered World War I in 1917, half of the adult males of the Alabama-Coushattas volunteered, but only six were accepted by the army. In 1924, in recognition of Indians' exemplary service during the Great War, Congress authorized that all Indians be considered citizens of the United States. Indians also responded to World War II in huge numbers, with more than twenty-five thousand serving in the military. Indians from every remaining Texas Indian nation fought and died during the war. While the marines' Navajo code-talkers in the Pacific are better known, Comanche code-talkers did the same things for the army in Europe.[4]

Unfortunately, stereotypes about Indians being natural warriors with superhuman abilities brought them high casualties. Indians in the infantry often led night patrols or served as point men or runners. Some were sent on dangerous missions time and time again until they were killed. Stereotypes about the Southern Plains Indians remained long after the wars ended. In a salute to its former adversaries, the army named some of its most potent and mobile twenty-first-century weaponry after them, such as Apache helicopter gunships, Comanche attack helicopters, and the Kiowa scout helicopters. War allowed Indian men to express their warrior feelings and gain status as well. It also allowed Indian communities to bring back traditional dances and ceremonies. Warrior songs were written, victory dances danced, and returning soldiers and marines were reintegrated into peaceful society with purification sweats, dances, and songs. Military societies, such as the Kiowa's Black Legs, sprang back to life, and Native American soldiers, sailors, and marines returning from World War II as well as later conflicts in Korea, Vietnam, Lebanon, Grenada, the Persian Gulf, Somalia, Kosovo, Afghanistan, and Iraq often joined them.[5]

More than any other conflict, World War II dramatically affected American Indians. Many people left their reservations and communities for the first time. Large numbers of Indians volunteered for military service. Forty-seven Alabama-Coushattas eventually served during the conflict. In the service, veterans saw the world and its potential. Forced to work shoulder to shoulder with non-Indians, they were exposed to new ways of doing things, and many learned how to work within the white man's system. It was no wonder that numerous veterans took up leadership positions in their communities after the war. Other men and women went to the cities to work in war production factories. They saw what American society had to offer, and those who returned to their communities brought this understanding with them. Some veterans and war plant workers who did return pressed for better education, healthcare, and economic development. Others went on to law school and returned to serve their people as attorneys, particularly in regard to the U.S. government's trust relationship. Indian people's realization of what could be and how to work with government bureaucracy helped bring on an Indian civil rights movement in the 1960s and 1970s.[6]

World War II also brought Indian people together on a massive scale for the first time. Comanches, Kiowas, and Caddos rubbed shoulders with Iroquois, Lakotas, and Navajos. They often discovered that they shared many of the same experiences at the hands of the states and the U.S. government, that they had the same needs and the same dreams. They looked anew at themselves and saw they were descendants of a proud people, with ancient, good traditions. A sense of "Indianness" began to bind people from many different nations and "tribes," and they began to develop a sense of "Indian" as an ethnic category. This pan-Indian consciousness-raising found expression in several ways. One was through the Powwow movement, which is strong to this day. Powwows are gath-

erings of Indians, maybe from one tribe, maybe from many, in which there
are organized singing, dances, honoring ceremonies, speeches, and such.
They are not necessarily religious in nature, though they may be, and often there are contests between dancers. Powwows began as dances honoring returning veterans but soon spread as Indian pride grew along with
the desire to visit and maintain relations with other Indian cultures. Non-
Indians soon discovered powwows, which were seen as particularly "Indian" events, and they began attending them as spectators. This sense of
"Indianness" also helped spur the Indian civil rights movement.[7]

World War II and postwar government policies also changed Indian
settlement patterns by getting them off farms and reservations and into
cities. After the war, many factory workers remained in the cities, while returning veterans often settled in urban areas. Once the war ended, the government actively tried to get Indians to move to urban areas. The Reloca-
tion Program advertised for relocatees, selected a city for them, arranged
transportation, then set up housing and jobs for them. The program even
tried to train relocatees in how to use telephones and alarm clocks. Soon,
for various reasons, including better-paying jobs, hundreds of thousands
of Indians lived in American cities. For some, this move was permanent;
for others, it was a terrible mistake and they quickly moved home. And
some might spend a few months working in the cities each year and then
spend the remainder at home among family. For many, the urban experience was beneficial. They got jobs, hung onto them, prospered, and eventually settled into cities and suburbs. Others found continuing poverty
and squalor. With little education or understanding of the world outside
their communities, Indians were often the first let go in economic down-
turns. Indian ghettos sprang up in some cities, and homelessness and al-
coholism increased. Nevertheless, the remainder of the twentieth century
saw large numbers of Indians migrate to the cities. Comanches, Kiowas,
Apaches, Caddos, Wichitas, Tonkawas, and Delawares made their way to
Oklahoma City or Dallas–Fort Worth. Alabama-Coushattas often went to
Houston and Tiguas to nearby El Paso.[8]

The impact of the Indians' move to the cities cannot be overstated. By
1990 more than 50 percent of all Indian people lived in urban areas. There
the city's melting pot erased a lot of Indian culture. Children of urban immigrants often did not learn their parents' native tongue. Traditions were
lost. Intermarriage between Indians of different tribes as well as with non-
Indians took place. Sometimes their children would not count themselves
as a member of any one Indian tribe. On the other hand, many urban Indian families, even those with a non-Indian parent or spouse, took pride in
their Indian ancestry and tried to retain some part of it. Many families took

pains to visit relatives in their old communities, to maintain and uphold their kinship ties, and to make sure their children understood them as well. Powwows provided a way for urban Indians to retain their "Indianness," and urban Indians are often the staunchest supporters of powwows. Indian centers opened in many major cities to help immigrants adjust to city life. Centers might provide a host of services, including legal help, alcohol and drug abuse programs, and job and housing services. They were also places were urban Indians could congregate, talk, and get to know each other.[9]

The government's so-called termination policy of the 1950s provided the impetus for the Indian civil rights movement. With World War II over, many politicians decided it was time to put an end to the "Indian problem" once and for all. With John Collier out as Commissioner of Indian Affairs, the government returned to its old assimilationist values and now planned to "terminate" its relationship with those Indian tribes it deemed advanced enough to handle it. Essentially, all government assistance and treaty obligations would come to an end. As the government saw it, eventually there would be no more Bureau of Indian Affairs, no more Indian Health Service. Reservations would be absorbed by states, and Indians would become subject to all the same laws and taxes as non-Indians. The federal government was, as one politician put it, getting out of the Indian business. Part of this was hopeful cost cutting. Part was Cold War suspicions, as Indian reservations, with their communal lands, seemed just a little too much like Socialism. And part was the same old good intentions that had long motivated people who wanted to change Indian society. In 1953 the termination policy went into effect.[10]

From the first, termination proved an abject failure and those few tribes "terminated" by the government, such as the Menominee of Wisconsin and the Klamath of Oregon, immediately went into a tailspin. Poor Indians could not pay property taxes suddenly levied on their lands and so lost them to developers. Indian stores and mills, which could not compete with those of their white neighbors, laid off their Indian workers or went out of business. Now the government found it was spending more than ever as homeless, jobless Indians flooded into the cities and onto the welfare rolls. Rather than offering the Indians a hand up to the good life, termination kicked many down into greater poverty and bad health. Almost immediately the government realized it could not completely withdraw its federal responsibility to the Indians. After much criticism by Indians and reformers alike, by 1960 the termination policy had quietly been shelved. But for those Indians who had been terminated, their lands and lives could not always be reassembled.[11]

During the 1960s the U.S. government seemed to finally accept the reality that Indians were always going to be with them. This ushered in a policy of "self-determination," which the government has pretty much followed up to this day. The federal government began to work closely with tribal governments, funneling in money for education, healthcare, welfare, cultural programs, and economic development. Much of this coincided with President Lyndon B. Johnson's Great Society and his war on poverty. The Bureau of Indian Affairs now hired and promoted Indians on a larger scale. By the mid-1960s the post of Commissioner of Indian Affairs was held by an Indian and has been ever since. The courts also now supported Indians. Between 1946 and 1978 the Indian Claims Commission heard more than six hundred suits filed by Indian tribes over land loss and swindles. The Claims Commission ruled in the Indians' favor in a majority of the cases, restoring land when it could, but usually awarding the tribes large sums of money in compensation. Besides the Indian Claims Commission, university-educated Indian lawyers brought suit in lower courts over land and water rights and past abuses and often won. It seemed that the Constitution had finally caught up with the Indians.[12]

While self-determination was certainly a move in the right direction—for once officials were asking Indians what they wanted—the ghosts of allotment, the Indian Reorganization Act, and termination haunted the government. During the mid-1960s young, educated, media-savvy urban Indians, frustrated with Indian poverty, police brutality, and violations of past treaties, began the Red Power movement. Led by the American Indian Movement (AIM), it coincided with similar civil rights movements of African Americans, Hispanics, and women. Members of AIM had a variety of demands. Some wanted the Bureau of Indian Affairs abolished because they said, it corrupted tribal governments with money and favors. Others wanted more cultural and social programs. But at its heart, AIM wanted the government to uphold its treaty obligations. Since so many Indians lived on isolated reservations or were just faces in a crowded city, AIM realized that most Americans could easily overlook the Indians and their problems.[13]

To make Americans realize that Indians were still here and still enduring poverty and repression, they staged media events to hammer home their points. In 1969 Indians took over the abandoned federal prison at Alcatraz in San Francisco Bay and held if for well over a year. In 1972 AIM marched on Washington D.C. in what was called the "Trail of Broken Treaties" and briefly occupied the offices of the Bureau of Indian Affairs. And in 1973 AIM members took over the small hamlet of Wounded Knee on the Lakota's Pine Ridge reservation in South Dakota. The Indians held it for about seventy days in the face of National Guard troops and armored vehicles. Now the government went on the offensive, infiltrating AIM and arresting and trying its leaders. Many AIM leaders spent time in prison. Others were killed under mysterious circumstances. By the late 1970s AIM's power had been broken.[14]

Under self-determination, the federal government recognizes Indian tribes as domestic-dependent nations within states and with certain rights that the states cannot infringe upon. This has benefited most Indians. AIM did draw attention to Indian living conditions and many Americans responded positively. For the remainder of the twentieth century American interest in Indian life and culture was on the upswing. Non-Indians attended powwows in huge numbers, and tourists often visited Indian reservations and historical sites. Indians were quick to take advantage of this tourism. As for major policy changes, most are done through the courts and the Bureau of Indian Affairs rather than through civil disobedience and the takeover of government buildings. For the Indians of Texas, like Indians throughout America, getting through the twentieth century to arrive at self-determination was a struggle.

Texas Indians in Oklahoma

With the allotment and sale of surplus reservation lands, the Texas Indians in Oklahoma—Comanches, Kiowas, Apaches, Wichitas, Caddos, and Tonkawas—now lived as residents on individual plots of lands. For the most part, they remained settled in tight-knit but separate communities. The reservations were gone, and the Kiowas, Comanches, and Apaches resided mainly in Comanche and Kiowa counties, usually separated from each other, with the Kiowas living to the north, the Comanches to south, and the Apaches to the east. Tribal government headquarters were eventually established for each, with the Kiowas' near the town of Carnegie, the Comanches' near Lawton, and the Apaches' south of Anadarko. Wichitas, Caddos, and Delawares kept themselves separate from the Comanches, Kiowas, and Apaches and often from each other. Eventually they created separate tribal headquarters north of the Washita River: the Wichitas just north of Anadarko, the Delawares near Gracemont, and the Caddos farther north near Binger. Completely separate, the few Tonkawas remained in Kay County in north-central Oklahoma.

In the late 1890s and early 1900s, at the behest of the U.S. government, the Kiowas, Comanches, and Apaches formed a joint Business Committee. Despite its name, the Business Committee served as a sort of intertribal government and an intermediary with the United States. Members were elected to the Business Council and initially concerned themselves with adopting outsiders, negotiating per capita payments of land and oil and gas revenues, and hiring lawyers to get back payments of "grass money" and annuities still owed them. The members of the Business Committee were not of all one mind. Comanches and Kiowas often disagreed over policy and the peyote issue split all communities. The Wichitas, Caddos, and Delawares formed a similar entity, while the Tonkawas created a Business Council of their own.[15]

Although Indian people might live in their own separate communities, they could not escape the outside world or each other. Government officials pressured the Indians to become profitable farmers or ranchers and not depend on the government. Missionaries and preachers urged them to become Christians, which many did. Teachers tried to imbue Indian students with American cultural traits. And the sheer number of non-Indians who settled around the Indians meant that many American characteristics rubbed off on them. At the same time, because of their proximity to each other, Indian men and women from various tribes often intermarried. Sometimes Kiowas married Comanches, Wichitas married Caddos, Caddos married Delawares, and some married non-Indians. Of course, newspapers, radios, movies, automobiles, and such had their effect.

Economically, the first four decades of the twentieth century were times of poverty for the Oklahoma Indians. With the break up of the reservations, the government quit providing rations. If this were not bad enough, many Indians, still new to the American economic system, were susceptible to the crooked negotiations of unscrupulous whites and lost their allotments or leased them out for paltry sums. For those who kept their allotments, just as they began turning to farming and stock raising, the bottom dropped out of the market. Farm prices were already falling during the late 1920s, and the Great Depression of the 1930s pushed the Indians into greater poverty. Hunger and illness remained the Indians' constant companions and many suffered from tuberculosis and trachoma. The Indian Health Service tried to improve Indian health by building tuberculosis sanitariums and instituting sanitation programs. Going a step farther, in 1935 the Indian Health Service formed the Kiowa School of Practical Nursing to help train Indian medical personnel.[16]

With the election of Franklin Roosevelt as president in 1933 and his appointment of John Collier as the commissioner of Indian Affairs, Indian policy, once again, veered in a different direction. The thrust of Collier's Indian Reorganization Act of 1934 was to stop the allotment of Indian lands and return the unsold surplus to them, essentially reestablishing Indian reservations. Unfortunately for the Texas Indians in Oklahoma, most all their lands had long been allotted and there remained little surplus. At the same time, while many of the Indians in southwest Oklahoma supported the Indian Reorganization Act, other Oklahoma Indians, particularly the more progressive ones in the eastern part of the state, objected to it, not wanting to go back to communal lands. Because of this, Oklahoma Indians were specifically excluded from the Indian Reorganization Act.[17]

Realizing the Indians still needed assistance, Congress passed the Oklahoma Indian Welfare Act (OIWA) of 1936. New reservations could be re-created, if land was available, but the OIWA also allowed Indian nations to write constitutions or corporate charters and so create tribal governments. The bill provided for these new governments to receive government loans, and there were promises of continuing health and education facilities. The Comanches, Kiowas, Apaches, and Wichitas refused to write constitutions and did not form new governments under the OIWA. The Kiowa-Comanche-Apache Business Committee remained their tribal government until 1966 when the three tribes split. In 1968 the Kiowas created their own government and became the Kiowa Tribe of Oklahoma. The next year the Comanches did the same and became the Comanche Indian Tribe of Oklahoma, while the Kiowa-Apaches became the Apache Tribe of Oklahoma. The Wichitas continued governing themselves along traditional lines without the use of a written constitution until 1961. In that year, the Wichita, Waco, Tawakoni, and Kichai divisions adopted a set of governing bylaws and became the Wichita and Affiliated Tribes. The Caddos applied for a corporate charter in 1938 under the OIWA and so brought together the Hainais, Cadodachos, and Nadacos into one government under the name Caddo Indian Tribe of Oklahoma. The Tonkawas also adopted a constitution in 1938 and became the Tonkawa Tribe of Indians of Oklahoma.[18]

Fortunately, the government's termination policy did not reach the Texas Indians in Oklahoma. The federal relationship was maintained and although none of them have reservations, each tribe possesses a small amount of land surrounding its tribal complex. For example, the Wichitas have about ten acres of tribal land. The advent of the policy of self-determination and the creation of their own governments seemingly brought better economic times to both the tribe and individuals. Tribal governments have been able to take advantage of government programs to provide better housing, education, and healthcare for their people. Often, tribes worked with their old reservation neighbors to promote economic development as the Wichitas, Caddos, and Delawares did in the 1970s when they created the WCD Enterprise Corporation. The tribes have also been quick to turn to the courts for redress of grievances and maintenance of their rights as domestic-dependent nations. Because of this, tax-free smoke shops, where visitors can purchase inexpensive cigarettes and other tobacco products, have sprung up on Indian land and provide revenue for the tribes.[19]

Both as tribes and individuals, the Texas Indians in Oklahoma not only still exist but also are growing. About half their enrolled, recognized members live near their traditional communities and tribal headquarters; the other half dispersed into cities and towns across America. Individually, as with all Americans, some are quite prosperous; some manage to keep their heads above water; and some live in poverty. Powwows are held and people still come home to visit their kin and renourish their community ties. Over the years, the native languages of these Indians almost died out, with few fluent speakers remaining. The tribes have tried to reteach their languages and bring them back to life. In the end, though they were long ago forced out of Texas, many still consider Texas as home and often make pilgrimages to the state to visit places historic and sacred to them.

The Persistent Alabama-Coushattas

Unlike the Texas Indians exiled to Oklahoma, the small Alabama-Coushatta reservation in Polk County never underwent the allotment process. In fact, during the first decades of the twentieth century the reservation land base was preserved, even expanded, as many Texans happily realized they still had Indians living among them. In the 1920s the Kirby Land Company inadvertently appropriated 192 acres of Alabama-Coushatta land but voluntarily gave it back when it discovered its error. Nearby citizens also lobbied the state and federal governments for aid to the Alabama-Coushattas. Their efforts bore fruit. As early as 1918 the federal government granted $8,000 for Alabama-Coushatta education. At the urging of local citizens, Alabama-Coushatta principal chief Charles Martin Thompson and second chief McConnico Battise, appeared before Congress to discuss their people's condition. This resulted in a grant of $40,000, with $29,000 being used to purchase 3,071 acres of land, bringing the reservation holdings to 4,315 acres. The state also chipped in, providing $47,000 for the construction of a hospital, a gymnasium, and reservation housing.[20]

Though they were tucked away in the piney woods of East Texas, the Alabama-Coushattas could not remain isolated forever and were influenced by their non-Indian neighbors. In the latter part of the nineteenth century the Presbyterian Church sent missionaries to the Alabama-Coushattas and over time drew many into that denomination. Logging became the biggest industry in that part of Texas, and some Alabama-Coushattas worked as loggers or in sawmills. To encourage this, the federal government set up a forestry resource management program on the reservation. Schoolteachers and doctors had their own impact. Because of these influences, by 1930 many traditions were on the wane. But while the Alabama-Coushattas might play basketball, drive cars, and dress like their non-Indian neighbors, they still lived in poverty, often receiving food and clothes from sympathetic Presbyterian congregations.[21]

With the coming of the Indian Reorganization Act of 1934, the Alabama-Coushattas drew up a constitution that officially united the two tribes. It was approved in 1938 and ratified by the tribe the next year. The new constitution called for a seven-member Tribal Council, with the elected chief, or *mikko*, serving as an adviser. Once again, this was applying an American style of government to a kin-based society that had never governed itself that way. The Tribal Council fell into disuse, while the mikko and clan elders retained their traditional powers. For the next decade or so, the Alabama-Coushattas had limited contact with the federal and state governments; when they did, the non-Indian superintendents of the reservation mainly served as go-betweens. In 1948, the State of Texas granted the right to vote to the Alabama-Coushattas.[22]

By the 1950s, when the federal government hoped to get out of the Indian business, the Alabama-Coushattas appeared to be perfect for termination. Virtually all other reservations across the country were administered by the federal government, but the Alabama-Coushatta reservation was controlled by the State of Texas. Superintendents were appointed by the state and most monetary support came from the state. About the only interaction the Alabama-Coushattas had with the federal government was through the Indian Health Service, the small forestry resource management program, and some education appropriations. In early 1953 officials from the Department of the Interior pressured the Alabama-Coushattas to accept termination of the federal government's trust responsibility. This trust, along with their lands, would officially be transferred to the State of Texas. The Alabama-Coushattas were probably not clear as to what termination meant for them. Many who initially approved it thought it only concerned the federal government handing the forest conservation program over to the state. The Alabama-Coushattas were nowhere near ready to compete with their non-Indian neighbors, and once they realized they would lose access to the Indian Health Service, they immediately began backtracking. However, for all intents and purposes, the Alabama-Coushattas had been terminated.[23]

Under the purview of Texas, the Alabama-Coushattas experienced mixed results. They lost some of their lands, with reservation acreage declining from a high of 4,315 to 1,250 acres, but the state maintained the forestry program and in 1963 appropriated $40,000 for a reservation museum, a restaurant, and an arts and crafts shop. Up to that time, the Alabama-Coushatta was the only Indian reservation in Texas and had been administered by the Board for Texas State Hospitals and Special Schools. In 1965 the state abolished the board and in its place created the Texas Commission for Indian Affairs to administer the Alabama-Coushatta reservation. About this time, with their land base dwindling and prices for timber declining, the Alabama-Coushatta's discovered the value of tourism. It was serendipitous for at about the same time interested Texans discovered there were Indians still living among them. To take advantage of the growing population of nearby Houston, in 1962, the Alabama-Coushattas founded the Tribal Enterprise Tourist Project, which was instrumental in establishing the tribal museum. Powwows now became big on the reservation and often drew large crowds of non-Indians, much to the chagrin of the Presbyterian missionaries who viewed Indian dances with a jaundiced eye.[24]

Though the federal termination program ended in the early 1960s, the federal trust responsibility with the Alabama-Coushattas was not immediately renewed. Still, the tribe benefited from the new policy of self-determination, the federal war on poverty, and the willingness of the State of Texas to provide needed money. Besides cultural programs, in 1970 the Department of Housing and Urban Development began building brick homes for reservation residents, and in 1975 a modern community center was built to be used for education, vocational training, recreation, and such. Nevertheless, by 1985 the Alabama-Coushattas were not happy with the administration of their resources by the Texas Indian Commission and appealed to the federal government for trust protection. In 1985 the federal government agreed and the Alabama-Coushattas once again became a federally recognized and supported tribe. This spelled the end for the Texas Indian Commission, which shut down in 1989. With its federal trust restored, the Alabama-Coushattas turned to the Indian Health Service for medical care and in 1989 the Chief Kina Medical Center was opened. At the same time, the Bureau of Indian Affairs began providing social services and economic programs on the reservation. With tourism still a main economic activity among the Alabama-Coushattas, in 1994 the tribe began building the large Alabama-Coushatta Cultural Center. At the turn of the twenty-first century tourism is still important. Regular powwows are still held and the Alabama-Coushattas remain as one of Texas' few existing Indian reservations.[25]

The Determined Tiguas

The turn of the twentieth century brought dramatic changes for the Tiguas. Though they had been in steady contact with the Spanish for three hundred years and had lived around El Paso for more than two hundred, during that time they had maintained a tight-knit, isolated community and rarely intermarried with their Hispanic neighbors. Despite that, the Tiguas had adopted many trappings of Mexican culture. John G. Bourke, an army officer with an anthropological bent, visited the home of one of his Tigua scouts in 1881. "I saw a shield, bows, arrows, guns, and a bundle of eagle feathers and a pair of wooden spurs, hanging from the rafters. But beyond these, nothing whatever to lead me to suspect I wasn't in the house of a humble and industrious family of Mexicans." No matter, these were Indians every bit as much as the Comanches or Caddos. Like the Southern Plains Indians, though they scouted for the army, they still performed their traditional dances and ceremonies. Sensing changes on the way and wanting to preserve what they had as best they could, in 1895 the Tiguas adopted a constitution complete with a tribal framework and elected officers. Tigua soldiers served in both world wars and became citizens with all other Indians across the nation in 1924.[26]

Not officially recognized as Indians by the U.S. government and already possessing a constitutional government, the Tiguas managed to bypass the Indian Reorganization Act and termination. In 1967 the State of Texas officially recognized the Tiguas as Indians and placed them under the administration of the Texas Commission of Indian Affairs, which in 1975 changed its name to the Texas Indian Commission. In 1968 the U.S. government also officially recognized the Tiguas but transferred jurisdiction to the state. Texas provided them with a small parcel of communal land and money to build a restaurant, visitor center, and administration buildings. In 1975 the tribe opened the Ysleta del Sur Pueblo Museum, which was later destroyed by fire and rebuilt in 1992. At the turn of the twenty-first century the Tiguas of Ysleta del Sur have about twenty-six acres of trust land some fifteen miles south of downtown El Paso. Every June 13 they celebrate the Fiesta de San Antonio, one of their most public celebrations.[27]

During the last years of the twentieth century the Tiguas found themselves embroiled in several high-profile lawsuits with the State of Texas. In the 1980s the Tiguas filed suit to regain the thirty-six-square-mile tract originally provided to them by Spanish land grant, which the United States agreed to when Texas entered the Union in 1845. The suit is still pending. In 1998 the Tiguas sued to prevent a nuclear waste dump from being placed on their lands. Another issue making for a rocky relationship between the tribe and the state is gambling. In the latter part of the twentieth century Indian nations across the United States, using their status as domestic-dependent nations, found that gambling was a way of raising much-needed capital. By the 1980s many Indian nations offered high-stakes bingo, slot machines, and table games, competing not only with Las Vegas and Atlantic City for gambling dollars but also with riverboat gambling. Non-Indian charities and churches also depended on bingo and such for revenue. In 1988 Congress passed the Indian Gaming Regulatory Act, which basically said that if a state allowed any form of gaming, such as charity bingo, then it had to allow Indian gaming, though the Indians had to come to agreements with their respective state governments. In 1996 the Tiguas opened the 70,000-square-foot Speaking Rock Casino, complete with slot machines, table games, and restaurants. The State of Texas took a dim view of the Tigua casino and filed suit to close it. The tribe contended that their casino was economically beneficial to them and to El Paso in general, employing 800 people, 50 of whom are tribal members; generating a payroll of $14 million per year; and adding $823 million to the El Paso economy. The state did not take on the Texas Kickapoo Lucky Eagle Casino near Eagle Pass, saying the Kickapoos are under the authority of the federal Bureau of Indian Affairs, whereas the Tiguas come under the jurisdiction of the State of Texas. In 2002 the courts ruled against the Tiguas and the state shut down the Speaking Rock casino. It was a blow to the Tiguas and they hope to find another venture to make up for the lost capital.

The Kickapoo Traditional Tribe of Texas

The Kickapoos of Mexico, after their defeat by Mackenzie in 1873, remained in their village on the Rio Sabina in Coahuila, Mexico. There they kept to themselves, not wanting to become "contaminated" by American culture. This often meant they did not send their children to public schools in Mexico and would not allow other Kickapoos from Oklahoma, whom they considered tainted, to join their band. Nevertheless, by the early twentieth century some Kickapoos began settling at a long-visited hunting camp on the Texas side of the international border at Eagle Pass, near the present-day International Bridge. While Mexican authorities recognized Kickapoo claims to land in Mexico, no one was really sure of the land situation in Texas. For years, the Kickapoos near Eagle Pass were pretty much ignored and migrated back and forth from Mexico to Texas. Many lived in a jerry-built village virtually underneath the International Bridge, with only one water spigot for several hundred Kickapoos. Then, in 1983, Texas officially granted them about 120 acres near El Indio, Texas, downriver from Eagle Pass. The next year the Texas Band of the Kickapoo Indians gained federal recognition. Unlike the Tiguas and Alabama-Coushattas who were under the jurisdiction of the Texas Indian Commission, the Kickapoos were trustees of the federal government and received no state money. Still, the Kickapoos worried about losing their culture through being lumped in with the Kickapoos in Oklahoma. So in 1989 the Texas Band of Kickapoos, drawing upon the 1934 Indian Reorganization Act, wrote up a constitution that officially separated them from the Kickapoos in Oklahoma. They created a tribal government with elected officials and renamed themselves the Kickapoo Traditional Tribe of Texas.[28]

Traditional and insular, the Mexican Kickapoos, as they are still often called, continue to migrate between Mexico and Texas and are considered to hold dual citizenship. While many spend the winter months farming and hunting in Mexico, during the spring and summer they travel across Texas and the United States as migrant farm workers. In 1996, citing the Indian Gaming Regulatory Act as their justification, the Kickapoos opened the fifteen-thousand-square-foot Lucky Eagle Casino at Eagle Pass, Texas, complete with slot machines, gaming tables, and a restaurant. How successful the casino will be and how it will affect their lives and culture remains to be seen.[29]

For most Texas Indians the twentieth century was just as devastating as the nineteenth. Conquered and often marginalized, the Indians lost much of their land through the allotment process or unscrupulous non-Indians. Their culture also came under attack from schoolteachers, missionaries, government officials, and their non-Indian neighbors. For many Indians, both in and out of Texas, much of the twentieth century was a time of poverty. Not until the late 1960s did Indians began to experience a cultural, political, and economic resurgence. Under the auspices of the 1934 Indian Reorganization Act, Texas Indian peoples established tribal governments. As more and more Indians attended universities and became schooled in the rules of the game, the battlefield shifted from Texas' forests and plains to courtrooms. Indian tribes now tried to regain lost lands and rights and were often successful. At the same time, non-Indians discovered the value of Indian culture, which gave a boost to the Indians themselves, who now set out to rediscover and retain aspects of their traditional culture. And as tourism grew, the Indians tried to take advantage of it through the establishment of museums, performance of public powwows and ceremonies, and the income provided by casino gambling. As they try to reclaim their lands and rights, they are often at odds with the State of Texas, the State of Oklahoma, and sometimes with the U.S. government.

So this is where the Indians of Texas stand today as they enter the twenty-first century. They have an ancient, often glorious, certainly complex, history. Here long before Europeans ever arrived in Texas, to say that the last five hundred years of contact with non-Indians has brought a time of devastation for them would be simplistic. Far better to consider Texas Indians' resilience and adaptive abilities. While disease, warfare, exile, and outright attempts to eradicate them and their culture resulted in the disappearance of many Texas Indians, many people still consider themselves Texas Indians, and Indian people still live within the boundaries of Texas. And their disappearance is certainly not assured. What will happen in future centuries is not known, but history is not over. And that story belongs to future books.

Notes

Chapter 1. Texas' Earliest Peoples

1. Stuart J. Fiedel, *Prehistory of the Americas* (New York: Cambridge University Press, 1987), 41–42, 44, 45; David Hurst Thomas, *Exploring Ancient Native America: An Archaeological Guide* (New York: Macmillan, 1994), 2–8; Jules B. Billard, ed., *The World of the American Indian* (Washington, D.C.: National Geographic Society, 1974), 33; Michael B. Collins, "Implications of Monte Verde, Chile, for the Earliest Prehistory of Texas," in *The Prehistoric Archeology of Texas*, ed. Timothy K. Perttula (College Station: Texas A&M University Press, 2004); "Monahan Draw," *Handbook of Texas Online*, http://www.tsha.utexas.edu/handbook/online.

2. Tom [Thomas] D. Dillehay, *The Settlement of the Americas: A New Prehistory* (New York: Basic Books, 2000), 2–3, 65–68; Michael H. Crawford, *The Origins of Native Americans: Evidence from Anthropological Genetics* (Cambridge, Eng.: Cambridge University Press, 1998), 21–27; Francis Jennings, *The Founders of America: From the Earliest Migrations to the Present* (New York and London: Norton, 1993), 25–31.

3. Fiedel, *Prehistory of the Americas*, 25–26, 45–47; Thomas, *Exploring Ancient Native America*, 6–10; Carl Waldman, *Atlas of the North American Indian* (New York: Facts on File Publications, 1985), 1; Collins, "Implications of Monte Verde"; C. Britt Bousman, Barry W. Baker, and Anne C. Kerr, "Paleoindian Archeology in Texas," in *Prehistoric Archeology of Texas*; Billard, *World of the American Indian*, 29–33; Jennings, *Founders of America*, 25–26.

4. Vynola Beaver Newkumet and Howard L. Meredith, *Hasinai: A Traditional History of the Caddo Confederacy* (College Station: Texas A&M Press, 1988), 5–6; Kelly F. Himmel, *The Conquest of the Karankawas and the Tonkawas, 1821–1859* (College Station: Texas A&M University Press, 1999), 31; Lawrence E. Aten, *Indians of the Upper Texas Coast* (New York: Academic Press, 1983), 72; John R. Swanton, "Mythology of the Indians of Louisiana and the Texas Coast," *Journal of American Folklore* 20 (1907): 286.

5. Parker Nunley, *A Field Guide to Archeological Sites of Texas* (Austin: Texas Monthly Press, 1989), 100–102; Vance T. Holliday, *Paleoindian Geoarchaeology of the Southern High Plains* (Austin: University of Texas Press, 1997), 177; Eileen Johnson and Vance T. Holliday, "Archeology and Late Quaternary Environments of the Southern High Plains," in *The Prehistoric Archeology of Texas*.

6. Fiedel, *Prehistory of the Americas*, 41–42, 44–45; Billard, *The World of the American Indian*, 33.

7. Bousman, Baker, and Kerr, "Paleoindian Archeology."

8. Fiedel, *Prehistory of the Americas*, 71–72.

9. Fiedel, *Prehistory of the Americas*, 69–75; Thomas, *Exploring Ancient Native America*, 20–35; Harry J. Shafer, "Early Lithic Assemblages in Eastern Texas," *Museum Journal* 17 (1977):

187–88; Solveig A. Turpin, "The Lower Pecos River Region of Texas and Northern Mexico," in *Prehistoric Archeology of Texas.*

10. Fiedel, *Prehistory of the Americas,* 63, 66–67, 69–70; Nunley, *Field Guide,* 71; Thomas, *Exploring Ancient Native America,* 19–20.

11. Fiedel, *Prehistory of the Americas,* 69–70; Bousman, Baker, and Kerr, "Paleoindian Archeology."

12. Fiedel, *Prehistory of the Americas,* 10, 72–75; William W. Newcomb, Jr., *The Rock Art of Texas Indians* (Austin: University of Texas Press, 1967), 39–40; Bousman, Baker, and Kerr, "Paleoindian Archeology"; Michael B. Collins, "Archeology in Central Texas," in *Prehistoric Archeology of Texas.*

13. Nunley, *Field Guide,* 38–40; Newcomb, *Rock Art,* 111–12; Fiedel, *Prehistory of the Americas,* 62; Holliday, *Paleoindian Geoarchaeology,* 177–82; Jon L. Gibson, *The Ancient Mounds of Poverty Point: Place of Rings* (Gainesville: University Press of Florida, 2000), 46–47; Bousman, Baker, and Kerr, "Paleoindian Archeology"; Timothy K. Perttula, "The Prehistoric and Caddoan Archeology of the Northeast Texas Pineywoods," in *Prehistoric Archeology of Texas.*

14. Fiedel, *Prehistory of the Americas,* 48–49; Nunley, *Field Guide,* 100–102; Holliday, *Paleoindian Geoarchaeology,* 183–85; Bousman, Baker, and Kerr, "Paleoindian Archeology"; Perttula, "Prehistoric and Caddoan Archeology."

15. Newcomb, *Rock Art,* 58; Nunley, *Field Guide,* 99–100, 111–12; Thomas R. Hester, "Tradition and Diversity among the Prehistoric Hunters and Gatherers of Southern Texas," *Plains Anthropologist* 26 (May, 1981): 121; Bousman, Baker, and Kerr, "Paleoindian Archeology"; Fiedel, *Prehistory of the Americas,* 75–76; Nunley, *Field Guide,* 40–42.

16. Nunley, *Field Guide,* 69, 79–83; Thomas, *Exploring Ancient Native America,* 22; Jack B. Bertram, *Archeological Investigation along the Proposed Alibates Tour Road,* Professional Paper No. 33, Southwest Cultural Resources Center, Division of Anthropology (Santa Fe: National Park Service, 1989), 6–18.

17. Fiedel, *Prehistory of the Americas,* 62, 76–78, 83; Nunley, *Field Guide,* 41; Dee Ann Story, "An Overview of the Archaeology of East Texas," *Plains Anthropologist* 26 (May, 1981): 143; Holliday, *Paleoindian Geoarchaeology,* 185–97; Bousman, Baker, and Kerr, "Paleoindian Archeology."

18. Fiedel, *Prehistory of the Americas,* 62–63; Nunley, *Field Guide,* 100–102; Tom [Thomas] D. Dillehay, "Late Quaternary Bison Population Changes on the Southern Plains," *Plains Anthropologist* 19 (August, 1974): 180–96; Johnson and Holliday, "Archeology and Late Quaternary Environments."

19. Waldman, *Atlas,* 5–6; Newcomb, *Rock Art,* 40; Edward B. Jelks, *Excavations at Texarkana Reservoir, Sulphur River, Texas,* in *River Basin Surveys Papers,* no. 21 (Washington, D.C.: GPO, 1961), 5.

20. Fiedel, *Prehistory of the Americas,* 89; Nunley, *Field Guide,* 42–43; Newcomb, *Rock Art,* 60–61; J. Michael Quigg, "A Late Archaic Bison Processing Event in the Texas Panhandle," *Plains Anthropologist* 43 ((1998): 367–83; Hester, "Tradition and Diversity," 124; Dillehay, "Late Quaternary Bison Population," 181–82; Collins, "Archeology in Central Texas"; Robert A. Ricklis, "Prehistoric Occupation of the Central and Lower Texas Coast: A Regional Overview," in *Prehistoric Archeology of Texas.*

21. Fiedel, *Prehistory of the Americas,* 89; Nunley, *Field Guide,* 42–43; Newcomb, *Rock Art,* 60–61; Collins, "Archeology in Central Texas."

22. Newcomb, *Rock Art,* 40, 60–61; Fiedel, *Prehistory of the Americas,* 89.

23. Nunley, *Field Guide,* 42–43, 139, 173, 191; Story, "Archeology of East Texas," 144; Fiedel, *Prehistory of the Americas,* 89.

24. Newcomb, *Rock Art*, 63–65; Jelks, *Excavations at Texarkana Reservoir*, 5; Myles R. Miller and Nancy A. Kenmotsu, "Prehistory of the Jornada Mogollon and Eastern Trans-Pecos Regions of West Texas," in *Prehistoric Archeology of Texas*.

25. Tom [Thomas] D. Dillehay, "Disease Ecology and Initial Human Migration," in *The First Americans: Search and Research*, ed. Tom D. Dillehay and David J. Meltzer (Boca Raton, Fla.: CRC Press, 1991), 234–43; Solveig A. Turpin, Maciej Henneberg, and David H. Riskind, "Late Archaic Mortuary Practices of the Lower Pecos River Region, Southwest Texas," *Plains Anthropologist* 31 (November, 1986): 306; Bousman, Baker, and Kerr, "Paleoindian Archeology."

26. Turpin, Henneberg, and Riskind, "Late Archaic Mortuary Practices," 306.

27. Billard, *World of the American Indian*, 43–51; Marshall Sahlins, "Notes on the Original Affluent Society," in *Man the Hunter*, ed. Richard B. Lee and Irven DeVore (Chicago: Aldine Publishing, 1968), 85–89; Newcomb, *Rock Art*, 61, 63–65; Quigg, "A Late Archaic Bison Processing Event," 371.

28. Story, "Archaeology of East Texas," 144.

29. Newcomb, *Rock Art*, 65; Story, "Archaeology of East Texas," 144; Turpin, Henneberg, and Riskind, "Late Archaic Mortuary Practices," 306.

30. Newcomb, *Rock Art*, 63–70; Harold E. Driver, *Indians of North America* (Chicago: University of Chicago Press, 1961), 480–81.

31. Nunley, *Field Guide*, 173–80; Newcomb, *Rock Art*, 40–43, 49, 56, 65, 71, 79, quote on 40; Driver, *Indians of North America*, 78–81.

32. Turpin, Henneberg, and Riskind, "Late Archaic Mortuary Practices," 308.

33. Turpin, Henneberg, and Riskind, "Late Archaic Mortuary Practices," 296–305; Thomas R. Hester, "The Prehistory of South Texas," in *Prehistoric Archeology of Texas*.

34. Turpin, Henneberg, and Riskind, "Late Archaic Mortuary Practices," 296–305; Solveig A. Turpin, "More About Mortuary Practices in the Lower Pecos River Region of Southwest Texas," *Plains Anthropologist* 37 (February, 1992): 7–17.

35. Denise Lardner Carmody, *The Oldest God: Archaic Religion Yesterday and Today* (Nashville: Abingdon Press, 1981), 24–25.

36. Newcomb, *Rock Art*, 40.

37. Story, "Archaeology of East Texas," 145; Robert W. Neuman, *An Introduction to Louisiana Archaeology* (Baton Rouge: Louisiana State University Press, 1984), 122–23, 163–64; Quigg, "A Late Archaic Bison Processing Event," 380.

38. Thomas, *Exploring Ancient North America*, 124–39.

39. Thomas, *Exploring Ancient North America*, 124–39; Neuman, *Louisiana Archaeology*, 142–43.

40. Neuman, *Louisiana Archaeology*, 163–64; Story, "Archaeology of East Texas," 146; Harry J. Shafer, "Comments on Woodland Cultures of East Texas," *Bulletin of Texas Archeological Society* 46 (1975): 252–53; Harald P. Jensen, Jr., "Coral Snake Mound, X16SA48," *Bulletin of the Texas Archeological Society* 39 (1968): 9–44.

41. J. Daniel Rogers, "Patterns of Change on the Western Margin of the Southeast, A.D. 600–900," in *Stability, Transformation, and Variation: The Late Woodland Southeast*, ed. Michael S. Nassaney and Charles R. Cobb (New York: Plenum Press, 1991), 224, 231; Hester, "Prehistory of South Texas"; Charles Hudson, *The Southeastern Indians* (Knoxville: University of Tennessee Press, 1976), 95–97.

42. Story, "Archaeology of East Texas," 146; Perttula, "Prehistoric and Caddoan Archeology."

43. Bertram, *Archeological Investigation*, 12; Hester, "Tradition and Diversity," 124; Story,

242 NOTES TO PAGES 17–22

"Archaeology of East Texas," 148; Quigg, "A Late Archaic Bison Processing Event," 380; Shafer, "Comments on Woodland Cultures," 250–51.

44. Lynda Norene Shaffer, *Native Americans before 1492: The Moundbuilding Centers of the Eastern Woodlands* (Armonk, N.Y.: M. E. Sharpe, 1992), 24–25; Hudson, *Southeastern Indians,* 80; Perttula, "Prehistoric and Caddoan Archeology."

45. Linda S. Cordell, *Prehistory of the Southwest* (New York: Academic Press, 1984), 169–71; Story, "Archaeology of East Texas," 149; Shaffer, *Native Americans before 1492,* 56–57; Timothy G. Baugh, "Holocene Adaptations in the Southern High Plains," in *Plains Indians, A.D. 500–1500: The Archaeological Past of Historic Groups,* ed. Karl H. Schleiser (Norman: University of Oklahoma Press, 1994), 288–89; Charles Avery Amsden, *Prehistoric Southwesterners from Basketmakers to Pueblo* (Los Angeles: Southwest Museum, 1949), 97–105; Perttula, "Prehistoric and Caddoan Archeology."

46. Cordell, *Prehistory of the Southwest,* 172–73; Shaffer, *Native Americans before 1492,* 56–57.

47. Hudson, *Southeastern Indians,* 19; William Cronon, *Changes in the Land: Indians, Colonists, and the Ecology of New England* (New York: Hill and Wang, 1983), 42–48; Isidro Felis de Espinosa, "Letter on the Asinai and their Allies, 1722," in "Descriptions of the Tejas or Asinai Indians, 1691–1722," trans. Mattie Austin Hatcher, *Southwestern Historical Quarterly* 31 (October, 1927): 156–57, hereafter cited as Espinosa Letter.

48. Hudson, *Southeastern Indians,* 264, 268.

49. Ibid., 186–87, 260–69, 319–22.

50. Preston Holder, *The Hoe and the Horse on the Plains: A Study of Cultural Development among North American Indians* (Lincoln: University of Nebraska Press, 1970), 95; Hudson, *Southeastern Indians,* 186–87, 260–69, 319–22; Paul H. Carlson, *The Plains Indians* (College Station: Texas A&M University Press, 1998), 81–82.

51. Cordell, *Prehistory of the Southwest,* 173–78.

52. Thomas, *Exploring Ancient Native America,* 151–52; Story, "Archaeology of East Texas," 148–50; Shaffer, *Native Americans before 1492,* 77; Timothy K. Perttula and James E. Bruseth, "Early Caddoan Subsistence Strategies, Sabine River Basin, East Texas," *Plains Anthropologist* 28 (February, 1983): 9–10.

53. Malcolm C. Webb, "Functional and Historical Parallelisms between Mesoamerican and Mississippian Cultures," in *The Southeastern Ceremonial Complex: Artifacts and Analysis, the Cottonlandia Conference,* ed. Patricia Galloway (Lincoln: University of Nebraska Press, 1989), 289; Chester DePratter, *Late Prehistoric and Early Historic Chiefdoms in the Southeastern United States* (New York: Garland Press, 1991), 8, 77–78.

54. David S. Brose, "From the Southeastern Ceremonial Complex to the Southern Cult: 'You Can't Tell the Players without a Program,'" in *The Southeastern Ceremonial Complex,* 29–30; DePratter, *Late Prehistoric and Early Historic Chiefdoms,* 77–78; Marvin T. Smith, *Archaeology of Aboriginal Culture Change in the Interior Southeast: Depopulation during the Early Historic Period* (Gainesville: University Press of Florida, 1987), 3–4.

55. Hudson, *Southeastern Indians,* 77–80; M. Smith, *Archaeology of Aboriginal Culture Change,* 3–4; M. Webb, "Functional and Historical Parallelisms," 291–92; Dennis A. Peterson, "A History of Excavations and Interpretations of Artifacts from the Spiro Mounds Site," in *The Southeastern Ceremonial Complex,* 117–21; Philip Phillips and James A. Brown, *Pre-Columbian Shell Engravings from the Craig Mound at Spiro, Oklahoma.* 2 vols. (Cambridge, Mass.: Peabody Museum, 1978), 1:19–20.

56. Peterson, "History of Artifacts from the Spiro Mounds," 119; Marvin T. Smith, "Early Historic Period Vestiges of the Southern Cult," in *The Southeastern Ceremonial Complex,* 141–46.

57. Thomas, *Exploring Ancient Native America*, 151–81.

58. Waldman, *Atlas*, 5–6; Robert Silverberg, *The Pueblo Revolt* (1970; University of Nebraska Press, 1994), 6–7.

59. Waldman, *Atlas*, 16–17; Baugh, "Holocene Adaptations," 271–72, 282–83; Albert H. Schroeder, "Development in the Southwest and Relations with the Plains," in *Plains Indians, A.D. 500–1500*, 290–94; Nunley, *Field Guide*, 216–23.

60. Amsden, *Prehistoric Southwesterners*, 48–50; Waldman, *Atlas*, 17–18; Silverberg, *Pueblo Revolt*, 8–11.

61. Waldman, *Atlas*, 18; Silverberg, *Pueblo Revolt*, 11–14; Schroeder, "Development in the Southwest," 296–99; David R. Wilcox, "Changing Contexts of Pueblo Adaptions, A.D. 1250–1600," in *Farmers, Hunters, and Colonists: Interactions between the Southwest and the Southern Plains*, ed. Katherine A. Spielmann (Tucson: University of Arizona Press, 1991), 146, 152–53.

62. Waldman, *Atlas*, 18; Silverberg, *Pueblo Revolt*, 14–17; Thomas D. Hall, *Social Change in the Southwest, 1350–1880* (Lawrence: University Press of Kansas, 1989), 39–40.

63. Baugh, "Holocene Adaptations," 282–83; Schroeder, "Development in the Southwest," 300–307; Nunley, *Field Guide*, 216–23; Hall, *Social Change*, 47; Robert L. Brooks, "From Stone Slab Architecture to Abandonment, the Antelope Creek Phase: A Revisionist View," in *Prehistoric Archeology of Texas*.

Chapter 2. The Blossoming of Texas Cultures

1. Russell Thornton, *American Indian Holocaust and Survival: A Population History since 1492* (Norman: University of Oklahoma Press, 1987), 25–32, 129; Waldman, *Atlas*, 29–30; H. F. Dobyns, *Their Number Become Thinned: Native American Population Dynamics in Eastern North America* (Knoxville: University of Tennessee Press, 1983); Timothy K. Perttula, *The Caddo Nation: Archaeological and Ethnohistoric Perspectives* (Austin: University of Texas Press, 1992), 96.

2. David La Vere, *The Caddo Chiefdoms: Caddo Economics and Politics, 700–1835* (Lincoln: University of Nebraska Press, 1998), 10–14.

3. Aten, *Indians of the Upper Texas Coast*.

4. Robert A. Ricklis, *The Karankawa Indians of Texas: An Ecological Study of Cultural Tradition and Change* (Austin: University of Texas Press, 1996), 4–9; Nancy P. Hickerson, "How Cabeza de Vaca Lived with, Worked among, and Finally Left the Indians of Texas," *Journal of Anthropological Research* 54 (1998): 199.

5. William W. Newcomb, Jr., "Historic Indians of Central Texas," *Bulletin of the Texas Archeological Society* 64 (1993): 26–29; Henri Joutel, *The La Salle Expedition to Texas: The Journal of Henri Joutel, 1684–1686*, ed. William C. Foster, trans. Johanna S. Warren (Austin: Texas State Historical Society, 1998), 293, hereafter cited as Joutel's Journal.

6. T. N. Campbell, "The Coahuiltecans and Their Neighbors," in *Handbook of North American Indians*, ed. Alfonso Ortiz (Washington, D.C.: Smithsonian Institution, 1983), 10:343–58.

7. Nancy P. Hickerson, *The Jumanos: Hunters and Traders of the South Plains* (Austin: University of Texas Press, 1994), xi.

8. Susan C. Vehik, "Cultural Continuity and Discontinuity in the Southern Prairies and Cross Timbers," in *Plains Indians, A.D. 500–1500*, 246–55; Judith Habicht-Mauche, "Coronado's Querechos and Teyas in the Archaeological Record of the Texas Panhandle," *Plains Anthropologist* 37 (August, 1992): 247–59; F. Todd Smith, *The Wichita Indians: Traders of Texas and the Southern Plains, 1540–1845* (College Station: Texas A&M University Press, 2000), 3–14.

9. James H. Gunnerson and Dolores Gunnerson, "Apachean Culture: A Study in Unity and Diversity," in *Apachean Culture History and Ethnology*, ed. Keith H. Basso and Morris E.

Opler (Tucson: University of Arizona Press, 1971), 7–11; Andrée F. Sjoberg, "Lipan Apache Culture in Historical Perspective," *Southwestern Journal of Anthropology* 9 (1953): 76, 80–85; Habicht-Mauche, "Coronado's Querechos and Teyas," 247–59.

10. Driver, *Indians of North America*, 242–68; Fiedel, *Prehistory of the Americas*, 71–72, 77–78; Carlson, *Plains Indians*, 68–69.

11. Driver, *Indians of North America*, 242–68; Hudson, *Southeastern Indians*, 185–91.

12. Carlson, *Plains Indians*, 68–69; Holder, *The Hoe and the Horse*, 57–58; Hudson, *Southeastern Indians*, 185–91.

13. Janet Siskind, "Kinship and Mode of Production," *American Anthropologist* 80 (December, 1978): 860–69; Robert Utley, *The Lance and the Shield: The Life and Times of Sitting Bull* (New York: Henry Holt, 1993), 11–12.

14. Espinosa Letter, 156–57; Hudson, *Southeastern Indians*, 295–301; Carlson, *Plains Indians*, 55.

15. Ernest Wallace and E. Adamson Hoebel, *The Comanches: Lords of the South Plains* (Norman: University of Oklahoma Press, 1952, 1986), 70–71; Hudson, *Southeastern Indians*, 301–302; Espinosa Letter, 177.

16. Mildred P. Mayhall, *The Kiowas* (Norman and London: University of Oklahoma Press, 1962), 115, 152–53; Hudson, *Southeastern Indians*, 266–69; Carlson, *Plains Indians*, 43, 50–56; Wallace and Hoebel, *Comanches*, 60–61, 80–81.

17. Hudson, *Southeastern Indians*, 186–87, 260–69, 319–22; Carlson, *Plains Indians*, 50–56, 81–82.

18. Hudson, *Southeastern Indians*, 395–96; Carlson, *Plains Indians*, 115.

19. Hudson, *Southeastern Indians*, 272–82; Richebourge G. McWilliams, trans. and ed. *Fleur de Lys and Calumet: Being the Pénicaut Narrative of French Adventure in Louisiana* (Baton Rouge: Louisiana State University Press, 1941), 112.

20. Carlson, *Plains Indians*, 39–43.

21. Carlson, *Plains Indians*, 107; David La Vere, *Life among the Texas Indians: The WPA Narratives* (College Station: Texas A&M University Press, 1998), 96–101.

22. Driver, *Indians of North America*, 44; Carlson, *Plains Indians*, 90–107; Fray Gaspar José de Solís, "Diary of a Visit of Inspection of the Texas Missions made by Fray Gaspar José de Solís in the Year 1767–68," trans. Margaret Kenney Kress, *Southwestern Historical Quarterly* 35 (July, 1931): 44, hereafter cited as Solís Diary; Alvar Nuñez Cabeza de Vaca, *Adventures in the Unknown Interior of America*, trans. and ed. Cyclone Covey (1961; Albuquerque: University of New Mexico Press, 1983), 99–100.

23. Marshall Sahlins, *Stone Age Economics* (Chicago: Aldine-Atherton, 1972), 186; W. Raymond Wood, "Plains Trade in Prehistoric and Protohistoric Intertribal Relations," in *Anthropology on the Great Plains*, ed. W. Raymond Wood and Margot Liberty (Lincoln: University of Nebraska Press, 1980), 104; Patricia C. Albers, "Symbiosis, Merger, and War: Contrasting Forms of Intertribal Relationship among Historic Plains Indians," in *The Political Economy of North American Indians*, ed. John H. Moore (Norman: University of Oklahoma Press, 1993), 98–99; Gary Clayton Anderson, *Kinsmen of Another Kind: Dakota-White Relations in the Upper Mississippi Valley, 1650–1862* (Lincoln: University of Nebraska Press, 1984), xi.

24. Carlson, *Plains Indians*, 67–68; Hudson, *Southeastern Indians*, 185–96.

25. Katherine A. Spielmann, "Interaction among Nonhierarchical Societies," in *Farmers, Hunters, and Colonists*, 4–5; Fiedel, *Prehistory of the Americas*, 71–72.

26. Spielmann, "Interaction among Nonhierarchical Societies," 4–5.

27. For a brief explanation of the role of kinship among Indian peoples, see Albers, "Symbiosis, Merger, and War"; Sahlins, *Stone Age Economics*, 193–97; David La Vere, "Friendly Per-

suasions: Gifts and Reciprocity in Comanche-Euroamerican Relations," *Chronicles of Oklahoma* 71 (fall, 1993): 322–37.

28. Sahlins, *Stone Age Economics*, 193–99; Marcel Mauss, *The Gift: Forms and Functions of Exchange in Archaic Societies*, trans. Ian Cunnison (London: Cohen and West, 1969), 79; Claude Leví- Strauss, *The Elementary Structures of Kinship* (Boston: Beacon Press, 1969), 66, 67; Spielmann, "Interaction among Nonhierarchical Societies," 4–5; Eric R. Wolf, *Europe and the People without History* (Berkeley: University of California Press, 1982), 88–100.

29. Fiedel, *Prehistory of the Americas*, 71–72; Wallace and Hoebel, *Comanches*, 209–28.

30. Francisco Casañas de Jesus Maria, "Letter to the Viceroy of Mexico, Mission Santíssima Nombre de Maria, 15 August 1691," in "Descriptions of the Tejas or Asinai Indians, 1691–1722," trans. Mattie Austin Hatcher, *Southwestern Historical Quarterly* 30 (January, 1927): 281–19, 299–300, hereafter cited as Casañas Letter; DePratter, *Late Prehistoric and Early Historic Chiefdoms*, 77–78, 126, 129–30, 138, 163–64; Don G. Wyckoff. and Timothy G. Baugh, "Early Historic Hasinai Elites: A Model for the Material Culture of Governing Elites," *Midcontinental Journal of Archaeology* 5 (1980): 235.

31. Utley, *The Lance and the Shield*, 8–13.

32. Thomas W. Kavanagh, *The Comanches: A History, 1706–1875* (Lincoln: University of Nebraska Press, 1996), 28–29; Howard Meredith, *Dancing on Common Ground: Tribal Cultures and Alliances on the Southern Plains* (Lawrence: University Press of Kansas, 1995), 47; Mayhall, *Kiowas*, 169.

33. Casañas Letter, 216–17; Carlson, *Plains Indians*, 71; Utley, *The Lance and the Shield*, 8–13; Kavanagh, *Comanches*, 36–39.

34. Carlson, *Plains Indians*, 67–80.

35. Ibid.

36. Ake Hultkrantz, *Native Religions of North America: The Power of Visions and Fertility* (San Francisco: Harper and Row, 1987), 12–19; Mayhall, *Kiowas*, 147–51; Waldman, *Atlas*, 57–58.

37. Hultkrantz, *Native Religions*, 20–21.

38. Ibid.

39. Hultkrantz, *Native Religions*, 17, David Roberts, *Once They Moved Like the Wind: Cochise, Geronomio, and the Apache Wars* (New York: Touchstone, 1993), 150; Wallace and Hoebel, *Comanches*, 51–54, 192–94; Wilbur S. Nye, *Bad Medicine and Good: Tales of the Kiowas* (Norman: University of Oklahoma Press, 1962, 1969), 49–51; Newkumet and Meredith, *Hasinai*, 4–5.

40. Hultkrantz, *Native Religions*, 25.

41. Wallace and Hoebel, *Comanches*, 200–203; Hultkrantz, *Native Religions*, 21–22.

42. Hultkrantz, *Native Religions*, 29–31; Jean Louis Berlandier, *The Indians of Texas in 1830*, ed. John C. Ewers (Washington, D.C.: Smithsonian Institution Press, 1969), 91.

43. Quote in Cabeza de Vaca, *Adventures*, 78; Hultkrantz, *Native Religions*, 29–31.

44. Hultkrantz, *Native Religions*, 29–32; Piers Vitebsky, *Shamanisn* (Norman: University of Oklahoma Press, 2001), 10–11.

45. Hudson, *Southeastern Indians*, 176–84, 336–46; Berlandier, *Indians of Texas*, 90–95; Wallace and Hoebel, *Comanches*, 155.

46. Hudson, *Southeastern Indians*, 230–32; Berlandier, *Indians of Texas*, 40; Carlson, *Plains Indians*, 114.

47. Berlandier, *Indians of Texas*, 37, 88–89; Paul J Foik, trans., "Captain Don Domingo Ramón's Diary of His Expedition into Texas in 1716," *Preliminary Studies of the Texas Catholic Historical Society* 2 (April, 1933): 21; Hudson, *Southeastern Indians*, 226, 318; Carlson, *Plains Indians*, 114–16, Cabeza de Vaca, *Adventures*, 99.

246 NOTES TO PAGES 49–59

48. Berlandier, *Indians of Texas*, 93; Hultkrantz, *Native Religions*, 32–34; Cabeza de Vaca, *Adventures*, 57–58; La Vere, *Life among the Texas Indians*, 124–30.

49. Quote in Solís Diary, 41; Wallace and Hoebel, *Comanches*, 56, 62, 78–79, 250–56; Newkumet and Meredith, *Hasinai*, 3, 13, 29, 102; H. Henrietta Stockel, *Chiricahua Apache Women and Children: Safekeepers of the Heritage* (College Station: Texas A&M University Press, 2000), 33–40.

50. Bernard Mishkin, *Rank and Warfare among the Plains Indians* (Lincoln: University of Nebraska Press, 1940, 1992), 28, 58; Richard White, "The Winning of the West: The Expansion of the Western Sioux in the Eighteenth and Nineteenth Centuries," *Journal of American History* 65 (September, 1978): 319–43; Berlandier, *Indians of Texas*, 67–71.

51. Hudson, *Southeastern Indians*, 239–57; James Robertson, trans. and ed., "The True Relation of the Hardships Suffered by Governor Hernando de Soto by a Gentleman of Elvas," in *The De Soto Chronicles: The Expedition of Hernando De Soto to North America in 1539–1543*, ed. Lawrence A. Clayton, Vernon James Knight, Jr., and Edward C. Moore. 2 vols. (Tuscaloosa: University of Alabama Press, 1993), 1:142–45, hereafter cited as Robertson, Elvas Relation.

52. Carlson, *Plains Indians*, 43–47.

53. Frank R. Secoy, *Changing Military Patterns on the Great Plains* (Lincoln: University of Nebraska Press, 1953, 1992), 10–14, 78–85.

54. Carlson, *Plains Indians*, 44–45; Rachel Plummer, "Narrative of the Capture and Subsequent Sufferings of Mrs. Rachel Plummer," in *The Rachel Plummer Narrative*, ed. Rachel Lofton, Susie Hendrix, and Jane Kennedy (1839; reprinted, n.p: [Palestine, Tex.], 1926), 3, 97, hereafter cited as Plummer Narrative; Dorman H. Winfrey and James M. Day, *The Indian Papers of Texas and the Southwest*, 5 vols. (Austin: Texas State Historical Association, 1995), 4:8–12, hereafter cited as Winfrey and Day, *Texas Indian Papers*.

55. Berlandier, *Indians of Texas*, 76–80, quote on 77; Wallace and Hoebel, *Comanches*, 189, 246, 269; Roberts, *Once They Moved Like the Wind*, 43–49.

56. Roberts, *Once They Moved Like the Wind*, 177–78, 192; Cabeza de Vaca, *Adventures*, 96, 112; Berlandier, *Indians of Texas*, 77.

57. Hudson, *Southeastern Indians*, 91; Hickerson, *The Jumanos*, xxvi–xxvii.

58. Helen Hornbeck Tanner, "The Land and Water Communication Systems of the Southeastern Indians," in *Powhatan's Mantle: Indians in the Colonial Southeast*, ed. Peter H. Wood, Gregory A. Waselkov, and M. Thomas Hatley (Lincoln: University of Nebraska Press, 1989), 8, 12–13; John Miller Morris, *El Llano Estacado: Exploration and Imagination on the High Plains of Texas and New Mexico, 1536–1860* (Austin: Texas State Historical Association, 1997), 184–90.

59. Berlandier, *Indians of Texas*, 40, 59; Sahlins, *Stone Age Economics*, 193–99; Mauss, *The Gift*, 79.

60. Albers, "Symbiosis, Merger, and War," 97–100.

61. Spielmann, "Interaction among Nonhierarchical Societies," 4–5; Gary Clayton Anderson, *The Indian Southwest, 1580–1830: Ethnogenesis and Reinvention* (Norman: University of Oklahoma Press, 1999), 30–31; Frank F. Schambach, "Spiro and the Tunica: A New Interpretation of the Role of the Tunica in the Culture History of the Southeast and the Southern Plains, A.D. 1100–1750," in *Arkansas Archaeology: Essays in Honor of Dan and Phyllis Morse*, ed. Robert C. Mainfort, Jr., and Marvin D. Jeter (Fayetteville: University of Arkansas Press, 1999), 212.

62. Anderson, *Indian Southwest*, 32–38.

Chapter 3. The Arrival of Strangers

1. Cabeza de Vaca, *Adventures*, 55–56.

2. Ricklis, *Karankawa*, 4–8; Himmel, *Conquest of the Karankawas and Tonkawas*, 14; William

W. Newcomb, Jr., "Karankawa," in *Handbook of North American Indians*, 10:359–60; Cabeza de Vaca, *Adventures*, 98.

3. Ricklis, *Karankawa*, 4, 14–21, 72–74, 99–100; Newcomb, "Karankawa," 10:363.

4. Cabeza de Vaca, *Adventures*, 56, 67; Ricklis, *Karankawa*, 9, 25–32, 40–41, 44–45; John R. Swanton, *The Indian Tribes of North America*, Bulletin 145 (Washington, D.C.: U.S. Bureau of American Ethnology, 1952), 320; Herbert Landar, "The Karankawa Invasion of Texas," *International Journal of American Linguistics* 34 (1968): 242–58; Newcomb, "Karankawa," 10:362–63.

5. Newcomb, "Karankawa," 10:363; Cabeza de Vaca, *Adventures*, 61, 63, 67; "Voyage to the Mississippi through the Gulf of Mexico," in *La Salle, the Mississippi, and the Gulf: Three Primary Documents*, ed. Robert Weddle, trans. Ann Linda Bell (College Station: Texas A&M University, 1987), 215, 238; Ricklis, *Karankawa*, 9–10; Solís Diary, 42.

6. Ricklis, *Karankawa*, 23–24; Newcomb, "Karankawa," 10:365; Cabeza de Vaca, *Adventures*, 61–62; Solís Diary, 42.

7. Cabeza de Vaca, *Adventures*, 66–67, 71, 83, 96–97; Joutel's Journal, 10–11; Ricklis, *Karankawa*, 99–100; Hickerson, "Cabeza de Vaca," 202–203.

8. Cabeza de Vaca, *Adventures*, 61–62, 66, 99; Solís Diary, 41; Newcomb, "Karankawa," 10:365–66.

9. Quote in Cabeza de Vaca, *Adventures*, 60; Solís Diary, 42–43; Newcomb, "Karankawa," 10:366; Himmel, *Conquest of the Karankawas and Tonkawas*, 84, 130–31; Ricklis, *Karankawas*, 147. See also W. Arens, *The Man-eating Myth: Anthropology and Anthropophagy*. New York: Oxford, 1979.

10. Cabeza de Vaca, *Adventures*, 56–58, quote on 56; Hickerson, "Cabeza de Vaca," 208.

11. John C. Ewers, "The Influence of Epidemics on the Indian Populations and Cultures of Texas," *Plains Anthropologist* 18 (May, 1973): 108, 110; Aten, *Indians of the Upper Texas Coast*, 94–95.

12. Cabeza de Vaca, *Adventures*, 56–65.

13. Ibid., 77.

14. Cabeza de Vaca, *Adventures*, 67–77, 83–84; Hickerson, "Cabeza de Vaca," 210–18.

15. Cabeza de Vaca, *Adventures*, 78–79, 84, 89, 91–92, 98; Hickerson, "Cabeza de Vaca," 202; T. Campbell, "The Coahuiltecans and Their Neighbors," 10:343; Thomas R. Hester, "'Coahuiltecan': A Critical Review of an Inappropriate Ethnic Label," *La Tierra, Journal of the Southern Texas Archaeological Association* 25 (October, 1998): 3–6; Donald W. Olson et al., "Piñon Pines and the Route of Cabeza de Vaca," *Southwestern Historical Quarterly* 101 (October, 1997): 176, 186.

16. T. Campbell, "Coahuiltecans and Their Neighbors," 10:349–58; Swanton, *Indian Tribes*, 309–11.

17. Hickerson, *Jumanos*, 5; Hester, "Prehistory of South Texas"; William W. Newcomb, Jr., *The Indians of Texas: From Prehistoric to Modern Times* (Austin: University of Texas Press, 1961), 49; Aten, *Indians of the Upper Texas Coast*, 40–41; Hester, "'Coahuiltecan,'" 4.

18. Newcomb, *Indians of Texas*, 31–35, 60.

19. Frederick Ruecking, Jr., "The Social Organization of the Coahuiltecan Indians of Southern Texas and Northeastern Mexico," *Texas Journal of Science* 7 (December, 1995): 361; T. Campbell, "Coahuiltecans and Their Neighbors," 10:351–53; Newcomb, *Indians of Texas*, 39, 49–50; Cabeza de Vaca, *Adventures*, 79–81.

20. Cabeza de Vaca, *Adventures*, 79–81; T. Campbell, "Coahuiltecans and Their Neighbors," 10:351–52; Newcomb, *Indians of Texas*, 39–44.

21. Cabeza de Vaca, *Adventures*, 78, 94–95; Ruecking, "Social Organization," 362–63, 379–80; T. Campbell, "Coahuiltecans and Their Neighbors," 10:351–52.

22. Cabeza de Vaca, *Adventures*, 77–82, 89–91, 94, 99, 100–101; Ruecking, "Social Organization," 379–80; T. Campbell, "Coahuiltecans and Their Neighbors," 10:352; Newcomb, *Indians of Texas*, 49.

23. Cabeza de Vaca, *Adventures*, 78–79, 88, 95–97, quote on 96.

24. France V. Scholes and H. P. Mera, "Some Aspects of the Jumano Problem," *Contributions to American Anthropology and History*, no. 34 (Washington, D.C.: Carnegie Institution of Washington, 1940), 269–89; Cabeza de Vaca, *Adventures*, 116; Hickerson, *Jumanos*, x–xxiv; Newcomb, *Indians of Texas*, 225–26.

25. Antonio Espejo, "Account of the Journey to the Provinces and Settlements of New Mexico, 1583," in *Spanish Exploration in the Southwest, 1542–1706*, ed. Herbert Eugene Bolton (New York: Barnes and Noble, 1967), 172–74, 174n. 3, hereafter cited as Espejo Expedition; Diego Pérez de Luxán, "Account of the Antonio de Espejo Expedition into New Mexico, 1582," in *The Rediscovery of New Mexico, 1580–1594*, ed. George P. Hammond and Agapito Rey (Albuquerque: University of New Mexico Press, 1966), 158–59, hereafter cited as Luxán Account; Newcomb, *Indians of Texas*, 234–37; Hickerson, *Jumanos*, 64–66.

26. Cabeza de Vaca, *Adventures*, 115.

27. Espejo Expedition, 172–73; Newcomb, *Indians of Texas*, 236–37; Luxán Account, 160–61; Scholes and Mera, "Some Aspects of the Jumano Problem," 269–89, 291–92.

28. Cabeza de Vaca, *Adventures*, 116; Espejo Expedition, 172.

29. Cabeza de Vaca, *Adventures*, 116–17; Newcomb, *Indians of Texas*, 239–41; Scholes and Mera, "Some Aspects of the Jumano Problem," 271, 291–92; Espejo Expedition, 172–73; Luxán Account, 162–63.

30. Quote in Cabeza de Vaca, *Adventures*, 116; Espejo Expedition, 172, 190.

31. Espejo Expedition, 190; Scholes and Mera, "Some Aspects of the Jumano Problem," 272, 276; Cabeza de Vaca, *Adventures*, 116.

32. Quote in Cabeza de Vaca, *Adventures*, 116; Hickerson, *Jumanos*, 66.

33. The best work on the great biological exchange is still Alfred W. Crosby, *The Columbian Exchange: Biological and Cultural Consequences of 1492*. Westport, Conn.: Greenwood Publishing, 1972.

34. Anderson, *Indian Southwest*, 16, 58–61; Edwin R. Bogusch, "Brush Invasion of the Rio Grande Plain of Texas," *Texas Journal of Science* 4 (March, 1952): 87–91; Hester, "Prehistory of South Texas."

35. Cabeza de Vaca, *Adventures*, 113; Alfred W. Crosby, "Virgin Soil Epidemics as a Factor in the Aboriginal Depopulation in America," *William and Mary Quarterly* 3, ser. 33 (April, 1976): 289–99.

36. Ewers, "Influence of Epidemics," 104, 107–109; Crosby, "Virgin Soil Epidemics," 289–99.

37. Ewers, "Influence of Epidemics," 104–13; Crosby, "Virgin Soil Epidemics," 289–99.

38. Anderson, *Indian Southwest*, 32–34.

39. Berlandier, *Indians of Texas*, 48, 53.

40. Secoy, *Changing Military Patterns*, 79–85.

41. H. F. Gregory, "Eighteenth-Century Caddoan Archaeology: A Study in Models and Interpretation" (Ph.D. diss. Southern Methodist University, Dallas, 1973), 250–51; William Griffith, "The Hasinai Indians of East Texas as Seen by Europeans, 1687–1772," in *Philological and Documentary Studies* (New Orleans: Tulane University, 1977), 2:151.

42. Foik, "Captain Don Domingo Ramón's Diary," 19–21; Joutel's Journal, 171–72, 146–48; Anderson, *Indian Southwest*, 32.

43. Anderson, *Indian Southwest*, 36; "Journal of an Expedition up the Red River,

1773–1774, by J. Gaignard, November 10, 1777," in *Athanase De Mézières and the Louisiana-Texas Frontier, 1768–1780,* ed. and trans. Herbert E Bolton, 2 vols. (Cleveland: Arthur H. Clark, 1914; New York: Kraus Reprint, 1970), 2:83–100, hereafter cited as Bolton, *ADM.*

44. Marc Simmons, *The Last Conquistador: Juan de Oñate and the Settling of the Far Southwest* (Norman: University of Oklahoma Press, 1991), 111.

Chapter 4. Expansion and Collapse in West Texas

1. Espejo Expedition, 172; Cabeza de Vaca, *Adventures,* 116; Anderson, *Indian Southwest,* 22–23.

2. Espejo Expedition, 174.

3. Cabeza de Vaca, *Adventures,* 116; Espejo Expedition, 175; Scholes and Mera, "Some Aspects of the Jumano Problem," 276–85, quote on 280; Anderson, *Indian Southwest,* 17–22; Hickerson, *Jumanos,* 216–19.

4. Ramón A. Gutiérrez, *When Jesus Came, the Corn Mothers Went Away: Marriage, Sexuality, and Power in New Mexico, 1500–1846* (Stanford, Calif.: Stanford University Press, 1991), 71–94.

5. Report of Gov. Jacinto Barrios y Jauregui, May 28, 1758, in *The San José Papers,* pt. 1, *1719–1791,* trans. Benedict Leutenegger, comp. and annot. Marion A. Habig (San Antonio, Tex.: Old Spanish Missions Historical Research Library, 1978), 134.

6. Santa Ana to Francisco Garcia Larios, September 9, 1748, in *Letters and Memorials of the Father Presidente Fray Benito Fernández de Santa Ana, 1736–1754,* ed. and trans. Benedict Leutenegger (San Antonio: Old Spanish Missions Historical Research Library, 1981), 79, 81–82, hereafter cited as Leutenegger, *Santa Ana Letters;* Jack D. Eaton, "The Gateway Missions of the Lower Rio Grande," in *Columbian Consequences: Archaeological and Historical Perspectives on the Spanish Borderlands West,* ed. David Hurst Thomas, 3 vols. (Washington, D.C.: Smithsonian Institution Press, 1989), 1:245–47; Anderson, *Indian Southwest,* 67–92.

7. Gutiérrez, *When Jesus Came,* 71–94, 122–30; Eaton, "Gateway Missions," 245–47; Anderson, *Indian Southwest,* 73, 83–84.

8. Anderson, *Indian Southwest,* 73–80.

9. Anderson, *Indian Southwest,* 25, 78–84; Anne A. Fox, "The Indians at Rancho de las Cabras," in *Columbian Consequences,* 1:259–67.

10. Anderson, *Indian Southwest,* 24–25.

11. Herbert E. Bolton, "The Spanish Occupation of Texas, 1519–1690," *Southwestern Historical Quarterly* 16 (July, 1912): 14–15; Anderson, *Indian Southwest,* 24–25, 39; Herbert E. Bolton, "Introduction: The Mendoza-López Expedition to the Jumanos, 1683–1684," in *Spanish Exploration in the Southwest,* 317; Fernando del Bosque, "Diary of Fernando del Bosque, 1675," in *Spanish Exploration in the Southwest,* 297, 302, hereafter cited as Bosque Diary; Jack D. Forbes, "The Appearance of the Mounted Indian in Northern Mexico and the Southwest, to 1680," *Southwestern Journal of Anthropology* 15 (summer, 1959): 190–94.

12. Hickerson, *Jumanos,* 104–106; Anderson, *Indian Southwest,* 24–25; Bolton, "Spanish Occupation of Texas," 15–17, 19–20.

13. Juan Dominguez de Mendoza, "Itinerary of Juan Dominguez de Mendoza, 1684," in *Spanish Exploration in the Southwest,* 339–40, hereafter cited as Mendoza Itinerary; Hickerson, *Jumanos,* 128–30, quote on 130; Anderson, *Indian Southwest,* 27; Bosque Diary, 298–99.

14. Kenneth G. Hirth, "Interregional Trade and the Formation of Prehistoric Gateway Communities," *American Antiquity* 43 (January, 1978): 35–36; Anderson, *Indian Southwest,* 35–39.

15. Anderson, *Indian Southwest,* 24–25; Hirth, "Gateway Communities," 37; Hickerson,

Jumanos, 128–30, 215–19; J. Charles Kelley, "Juan Sabeata and Diffusion in Aboriginal Texas," *American Anthropologist* 57 (October, 1955): 981–82, 985; Bolton, "Spanish Occupation of Texas," 15–17.

16. Mendoza Itinerary, 339–40.

17. Anderson, *Indian Southwest*, 32–37; Hickerson, *Jumanos*, 128–30; Kelley, "Juan Sabeata," 987–89; Bolton, "Spanish Occupation of Texas," 20–21.

18. Mendoza Itinerary, 338–39; Anderson, *Indian Southwest*, 32–37; Hickerson, *Jumanos*, 128–30; Bolton, "Spanish Occupation of Texas," 20–21; Kelley, "Juan Sabeata," 988; Curtis Tunnell, "A Cache of Cannons: La Salle's Colony in Texas," *Southwestern Historical Quarterly* 102 (July, 1998): 23, 43.

19. Morris E. Opler, "The Apachean Culture Pattern and Its Origins," in *Handbook of North American Indians*, 10:368, 381–83, 385; John Upton Terrell, *The Plains Apache* (New York: Crowell, 1975), 8; Pedro de Castañeda, "Narrative of the Expedition of Coronado," in *Spanish Explorers in the Southern United States*, ed. Frederick W. Hodge (New York: Barnes and Noble, 1971), 330, hereafter cited as Castañeda, Coronado Narrative.

20. William Edward Dunn, "Apache Relations in Texas, 1718–1750," *Texas Historical Association Quarterly* 14 (January, 1911): 202–203.

21. Castañeda, Coronado Narrative, 332; Juan de Oñate, "True Account of the Expedition of Oñate toward the East," in *Spanish Exploration in the Southwest*, 258, hereafter cited as Oñate Eastern Account; Vicente de Saldivar Mendoca, "Account of the Discovery of the Buffalo, 1599," in *Spanish Exploration in the Southwest*, 225, hereafter cited as Mendoca Account; Newcomb, *Indians of Texas*, 109–10; Terrell, *Plains Apaches*, 34.

22. Castañeda, Coronado Narrative, 330.

23. Oñate Eastern Account, 257.

24. Mendoca Account, 230.

25. Castañeda, Coronado Narrative, 362–63.

26. Castañeda, Coronado Narrative, 330, 362–63; Mendoca Account, 226–27; Terrell, *Plains Apaches*, 34.

27. Opler, "Apachean Culture Pattern," 10:369–70, 372; Terrell, *Plains Apaches*, 40; Stockel, *Chiricahua Apache Women and Children*, 8.

28. Oñate Eastern Account, 257

29. Mendoca Account, 225–27; Terrell, *Plains Apaches*, 40.

30. Opler, "Apachean Culture Pattern," 10:372–73, 376–80; Terrell, *Plains Apache*, 41; Newcomb, *Indians of Texas*, 122–24, 128–30; Roberts, *Once They Moved Like the Wind*, 150.

31. Castañeda, Coronado Narrative, 330.

32. Ibid., 363.

33. Quote in Oñate Eastern Account, 252; Opler, "Apachean Culture Pattern," 10:373; Roberts, *Once They Moved Like the Wind*, 43–49.

34. Luxán Account, 182.

35. Anderson, *Indian Southwest*, 41; Robert A. Ricklis, "The Archeology of Native American Occupation of Southeast Texas," in *Prehistoric Archeology of Texas*.

36. Castañeda, Coronado Narrative, 333.

37. Castañeda, Coronado Narrative, 334; Timothy G. Baugh, "Culture History and Protohistoric Societies in the Southern Plains," *Plains Anthropologist* 31 (November, 1986): 169, fig. 1; Richard R. Drass and Timothy G. Baugh, "The Wheeler Phase and Cultural Continuity in the Southern Plains," *Plains Anthropologist* 42 (May, 1997): 198–200; Opler, "Apachean Culture Pattern," 10:387; Habicht-Mauche, "Coronado's Querechos and Teyas," 256.

38. Castañeda, Coronado Narrative, 357; Baugh, "Culture History," 181; Katherine A.

Spielmann, "Late Prehistoric Exchange between the Southwest and Southern Plains," *Plains Anthropologist* 28 (November, 1983): 268–70; Albert H. Schroeder and Dan S. Matson, eds., *A Colony on the Move: Gaspar Castaño de Sosa's Journal, 1590–1591* (Salt Lake City: Alphabet Printing, 1965), 84; quote in Mendoca Account, 226.

39. Oñate Eastern Account, 260–64; Anderson, *Indian Southwest*, 63, 95–96, 117; Schroeder and Matson, *Colony on the Move*, 55.

40. Elizabeth A. H. John, *Storms Brewed in Other Men's Worlds: The Confrontation of Indians, Spanish, and French in the Southwest, 1540–1795* (College Station: Texas A&M University Press, 1975; Lincoln: University of Nebraska Press, 1981), 71, 74, 79–80, 90–91, 228–29.

41. John, *Storms*, 77, 80, 86–91, 110.

42. Several historians provide their own analysis of Pueblo conditions and what led to the Pueblo Revolt in David J. Weber, ed., *What Caused the Pueblo Revolt of 1680?* (Boston: Bedford/St. Martins, 1999).

43. Silverberg, *Pueblo Revolt*, 89–93, 116; Bill Wright, *The Tiguas: Pueblo Indians of Texas* (El Paso: University of Texas at El Paso, 1993), 10; "The Tiguas: People of the Sun, Ysleta Del Sur Pueblo" (El Paso, Tex.: Tigua Indian Cultural Center, n.d.), 12–13. See also Weber, *What Caused the Pueblo Revolt?*

44. B. Wright, *Tiguas*, 10–11; Jeffrey M. Schulze, "The Rediscovery of the Tiguas: Federal Recognition and Indianness in the Twentieth Century," *Southwestern Historical Quarterly* 105 (July, 2001): 21.

45. Castañeda, Coronado Narrative, 312–24, 358; B. Wright, *Tiguas*, 5–6.

46. Schulze, "Rediscovery of the Tiguas," 15–21.

47. Schulze, "Rediscovery of the Tiguas," 22, 25; B. Wright, *Tiguas*, 9–19.

48. Quote in B. Wright, *Tiguas*, 12.

49. Schulze, "Rediscovery of the Tiguas," 18; "Tigua Indians," *Handbook of Texas Online.*

50. John, *Storms*, 97,

51. Peter Iverson, *When Indians Became Cowboys: Native Peoples and Cattle Ranching in the American West* (Norman: University of Oklahoma Press, 1994), 9–12.

52. Luxán Account, 168.

53. Luxán Account, 159; Espejo Expedition, 172

54. Jack Jackson, *Los Mesteños: Spanish Ranching in Texas, 1721–1821* (College Station: Texas A&M University Press, 1986), 9–11; Dan Flores, *Journal of an Indian Trader: Anthony Glass and the Texas Trading Frontier, 1790–1810* (College Station: Texas A&M University Press, 1985), 8; Forbes, "Appearance of the Mounted Indian in Northern Mexico," 191–93.

55. David Anthony, Dimitri Y. Telegin, and Dorcas Brown, "The Origin of Horseback Riding," *Scientific American* 265 (December, 1991): 98; Holder, *The Hoe and the Horse*," 28, 78–81; Mishkin, *Rank and Warfare*, 5–23; Secoy, *Changing Military Patterns*, 6–10.

56. Oñate Eastern Account, 257; Mendoza Itinerary, 332, 335; Joutel's Journal, 11; Anthony, Telegin, and Brown, "Origin of Horseback Riding," 98; Mishkin, *Rank and Warfare*, 18; Secoy, *Changing Military Patterns*, 22–24.

57. Mishkin, *Rank and Warfare*, 19–20, 21–22; Carlson, *Plains Indians*, 36–39.

58. Mendoza Itinerary, 330–31; Joutel's Journal, 11, 180, 218.

59. Oñate Eastern Account, 263–64; Mendoza Itinerary, 321, 330–31, 335; Mendoca Account, 225.

60. John, *Storms*, 174.

61. Kelley, "Juan Sabeata," 984; Bolton, *Spanish Exploration in the Southwest*, 314–15.

62. Bosque Diary, 297–98, 300; Donald E. Chipman, *Spanish Texas, 1519–1821* (Austin: University of Texas Press, 1992), 67–68.

63. Kelley, "Juan Sabeata," 984; John, *Storms*, 174–78.

64. Chipman, *Spanish Texas*, 75–99, 108–109, fig. 14.

65. Bogusch, "Brush Invasion," 87–91; Ewers, "Influence of Epidemics," 108.

66. Anderson, *Indian Southwest*, 55, 57–63, 113–15.

67. Chipman, *Spanish Texas*, 70, 75–99, 108–109, fig 14, 112–17; Eaton, "Gateway Missions," 245–47; V. Kay Hindes, "Native American and European Contact in the Lower Medina River Valley," *La Tierra: Journal of the Southern Texas Archaeological Association* 22 (April, 1995): 25–33; Anderson, *Indian Southwest*, 68, 82; T. N. Campbell and T. J. Campbell, "Indians of the San Antonio Missions," in *The Indians of Southern Texas and Northeastern Mexico: Selected Writings of Thomas Nolan Campbell*, ed. T. N. Campbell (Austin: Texas Archeological Research Laboratory, 1988), 82–83, 86–93.

68. Anderson, *Indian Southwest*, 82–86; Thomas R. Hester, "Texas and Northeastern Mexico: An Overview," in *Columbian Consequences*, 1:200–201; John, *Storms*, 207, 276–77.

69. Anderson, *Indian Southwest*, 63–64; Reginald C. Reindorp, trans., "Documents: The Founding of the Missions at La Junta de los Rios," *Mid-America* 20 (1940): 107–31.

70. Reindorp, "Documents," 118.

71. Ibid., 119.

72. Reindorp, "Documents," 121; Anderson, *The Indian Southwest*, 64.

73. Hindes, "Native American and European Contact," 29–30.

Chapter 5. Resurgence in East Texas

1. Herbert E. Bolton, "The Native Tribes about the East Texas Missions," *Texas State Historical Quarterly* 2 (1908): 251–52.

2. Story, "An Overview of the Archaeology of East Texas," 148–50; Shaffer, *Native Americans before 1492*, 77; Perttula, *The Caddo Nation*, 97–102; Harry J. Shafer, "Lithic Technology at the George C. Davis Site, Cherokee County, Texas" (Ph.D diss., University of Texas, Austin, 1973), 346; John Sibley, "Historical Sketches of the Several Indian Tribes in Louisiana, Mouth of the Arkansas River, and between the Mississippi and River Grand," in *Travels in the Interior Parts of America*, ed. Thomas Jefferson (London: J. G. Barnard, 1807), 66–68.

3. Neuman, *Louisiana Archaeology*, 226, 242; Casañas Letter, 213, 285; Griffith, "Hasinai Indians," 49.

4. Casañas Letter, 213, 285; Talon Interrogation, in "Voyage to the Mississippi through the Gulf of Mexico," in *La Salle, the Mississippi, and the Gulf: Three Primary Documents*, ed. Robert Weddle, trans. Ann Linda Bell (College Station: Texas A&M University, 1987), 238; Elsie Clews Parsons, *Notes on the Caddo: Memoirs of the American Anthropological Association*, no. 57 (Menasha, Wis.: American Anthropological Association, 1941; New York: Kraus Reprint, 1969), 54; Griffith, "Hasinai Indians," 49; Neuman, *Louisiana Archaeology*, 243.

5. Joutel's Journal, 148–49; Neuman, *Louisiana Archaeology*, 247–51; Holder, *The Hoe and the Horse*, 57; Casañas Letter, 30, 215; Griffith, "Hasinai Indians," 48–51; John R. Swanton, *Source Material on the History and Ethnology of the Caddo Indians*, Bulletin 132 (Washington, D.C.: Smithsonian Institution, U.S. Bureau of American Ethnology, 1942), 164; Cecile Elkins Carter, *Caddo Indians: Where We Come From* (Norman: University of Oklahoma Press, 1995), 382n. 40; Fred B. Kniffen, Hiram F. Gregory, and George A. Stokes, *The Historic Indian Tribes of Louisiana from 1542 to the Present* (Baton Rouge: Louisiana State University Press, 1987), 226; Rachel B. Galan, "Caddo Mythology: Ethnohistorical and Archaeological Considerations," *Mid-America Folklore* 22 (fall, 1994): 64–66.

6. Wyckoff and Baugh, "Early Historic Hasinai Elites," 235–37, 240, 243, 245.

7. Casañas Letter, 288; Espinosa Letter, 158–61; F. Todd Smith, *The Caddo Indians: Tribes at*

the Convergence of Empires, 1542–1854 (College Station: Texas A&M University Press, 1995), 9–10; DePratter, *Late Prehistoric and Early Historic Chiefdoms,* 77–78; Galan, "Caddo Mythology," 62–63; Jay Miller, "Changing Moons: A History of Caddo Religion," *Plains Anthropologist* 41 (1996): 243–59.

8. Robertson, Elvas Relation, 1:140–41, 145–49; John E. Worth, ed. and trans., "Relation of the Island of Florida by Luys Hernández de Biedma," in *The De Soto Chronicles,* 2:244; Charles Hudson, "The Hernando de Soto Expedition, 1539–1543," in *The Forgotten Centuries: Indians and Europeans in the American South, 1521–1704,* ed. Charles Hudson and Carmen Chaves Tesser (Athens: University of Georgia Press, 1994), 96–98; Nancy Adele Kenmotsu, James E. Bruseth, and James E. Corbin, "Moscoso and the Route in Texas: A Reconstruction," in *The Expedition of Hernando de Soto West of the Mississippi, 1541–1543,* ed. Gloria A. Young and Michael P. Hoffman (Fayetteville: University of Arkansas Press, 1993), 15–30.

9. M. Smith, *Archaeology of Aboriginal Cultural Change,* 86, 143–47; Perttula, *The Caddo Nation,* 850–83; Swanton, *Source Material,* 12–13, fig. 1.

10. Herbert E. Bolton, *The Hasinai: Southern Caddoans As Seen by the Earliest Europeans* (Norman: University of Oklahoma Press, 1987), 31, 63–64.

11. Joutel's Journal, 180, 187, 204–206; Henri de Tonty, "Memoir by the Sieur de la Tonty," in *Historical Collections of Louisiana, Embracing Many Rare and Valuable Documents Relating to the Natural, Civil, and Political History of That State,* ed. B. F. French. 4 vols. (New York: Wiley and Putnam, 1846; New York: AMS Press, 1976), 1:73, 74, 77, hereafter cited as Tonty Memoir.

12. Quote in Kelley, "Juan Sabeata," 989.

13. Joutel's Journal, 11, 179, 295–96; Kenmotsu, Bruseth, and Corbin, "Moscoso and the Route in Texas," 128–29; Casañas Letter, 287; Newcomb, "Historic Indians of Central Texas," 23–24; Tonty Memoir, 1:72–73; Espinosa Letter, 160; Frederick W. Hodge, *Handbook of American Indians North of Mexico.* 2 vols. (Washington, D.C.: Government Printing Office, 1907), 2:998–98; Kenmotsu, Bruseth, and Corbin, "Moscoso and the Route in Texas," 116, 126.

14. Joutel's Journal, 13, 93, 289; Talon Interrogation, 224; Kelley, "Juan Sabeata," 984, 987, 989; Ricklis, *Karankawa Indians,* 9, 131, 146–47.

15. Joutel's Journal, 186–87.

16. Ibid., 206–15, 254–55.

17. Chipman, *Spanish Texas,* 86–99; Damian Manzanet, "The Expedition of Don Domingo Terán de los Rios into Texas (1691–92)," trans. Mattie Austin Hatcher, *Preliminary Studies of the Texas Catholic Historical Society* 2 (January, 1932): 3–67; Casañas Letter, 206–18, 283–304.

18. Tonty Memoir, 73; Jean-Baptiste Bénard de La Harpe, *The Historical Journal of the Establishment of the French in Louisiana,* trans. Joan Cain and Virginia Koenig, ed. and annot. Glenn R. Conrad (Lafayette: University of Southwestern Louisiana, 1971), 35–38, 134; La Vere, *Caddo Chiefdoms,* 50–51, 81–84.

19. Chipman, *Spanish Texas,* 123; Charmion Clair Shelby, "St. Denis's Declaration Concerning Texas in 1717," *Southwestern Historical Quarterly* 26 (January, 1923): 178, 182; Foik, "Captain Don Domingo Ramón's Diary," 19–21; James E. Corbin, "Spanish-Indian Interaction on the Eastern Frontier of Texas," in *Columbian Consequences,* 1:269–79.

20. La Vere, *Caddo Chiefdoms,* 7, 87–91; Timothy K. Perttula and Bob D. Skiles, "Another Look at an Eighteenth-Century Archaeological Site in Wood County, Texas," *Southwestern Historical Quarterly* 92 (January, 1989): 417–35.

21. Newcomb, *Indians of Texas,* 315–16; Aten, *Indians of the Upper Texas Coast,* 34–39; Andrée F. Sjoberg, "The Bidai Indians of Southeastern Texas," *Southwestern Journal of Anthropology* 7 (1951): 391–93; Shafer, "Lithic Technology," 33.

22. Aten, *Indians of the Upper Texas Coast*, 34–39; Newcomb, *Indians of Texas*, 316; Kniffen, Gregory, and Stokes, *Historic Indian Tribes*, 114–15, 122, 257; letter of Santa Ana, March 10, 1749, Leutenegger, *Santa Ana Letters*, 93; Henri Folmer, "De Bellisle on the Texas Coast," *Southwestern Historical Quarterly* 44 (1940): 221; Sjoberg, "Bidai Indians," 391–93.

23. Folmer, "De Bellisle," 216, 218; Aten, *Indians of the Upper Texas Coast*, 34–36; Cabeza de Vaca, *Adventures*, 61, 98.

24. Aten, *Indians of the Upper Texas Coast*, 37–38; Sjoberg, "Bidai Indians," 391–93.

25. Newcomb, *Indians of Texas*, 319–21; Folmer, "De Bellisle," 216.

26. Folmer, "De Bellisle," 217, 218–19, 220; Aten, *Indians of the Upper Texas Coast*, 72–75; Kniffen, Gregory, and Stokes, *Historic Indian Tribes*, 257.

27. Folmer, "De Bellisle," 219.

28. Joutel's Journal, 227; Bolton, *ADM*, 1:286, 289; William W. Newcomb, Jr., "A Reappraisal of the 'Cultural Sink' of Texas." *Southwestern Journal of Anthropology* 12 (1956): 148; Hodge, *Handbook of American Indians North of Mexico*, 1:114.

29. Folmer, "De Bellisle," 223.

30. Bolton, *ADM*, 1:52–56; 2:104–106; Daniel H. Usner, Jr., *Indians, Settlers, and Slaves in a Frontier Exchange Economy: The Lower Mississippi Valley before 1783* (Chapel Hill: University of North Carolina Press, 1992), 179–81.

31. T. N. Campbell, "Name All the Indians of the Bastrop Area," in *Indians of Southern Texas and Northeastern Mexico*, 71–77.

32. Casañas Letter, 287; Damian Manzanet, "Carta de Don Damian Manzanet a Don Carlos De Siguenza sobre el descubrimiento de la Bahía del Espíritu Santo," trans. Lilia M. Casis, *Quarterly of the Texas State Historical Association* 2 (April, 1899): 286–87, 309; Andrée F. Sjoberg, "The Culture of the Tonkawa, a Texas Indian Tribe," *Texas Journal of Science* 5 (September, 1953): 281; Newcomb, "Historic Indians of Central Texas," 16–17, 29; T. Campbell, "Name All the Indians of the Bastrop Area," 71–77.

33. Newcomb, "Historic Indians of Central Texas," 8, 17–22, 26–32; Espinosa Letter, 160.

34. Joutel's Journal, 171; Newcomb, "Historic Indians of Central Texas," 24–25; Fray Francisco Céliz, *Diary of the Alarcón Expedition into Texas, 1718–1719*, trans. Fritz Leo Hoffman (Los Angeles: Quivira Society, 1935), 68

35. Shelby, "St. Denis's Declaration," 176.

36. Shelby, "St. Denis's Declaration," 177–78; Céliz, *Diary of the Alarcón Expedition*, 68–70; Newcomb, "Historic Indians of Central Texas," 25–27; Oñate's Eastern Expedition, 264n. 2; William C. Foster, *Spanish Expeditions into Texas, 1689–1768* (Austin: University of Texas Press, 1995), 271, 274, 277, 285, 287–88; Sjoberg, "Culture of the Tonkawa," 281; T. Campbell, "Name All the Indians of the Bastrop Area," 73–75; Anderson, *Indian Southwest*, 39.

37. Sjoberg, "Culture of the Tonkawas," 289–90; Newcomb, "Reappraisal of the 'Cultural Sink,'" 148.

38. Sjoberg, "Culture of the Tonkawas," 291–97.

39. Solís Diary, 58; Himmel, *Karankawas and the Tonkawas*, 32–33.

40. Quote in Solís Diary, 58; Walter Prescott Webb, *The Great Plains* (Boston: Ginn, 1931; Lincoln: University of Nebraska Press, 1981), 68–84; T. N. Campbell, "Espinosa, Olivares, and the Colorado River Indians, 1709," in *Indians of Southern Texas and Northeastern Mexico*, 63; Usner, *Indians, Settlers, and Slaves*, 258–59.

41. Himmel, *Conquest of the Karankawas and the Tonkawas*, 33.

42. Anderson, *Indian Southwest*, 105–106; Secoy, *Changing Military Patterns*, 7–10, 16–17.

43. Anderson, *Indian Southwest*, 109–10; Daniel K. Richter, *The Ordeal of the Longhouse: The*

Peoples of the Iroquois League in the Era of European Colonization (Chapel Hill: University of North Carolina Press, 1992).

44. Santa Ana to Viceroy Pedro Cebrian, May 16, 1745, Leutenegger, *Santa Ana Letters,* 49–50; Anderson, *Indian Southwest,* 110–16.

45. Anderson, *Indian Southwest,* 116–19; letter of Santa Ana, March 10, 1749, Leutenegger, *Santa Ana Letters,* 92.

46. Quote in Santa Ana to Fray Alonso Giraldo, February 2, 1746, Leutenegger, *Santa Ana Letters,* 66; Anderson, *Indian Southwest,* 113.

47. Santa Ana to Fray Alonso Giraldo, February 2, 1746, Leutenegger, *Santa Ana Letters,* 57–62; Herbert E. Bolton, *Texas in the Middle Eighteenth Century: Studies in Spanish Colonial History and Administration* (Berkeley: University of California Press, 1915, Austin: Texas History Paperbacks, 1970), 44.

48. Herbert E. Bolton, "The Founding of Mission Rosario: A Chapter in the History of the Gulf Coast," *Texas State Historical Association Quarterly* 10 (October, 1906): 117; Chipman, *Spanish Texas,* 148–49.

49. Bolton, "Founding of Mission Rosario," 119; Chipman, *Spanish Texas,* 147–70.

50. Santa Ana to Francisco Garcia Larios, September 9, 1748, Leutenegger, *Santa Ana Letters,* 85; Bolton, *Texas in the Middle Eighteenth Century,* 49–78.

51. Santa Ana to Francisco Garcia Larios, September 9, 1748, Leutenegger, *Santa Ana Letters,* 85; Bolton, *Texas in the Middle Eighteenth Century,* 49–78.

52. Ewers, "The Influence of Epidemics," 108.

53. La Vere, *Caddo Chiefdoms,* 106–108.

54. Bolton, *ADM,* 1:305, 2:269; La Vere, *Caddo Chiefdoms,* 58–59; Lawrence Kinnaird, ed., *Spain in the Mississippi Valley, 1765–1794: Post War Decade, 1782–1792,* Annual Report of the American Historical Association for the Year 1945, 3 vols. (Washington: Government Printing Office, 1946), 2:94, 3:18–19, hereafter cited as Kinnaird, *SMV.*

Chapter 6. The Nations of the North

1. Earl H. Elam, "The Origin and Identity of the Wichita," *Kansas Quarterly* 3 (1971): 13–15; David La Vere, *Contrary Neighbors: Southern Plains and Removed Indians in Indian Territory* (Norman: University of Oklahoma Press, 2000), 149.

2. Oñate's Eastern Expedition, 261; Newcomb, *Indians of Texas,* 262.

3. Kenmotsu, Bruseth, and Corbin, "Moscoso and the Route in Texas," 128–29; Newcomb, "Historic Indians of Central Texas," 8–9, 17–24; Susan C. Vehik, "Wichita Culture History," *Plains Anthropologist* 37 (November, 1992): 328–29; F. Smith, *Wichita Indians,* 8; Coronado Expedition, 334–43.

4. Coronado Expedition, 334.

5. George A. Dorsey, *The Mythology of the Wichita* (Washington, D.C.: Carnegie Institution, 1904), 2–3; Mildred Mott Wedel, "The Ethnohistoric Approach to Plains Caddoan Origins," *Nebraska History* 60 (summer, 1979): 189; F. Smith, *Wichita Indians,* 6, 25; Bolton, *ADM,* 1:250; Swanton, *Indian Tribes of North America,* 305.

6. Dorsey, *Mythology of the Wichita,* 18–20.

7. Bolton, *ADM,* 1:295.

8. Peterson, "Spiro Mounds Site," 119; Dorsey, *Mythology of the Wichita,* 6.

9. Coronado Expedition, 337.

10. Oñate's Eastern Expedition, 259–60.

11. Ibid., 263–64.

12. F. Smith, *Wichita Indians,* 10, 15–30.

13. Jean-Baptiste Bénard de la Harpe, "Account of the Journey of Bénard de la Harpe: Discovery Made by Him of Several Nations Situated in the West," trans. Ralph A. Smith, *Southwestern Historical Quarterly* 62 (July, 1958): 528.

14. Elizabeth Ann Harper, "The Taovayas Indians in Frontier Trade and Diplomacy, 1719–1768," *Chronicles of Oklahoma* 31 (autumn, 1953): 270–72; Ralph Smith, "The Tawehash in French, Spanish, English, and American Imperial Affairs," *West Texas Historical Association Year Book* 28 (October, 1952): 21–22.

15. Kavanagh, *Comanches*, 58, 126–27; Wallace and Hoebel, *Comanches*, 4–10; Meredith, *Dancing on Common Ground*, 34–35.

16. Kavanagh, *Comanches*, 121–24; Morris W. Foster, *Being Comanche: A Social History of an American Indian Community* (Tucson: University of Arizona Press, 1991), 36–38; Wallace and Hoebel, *Comanches*, 25–31; Catherine Price, "The Comanches Threat to Texas and New Mexico in the Eighteenth Century and the Development of Spanish Indian Policy," *Journal of the West* 24 (April, 1989): 38; Gerald Betty, *Comanche Society: Before the Reservation* (College Station: Texas A&M University Press, 2002), 13–45.

17. Wallace and Hoebel, *Comanches*, 25–31; Betty, *Comanche Society*, 13–45.

18. Kavanagh, *Comanches*, 53.

19. Vial quote in Kavanagh, *Comanches*, 102.

20. Kavanagh, *Comanches*, 38–39, 52–55.

21. Kavanagh, *Comanches*, 48–52, 59–62, 107; Berlandier, *Indians of Texas*, 91, 116, 170–72, plate 3; Betty, *Comanche Society*, 129–30.

22. Kavanagh, *Comanches*, 28–36, 48, 53; Melburn D. Thurman, "A New Interpretation of Comanche Social Organization," *Current Anthropology* 23 (October, 1982): 578–79; Daniel J. Gelo, "On a New Interpretation of Comanche Social Organization," *Current Anthropology* 28 (August–October, 1987): 551–52; Daniel J. Gelo, "'Comanche Land and Ever Has Been': A Native Geography of the Nineteenth-Century Comanchería," *Southwestern Historical Quarterly* 103 (January, 2000): 273–307; Wallace and Hoebel, *Comanches*, 155–71, 175–84.

23. George Catlin, *North American Indians*, ed. Peter Matthiessen (New York: Penguin Books, 1989), 332.

24. Wallace and Hoebel, *Comanches*, 77–86.

25. Betty, *Comanche Society*, 6, 49.

26. Pekka Hamalainen, "The Western Comanche Trade Center: Rethinking the Plains Indian Trade System," *Western Historical Quarterly* 29 (winter, 1998): 488; Price, "The Comanches Threat," 38–39; John, *Storms*, 245–54.

27. Hamalainen, "The Western Comanche Trade Center," 489–90; Robert Ryal Miller, trans. and ed., "New Mexico in Mid-Eighteenth Century: A Report Based on Governor Vélez Capuchín's Inspection," *Southwestern Historical Quarterly* 79 (October, 1975): 170.

28. Hamalainen, "The Western Comanche Trade Center," 490–92; R. Miller, "New Mexico in Mid-Eighteenth Century," 172–73.

29. Price, "Comanches Threat," 39; Hamalainen, "The Western Comanche Trade Center," 490; Kavanagh, *Comanches*, 65–72; John, *Storms*, 312–17.

30. James M. Daniel, "The Spanish Frontier in West Texas and Northern Mexico," *Southwestern Historical Quarterly* 71 (April, 1968): 483–84; Hall, *Social Change*, 94; Dunn, "Apache Relations," 202–12; John, *Storms*, 284–88.

31. John, *Storms*, 286–87; Bolton, *ADM*, 1:266–69.

32. Bolton, *Texas in the Middle Eighteenth Century*, 78–79; Petition of Santa Ana, January 9, 1748, Leutenegger, *Santa Ana Letters*, 75; William Edward Dunn, "Missionary Activities

among the Eastern Apaches Previous to the Founding of the San Saba Mission," *Quarterly of the Texas State Historical Association* 15 (January, 1912): 187–88.

33. Daniel, "The Spanish Frontier," 484–85.

34. Odie Faulk, "Spanish-Comanche Relations and the Treaty of 1785," *Texana* 2 (spring, 1964): 45–47; Daniel, "The Spanish Frontier," 484–85.

35. John, *Storms*, 266, 347–48.

36. John, *Storms*, 258–62, 294–98; Chipman, *Spanish Texas*, 158–60.

37. John, *Storms*, 297–303; Betty, *Comanche Society*, 121–24.

38. Henry Easton Allen, "The Parilla Expedition to the Red River," *Southwestern Historical Quarterly* 43 (July, 1939): 53–71; Chipman, *Spanish Texas*, 160–63; John, *Storms*, 297–303.

39. Chipman, *Spanish Texas*, 177–78.

40. Kniffen, Gregory, and Stokes, *Historic Indian Tribes*, 211, 232.

41. John, *Storms*, 361–68; Price, "The Comanches Threat," 39.

42. John, *Storms*, 355–57.

43. R. Smith, "The Tawehash," 26–28; Harper, "The Taovayas," 184–85; Bolton, *ADM*, 1:63–66; Price, "Comanches Threat," 41–42.

44. Sibley, "Historical Sketches," 66–68.

45. Bolton, *ADM*, 1:206–35; La Vere, *Caddo Chiefdoms*, 118–19; John, *Storms*, 402, 666.

46. Willard H. Rollings, *The Osage: An Ethnohistorical Study of Hegemony on the Prairie-Plains* (Columbia: University of Missouri Press, 1992), 5–7, 136–39.

47. La Harpe, *Historical Journal*, 137, 142–43; Holder, *The Hoe and the Horse*, 78; Rollings, *Osage*, 7, 126–28.

48. Bolton, *ADM*, 1:167.

49. Ibid., 1:167–68, 182, 193–95, 202–203, 2:24–25.

50. Kinnaird, *SMV*, 2:281, 316, 3:9–11; Kavanagh, *Comanches*, 147–48.

51. Kavanagh, *Comanches*, 111–21; John, *Storms*, 668–76, 762; Max L. Moorhead, *The Apache Frontier: Jacobo Ugarte and Spanish-Indian Relations in Northern New Spain, 1769–1791* (Norman: University of Oklahoma Press, 1968), 155–67; Betty, *Comanche Society*, 13–19.

52. John, *Storms*, 397–403, 653; Elizabeth A H. John, ed., and John Wheat, trans., "Governing Texas, 1779: The Karankawa Aspect," *Southwestern Historical Quarterly* 104 (April, 2001): 568–74.

53. François Grappe, "An Expedition to the Kichai: The Journal of François Grappe, September 24, 1783," ed. David La Vere and Katia Campbell, *Southwestern Historical Quarterly* 98 (July, 1994): 59–78; Price, "Comanche Threat," 39–43; Faulk, "Spanish-Comanche Relations," 44–53; Chipman, *Spanish Texas*, 195–215.

54. Kavanagh, *Comanches*, 105, 119–21, 140–54.

55. José Cortés, *Views from the Apache Frontier: Report on the Northern Provinces of New Spain*, ed. Elizabeth A. H. John, trans. John Wheat (Norman: University of Oklahoma Press, 1989), 28–31, 83; Moorhead, *Apache Frontier*, 200–69; Antonio Cordero, "Cordero's Description of the Apache, 1796," ed. Daniel S. Matson and Albert H. Schroeder, *New Mexico Historical Review* 32 (October, 1957): 350–56.

56. Cortés, *Views from the Apache Frontier*, 84–88.

57. La Vere, *Caddo Chiefdoms*, 106–26.

58. Quote in Cortés, *Views from the Apache Frontier*, 83; Himmel, *Karankawas and the Tonkawas*, 26–28.

59. Thomas Wolff, "The Karankawa Indians: Their Conflict with the White Man in Texas," *Ethnohistory* 16 (winter, 1969): 15–21; John and Wheat, "Governing Texas, 1779," 566–76; Himmel, *Karankawas and the Tonkawas*, 15–16.

60. Juan Bautista de Elguézabal, "A Description of Texas in 1803," trans. and ed. Odie Faulk, *Southwestern Historical Quarterly* 66 (April, 1963): 513–15.

Chapter 7. Immigrants from the East

1. La Harpe, "Account of the Journey," 251; J. Leitch Wright, *The Only Land They Knew: The Tragic Story of the American Indians in the Old South* (New York: Free Press, 1981), 137–45.

2. Arrell M. Gibson, *The Chickasaws* (Norman: University of Oklahoma Press, 1971), 4; Richard White, *The Roots of Dependency: Subsistence, Environment, and Social Change among the Choctaws, Pawnees, and Navajos* (Lincoln: University of Nebraska Press, 1983), 2, 5; Angie Debo, *The Rise and Fall of the Choctaw Republic* (Norman: University of Oklahoma Press, 1934, 1964), 1–2.

3. James Taylor Carson, *Searching for the Bright Path: The Mississippi Choctaws from Prehistory to Removal* (Lincoln: University of Nebraska Press, 1999), 8–25; Debo, *Rise and Fall of the Choctaw Republic*, 1, 9–10, 18; A. Gibson, *Chickasaws*, 21–22.

4. White, *Roots of Dependency*, 9, 35–68, 103–106; Carson, *Searching for the Bright Path*, 26–50; A. Gibson, *Chickasaws*, 39; David K. Bjork, ed. and trans., "Documents Regarding Indian Affairs in the Lower Mississippi Valley, 1771–1772," *Mississippi Valley Historical Review* 13 (June, 1926–March, 1927): 398–410.

5. Kinnaird, *SMV*, 2:316, 3:25–27, 92, 99–100; La Vere, *Caddo Chiefdoms*, 102–105; Dianna Everett, *The Texas Cherokees: A People between Two Fires, 1819–1840* (Norman: University of Oklahoma Press, 1990), 22; Berlandier, *Indians of Texas*, 127.

6. Theda Perdue, *Cherokee Women: Gender and Culture Change, 1700–1835* (Lincoln: University of Nebraska Press, 1998), 13–15, 41–59, 99; William G. McLoughlin, *Cherokee Renascence in the New Republic* (Princeton, N.J.: Princeton University Press, 1986), 3–32.

7. Theda Perdue and Michael D. Green, *The Cherokee Removal: A Brief History with Documents* (Boston and New York: Bedford Books of St. Martin's Press, 1995), 10; Thurman Wilkins, *Cherokee Tragedy: The Ridge Family and the Decimation of a People*, 2d ed. (Norman: University of Oklahoma Press, 1983), 25–27; McLoughlin, *Cherokee Renascence*, 3–32.

8. John Sibley, *A Report from Natchitoches in 1807*, ed. Annie Heloise Abel (Ville Platte, La.: Evangeline Genealogical and Historical Society, 1987), 16, 39, 51; Everett, *Texas Cherokees*, 10–11, 14–15.

9. Everett, *Texas Cherokees*, 15–23.

10. Quote in Berlandier, *Indians of Texas*, 112–13; Everett, *Texas Cherokees*, 15–23.

11. Timothy K. Perttula, "Material Culture of the Koasati Indians of Texas," *Historical Archaeology* 28 (1994): 66; Kathryn E. Holland Braund, *Deerskins and Duffels: The Creek Indian Trade with Anglo-America, 1685–1815* (Lincoln: University of Nebraska Press, 1993), 4; Michael D. Green, *The Politics of Indian Removal: Creek Government and Society in Crisis* (Lincoln: University of Nebraska Press, 1982), 14–15.

12. Braund, *Deerskins and Duffels*, 9–23.

13. Braund, *Deerskins and Duffels*, 9–23; Jonathan B. Hook, *The Alabama-Coushatta Indians* (College Station: Texas A&M University Press, 1997), 20–28.

14. Joel W. Martin, *Sacred Revolt: The Muskogee's Struggle for a New World* (Boston: Beacon Press, 1991), 70–84.

15. Quotes in Juan Antonio Padilla, "Texas in 1820," trans. Mattie Austin Hatcher, *Southwestern Historical Quarterly* 23 (July, 1919–April, 1920): 50; Perttula, "Material Culture of the Koasati," 66; Hook, *Alabama-Coushatta Indians*, 28–31.

16. Francis Paul Prucha, *The Great Father: The United States Government and the American Indians* (Lincoln: University of Nebraska Press, 1984), 243–48; La Vere, *Caddo Chiefdoms*, 80–81, 138–39; Everett, *Texas Cherokees*, 36, 39–40.

17. Berlandier, *Indians of Texas*, 23, fig. 13, 108–109, 111–13, 124–25, 127–28; Everett, *Texas Cherokees*, 40, 50–51; Hook, *Alabama-Coushatta Indians*, 30–31; John H. Reagan, "The Expulsion of the Cherokees from East Texas," *Texas Historical Association Quarterly* 1 (1897): 38; Anna Muckleroy, "The Indian Policy of the Republic of Texas," *Southwestern Historical Quarterly* 25 (April, 1922): 237–41.

18. Robert A. Calvert and Arnoldo De León, *The History of Texas* 2d ed. (Wheeling, Ill.: Harlan Davidson, 1996), 45–46; Berlandier, *Indians of Texas*, 124; Anderson, *Indian Southwest*, 194–95; Everett, *Texas Cherokees*, 22–23.

19. Dan L. Flores, *Journal of an Indian Trader: Anthony Glass and the Texas Trading Frontier, 1790–1810* (College Station: Texas A&M University Press, 1985), 26–30, 37–60, 128n.18; David La Vere, "Edward Murphy (1761–1808): Irish Entrepreneur in Spanish Natchitoches," *Louisiana History* 32 (fall, 1991): 371–91; Anderson, *Indian Southwest*, 192.

20. Dan Flores, ed., *Jefferson and Southwestern Exploration: The Freeman and Custis Accounts of the Red River Expedition of 1806* (Norman: University of Oklahoma Press, 1984), 160–68; Sibley, *Report from Natchitoches*, 12–13, 20–21, 48–67; Clarence Carter, ed., *Territorial Papers of the United States: Territory of Arkansas*. 26 vols. (Washington, D.C.: Government Printing Office, 1940), 19:70–75, hereafter cited as Carter, *Territorial Papers*; La Vere, *Caddo Chiefdoms*, 131–38.

21. W. C. C. Claiborne, *Official Letterbooks of W. C. C. Claiborne*, ed. Dunbar Rowland, 6 vols. (Jackson, Miss.: State Department of Archives and History, 1917), 3:87.

22. Sibley, *Report from Natchitoches*, 48–67; Flores, *Journal of an Indian Trader*, 37–46; Flores, *Jefferson and Southwestern Exploration*, 160–68, 193–94.

23. White, *Roots of Dependency*, 82–86.

24. Carter, *Territorial Papers*, 19:73–75, 86; White, *Roots of Dependency*, 82–86; Padilla, "Texas in 1820," 48, 50–52; La Vere, *Caddo Chiefdoms*, 134–37.

25. La Vere, *Caddo Chiefdoms*, 135–39; Carter, *Territorial Papers*, 19:73–75.

26. Carter, *Territorial Papers*, 9:878–79, 19:193, 197–98, 455, 497, 578, 611–12, 20:52, 90–92, 152–53, 237–38, 742; La Vere, *Caddo Chiefdoms*, 138–41.

27. Eugene C. Barker, ed., *The Austin Papers: Annual Report of the American Historical Association for the Year 1919* (Washington, D.C.: Government Printing Office, 1924), vol. 2, pt. 2, 1194–95; hereafter cited as *Austin Papers, 1919*; La Vere, *Caddo Chiefdoms*, 143; Everett, *Texas Cherokees*, 22, 30–33.

28. Don Manuel de Mier y Terán, "Documentos Para la Historia, año de 1828: Noticia de las tribus de salvajes conocidos que habitan en el Departamento de Tejas, y del número de familias de que consta cada tribu, puntos en que habitan y terrenos en que acampan," *Boletin de la Sociedad Macicana de Geografia y Estadistica* (1870): 264–69.

29. La Vere, *Caddo Chiefdoms*, 136–46.

30. Newkumet and Meredith, *Hasinai*, 76; F. Smith, *Caddo Indians*, 131, 143–44; Kenneth F. Neighbours, "José María: Anadarko Chief," *Chronicles of Oklahoma* 44 (autumn, 1966): 254–74.

31. José María Sánchez, "A Trip to Texas in 1828," trans. Carlos E. Castaneda, *Southwestern Historical Quarterly* 29 (April, 1926): 286–88; Everett, *Texas Cherokees*, 30–32, 36–37, 41–43.

32. Calvert and De León, *History of Texas*, 52–57; Muckleroy, "Indian Policy of the Republic of Texas," 247.

33. Himmel, *Conquest of the Karankawas and the Tonkawas*, 42–45, 71–74; Calvert and De León, *History of Texas*, 63–69; Juan N. Almonte, "Statistical Report on Texas," trans. C. E. Castañeda, *Southwestern Historical Quarterly* 28 (January, 1925): 222.

34. Winfrey and Day, *Texas Indian Papers*, 1:14; Barker, *Austin Papers, 1919*, vol. 2, pt. 2, 1197–98, 1220–21, 1231–32. 1307–1309.

35. Everett, *Texas Cherokees*, 43–48, 64–65; Calvert and De León, *The History of Texas*, 58.

36. F. Smith, *Caddo Indians*, 126–27.

37. Quotes in Winfrey and Day, *Texas Indian Papers*, 1:14–17; Randolph B. Campbell, *Sam Houston and the American Southwest* (New York: HarperCollins, 1993), 4–5, 28–34.

38. F. Smith, *Caddo Indians*, 128–30; Everett, *Texas Cherokees*, 76–79.

39. F. Smith, *Caddo Indians*, 129–33; Everett, *Texas Cherokees*, 79–84.

40. Winfrey and Day, *Texas Indian Papers*, 1:21–54; R. Earl McClendon, "The First Treaty of the Republic of Texas," *Southwestern Historical Quarterly* 52 (July, 1948): 39–42; F. Smith, *Caddo Indians*, 133–36; Everett, *Texas Cherokees*, 83–88.

41. Everett, *Texas Cherokees*, 90–95; F. Smith, *Caddo Indians*, 137–39; Calvert and De León, *History of Texas*, 100.

42. Reagan, "Expulsion of the Cherokees," 38; F. Smith, *Caddo Indians*, 138–41; Everett, *Texas Cherokees*, 95–96; Albert Woldert, "The Last of the Cherokees in Texas, and the Life and Death of Chief Bowles," *Chronicles of Oklahoma* 1 (June, 1923): 205.

43. Reagan, "Expulsion of the Cherokees," 38; F. Smith, *Caddo Indians*, 138–41; Everett, *Texas Cherokees*, 95–96.

44. Everett, *Texas Cherokees*, 100–103; F. Smith, *Caddo Indians*, 141.

45. Winfrey and Day, *Texas Indian Papers*, 1:61–66.

46. Reagan, "Expulsion of the Cherokees," 38–42.

47. Winfrey and Day, *Texas Indian Papers*, 1:67.

48. Quotes in Reagan, "Expulsion of the Cherokees," 44–46; Winfrey and Day, *Texas Indian Papers*, 1:76–77; Everett, *Texas Cherokees*, 108; Woldert, "Last of the Cherokees in Texas," 179, 210–26.

49. F. Smith, *Caddo Indians*, 143; Everett, *Texas Cherokees*, 109; Winfrey and Day, *Texas Indian Papers*, 1:80–81, 92–94.

50. Hook, *Alabama-Coushatta Indians*, 32–33; Winfrey and Day, *Texas Indian Papers*, 1:102–103; "Tigua Indians," *Handbook of Texas Online*.

Chapter 8. The Wars for Texas

1. Almonte, "Statistical Report on Texas," 194.

2. David B. Gracy, "Jean Lafitte and the Karankawa Indians," *East Texas Historical Journal* 2 (1964): 40–44; Wolff, "Karankawa Indians," 21–22.

3. George P. Garrison, ed., "Reminiscences of Early Texans," *Texas Historical Association Quarterly* 6 (1903): 237–41.

4. Noah Smithwick, *The Evolution of a State, or, Recollections of Old Texas Days* (1900; Austin: University of Texas Press, 1984), 3–4; Garrison, "Reminiscences of Early Texans," 237–41; Barker, *Austin Papers, 1919*, vol. 2, pt. 2, 1198, 1639–41; Himmel, *Conquest of the Karankawas and the Tonkawas*, 49–51.

5. Himmel, *Conquest of the Karankawas and the Tonkawas*, 52–54, 74–75; Berlandier, *Indians of Texas*, 114, 123.

6. Himmel, *Conquest of the Karankawas and the Tonkawas*, 77–82; William Bollaert, *William Bollaert's Texas*, ed. W. Eugene Hollon (Norman: University of Oklahoma Press, 1956, 1989), 73.

7. Himmel, *Conquest of the Karankawas and the Tonkawas*, 100–105; Wolff, "Karankawa Indians," 23–25.

8. Mishkin, *Rank and Warfare*, 18–34.

9. Carlson, *Plains Indians*, 36–39.

10. Jacob Fowler, *The Journal of Jacob Fowler*, ed. Elliott Coues (New York: Francis P.

Harper, 1898; Minneapolis: Ross and Haines, 1969), 59–60, 65, 92–95; Smithwick, *Evolution of a State*, 174–75; Mishkin, *Rank and Warfare*, 20.

11. Herman Lehmann, *Nine Years among the Indians, 1870–1879*, ed. J. Marvin Hunter, 1st paperback ed. (Albuquerque: University of New Mexico Press, 1993), 2–23; *Catlin, North American Indians*, 334; Carlson, *Plains Indians*, 38, 48.

12. Dan Flores, "Bison Ecology and Bison Diplomacy: The Southern Plains from 1800 to 1850," *Journal of American History* 78 (September, 1991): 471, 479, 483; Alan M. Klein, "Political Economy of the Buffalo Hide Trade: Race and Class on the Plains," in *The Political Economy of North American Indians*, ed. John H. Moore (Norman: University of Oklahoma Press, 1993), 142–43.

13. Plummer Narrative, 3, 97; Newcomb, *Indians of Texas*, 344–45.

14. Winfrey and Day, *Texas Indian Papers*, 1:114; La Vere, *Contrary Neighbors*, 124.

15. Smithwick, *Evolution of a State*, 134–35, 151, 167; La Vere, *Contrary Neighbors*, 155–57; Mishkin, *Rank and Warfare*, 28–30.

16. Himmel, *Conquest of the Karankawas and the Tonkawas*, 43–44, 67; F. Smith, *Wichita Indians*, 123–25.

17. Smithwick, *Evolution of a State*, 135.

18. Gregg Cantrell, *Stephen F. Austin: Empresario of Texas* (New Haven, Conn.: Yale University Press, 1999), 111.

19. La Vere, *Contrary Neighbors*, 90–126; James Mooney, *Calendar History of the Kiowa Indians* (Washington, D.C.: Smithsonian Institution Press, 1979), 297–99.

20. Smithwick, *Evolution of a State*, 154–62.

21. Himmel, *Conquest of the Karankawas and the Tonkawas*, 54–61, 82–92.

22. Himmel, *Conquest of the Karankawas and the Tonkawas*, 130–31, 159; Grant Foreman, ed., "The Journal of Elijah Hicks," *Chronicles of Oklahoma* 13 (March, 1935): 82; Winfrey and Day, *Texas Indian Papers*, 1:30–32, 46–48; Lehmann, *Nine Years among the Indians*, 153–64.

23. Smithwick, *Evolution of a State*, 134

24. Ibid., 138.

25. Quote in Smithwick, *Evolution of a State*, 135; Mooney, *Calendar History*, 302–305.

26. Stanley Noyes, *Los Comanches: The Horse People, 1751–1845* (Albuquerque: University of New Mexico Press, 1993), 280–84.

27. Noyes, *Los Comanches*, 280–84; Wallace and Hoebel, *Comanches*, 294; Smithwick, *Evolution of a State*, 183–84.

28. Noyes, *Los Comanches*, 288–96; Newcomb, *Indians of Texas*, 350.

29. Winfrey and Day, *Texas Indian Papers*, 1:241–46, 2:114–18, 154, quote on 2:116; Smithwick, *Evolution of a State*, 184–85.

30. Mayhall, *Kiowas*, 1–15, 135–36; Mooney, *Calendar History*, 162–65, 228–30.

31. Carlson, *Plains Indians*, 2–4, 121, 128–29.

32. Mayhall, *Kiowas*, 128–30; Newcomb, *Indians of Texas*, 193–96.

33. Mayhall, *Kiowas*, 138–40.

34. Mayhall, *Kiowas*, 138–40; La Vere, *Life among the Texas Indians*, 49–50; Mooney, *Calendar History*, 284–85.

35. Mayhall, *Kiowas*, 136–37.

36. Meredith, *Dancing on Common Ground*, 45–54; Mayhall, *Kiowas*, 147–51; Maurice Boyd, *Kiowa Voices*, vol. 2, *Myths, Legends, and Folktales* (Fort Worth: Texas Christian University Press, 1983), 2:49–50, 137–38; Mooney, *Calendar History*, 238–44, 257–61.

37. Quotes in Josiah Gregg, *Commerce of the Prairies*, ed. Max L. Moorhead (1844; Norman: University of Oklahoma Press, 1954), 415, 251.

38. David Lavender, *Bent's Fort* (Garden City, N.Y.: Doubleday, 1954), 15, 86, 127–28; Gregg, *Commerce of the Prairies*, 52–57.

39. Prucha, *Great Father*, 354–59.

40. Foreman, "Journal of Elijah Hicks," 86–89, La Vere, *Contrary Neighbors*, 108–11; Charles J. Kappler, ed., *Indian Treaties, 1778–1883* (New York: International Publishing, 1972), 435–39, 489–91, 554–57.

41. Thomas T. Smith, *The U.S. Army and the Texas Frontier Economy, 1845–1900* (College Station: Texas A&M University Press, 1999), 17–22; Thomas T. Smith, "U.S. Army Combat Operations in the Indian Wars of Texas, 1849–1881," *Southwestern Historical Quarterly* 94 (April, 1996): 507–10, 518.

42. T. Smith, "U.S. Army Combat Operations," 510–19.

43. Winfrey and Day, *Texas Indian Papers*, 3:130–36, 148–54.

44. Winfrey and Day, *Texas Indian Papers*, 3:186–209; F. Todd Smith, *The Caddos, the Wichitas, and the United States, 1846–1901* (College Station: Texas A&M University Press, 1996), 39–44; Kavanagh, *Comanches*, 356–60; "Tigua Indians," *Handbook of Texas Online*.

45. F. Smith, *Caddos, the Wichitas, and the United States*, 39–54; La Vere, *Contrary Neighbors*, 154–64; John Salmon Ford, *Rip Ford's Texas* (Austin: University of Texas Press, 1963, 1987), 231–34.

46. La Vere, *Contrary Neighbors*, 154–64; Ford, *Rip Ford's Texas*, 231–34; Wallace and Hoebel, *Comanches*, 301–302.

47. La Vere, *Contrary Neighbors*, 98–99, 142–50.

48. Ford, *Rip Ford's Texas*, 231–40; La Vere, *Contrary Neighbors*, 154–56; William Y. Chalfant, *Without Quarter: The Wichita Expedition and the Fight on Crooked Creek* (Norman: University of Oklahoma Press, 1991), 36.

49. Chalfant, *Without Quarter*, 38–44, 63–103; F. Smith, *Caddos, the Wichitas, and the United States*, 58–59; La Vere, *Contrary Neighbors*, 160–61.

50. George Klos, "'Our People Could Not Distinguish One Tribe from Another': The 1859 Expulsion of the Reserve Indians from Texas," *Southwestern Historical Quarterly* 97 (April, 1994): 602–19; F. Smith, *Caddos, the Wichitas, and the United States*, 67–78.

51. Klos, "'Our People Could Not Distinguish One Tribe from Another,'" 602–19; William E. Burnett, "Lieutenant Wm. E. Burnett: Notes on Removal of Indians from Texas to Indian Territory," ed. Raymond Estep, *Chronicles of Oklahoma* 38 (autumn, 1960): 274–309; F. Smith, *Caddos, the Wichitas, and the United States*, 67–78; Prucha, *Great Father*, 364–66.

Chapter 9. Conquered

1. Prucha, *Great Father*, 415–27; Hook, *Alabama-Coushatta Indians*, 38.

2. Jeanne V. Harrison, "Matthew Leeper, Confederate Agent at the Wichita Agency, Indian Territory," *Chronicles of Oklahoma* 47 (autumn, 1969): 242–57; Thomas W. Dunlay, *Wolves for the Blue Soldiers: Indian Scouts and Auxiliaries with the United States Army, 1860–90* (Lincoln: University of Nebraska Press, 1982), 117–18; Prucha, *Great Father*, 421; La Vere, *Life among the Texas Indians*, 40–41.

3. James L. Haley, *The Buffalo War: The History of the Red River Indian Uprising of 1874* (Norman: University of Oklahoma Press, 1976), 85; "Cynthia Ann Parker," *Handbook of Texas Online*.

4. Felipe A. Latorre and Dolores L. Latorre, *The Mexican Kickapoo Indians* (Austin: University of Texas Press, 1976), 11–13; Arrell M. Gibson, *The Kickapoos: Lords of the Middle Border* (Norman: University of Oklahoma Press, 1963), 201.

5. A. Gibson, *Kickapoos*, 182.

6. Ibid., 188–90.

7. A. Gibson, *Kickapoos*, 193–207; Latorre and Latorre, *Mexican Kickapoo Indians*, 17–19.

8. A. Gibson, *Kickapoos*, 208–26; 234–45; Latorre and Latorre, *Mexican Kickapoo Indians*, 21–22.

9. A. Gibson, *Kickapoos*, 208–26; 234–45; Latorre and Latorre, *Mexican Kickapoo Indians*, 21–22.

10. A. Gibson, *Kickapoos*, 244–70; Latorre and Latorre, *Mexican Kickapoo Indians*, 22–23.

11. T. Lindsay Baker and Billy R. Harrison, *Adobe Walls: The History and Archeology of the 1874 Trading Post* (College Station: Texas A&M University Press, 1986), 14, 126; Robert Utley, *The Indian Frontier of the American West, 1846–1890* (Albuquerque: University of New Mexico Press, 1984), 95.

12. Kappler, *Indian Treaties*, 887–95.

13. William T. Hagan, *United States-Comanche Relations: The Reservation Years* (Norman: University of Oklahoma Press, 1990), 21–23; Thomas T. Smith, *Fort Inge: Sharps, Spurs, and Sabers on the Texas Frontier, 1849–1869* (Austin: Eakin Press, 1993), 154–55.

14. T. Smith, *Fort Inge*, 155–56; E. A. Bode, *A Dose of Frontier Soldiering: The Memoirs of Corporal E. A. Bode, Frontier Regular Infantry, 1877–1882*, ed. Thomas T. Smith (Lincoln: University of Nebraska Press, 1994), 178–79.

15. Bode, *A Dose of Frontier Soldiering*, 178–79.

16. Dunlay, *Wolves for the Blue Soldiers*, 117; La Vere, *Contrary Neighbors*, 182.

17. Kappler, *Indian Treaties*, 977–87; Alfred A. Taylor, "The Medicine Lodge Peace Council," *Chronicles of Oklahoma* 2 (June, 1924): 89–118.

18. F. Smith, *Caddos, the Wichitas, and the United States*, 95–109.

19. Hagan, *United States-Comanche Relations*, 29–58, 64–65.

20. Ibid., 59–91, quote on 73.

21. Utley, *Indian Frontier*, 143–45; Hagan, *United States-Comanche Relations*, 76.

22. Charles M. Robinson III, *Satanta: The Life and Death of a War Chief* (Austin: State House Press, 1997), 125–52, quote on 129; Utley, *Indian Frontier*, 146–48.

23. Hagan, *United States-Comanche Relations*, 87–102; Robinson, *Satanta*, 174–80.

24. David D. Smits, "The Frontier Army and the Destruction of the Buffalo, 1865–1883," *Western Historical Quarterly* 25 (autumn, 1994): 314–34; Hagan, *United States-Comanche Relations*, 75–77; Haley, *Buffalo War*, 24–36.

25. Haley, *Buffalo War*, 52–93.

26. Ibid., 107–23.

27. Ibid.

28. Haley, *Buffalo War*, 125–46, 169–83; Utley, *Indian Frontier*, 175–76.

29. Haley, *Buffalo War*, 185–221; Hagan, *United States-Comanche Relations*, 108–20; Utley, *Indian Frontier*, 176–77.

30. Roberts, *Once They Moved Like the Wind*, quote on 185; "Victorio," *Handbook of Texas Online*; B. Wright, *Tiguas*, 16; Tigua Indian Cultural Center Museum, El Paso, Tex.

31. Roberts, *Once They Moved Like the Wind*, 170–89, quote on 185; "Victorio," *Handbook of Texas Online*; B. Wright, *Tiguas*, 16; Tigua Indian Cultural Center Museum.

32. Hook, *Alabama-Coushatta Indians*, 39; "Tigua Indians," *Handbook of Texas Online*.

33. Hagan, *United States-Comanche Relations*, 127–34, 148–53, 175–76; Forrest D. Monahan, Jr., "The Kiowa-Comanche Reservation in the 1890s," *Chronicles of Oklahoma* 45 (winter, 1967–78): 451–63; quote in La Vere, *Life among the Texas Indians*, 188.

34. Benjamin R. Kracht, "The Kiowa Ghost Dance, 1894–1916: An Unheralded Revitalization Movement," *Ethnohistory* 39 (fall, 1992): 456–59; William T. Hagan, *Quanah Parker, Co-*

manche Chief (Norman: University of Oklahoma Press, 1993), 52–61; Hagan, *United States-Comanche Relations,* 189–94; quote in Carol K. Rachlin, "The Native American Church in Oklahoma," *Chronicles of Oklahoma* 42 (autumn, 1964): 262.

35. Clyde Ellis, *To Change Them Forever: Indian Education at Rainy Mountain Boarding School, 1893–1920* (Norman: University of Oklahoma Press, 1996), 91–130; Hagan, *United States- Comanche Relations,* 133–35, 194–200; La Vere, *Life among the Texas Indians,* 148–67.

36. La Vere, *Contrary Neighbors,* 215–16.

37. Quote in Francis Paul Prucha, *Indian Policy in the United States: Historical Essays* (Lincoln: University of Nebraska Press, 1981), 239.

38. Hagan, *United States-Comanche Relations,* 166; F. Smith, *Caddos, the Wichitas, and the United States,* 142–44; Prucha, *Great Father,* 666–71.

39. Prucha, *Great Father,* 671.

40. Hagan, *United States-Comanche Relations,* 204–16; F. Smith, *Caddos, the Wichitas, and the United States,* 146–48.

41. Prucha, *Great Father,* 775–76; Hagan, *United States-Comanche Relations,* 262–94.

42. B. Wright, *Tiguas,* 16; Richard White, *"It's Your Misfortune and None of My Own": A History of the American West* (Norman: University of Oklahoma Press, 1991), 343.

Chapter 10. From One Millennium to the Next

1. Prucha, *Great Father,* 810, 864–96.

2. Prucha, *Great Father,* 810, 864–96; quote in "Meriam Commission," *Native America in the Twentieth Century: An Encyclopedia,* ed. Mary B. Davis (New York: Garland Publishing, 1994), 335; "Indian Reorganization Act," *Native America,* 263.

3. "Indian Reorganization Act," *Native America,* 262–64; Prucha, *Great Father,* 954–68.

4. Hooks, *Alabama-Coushatta Indians,* 40; M. Foster, *Being Comanche,* 125, 131, 145.

5. M. Foster, *Being Comanche,* 125, 131, 145.

6. "Military Service," *Native America,* 341–43; "Alabama-Coushattas," *Handbook of Texas Online.*

7. "Powwow," *Native America,* 476–81; M. Foster, *Being Comanche,* 145; Meredith, *Dancing on Common Ground,* 119–20.

8. "Urbanization," *Native America,* 670–72; Prucha, *Great Father,* 1079–86.

9. "Urbanization," *Native America,* 670–72.

10. Prucha, *Great Father,* 1041–56.

11. Ibid., 1056–59.

12. Ibid., 1017–23, 1060–1110.

13. Ibid., 1106–20.

14. Ibid.

15. M. Foster, *Being Comanche,* 100–14; David La Vere, "The Comanche-Kiowa Business Council of the Early 1900s," in *Native Pathways: Economic Development and American Indian Culture,* ed. Brian C. Hosmer and Colleen O'Neill (Boulder: University Press of Colorado, forthcoming).

16. Prucha, *Great Father,* 849–50; M. Foster, *Being Comanche,* 100–109; "Indian Health Service," *Native America,* 256–61.

17. Prucha, *Great Father,* 971–73.

18. F. Smith, *Caddos, the Wichitas, and the United States,* 154; M. Foster, *Being Comanche,* 113–14, 130, 136–37; "Tonkawa Tribe of Indians," online home page, http://members.tripod.com/tonkawa/main.html.

19. Meredith, *Dancing on Common Ground,* 121–46.

20. Hook, *Alabama-Coushatta Indians*, 40–41; "Alabama-Coushatta Indians," *Handbook of Texas Online*.

21. Hook, *Alabama-Coushatta Indians*, 36–59.

22. Hook, *Alabama-Coushatta Indians*, 65; "Alabama-Coushatta Indians," *Handbook of Texas Online*.

23. "Alabama-Coushatta Indians," *Handbook of Texas Online*; Hook, *Alabama-Coushattas*, 70–77; Prucha, *Great Father*, 1047–48.

24. "Texas Indian Commission," *Handbook of Texas Online*; "Alabama-Coushatta Indians," *Handbook of Texas Online*; Hook, *Alabama-Coushattas*, 86–91.

25. "Texas Indian Commission," *Handbook of Texas Online*; "Alabama-Coushatta Indians," *Handbook of Texas Online*; Hook, *Alabama-Coushattas*, 91–98.

26. Quote in B. Wright, *Tiguas*, 16

27. B. Wright, *Tiguas*, 18–25; "Tigua Indians" and "Ysleta del Sur Museum," *Handbook of Texas Online*.

28. "Kickapoo Indians" and "Texas Indian Commission," *Handbook of Texas Online*; Latorre and Latorre, *Mexican Kickapoo Indians*, 21–22, 26.

29. "Kickapoo Indians," *Handbook of Texas Online*.

Bibliography

Albers, Patricia C. "Symbiosis, Merger, and War: Contrasting Forms of Intertribal Relationship among Historic Plains Indians." In *The Political Economy of North American Indians*, ed. John H. Moore, 97–100. Norman: University of Oklahoma Press, 1993.

Allen, Henry Easton. "The Parilla Expedition to the Red River." *Southwestern Historical Quarterly* 43 (July, 1939): 53–71.

Almonte, Juan N. "Statistical Report on Texas, 1834." Trans. C. E. Castañeda. *Southwestern Historical Quarterly* 28 (January, 1925): 177–222.

Amsden, Charles Avery. *Prehistoric Southwesterners from Basketmakers to Pueblo*. Los Angeles: Southwest Museum, 1949.

Anderson, Gary Clayton. *The Indian Southwest, 1580–1830: Ethnogenesis and Reinvention*. Norman: University of Oklahoma Press, 1999.

———. *Kinsmen of Another Kind: Dakota-White Relations in the Upper Mississippi Valley, 1650–1862*. Lincoln: University of Nebraska Press, 1984.

Anthony, David, Dimitri Y. Telegin, and Dorcas Brown. "The Origin of Horseback Riding." *Scientific American* 265 (December, 1991): 94–100.

Arens, W. *The Man-eating Myth: Anthropology and Anthropophagy*. New York: Oxford, 1979.

Aten, Lawrence E. *Indians of the Upper Texas Coast*. New York: Academic Press, 1983.

Baker, T. Lindsay, and Billy R. Harrison. *Adobe Walls: The History and Archeology of the 1874 Trading Post*. College Station: Texas A&M University Press, 1986.

Barker, Eugene C., ed. *The Austin Papers: Annual Report of the American Historical Association for the Year 1919*. 2 vols. and 2 pts. Washington, D.C.: Government Printing Office, 1924.

Baugh, Timothy G. "Culture History and Protohistoric Societies in the Southern Plains." *Plains Anthropologist* 31 (November, 1986): 167–87.

———. "Holocene Adaptations in the Southern High Plains." In *Plains Indians, A.D. 500–1500: The Archaeological Past of Historic Groups*, ed. Karl H. Schleiser, 264–89. Norman: University of Oklahoma Press, 1994.

Berlandier, Jean Louis. *The Indians of Texas in 1830*. Ed. John C. Ewers. Washington, D.C.: Smithsonian Institution Press, 1969.

Bertram, Jack B. *Archeological Investigation Along the Proposed Alibates Tour Road*. Professional Paper No. 33, Southwest Cultural Resources Center, Division of Anthropology. Santa Fe: National Park Service, 1989.

Betty, Gerald. *Comanche Society: Before the Reservation*. College Station: Texas A&M University Press, 2002.

Billard, Jules H., ed. *The World of the American Indian*. Washington, D.C.: National Geographic Society, 1974.

Bjork, David K., ed. and trans. "Documents Regarding Indian Affairs in the Lower Mississippi Valley, 1771–1772." *Mississippi Valley Historical Review* 13 (June, 1926–March, 1927): 398–410.

Bode, E. A. *A Dose of Frontier Soldiering: The Memoirs of Corporal E. A. Bode, Frontier Regular Infantry, 1877–1882*. Ed. Thomas T. Smith. Lincoln: University of Nebraska Press, 1994.

Bogusch, Edwin R. "Brush Invasion of the Rio Grande Plain of Texas." *Texas Journal of Science* 4 (March, 1952): 85–91.

Bollaert, William. *William Bollaert's Texas*. Ed. W. Eugene Hollon. Norman: University of Oklahoma Press, 1989.

Bolton, Herbert E. "The Founding of Mission Rosario: A Chapter in the History of the Gulf Coast." *Texas State Historical Association Quarterly* 10 (October, 1906): 113–39.

———. *The Hasinai: Southern Caddoans As Seen by the Earliest Europeans*. Norman: University of Oklahoma Press, 1987.

———. "The Native Tribes about the East Texas Missions." *Texas State Historical Quarterly* 2 (1908): 249–76.

———. "The Spanish Occupation of Texas, 1519–1690." *Southwestern Historical Quarterly* 16 (July, 1912): 1–26.

———. *Texas in the Middle Eighteenth Century: Studies in Spanish Colonial History and Administration*. Berkeley: University of California Press, 1915; Austin: Texas History Paperbacks, 1970.

———, ed. *Spanish Exploration in the Southwest, 1542–1706*. New York: Barnes and Noble, 1967.

———, trans. and ed. *Athanase De Mézières and the Louisiana-Texas Frontier, 1768–1780*. 2 vols. Cleveland: Arthur H. Clark, 1914; New York: Kraus Reprint, 1970.

Bosque, Fernando del. "Diary of Fernando del Bosque, 1675." In *Spanish Exploration in the Southwest, 1542–1706*, ed. Herbert E. Bolton, 291–309. New York: Barnes and Noble, 1967.

Bousman, C. Britt, Barry W. Baker, and Anne C. Kerr. "Paleoindian Archeology in Texas." In *The Prehistoric Archeology of Texas*. Ed. Timothy K. Perttula. College Station: Texas A&M University Press, 2004.

Boyd, Maurice. *Kiowa Voices*. Vol. 2, *Myths, Legends, and Folktales*. Fort Worth: Texas Christian University Press, 1983.

Braund, Kathryn E. Holland. *Deerskins and Duffels: The Creek Indian Trade with Anglo-America, 1685–1815*. Lincoln: University of Nebraska Press, 1993.

Brooks, Robert L. "From Stone Slab Architecture to Abandonment, the Antelope Creek Phase: A Revisionist View." In *The Prehistoric Archeology of Texas*, ed. Timothy K. Perttula. College Station: Texas A&M University Press, 2004.

Brose, David S. "From the Southeastern Ceremonial Complex to the Southern Cult: 'You Can't Tell the Players without a Program.'" In *The Southeastern Ceremonial Complex: Artifacts and Analysis, the Cottonlandia Conference*, ed. Patricia Galloway , 27–37. Lincoln: University of Nebraska Press, 1989.

Burnett, William E. "Lieutenant Wm. E. Burnett: Notes on Removal of Indians from Texas to Indian Territory." Ed. Raymond Estep. *Chronicles of Oklahoma* 38 (autumn, 1960): 274–309.

Cabeza de Vaca, Alvar Nuñez. *Adventures in the Unknown Interior of America*. Trans. and ed. Cyclone Covey. Albuquerque: University of New Mexico Press, 1986.

Calvert, Robert A., and Arnoldo De León. *The History of Texas*. 2d ed. Wheeling, Ill.: Harlan Davidson, 1996.

Campbell, Randolph B. *Sam Houston and the American Southwest*. New York: HarperCollins, 1993.

Campbell, T. N. "The Coahuiltecans and Their Neighbors." In *Handbook of North American Indians*, ed. Alfonso Ortiz, 343–58. Vol. 10. Washington, D.C.: Smithsonian Institution, 1983.
———. "Espinosa, Olivares, and the Colorado River Indians, 1709." In *The Indians of Southern Texas and Northeastern Mexico: Selected Writings of Thomas Nolan Campbell*, ed. T. N. Campbell, 61–70. Austin: Texas Archeological Research Laboratory, University of Texas, 1988.
———. "Name All the Indians of the Bastrop Area." In *The Indians of Southern Texas and Northeastern Mexico: Selected Writings of Thomas Nolan Campbell*, ed. T. N. Campbell, 71–77. Austin: Texas Archeological Research Laboratory, University of Texas, 1988.
Campbell, T. N., and T. J. Campbell. "Indians of the San Antonio Missions." In *The Indians of Southern Texas and Northeastern Mexico: Selected Writings of Thomas Nolan Campbell*, ed. T. N. Campbell. Austin: Texas Archeological Research Laboratory, University of Texas, 1988, 79–93.
Cantrell, Gregg. *Stephen F. Austin: Empresario of Texas*. New Haven, Conn.: Yale University Press, 1999.
Carlson, Paul H. *The Plains Indians*. College Station: Texas A&M University Press, 1998.
Carmody, Denise Lardner. *The Oldest God: Archaic Religion Yesterday and Today*. Nashville: Abingdon Press, 1981.
Carson, James Taylor. *Searching for the Bright Path: The Mississippi Choctaws from Prehistory to Removal*. Lincoln: University of Nebraska Press, 1999.
Carter, Cecile Elkins. *Caddo Indians: Where We Come From*. Norman: University of Oklahoma Press, 1995.
Carter, Clarence, ed. *The Territorial Papers of the United States*. Vol. 19, *Territory of Arkansas*. 26 vols. Washington, D.C.: Government Printing Office, 1940.
Casañas de Jesus Maria, Francisco. "Letter to the Viceroy of Mexico, Mission Santíssima Nombre de Maria, 15 August 1691." In "Descriptions of the Tejas or Asinai Indians, 1691–1722," trans. Mattie Austin Hatcher. *Southwestern Historical Quarterly* 30 (January, 1927).
Castañeda, Pedro de. "Narrative of the Expedition of Coronado." In *Spanish Explorers in the Southern United States, 1528–1543*, ed. Frederick W. Hodge, 281–387. New York: Barnes and Noble, 1971.
Catlin, George. *North American Indians*. Ed. Peter Matthiessen. New York: Penguin Books, 1989.
Céliz, Fray Francisco. *Diary of the Alarcón Expedition into Texas, 1718–1719*. Trans. Fritz Leo Hoffman. Los Angeles: Quivira Society, 1935.
Chalfant, William Y. *Without Quarter: The Wichita Expedition and the Fight on Crooked Creek*. Norman: University of Oklahoma Press, 1991.
Chipman, Donald E. *Spanish Texas, 1519–1821*. Austin: University of Texas Press, 1992.
Claiborne, W. C. C. *Official Letterbooks of W. C. C. Claiborne*. 6 vols. Ed. Dunbar Rowland. Jackson, Miss.: State Department of Archives and History, 1917.
Collins, Michael B. "Archeology in Central Texas." In *The Prehistoric Archeology of Texas*, ed. Timothy K. Perttula. College Station: Texas A&M University Press, 2004.
———. "Implications of Monte Verde, Chile, for the Earliest Prehistory of Texas." In *The Prehistoric Archeology of Texas*, ed. Timothy K. Perttula. College Station: Texas A&M University Press, 2004.
Corbin, James E. "Spanish-Indian Interaction on the Eastern Frontier of Texas." In *Columbian Consequences: Archaeological and Historical Perspectives on the Spanish Borderlands West*, ed. David Hurst Thomas, 269–79. 3 vols. Washington, D.C.: Smithsonian Institution Press, 1989.

Cordell, Linda S. *Prehistory of the Southwest*. New York: Academic Press, 1984.

Cordero, Antonio. "Cordero's Description of the Apache, 1796." Ed. Daniel S. Matson and Albert H. Schroeder. *New Mexico Historical Review* 32 (October, 1957): 335–56.

Cortés, José. *Views from the Apache Frontier: Report on the Northern Provinces of New Spain.* Ed. Elizabeth A. H. John, trans. John Wheat. Norman: University of Oklahoma Press, 1989.

Crawford, Michael H. *The Origins of Native Americans: Evidence from Anthropological Genetics.* Cambridge, Eng.: Cambridge University Press, 1998.

Cronon, William. *Changes in the Land: Indians, Colonists, and the Ecology of New England.* New York: Hill and Wang, 1983.

Crosby, Alfred W. *The Columbian Exchange: Biological and Cultural Consequences of 1492.* Westport, Conn.: Greenwood Publishing, 1972.

———. "Virgin Soil Epidemics as a Factor in the Aboriginal Depopulation in America." *William and Mary Quarterly*, 3, ser. 33 (April, 1976): 289–99.

Daniel, James M. "The Spanish Frontier in West Texas and Northern Mexico." *Southwestern Historical Quarterly* 71 (April, 1968): 481–95.

Debo, Angie. *The Rise and Fall of the Choctaw Republic.* Norman: University of Oklahoma Press, 1961.

DePratter, Chester B. *Late Prehistoric and Early Historic Chiefdoms in the Southeastern United States.* New York: Garland Press, 1991.

DeShields, James T. *Border Wars of Texas.* Tioga, Tex.: Herald Co., 1912.

Dillehay, Tom [Thomas] D. "Disease Ecology and Initial Human Migration." In *The First Americans: Search and Research*, ed. Tom D. Dillehay and David J. Meltzer. Boca Raton, Fla.: CRC Press, 1991.

———. "Late Quaternary Bison Population Changes on the Southern Plains." *Plains Anthropologist* 19 (August, 1974): 180–96.

———. *The Settlement of the Americas: A New Prehistory.* New York: Basic Books, 2000.

Dobyns, H. F. *Their Number Become Thinned: Native American Population Dynamics in Eastern North America.* Knoxville: University of Tennessee Press, 1983.

Dorsey, George A. *The Mythology of the Wichita.* Washington, D.C.: Carnegie Institution, 1904.

Drass, Richard R., and Timothy G. Baugh. "The Wheeler Phase and Cultural Continuity in the Southern Plains." *Plains Anthropologist* 42 (May, 1997): 183–204.

Driver, Harold E. *Indians of North America.* Chicago: University of Chicago Press, 1961.

Dunlay, Thomas W. *Wolves for the Blue Soldiers: Indian Scouts and Auxiliaries with the United States Army, 1860–90.* Lincoln: University of Nebraska Press, 1982.

Dunn, William Edward. "Apache Relations in Texas, 1718–1750." *Texas Historical Association Quarterly* 14 (January, 1911): 198–274.

———. "Missionary Activities among the Eastern Apaches Previous to the Founding of the San Saba Mission." *Texas Historical Association Quarterly* 15 (January, 1912): 186–200.

Eaton, Jack D. "The Gateway Missions of the Lower Rio Grande." In *Columbian Consequences: Archaeological and Historical Perspectives on the Spanish Borderlands West*, ed. David Hurst Thomas, 1:245–58. 3 vols. Washington, D.C.: Smithsonian Institution Press, 1989.

Elam, Earl H. "The Origin and Identity of the Wichita." *Kansas Quarterly* 3 (1971): 13–20.

Elguézabal, Juan Bautista de. "A Description of Texas in 1803." Trans. and ed. Odie Faulk. *Southwestern Historical Quarterly* 66 (April, 1963): 513–15.

Ellis, Clyde. *To Change Them Forever: Indian Education at Rainy Mountain Boarding School, 1893–1920.* Norman: University of Oklahoma Press, 1996.

Espejo, Antonio. "Account of the Journey to the Provinces and Settlements of New Mexico,

1583." In *Spanish Exploration in the Southwest, 1542–1706*, ed. Herbert E. Bolton, 168–95. New York: Barnes and Noble, 1967.

Espinosa, Isidro Felis de. "Letter on the Asinai and their Allies, 1722." In "Descriptions of the Tejas or Asinai Indians, 1691–1722," trans. Mattie Austin Hatcher. *Southwestern Historical Quarterly* 31 (October, 1927): 151–80.

Everett, Dianna. *The Texas Cherokees: A People between Two Fires, 1819–1840*. Norman: University of Oklahoma Press, 1990.

Ewers, John C. "The Influence of Epidemics on the Indian Populations and Cultures of Texas." *Plains Anthropologist* 18 (May, 1973): 104–15.

Faulk, Odie. "Spanish-Comanche Relations and the Treaty of 1785." *Texana* 2 (spring, 1964): 44–53.

Fiedel, Stuart J. *Prehistory of the Americas*. New York: Cambridge University Press, 1987.

Flores, Dan. "Bison Ecology and Bison Diplomacy: The Southern Plains from 1800 to 1850." *Journal of American History* 78 (September, 1991): 465–85.

———, ed. *Jefferson and Southwestern Exploration: The Freeman and Custis Accounts of the Red River Expedition of 1806*. Norman: University of Oklahoma Press, 1984.

———. *Journal of an Indian Trader: Anthony Glass and the Texas Trading Frontier, 1790–1810*. College Station: Texas A&M University Press, 1985.

Foik, Paul J, trans. "Captain Don Domingo Ramón's Diary of His Expedition into Texas in 1716." *Preliminary Studies of the Texas Catholic Historical Society* 2 (April, 1933): 3–23.

Folmer, Henri. "De Bellisle on the Texas Coast." *Southwestern Historical Quarterly* 44 (1940): 204–31.

Forbes, Jack D. "The Appearance of the Mounted Indian in Northern Mexico and the Southwest, to 1680." *Southwestern Journal of Anthropology* 15 (summer, 1959): 189–212.

Ford, John Salmon. *Rip Ford's Texas*. Austin: University of Texas Press, 1987.

Foreman, Grant, ed. "The Journal of Elijah Hicks." *Chronicles of Oklahoma* 13 (March, 1935): 68–99.

Foster, Morris W. *Being Comanche: A Social History of an American Indian Community*. Tucson: University of Arizona Press, 1991.

Foster, William C. *Spanish Expeditions into Texas, 1689–1768*. Austin: University of Texas Press, 1995.

Fowler, Jacob. *The Journal of Jacob Fowler*. Ed. Elliott Coues. New York: Francis P. Harper, 1898; Minneapolis: Ross and Haines, 1969.

Fox, Anne A. "The Indians at Rancho de las Cabras." In *Columbian Consequences: Archaeological and Historical Perspectives on the Spanish Borderlands West*, ed. David Hurst Thomas, 1:259–67. 3 vols. Washington, D.C.: Smithsonian Institution Press, 1989.

Galan, Rachel B. "Caddo Mythology: Ethnohistorical and Archaeological Considerations." *Mid-America Folklore* 22 (fall, 1994): 61–67.

Garrison, George P., ed. "Reminiscences of Early Texans." *Texas Historical Association Quarterly* 6 (1903): 236–53.

Gelo, Daniel J. "'Comanche Land and Ever Has Been': A Native Geography of the Nineteenth-Century Comanchería." *Southwestern Historical Quarterly* 103 (January, 2000): 273–307.

———. "On a New Interpretation of Comanche Social Organization." *Current Anthropology* 28 (August–October, 1987): 551–52.

Gibson, Arrell M. *The Chickasaws*. Norman: University of Oklahoma Press, 1971.

———. *The Kickapoos: Lords of the Middle Border*. Norman: University of Oklahoma Press, 1963.

Gibson, Jon L. *The Ancient Mounds of Poverty Point: Place of Rings.* Gainesville: University Press of Florida, 2000.

Gracy, David B. "Jean Lafitte and the Karankawa Indians." *East Texas Historical Journal* 2 (1964): 40–44.

Grappe, François. "An Expedition to the Kichai: The Journal of François Grappe, September 24, 1783." Ed. David La Vere and Katia Campbell. *Southwestern Historical Quarterly* 98 (July, 1994): 59–78.

Green, Michael D. *The Politics of Indian Removal: Creek Government and Society in Crisis.* Lincoln: University of Nebraska Press, 1982.

Gregg, Josiah. *Commerce of the Prairies.* Ed. Max L. Moorhead. 1844; Norman: University of Oklahoma Press, 1954.

Gregory, H. F. "Eighteenth-Century Caddoan Archaeology: A Study in Models and Interpretation." Ph.D. diss., Southern Methodist University, Dallas, 1973.

Griffith, William. "The Hasinai Indians of East Texas As Seen by Europeans, 1687–1772." In *Philological and Documentary Studies.* Vol. 2. New Orleans: Tulane University, 1977.

Gunnerson, James H., and Dolores Gunnerson. "Apachean Culture: A Study in Unity and Diversity." In *Apachean Culture History and Ethnology,* ed. Keith H. Basso and Morris E. Opler, 7–27. Tucson: University of Arizona Press, 1971.

Gutiérrez, Ramón A. *When Jesus Came, the Corn Mothers Went Away: Marriage, Sexuality, and Power in New Mexico, 1500–1846.* Stanford, Calif.: Stanford University Press, 1991.

Habicht-Mauche, Judith A. "Coronado's Querechos and Teyas in the Archaeological Record of the Texas Panhandle." *Plains Anthropologist* 37 (August, 1992): 247–59.

Hagan, William T. *Quanah Parker, Comanche Chief.* Norman: University of Oklahoma Press, 1993.

————. *United States-Comanche Relations: The Reservation Years.* Norman: University of Oklahoma Press, 1990.

Haley, James L. *The Buffalo War: The History of the Red River Indian Uprising of 1874.* Norman: University of Oklahoma Press, 1976.

Hall, Thomas D. *Social Change in the Southwest, 1350–1880.* Lawrence: University Press of Kansas, 1989.

Hamalainen, Pekka. "The Western Comanche Trade Center: Rethinking the Plains Indian Trade System." *Western Historical Quarterly* 29 (winter, 1998): 485–513.

Handbook of Texas Online. http://www.tsha.utexas.edu/handbook/online. A joint project of the General Libraries at the University of Texas at Austin and the Texas State Historical Association.

Harper, Elizabeth Ann. "The Taovayas Indians in Frontier Trade and Diplomacy, 1719–1768." *Chronicles of Oklahoma* 31 (autumn, 1953): 268–89.

Harrison, Jeanne V. "Matthew Leeper, Confederate Agent at the Wichita Agency, Indian Territory." *Chronicles of Oklahoma* 47 (autumn, 1969): 242–57.

Hester, Thomas R. "'Coahuiltecan': A Critical Review of an Inappropriate Ethnic Label." *La Tierra, Journal of the Southern Texas Archaeological Association* 25 (October, 1998): 3–7.

————. "The Prehistory of South Texas." In *The Prehistoric Archeology of Texas,* ed. Timothy K. Perttula. College Station: Texas A&M University Press, 2004.

————. "Texas and Northeastern Mexico: An Overview." In *Columbian Consequences: Archaeological and Historical Perspectives on the Spanish Borderlands West,* ed. David Hurst Thomas, 1:191–211. 3 vols. Washington, D.C.: Smithsonian Institution Press, 1989.

————. "Tradition and Diversity among the Prehistoric Hunters and Gatherers of Southern Texas." *Plains Anthropologist* 26 (May, 1981): 119–28.

Hickerson, Nancy P. "How Cabeza de Vaca Lived With, Worked among, and Finally Left the Indians of Texas." *Journal of Anthropological Research* 54 (1998): 199–218.

———. *The Jumanos: Hunters and Traders of the South Plains.* Austin: University of Texas Press, 1994.

Himmel, Kelly F. *The Conquest of the Karankawas and the Tonkawas, 1821–1859.* College Station: Texas A&M University Press, 1999.

Hindes, V. Kay. "Native American and European Contact in the Lower Medina River Valley." *La Tierra: Journal of the Southern Texas Archaeological Association* 22 (April, 1995): 25–33.

Hirth, Kenneth G. "Interregional Trade and the Formation of Prehistoric Gateway Communities." *American Antiquity* 43 (January, 1978): 35–45.

Hodge, Frederick W. *Handbook of American Indians North of Mexico.* 2 vols. Washington, D.C.: Government Printing Office, 1907.

Holder, Preston. *The Hoe and the Horse on the Plains: A Study of Cultural Development among North American Indians.* Lincoln: University of Nebraska Press, 1970.

Holliday, Vance T. *Paleoindian Geoarchaeology of the Southern High Plains.* Austin: University of Texas Press, 1997.

Hook, Jonathan B. *The Alabama-Coushatta Indians.* College Station: Texas A&M University Press, 1997.

Hudson, Charles. "The Hernando de Soto Expedition, 1539–1543." In *The Forgotten Centuries: Indians and Europeans in the American South, 1521–1704,* ed. Charles Hudson and Carmen Chaves Tesser, 74–103. Athens: University of Georgia Press, 1994.

———. *The Southeastern Indians.* Knoxville: University of Tennessee Press, 1976.

Hultkrantz, Ake. *Native Religions of North America: The Power of Visions and Fertility.* San Francisco: Harper and Row, 1987.

Iverson, Peter. *When Indians Became Cowboys: Native Peoples and Cattle Ranching in the American West.* Norman: University of Oklahoma Press, 1994.

Jackson, Jack. *Los Mesteños: Spanish Ranching in Texas, 1721–1821.* College Station: Texas A&M University Press, 1986.

Jelks, Edward B. *Excavations at Texarkana Reservoir, Sulphur River, Texas.* In *River Basin Surveys Papers .No. 21.* Washington, D.C.: GPO, 1961.

Jennings, Francis. *The Founders of America: From the Earliest Migrations to the Present.* New York: Norton, 1993.

Jensen, Harald P., Jr. "Coral Snake Mound, X16SA48." *Bulletin of the Texas Archeological Society* 39 (1968): 9–44.

John, Elizabeth A. H. *Storms Brewed in Other Men's Worlds: The Confrontation of Indians, Spanish, and French in the Southwest, 1540–1795.* College Station: Texas A&M University Press, 1975; Lincoln: University of Nebraska Press, 1981.

John, Elizabeth A H., ed., and John Wheat, trans. "Governing Texas, 1779: The Karankawa Aspect." *Southwestern Historical Quarterly* 104 (April, 2001): 561–76.

Johnson, Eileen, and Vance T. Holliday. "Archeology and Late Quaternary Environments of the Southern High Plains." In *The Prehistoric Archeology of Texas,* ed. Timothy K. Perttula. College Station: Texas A&M University Press, 2004.

Joutel, Henri. *The La Salle Expedition to Texas: The Journal of Henri Joutel, 1684–1686.* Ed. William C. Foster, trans. Johanna S. Warren. Austin: Texas State Historical Society, 1998.

Kappler, Charles J., ed. *Indian Treaties, 1778–1883.* New York: International Publishing, 1972.

Kavanagh, Thomas W. *The Comanches: A History, 1706–1875.* Lincoln: University of Nebraska Press, in cooperation with the American Indian Studies Research Institute, Indiana University, Bloomington, 1996.

Kelley, J. Charles. "Juan Sabeata and Diffusion in Aboriginal Texas." *American Anthropologist* 57 (October, 1955): 981–95.

Kenmotsu, Nancy Adele, James E. Bruseth, and James E. Corbin. "Moscoso and the Route in Texas: A Reconstruction." In *The Expedition of Hernando de Soto West of the Mississippi, 1541–1543,* ed. Gloria A. Young and Michael P. Hoffman , 106–31. Fayetteville: University of Arkansas Press, 1993.

Kinnaird, Lawrence, ed. *Spain in the Mississippi Valley, 1765–1794: Post War Decade, 1782–1792.* 3 vols. Annual Report of the American Historical Association for the Year 1945. Washington: Government Printing Office, 1946.

Klein, Alan M. "Political Economy of the Buffalo Hide Trade: Race and Class on the Plains." In *The Political Economy of North American Indians,* ed. John H. Moore, 133–60. Norman: University of Oklahoma Press, 1993.

Klos, George. "'Our People Could Not Distinguish One Tribe from Another': The 1859 Expulsion of the Reserve Indians from Texas." *Southwestern Historical Quarterly* 97 (April, 1994): 599–619.

Kniffen, Fred B., Hiram F. Gregory, and George A. Stokes. *The Historic Indian Tribes of Louisiana from 1542 to the Present.* Baton Rouge: Louisiana State University Press, 1987.

Kracht, Benjamin R. "The Kiowa Ghost Dance, 1894–1916: An Unheralded Revitalization Movement." *Ethnohistory* 39 (fall, 1992): 456–59.

La Harpe, Jean-Baptiste Bénard de. "Account of the Journey of Bénard de la Harpe: Discovery Made by Him of Several Nations Situated in the West." Trans. Ralph A. Smith. *Southwestern Historical Quarterly* 62 (July, 1958).

———. *The Historical Journal of the Establishment of the French in Louisiana.* Trans. Joan Cain and Virginia Koenig, ed. and annot. Glenn R. Conrad. Lafayette: University of Southwestern Louisiana, 1971.

La Vere, David. *The Caddo Chiefdoms: Caddo Economics and Politics, 700–1835.* Lincoln: University of Nebraska Press, 1998.

———. "The Comanche-Kiowa Business Council of the Early 1900s." In *Native Pathways: Economic Development and American Indian Culture,* ed. Brian C. Hosmer and Colleen O'Neill. Boulder: University Press of Colorado, forthcoming.

———. *Contrary Neighbors: Southern Plains and Removed Indians in Indian Territory.* Norman: University of Oklahoma Press, 2000.

———. "Edward Murphy (1761–1808): Irish Entrepreneur in Spanish Natchitoches." *Louisiana History* 32 (fall, 1991): 371–91.

———. "Friendly Persuasions: Gifts and Reciprocity in Comanche-Euroamerican Relations." *Chronicles of Oklahoma* 71 (fall, 1993): 322–37.

———. *Life among the Texas Indians: The WPA Narratives.* College Station: Texas A&M University Press, 1998.

Landar, Herbert. "The Karankawa Invasion of Texas." *International Journal of American Linguistics* 34 (1968): 242–58.

Latorre, Felipe A., and Dolores L. Latorre. *The Mexican Kickapoo Indians.* Austin: University of Texas Press, 1976.

Lavender, David. *Bent's Fort.* Garden City, N.Y.: Doubleday, 1954.

Lehmann, Herman. *Nine Years among the Indians, 1870–1879.* Ed. J. Marvin Hunter. 1st paperback ed. Albuquerque: University of New Mexico Press, 1993.

Leutenegger, Benedict, ed. and trans. *Letters and Memorials of the Father Presidente Fray Benito Fernández de Santa Ana, 1736–1754.* San Antonio, Tex.: Old Spanish Missions Historical Research Library, 1981.

Leutenegger, Benedict, trans., and Marion A. Habig, comp. and annot. *The San José Papers*. Pt. 1, *1719–1791*. San Antonio, Tex.: Old Spanish Missions Historical Research Library, 1978.

Leví-Strauss, Claude. *The Elementary Structures of Kinship*. Boston: Beacon Press, 1969.

Luxán, Diego Péréz de. "Account of the Antonio de Espejo Expedition into New Mexico, 1582." In *The Rediscovery of New Mexico, 1580–1594*, ed. George P. Hammond and Agapito Rey , 153–212. Albuquerque: University of New Mexico Press, 1966.

Manzanet, Damian [Damián Mansanet]. "Carta de Don Damian Manzanet a Don Carlos De Siguenza sobre el descubrimiento de la Bahía del Espíritu Santo." Trans. Lilia M. Casis. *Quarterly of the Texas State Historical Association* 2 (April, 1899): 279–312.

———. "The Expedition of Don Domingo Terán de los Rios into Texas (1691–92)." Trans. Mattie Austin Hatcher. *Preliminary Studies of the Texas Catholic Historical Society* 2 (January, 1932): 3–67.

Martin, Joel W. *Sacred Revolt: The Muskogee's Struggle for a New World*. Boston: Beacon Press, 1991.

Mauss, Marcel. *The Gift: Forms and Functions of Exchange in Archaic Societies*. Trans. Ian Cunnison. London: Cohen and West, 1969.

Mayhall, Mildred P. *The Kiowas*. Norman: University of Oklahoma Press, 1962.

McClendon, R. Earl. "The First Treaty of the Republic of Texas." *Southwestern Historical Quarterly* 52 (July, 1948): 39–42.

McLoughlin, William G. *Cherokee Renascence in the New Republic*. Princeton, N.J.: Princeton University Press, 1986.

McWilliams, Richebourge G., trans. and ed. *Fleur de Lys and Calumet: Being the Pénicaut Narrative of French Adventure in Louisiana*. Baton Rouge: Louisiana State University Press, 1941.

Mendoca, Vicente de Saldivar. "Account of the Discovery of the Buffalo, 1599." In *Spanish Exploration in the Southwest, 1542–1706*, ed. Herbert E. Bolton, 223–32. New York: Barnes and Noble, 1967.

Mendoza, Juan Dominguez de. "Itinerary of Juan Dominguez de Mendoza, 1684." In *Spanish Exploration in the Southwest, 1542–1706*, ed. Herbert E. Bolton, 320–43. New York: Barnes and Noble, 1967.

Meredith, Howard. *Dancing on Common Ground: Tribal Cultures and Alliances on the Southern Plains*. Lawrence: University Press of Kansas, 1995.

Miller, Jay. "Changing Moons: A History of Caddo Religion." *Plains Anthropologist* 41 (1996): 243–59.

Miller, Myles R., and Nancy A. Kenmotsu. "Prehistory of the Jornada Mogollon and Eastern Trans-Pecos Regions of West Texas." In *The Prehistoric Archeology of Texas*, ed. Timothy K. Perttula. College Station: Texas A&M University Press, 2004.

Miller, Robert Ryal, trans. and ed. "New Mexico in Mid-Eighteenth Century: A Report Based on Governor Vélez Capuchín's Inspection." *Southwestern Historical Quarterly* 79 (October, 1975): 166–81.

Mishkin, Bernard. *Rank and Warfare among the Plains Indians*. Lincoln: University of Nebraska Press, 1992.

Monahan, Forrest D., Jr. "The Kiowa-Comanche Reservation in the 1890s." *Chronicles of Oklahoma* 45 (winter, 1967–68): 451–63.

Mooney, James. *Calendar History of the Kiowa Indians* Washington, D.C.: Smithsonian Institution Press, 1979.

Moorhead, Max L. *The Apache Frontier: Jacobo Ugarte and Spanish-Indian Relations in Northern New Spain, 1769–1791*. Norman: University of Oklahoma Press, 1968.

Morris, John Miller. *El Llano Estacado: Exploration and Imagination on the High Plains of Texas and New Mexico, 1536–1860*. Austin: Texas State Historical Association, 1997.

Muckleroy, Anna. "The Indian Policy of the Republic of Texas." *Southwestern Historical Quarterly* 25 (April, 1922): 229–60.

Native America in the Twentieth Century: An Encyclopedia. Ed. Mary B. Davis. New York: Garland Publishing, 1994.

Neighbours, Kenneth F. "José María: Anadarko Chief." *Chronicles of Oklahoma* 44 (autumn, 1966): 254–74.

Neuman, Robert W. *An Introduction to Louisiana Archaeology*. Baton Rouge: Louisiana State University Press, 1984.

Newcomb, William W., Jr. "Historic Indians of Central Texas." *Bulletin of the Texas Archeological Society* 64 (1993): 1–63.

———. *The Indians of Texas: From Prehistoric to Modern Times*. Austin: University of Texas Press, 1961.

———. "Karankawa." In *Handbook of North American Indians*, ed. Alfonso Ortiz, 359–60. Vol. 10. Washington, D.C.: Smithsonian Institution, 1983.

———. "A Reappraisal of the 'Cultural Sink' of Texas." *Southwestern Journal of Anthropology* 12 (1956): 145–53.

———. *The Rock Art of Texas Indians*. Austin: University of Texas Press, 1967.

Newkumet, Vynola Beaver, and Howard L. Meredith. *Hasinai: A Traditional History of the Caddo Confederacy*. College Station: Texas A&M Press, 1988.

Noyes, Stanley. *Los Comanches: The Horse People, 1751–1845*. Albuquerque: University of New Mexico Press, 1993.

Nunley, Parker. *A Field Guide to Archeological Sites of Texas*. Austin: Texas Monthly Press, 1989.

Nye, Wilbur S. *Bad Medicine and Good: Tales of the Kiowas*. Norman; University of Oklahoma Press, 1969.

Olson, Donald W., et al. "Piñon Pines and the Route of Cabeza de Vaca." *Southwestern Historical Quarterly* 101 (October, 1997): 175–86.

Oñate, Juan de. "True Account of the Expedition of Oñate toward the East, 1601." In *Spanish Exploration in the Southwest, 1542–1706*, ed. Herbert E. Bolton, 250–67. New York: Barnes and Noble, 1967.

Opler, Morris E. "The Apachean Culture Pattern and Its Origins." In *Handbook of North American Indians*, ed. Alfonso Ortiz, 368–92. Vol. 10. Washington, D.C.: Smithsonian Institution, 1983.

Padilla, Juan Antonio. "Texas in 1820." Trans. Mattie Austin Hatcher. *Southwestern Historical Quarterly* 23 (July, 1919–April, 1920): 47–68.

Parsons, Elsie Clews. *Notes on the Caddo: Memoirs of the American Anthropological Association*. No. 57. Menasha, Wis.: American Anthropological Association, 1941; New York: Kraus Reprint, 1969.

Perdue, Theda. *Cherokee Women: Gender and Culture Change, 1700–1835*. Lincoln: University of Nebraska Press, 1998.

Perdue, Theda, and Michael D. Green. *The Cherokee Removal: A Brief History with Documents*. Boston: Bedford Books of St. Martin's Press, 1995.

Perttula, Timothy K. *The Caddo Nation: Archaeological and Ethnohistoric Perspectives*. Austin: University of Texas Press, 1992.

———. "Material Culture of the Koasati Indians of Texas." *Historical Archaeology* 28 (1994): 67–77.

———. "The Prehistoric and Caddoan Archeology of the Northeast Texas Pineywoods." In

The Prehistoric Archeology of Texas, ed. Timothy K. Perttula. College Station: Texas A&M University Press, 2004.

Perttula, Timothy K., and James E. Bruseth. "Early Caddoan Subsistence Strategies, Sabine River Basin, East Texas." *Plains Anthropologist* 28 (February, 1983): 9–21.

Perttula, Timothy K., and Bob D. Skiles. "Another Look at an Eighteenth-Century Archaeological Site in Wood County, Texas." *Southwestern Historical Quarterly* 92 (January, 1989): 417–35.

Peterson, Dennis A. "A History of Excavations and Interpretations of Artifacts from the Spiro Mounds Site." In *The Southeastern Ceremonial Complex: Artifacts and Analysis, the Cottonlandia Conference,* ed. Patricia Galloway, 114–21. Lincoln: University of Nebraska Press, 1989.

Phillips, Philip, and James A. Brown. *Pre-Columbian Shell Engravings from the Craig Mound at Spiro, Oklahoma.* 2 vols. Cambridge, Mass.: Peabody Museum, 1978.

Plummer, Rachel. "Narrative of the Capture and Subsequent Sufferings of Mrs. Rachel Plummer." In *The Rachel Plummer Narrative,* ed. Rachel Lofton, Susie Hendrix, and Jane Kennedy, 89–118. 1839; reprinted, n.p: [Palestine, Tex.], 1926.

Price, Catherine. "The Comanches Threat to Texas and New Mexico in the Eighteenth Century and the Development of Spanish Indian Policy." *Journal of the West* 24 (April, 1989): 34–45.

Prucha, Francis Paul. *The Great Father: The United States Government and the American Indians.* Lincoln: University of Nebraska Press, 1984.

———. *Indian Policy in the United States: Historical Essays.* Lincoln: University of Nebraska Press, 1981.

Quigg, J. Michael. "A Late Archaic Bison Processing Event in the Texas Panhandle." *Plains Anthropologist* 43 (1998): 367–83.

Rachlin, Carol K. "The Native American Church in Oklahoma." *Chronicles of Oklahoma* 42 (autumn, 1964): 262–72.

Reagan, John H. "The Expulsion of the Cherokees from East Texas." *Texas Historical Association Quarterly* 1 (1897): 38–46.

Reindorp, Reginald C., trans. "Documents: The Founding of the Missions at La Junta de los Rios." *Mid-America* 20 (1940): 107–31.

Richter, Daniel K. *The Ordeal of the Longhouse: The Peoples of the Iroquois League in the Era of European Colonization.* Chapel Hill: University of North Carolina Press, 1992.

Ricklis, Robert A. "The Archeology of Native American Occupation of Southeast Texas." In *The Prehistoric Archeology of Texas,* ed. Timothy K. Perttula. College Station: Texas A&M University Press, 2004.

———. *The Karankawa Indians of Texas: An Ecological Study of Cultural Tradition and Change.* Austin: University of Texas Press, 1996.

———. "Prehistoric Occupation of the Central and Lower Texas Coast: A Regional Overview." In *The Prehistoric Archeology of Texas,* ed. Timothy K. Perttula. College Station: Texas A&M University Press, 2004.

Roberts, David. *Once They Moved Like the Wind: Cochise, Geronomio, and the Apache Wars.* New York: Touchstone, 1993.

Robertson, James, trans. and ed. "The True Relation of the Hardships Suffered by Governor Hernando de Soto by a Gentleman of Elvas." *The De Soto Chronicles: The Expedition of Hernando De Soto to North America in 1539–1543.* Ed. Lawrence A. Clayton, Vernon James Knight, Jr., and Edward C. Moore. 2 vols. Tuscaloosa: University of Alabama Press, 1993.

Robinson, Charles M., III. *Satanta: The Life and Death of a War Chief.* Austin: State House Press, 1997.

Rogers, J. Daniel. "Patterns of Change on the Western Margin of the Southeast, A.D. 600–900." In *Stability, Transformation, and Variation: The Late Woodland Southeast*, ed. Michael S. Nassaney and Charles R. Cobb, 221–48. New York: Plenum Press, 1991.

Rollings, Willard H. *The Osage: An Ethnohistorical Study of Hegemony on the Prairie-Plains*. Columbia: University of Missouri Press, 1992.

Ruecking, Frederick, Jr. "The Social Organization of the Coahuiltecan Indians of Southern Texas and Northeastern Mexico." *Texas Journal of Science* 7 (December, 1995): 357–88.

Sahlins, Marshall. "Notes on the Original Affluent Society." In *Man the Hunter*, ed. Richard B. Lee and Irven DeVore. Chicago: Aldine Publishing, 1968.

———. *Stone Age Economics*. Chicago: Aldine-Atherton, 1972.

Sánchez, José María. "A Trip to Texas in 1828." Trans. Carlos E. Castaneda. *Southwestern Historical Quarterly* 29 (April, 1926): 249–88.

Schambach, Frank F. "Spiro and the Tunica: A New Interpretation of the Role of the Tunica in the Culture History of the Southeast and the Southern Plains, A.D. 1100–1750." In *Arkansas Archaeology: Essays in Honor of Dan and Phyllis Morse*, ed. Robert C. Mainfort, Jr., and Marvin D. Jeter, 169–224. Fayetteville: University of Arkansas Press, 1999.

Scholes, France V., and H. P. Mera. "Some Aspects of the Jumano Problem." *Contributions to American Anthropology and History*. No. 34. Washington, D.C.: Carnegie Institution of Washington, 1940.

Schroeder, Albert H. "Development in the Southwest and Relations with the Plains." In *Plains Indians, A.D. 500–1500: The Archaeological Past of Historic Groups*, ed. Karl H. Schleiser, 290–307. Norman: University of Oklahoma Press, 1994.

Schroeder, Albert H., and Dan S. Matson, eds. *A Colony on the Move: Gaspar Castaño de Sosa's Journal, 1590–1591*. Salt Lake City: Alphabet Printing, 1965.

Schulze, Jeffrey M. "The Rediscovery of the Tiguas: Federal Recognition and Indianness in the Twentieth Century." *Southwestern Historical Quarterly* 105 (July, 2001): 14–39.

Secoy, Frank R. *Changing Military Patterns on the Great Plains*. Lincoln: University of Nebraska Press, 1992.

Shafer, Harry J. "Comments on Woodland Cultures of East Texas." *Bulletin of Texas Archeological Society* 46 (1975): 249–54.

———. "Early Lithic Assemblages in Eastern Texas." *Museum Journal* 17 (1977): 187–97.

———. "Lithic Technology at the George C. Davis Site, Cherokee County, Texas." Ph.D. diss., University of Texas, Austin, 1973.

Shaffer, Lynda Norene. *Native Americans before 1492: The Moundbuilding Centers of the Eastern Woodlands*. Armonk, N.Y.: M. E. Sharpe, 1992.

Shelby, Charmion Clair. "St. Denis's Declaration Concerning Texas in 1717." *Southwestern Historical Quarterly* 26 (January, 1923): 165–83.

Sibley, John. "Historical Sketches of the Several Indian Tribes in Louisiana, Mouth of the Arkansas River, and between the Mississippi and River Grand." In *Travels in the Interior Parts of America*, ed. Thomas Jefferson. London: J. G. Barnard, 1807.

———. *A Report from Natchitoches in 1807*. Ed. Annie Heloise Abel. Ville Platte, La.: Evangeline Genealogical and Historical Society, 1987.

Silverberg, Robert. *The Pueblo Revolt*. Lincoln: University of Nebraska Press, 1994.

Simmons, Marc. *The Last Conquistador: Juan de Oñate and the Settling of the Far Southwest*. Norman: University of Oklahoma Press, 1991.

Siskind, Janet. "Kinship and Mode of Production." *American Anthropologist* 80 (December, 1978): 860–72.

Sjoberg, Andrée F. "The Bidai Indians of Southeastern Texas." *Southwestern Journal of Anthropology* 7 (1951): 391–400.

———. "The Culture of the Tonkawa, a Texas Indian Tribe." *Texas Journal of Science* 5 (September, 1953): 280–304.

———. "Lipan Apache Culture in Historical Perspective." *Southwestern Journal of Anthropology* 9 (1953): 76–98.

Smith, F. Todd. *The Caddo Indians: Tribes at the Convergence of Empires, 1542–1854*. College Station: Texas A&M University Press, 1995.

———. *The Caddos, the Wichitas, and the United States, 1846–1901*. College Station: Texas A&M University Press, 1996.

———. *The Wichita Indians: Traders of Texas and the Southern Plains, 1540–1845*. College Station: Texas A&M University Press, 2000.

Smith, Marvin T. *Archaeology of Aboriginal Culture Change in the Interior Southeast: Depopulation during the Early Historic Period*. Gainesville: University Press of Florida, 1987.

———. "Early Historic Period Vestiges of the Southern Cult." In *The Southeastern Ceremonial Complex: Artifacts and Analysis, the Cottonlandia Conference*, ed. Patricia Galloway, 141–46. Lincoln: University of Nebraska Press, 1989.

Smith, Ralph. "The Tawehash in French, Spanish, English, and American Imperial Affairs." *West Texas Historical Association Year Book* 28 (October, 1952): 18–49.

Smith, Thomas T. *Fort Inge: Sharps, Spurs, and Sabers on the Texas Frontier, 1849–1869*. Austin: Eakin Press, 1993.

———. *The U.S. Army and the Texas Frontier Economy, 1845–1900*. College Station: Texas A&M University Press, 1999.

———. "U.S. Army Combat Operations in the Indian Wars of Texas, 1849–1881." *Southwestern Historical Quarterly* 94 (April, 1996): 501–31.

Smithwick, Noah. *The Evolution of a State, or, Recollections of Old Texas Days*. 1900; Austin: University of Texas Press, 1984.

Smits, David D. "The Frontier Army and the Destruction of the Buffalo, 1865–1883." *Western Historical Quarterly* 25 (autumn, 1994): 314–34.

Solís, Fray Gaspar José de. "Diary of a Visit of Inspection of the Texas Missions made by Fray Gaspar José de Solís in the Year 1767–68." Trans. Margaret Kenney Kress. *Southwestern Historical Quarterly* 35 (July, 1931): 28–76.

Spielmann, Katherine A. "Interaction among Nonhierarchical Societies." In *Farmers, Hunters, and Colonists: Interaction between the Southwest and the Southern Plains*, ed. Katherine A. Spielmann, 1–17. Tucson: University of Arizona Press, 1991.

———. "Late Prehistoric Exchange between the Southwest and Southern Plains." *Plains Anthropologist* 28 (November, 1983): 257–72.

Stockel, H. Henrietta. *Chiricahua Apache Women and Children*. College Station: Texas A&M University Press, 2000.

Story, Dee Ann. "An Overview of the Archaeology of East Texas" *Plains Anthropologist* 26 (May, 1981): 139–56.

Swanton, John R. *The Indian Tribes of North America*. Bulletin 145. Washington, D.C.: U.S. Bureau of American Ethnology, 1952.

———. "Mythology of the Indians of Louisiana and the Texas Coast." *Journal of American Folklore* 20 (1907): 285–89.

———. *Source Material on the History and Ethnology of the Caddo Indians*. Bulletin 132. Washington, D.C.: Smithsonian Institution, U.S. Bureau of American Ethnology, 1942.

Talon Interrogation. In "Voyage to the Mississippi through the Gulf of Mexico." In *La Salle, the Mississippi, and the Gulf: Three Primary Documents,* ed. Robert Weddle, trans. Ann Linda Bell. College Station: Texas A&M University Press, 1987.

Tanner, Helen Hornbeck. "The Land and Water Communication Systems of the Southeastern Indians." In *Powhatan's Mantle: Indians in the Colonial Southeast,* ed. Peter H. Wood, Gregory A. Waselkov, and M. Thomas Hatley, 6–20. Lincoln: University of Nebraska Press, 1989.

Taylor, Alfred A. "The Medicine Lodge Peace Council." *Chronicles of Oklahoma* 2 (June, 1924): 89–118.

Terán, Don Manuel de Mier y. "Documentos Para la Historia, año de 1828: Noticia de las tribus de salvajes conocidos que habitan en el Departamento de Tejas, y del número de familias de que consta cada tribu, puntos en que habitan y terrenos en que acampan." *Boletin de la Sociedad Macicana de Geografia y Estadistica* (1870): 264–69.

Terrell, John Upton. *The Plains Apache.* New York: Crowell, 1975.

Thomas, David Hurst. *Exploring Ancient Native America: An Archaeological Guide.* New York: Macmillan, 1994.

Thornton, Russell. *American Indian Holocaust and Survival: A Population History since 1492.* Norman: University of Oklahoma Press, 1987.

Thurman, Melburn D. "A New Interpretation of Comanche Social Organization." *Current Anthropology* 23 (October, 1982): 578–79.

Tigua Indian Cultural Center Museum. El Paso, Tex.

"Tiguas: People of the Sun, Ysleta Del Sur Pueblo." El Paso, Tex.: Tigua Indian Cultural Center, n.d.

"Tonkawa Tribe of Indians" Online home page. http://members.tripod.com/tonkawa/main.html.

Tonty, Henri de. "Memoir by the Sieur de la Tonty." Vol. 1 in *Historical Collections of Louisiana, Embracing Many Rare and Valuable Documents Relating to the Natural, Civil, and Political History of That State,* ed. B. F. French. 4 vols. New York: Wiley and Putnam, 1846; New York: AMS Press, 1976.

Tunnell, Curtis. "A Cache of Cannons: La Salle's Colony in Texas." *Southwestern Historical Quarterly* 102 (July, 1998): 19–43.

Turpin, Solveig A. "The Lower Pecos River Region of Texas and Northern Mexico." In *The Prehistoric Archeology of Texas,* ed. Timothy K. Perttula. College Station: Texas A&M University Press, 2004.

———. "More about Mortuary Practices in the Lower Pecos River Region of Southwest Texas." *Plains Anthropologist* 37 (February, 1992): 7–17.

Turpin, Solveig A., Maciej Henneberg, and David H. Riskind. "Late Archaic Mortuary Practices of the Lower Pecos River Region, Southwest Texas." *Plains Anthropologist* 31 (November, 1986): 295–315.

Usner, Daniel H., Jr. *Indians, Settlers, and Slaves in a Frontier Exchange Economy: The Lower Mississippi Valley before 1783.* Chapel Hill: University of North Carolina Press, 1992.

Utley, Robert M. *The Indian Frontier of the American West, 1846–1890.* Albuquerque: University of New Mexico Press, 1984.

———. *The Lance and the Shield: The Life and Times of Sitting Bull.* New York: Henry Holt, 1993.

Vehik, Susan C. "Cultural Continuity and Discontinuity in the Southern Prairies and Cross Timbers." In *Plains Indians, A.D. 500–1500: The Archaeological Past of Historic Groups,* ed. Karl H. Schleiser, 239–63. Norman: University of Oklahoma Press, 1994.

———. "Wichita Culture History." *Plains Anthropologist* 37 (November, 1992): 311–32.

Vitebsky, Piers. *Shamanisn*. Norman: University of Oklahoma Press, 2001.

"Voyage to the Mississippi through the Gulf of Mexico." In *La Salle, the Mississippi, and the Gulf: Three Primary Documents*, ed. Robert Weddle, trans. Ann Linda Bell. College Station: Texas A&M University, 1987.

Waldman, Carl. *Atlas of the North American Indian*. New York: Facts on File Publications, 1985.

Wallace, Ernest, and E. Adamson Hoebel. *The Comanches: Lords of the South Plains*. Norman: University of Oklahoma Press, 1986.

Webb, Malcolm C. "Functional and Historical Parallelisms between Mesoamerican and Mississippian Cultures." In *The Southeastern Ceremonial Complex: Artifacts and Analysis, the Cottonlandia Conference*, ed. Patricia Galloway, 279–93. Lincoln: University of Nebraska Press, 1989.

Webb, Walter Prescott. *The Great Plains*. Boston: Ginn, 1931; Lincoln: University of Nebraska Press, 1981.

Weber, David J., ed. *What Caused the Pueblo Revolt of 1680?* Boston: Bedford/St. Martins, 1999.

Wedel, Mildred Mott. "The Ethnohistoric Approach to Plains Caddoan Origins." *Nebraska History* 60 (summer, 1979): 183–96.

White, Richard. *"It's Your Misfortune and None of My Own": A History of the American West*. Norman: University of Oklahoma Press, 1991.

———. *The Roots of Dependency: Subsistence, Environment, and Social Change among the Choctaws, Pawnees, and Navajos*. Lincoln: University of Nebraska Press, 1983.

———. "The Winning of the West: The Expansion of the Western Sioux in the Eighteenth and Nineteenth Centuries." *Journal of American History* 65 (September, 1978): 319–43.

Wilcox, David R. "Changing Contexts of Pueblo Adaptions, A.D. 1250–1600." In *Farmers, Hunters, and Colonists: Interactions between the Southwest and the Southern Plains*, ed. Katherine A. Spielmann, 128–54. Tucson: University of Arizona Press, 1991.

Wilkins, Thurman. *Cherokee Tragedy: The Ridge Family and the Decimation of a People*. 2d ed. Norman: University of Oklahoma Press, 1983.

Winfrey, Dorman H., and James M. Day. *The Indian Papers of Texas and the Southwest*. 5 vols. Austin: Texas State Historical Association, 1995.

Woldert, Albert. "The Last of the Cherokees in Texas, and the Life and Death of Chief Bowles." *Chronicles of Oklahoma* 1 (June, 1923): 179–226.

Wolf, Eric R. *Europe and the People without History*. Berkeley: University of California Press, 1982.

Wolff, Thomas. "The Karankawa Indians: Their Conflict with the White Man in Texas." *Ethnohistory* 16 (winter, 1969): 1–32.

Wood, W. Raymond. "Plains Trade in Prehistoric and Protohistoric Intertribal Relations." In *Anthropology on the Great Plains*, ed. W. Raymond Wood and Margot Liberty, 98–109. Lincoln: University of Nebraska Press, 1980.

Worth, John E., ed. and trans. "Relation of the Island of Florida by Luys Hernández de Biedma." *The De Soto Chronicles: The Expedition of Hernando De Soto to North America in 1539–1543*. Ed. Lawrence A. Clayton, Vernon James Knight, Jr., Edward C. Moore. 2 vols. Tuscaloosa: University of Alabama Press, 1993.

Wright, Bill. *The Tiguas: Pueblo Indians of Texas*. El Paso: University of Texas at El Paso, 1993.

Wright, J. Leitch. *The Only Land They Knew: The Tragic Story of the American Indians in the Old South*. New York: Free Press, 1981.

Wyckoff, Don G., and Timothy G. Baugh. "Early Historic Hasinai Elites: A Model for the Material Culture of Governing Elites." *Midcontinental Journal of Archaeology* 5 (1980): 225–88.

Index

Abriaches (Jumanos), 68

Acculturation (*see also* Identity): Americanization, 156–57, 159, 189, 199, 208–209; effects of, 222–23, 230; forced, 218; Hispanicization, *x*, 78–80, 94–95, 101–102, 201, 235; to Indian life, 182–84; resistance to, 201; post-World War II, 225–26

Adaes (Caddos), 155

Adena Complex, 15

Adobe Walls, 206, 212–13

Adoption, 38, 53, 84, 89, 98–99, 110; by Apaches, 102, 182; by Caddos, 110, 124

Agriculture, 18–20, 27, 32; by Apaches, 86; by Caddos, 104–105; development of, 17–20; by Jumanos, 69; methods of, 18–19; in Mississippian Cultural Tradition, 20–21; in Pueblo Cultural Tradition, 23; on reservation, 219; by Tiguas, 94–95; women's role in, 18–19, 32

Agricultural Revolution, 17–20

Ais (Caddos), 155, 162

Akokisas (Atakapas), 112, 122, 140, 142

Alabama-Coushattas, *ix*, 31, 158–60, 232–34; battle Mexicans, 161; battle Texans, 172; in Civil War, 202; government, 159, 233; land, 175, 222, 232, 234; location, 158–61, 175, 201; logging, 232–33; migration, 226; population, 160–61; powwows, 234; relations with Mexico, 170–76; religion, 159, 232–33; reservation, 216, 234; terminated, 233–34; treaties, 169–70; in World War I, 224; in World War II, 225

Alarcón, Martín de, 116

Alcohol, 163–64

Alibates quarry, 8

Allotment. *See under* Land

American Indian Movement, 228–29

Anadarkos (Caddos), 123, 150, 165, 197–98

Anagados (Coahuiltecans), 64

Angelina River, 21, 28, 104, 156, 161

Anza, Juan Bautista de, 148

Apaches (*see also* Chiricahuas, Escanjaques, Jicarillas, Natagés, Kiowa-Apaches, Lipans, Mescaleros, Plains Apaches, Querechos), *ix*, *x*, 84–85, 214–16; absorbing others, 31; female warriors, 53; girl's puberty ceremony, 50, 86; location, 30, 85, 150; migration, 30; raids, 214–16; religion, 45; subsistence, 31; trade, 55, 88–91

Aranamas (Coahuiltecans), 65

Aransas Bay, 59

Arbadaos (Coahuiltecans), 64

Archaic Indians, 9–14, 23

ISBN 1-58544-301-8

90000